D0667327

The Executive Branch of the U.S. Government

Recent Titles in
Bibliographies and Indexes in Law and Political Science

Scottish Nationalism and Cultural Identity in the Twentieth Century: An Annotated Bibliography of Secondary Sources
Gordon Bryan, compiler

Edward S. Corwin and the American Constitution:
A Bibliographical Analysis
Kenneth D. Crews

Political Risk Assessment: An Annotated Bibliography
David A. Jodice, compiler

Human Rights: An International and Comparative Law Bibliography
Julian R. Friedman and Marc I. Sherman, compilers and editors

Latin American Society and Legal Culture
Frederick E. Snyder, compiler

Congressional Committees, 1789-1982: A Checklist
Walter Stubbs, compiler

Criminal Justice Documents:
A Selective, Annotated Bibliography of U.S. Government Publications Since 1975
John F. Berens, compiler

Terrorism, 1980-1987:
A Selectively Annotated Bibliography
Edward F. Mickolus, compiler with Peter A. Flemming

Guide to the *Archiv für Sozialwissenschaft und Sozialpolitik* Group, 1904-1933
Regis A. Factor

Contemporary Canadian Politics: An Annotated Bibliography, 1970-1987
Gregory Mahler, compiler

The Executive Branch of the U.S. Government

A Bibliography

Compiled by
Robert Goehlert and Hugh Reynolds

Bibliographies and Indexes in Law and Political Science, Number 11

Greenwood Press
New York • Westport, Connecticut • London

Library of Congress Cataloging-in-Publication Data

Goehlert, Robert, 1948-
The executive branch of the U.S. government : a bibliography / compiled by Robert Goehlert and Hugh Reynolds.
p. cm.—(Bibliographies and indexes in law and political science, ISSN 0742-6909 ; no. 11)
Includes indexes.
ISBN 0-313-26568-2 (lib. bdg. : alk. paper)
1. United States—Executive departments—Bibliography.
I. Reynolds, Hugh. II. Title. III. Series.
Z7165.U5G56 1989
[JK421]
016.35304—dc19 88-24704

British Library Cataloguing in Publication Data is available.

Library of Congress Catalog Card Number: 88-24704
ISBN: 0-313-26568-2
ISSN: 0742-6909

First published in 1989

Greenwood Press, Inc.
88 Post Road West, Westport, Connecticut 06881

Printed in the United States of America

The paper used in this book complies with the Permanent Paper Standard issued by the National Information Standards Organization (Z39.48-1984).

10 9 8 7 6 5 4 3 2 1

Contents

Introduction

SCOPE

This bibliography is designed to assist librarians, students, researchers, and government personnel interested in the executive branch of the government. This work fills a real need because no book-length bibliography on the executive branch has been published previously.

Our aim in compiling this volume was to prepare a comprehensive bibliography on the executive branch, including the history, development, organization, procedures, rulings, and policy of the departments. The primary focus of the bibliography is on the executive branch at the cabinet-department level, but we have also included some material that deals with sub-agencies of a department, particularly the Federal Bureau of Investigation, Census Bureau, Federal Aviation Administration, Internal Revenue Service, Patent Office, Bureau of Indian Affairs, Bureau of Reclamation, Forest Service, Public Health Service, National Park Service, Food and Drug Administration, Bureau of Land Management, Social Security Administration, Federal Highway Administration, and the National Transportation Safety Board. The bibliography includes citations drawn from a variety of fields, including business, economics, political science, law, history, public administration and the general social sciences.

The bibliography includes books, scholarly articles, dissertations, and selected research reports. Since there is a wealth of documents dealing with each department, we felt that it would be best to leave these out of the volume. There are all sorts of U. S. documents of the Executive Branch that would be invaluable to study. Individual departments, agencies, bureaus, boards all publish documents. The best indexes for identifying documents published by the executive branch are the **Monthly Catalog of United States Government Publications** and the **GPO Publications Reference File.** The **Monthly Catalog** can be used to identify documents by issuing agency, author, title, subject, report, or series number. The **GPO Publications Ref-**

erence File is a microfiche service which lists documents that are in print and available for purchase. The price and stock number is included. In addition to executive branch publications, there are also reports done by Congress that are useful in studying the executive branch. These include hearings, committee prints, and reports. The best tool for identifying those documents is **CIS Index**, a monthly index to Congressional publications. One can identify documents by using a number of indexes.

Since the bibliography is intended primarily for an English-speaking audience, all the citations are to English-language works. In general, the time period covered by the bibliography extends primarily from 1945 to 1985. While most of the citations identified were published within the last forty years, there are some citations to earlier works, especially for books. We attempted to include all books written about individual departments since 1900.

The chief criteria we used to determine which materials to include were that they be analytical, scholarly in nature, and not merely descriptive. Consequently, the emphasis is on research monographs, articles from major journals, and dissertations. Because of the enormous amount of descriptive material aimed at policymakers, we selectively included such materials in some categories, especially when there was little scholarly work done in those areas. Generally, we tended to include only materials that were commercially available and that could be found in medium to large academic libraries.

ARRANGEMENT

We have divided the bibliography into fifteen major chapters. The first chapter is a listing of key materials on the executive branch in general. This includes materials written about the executive branch as a whole as well as key works about American public administration and bureaucracy in general. The next fourteen chapters focus on each of the departments individually. Materials relating to the area of education are in the chapter for the Department of Education. Materials dealing with the old Department of Health, Education, and Welfare are in the chapter for the Department of Health and Human Services. We have also included a Subject Index, which includes more specific subjects and an Author Index.

The arrangement of the bibliography reflects the nature of the literature. Most of the citations in the first chapter are theoretical and comparative in nature, while the remaining chapters contain materials on individual departments. Consequently, this bibliography can be used to quickly find materials on either a particular topic or department.

COMPILATION

In compiling this bibliography, we checked a variety of sources. Primarily, we searched eleven indexes: **Business Periodical Index, Business Index, Legal Resources Index, Index to Legal Periodicals, United States Political Science Documents, Social Sciences Index, Humanities Index, Public Affairs Information Service Bulletin, Writings on American History, America: History and Life,** and **Sage Public Administration Abstracts.** For dissertations, we made an exhaustive key word search of **Comprehensive Dissertation Index.** For books and research reports, we checked **Books in Print, Cumulative Book Index, American Book Publishing Record, Public Affairs Information Service Bulletin,** as well as the holdings of the Indiana University Libraries.

The eleven indexes were chosen to incorporate a variety of disciplines, including history, political science and law, as they provide the best coverage of government regulation. We hope that this bibliography will prove beneficial to researchers and students in the field of regulation. This bibliography is also intended to generate interest in the study of the executive branch, by surveying what has been done and pointing out areas of neglected research.

Chapter 1.
General Studies

1. Abbott, Roger S. "The Federal Loyality Program: Background and Problems." Ph.D. dissertation, University of California, 1949.

2. Abel, Robert B. "The Politics of Executive-Legislative Relationships in a Multiple Committee-Single Bureau Situation." Ph.D. dissertation, American University, 1972.

3. Aberbach, Joel D., Robert D. Putnam and Bert A. Rockman. **Bureaucrats and Politicians in Western Democracies.** Cambridge, MA: Harvard University Press, 1981.

4. Aberbach, Joel D. and Bert A. Rockman. "Bureaucrats and Client Groups: A View from Capitol Hill." **American Journal of Political Science** 22 (November 1978): 818-832.

5. Aberbach, Joel D. and Bert A. Rockman. "Clashing Beliefs within the Executive Branch: The Nixon Administration Bureaucracy." **American Political Science Review** 70 (June 1976): 456-468.

6. Aberbach, Joel D. and Bert A. Rockman. "The Overlapping Worlds of American Federal Executives and Congressmen." **British Journal of Political Science** 7 (January 1977): 23-48.

7. Abramowitz, Michael E. "Bureaucrats and Lawyers - Legal Myths and Realities." **Bureaucrat** 2 (Fall 1973): 256-268.

8. Adams, Bruce and Kathryn Kavanagh-Baran. **Promise and Performance: Carter Builds a New Administration.** Lexington, MA: Lexington Books, 1979.

9. Adams, Charles M. "Bookkeeper for the Bureaucracy."

Nation's Business 24 (October 1936): 56-62.

10. Adams, Quincy. "Possible Revisions of Federal Agricultural Policies with Special Reference to the Brannan Plan." Ph.D. dissertation, American University, 1952.

11. Agria, John J. "Constitutional Basis of Executive Impoundment." **Michigan Academician** 7 (Fall 1974): 157-165.

12. Ahlberg, Clark D. "The Federal Position Classification System: A Critique of Administrative Achievement." Ph.D. dissertation, Syracuse University, 1952.

13. Aiken, Carl. "Task Force: Methodology." **Public Administration Review** 9 (Autumn 1949): 241-251.

14. Aiken, Carl. "Minority Perspectives on Bureaucracy." **Bureaucrat** 2 (Summer 1973): 131-135.

15. Alexander, Thomas G. "The Federal Frontier: Interior Department Financial Policy in Idaho, Utah, and Arizona, 1863-1896." Ph.D. dissertation, University of California, 1965.

16. Alexander, Thomas G. "Why Bureaucracy Keeps Growing." **Fortune** 99 (May 1979): 164-166.

17. Allan, Peter and Steven Rosenberg. **Public Personnel and Administrative Behavior.** Monterey, CA: Duxbury Press, 1981.

18. Allensworth, Don T. **Public Administration.** Philadelphia: Lippincott, 1973.

19. Altshuler, Alan A. and Norman C. Thomas. **The Politics of the Federal Bureaucracy**. 2nd ed. New York: Harper and Row, 1977.

20. Anderson, David. "A Theoretical and Empirical Analysis of the Federal Budget Process." Ph.D. dissertation, Boston College, 1973.

21. Anderson, Jack. "How to Outsmart the Bureaucrats." **Parade** (July 27, 1980): 6-8.

22. Anderson, James E. **Public Policy Making.** New York: Praeger, 1975.

23. Anderson, James E. **Cases in Public Policy Management.** New York: Praeger, 1976.

24. Anderson, Stanley V. **Ombudsman for American Government.** Englewood Cliffs, NJ: Prentice-Hall, 1968.

25. Anderson, William H. "Executives: National and State." **Public Administration Review** 12 (Winter 1952): 55-59.

26. Anderson, William H. **Financing Modern Governments: The Political Economy of the Public Sector.** Boston: Houghton Mifflin, 1973.

27. Annis, Edward R. "Government Health Care: First the Aged, then Everyone." **Current History** 45 (August 1963): 104-109, 119.

28. Appleby, Paul H. **Policy and Administration.** University: University of Alabama Press, 1975.

29. Appleby, Paul H. **Morality and Administration in Democratic Government.** Baton Rouge: Louisiana State University Press, 1952.

30. Appleby, Paul H. "Organizing Around the Head of a Large Federal Department." **Public Administration Review** 6 (Summer 1946): 205-212.

31. Arnold, Peri E. "First Hoover Commission and the Managerial Presidency." **Journal of Politics** 38 (February 1976): 46-70.

32. Arnold, Peri E. "Reorganization and Politics: A Reflection on the Adequacy of Administrative Theory." **Public Administration Review** 34 (May 1974): 205-211.

33. Arnold, Peri E. and L. John Roos. "Toward a Theory of Congressional-Executive Relations." **Review of Politics** 36 (July 1974): 410-429.

34. Arnold, R. Douglas. **Congress and the Bureaucracy: A Theory of Influence.** New Haven, CT: Yale University Press, 1979.

35. Arnold, R. Douglas. "Legislators, Bureaucrats, and Locational Decisions." **Public Choice** 37 (1981): 107-132.

36. Aronson, Sidney H. **Status and Kinship in the Higher Civil Service.** Cambridge, MA: Harvard University Press, 1964.

37. Arvis, Paul F. "Factors Affecting the Recruitment and Advancement of Women to Managerial Positions in Federal Agencies." Ph.D. dissertation, Ameri-

can University, 1973.

38. Ashby, Paul F. "The Federal Administration, 1865 to 1877." Ph.D. dissertation, University of Chicago, 1950.

39. Ashford, Douglas E. "Bureaucrats and Citizens." **Annals of the American Academy of Political and Social Science** 358 (March 1965): 89-100.

40. Asimow, Michael. **Advice to the Public from Federal Administrative Agencies.** New York: Bender, 1973.

41. Aswell, James B. "Bureaucratic Government." **Congressional Record** 67 (1926): 8015-8016.

42. Bacharach, Peter. **The Theory of Democratic Elitism: A Critique.** Lanham, MD: University Press of America, 1980.

43. Bacharach, Samuel B. **Power and Politics in Organizations.** San Francisco, CA: Jossey-Bass, 1980.

44. Bailey, Steven K. "Improving Federal Governance." **Public Administration Review** 40 (November/December 1980): 548-552.

45. Baldwin, Raymond and Livingston Hall. "Using Government Lawyers to Animate Bureaucracy." **Yale Law Journal** 63 (December 1953): 197-204.

46. Balk, Walter L. **Improving Government Productivity: Some Policy Perspectives.** Beverly Hills, CA: Sage, 1975.

47. Ball, Jospeh H. "The Implementation of Federal Manpower Policy, 1961-1971: A Study in Bureaucratic Competition and Intergovernmental Relations." Ph.D. dissertation, Columbia University, 1972.

48. Balutis, Alan P. and Daron K. Butler. **The Political Purse-Strings.** New York: Halstead Press, 1975.

49. Balutis, Alan P. and James J. Heaphey. **Public Administration and the Legislative Process.** Beverly Hills, CA: Sage, 1974.

50. Balzano, Michael P. **Reorganizing the Federal Bureaucracy: The Rhetoric and the Reality.** Washington, DC: American Enterprise Institute

for Public Policy Research, 1977.

51. Barbee, Alfred C. "Relationships between Organization Structure and Job Satisfaction among Federal Civil Service Managers." Ph.D. dissertation, American University, 1972.

52. Barbour, Dana M. "Interdepartmental Centralization in Federal Procurement." Ph.D. dissertation, Stanford University, 1948.

53. Barnard, Chester I. "Bureaucracy in a Democracy." **American Political Science Review** 44 (December 1950): 990-1004.

54. Barnard, Chester I. **The Functions of the Executive.** Cambridge, MA: Harvard University Press, 1938.

55. Barnett, Vincent M. "Changing Problems of United States Representation Abroad." **Public Administration Review** 17 (Winter 1957): 20-30.

56. Bartholomew, Paul C. **Public Administration.** Paterson, NJ: Littlefield, Adams, 1959.

57. Bartlett, Ewell T. "Can Government Be Human?" **Public Administration Review** 15 (Winter 1955): 39-42.

58. Bartlett, Joseph W. and Douglas M. Jones. "Managing a Cabinet Agency: Problems of Performance at Commerce." **Public Administration Review** 34 (January 1974): 62-70.

59. Barton, Allen H. "A Diagnosis of Bureaucratic Maladies." **American Behavioral Scientist** 22 (May/June 1979): 483-492.

60. Baruch, Ismar. **Position Classification in the Public Service.** Chicago: Public Personnel Association, 1941.

61. Bauer, Raymond A. and Kenneth J. Gergen. **The Study of Policy Formation.** New York: Free Press, 1968.

62. Beam, David R. "Public Administration Is Alive and Well - and Living in the White House." **Public Administration Review** 38 (January 1978): 72-77.

63. Beard, Charles A. **Public Policy and General Welfare.** New Haven, CT: Yale University Press, 1941.

64. Beard, Charles and William Beard. "The Case for Bureaucracy." **Scribner's Magazine** 93 (April 1933): 209-214.

65. Beauchamp, Tom L. **Ethics and Public Policy.** Englewood Cliffs, NJ: Prentice-Hall, 1975.

66. Beck, James M. **Our Wonderful World of Bureaucracy.** New York: Macmillan, 1932.

67. Becker, Theodore M. and Peter R. Meyers. "Empathy and Bravado: Interviewing Reluctant Bureaucrats." **Public Opinion Quarterly** 38 (Winter 1974-1975): 605-613.

68. Beckman, Norman and Harold Handerson, eds. **New Directions in Public Administration: The Federal View.** Reston, VA: Bureaucrat, 1975.

69. Bell, Frank. "Federal Legislation Concerning the Disposition of Grazing Lands (1862-1900)." Ph.D. dissertation, Indiana University, 1959.

70. Bellone, Carl J. **Organization Theory and the New Public Administration.** Boston: Allyn and Bacon, 1980.

71. Belsley, Gilbert L. **Federal Personnel Management and the Transition.** Chicago: Public Administration Clearing House, 1953.

72. Beltram, Edward J. **Models for Public System Analysis.** New York: Academic Press, 1977.

73. Bender, George H. "Bureaucracy Runs Wild." **Congressional Record** 86 (1940): 2765-2767.

74. Bendix, Reinhard. **Higher Civil Servants in American Society: A Study of the Social Origins, the Careers, and the Power-Position of Higher Federal Administrators.** Boulder: University of Colorado Press, 1949.

75. Bendix, Reinhard. "The Public Servant in a Democracy: A Study of the Social Origins and Careers of Higher Federal Administrators." Ph.D. dissertation, University of Chicago. 1947.

76. Bendix, Reinhard. "Who Are the Government Bureaucrats?" **Studies in Leadership.** Edited by Alvin Gouldner. New York: Russell and Russell, 1965.

77. Bennis, Warren G., ed. **American Bureaucracy.** Chicago: Aldine, 1970.

78. Benson, Bruce L. "Why Are Congressional Committees Dominated by High-Demand Legislators - A Comment on Niskanen's View of Bureaucrats and Politicians." **Southern Economic Review** 48 (1981): 68-77.

79. Berenyi, Eileen B. "The 1974 Congressional Budget and Impoundment Control Act: A Study of Institutional Change in the Federal Budgetary Process." Ph.D. dissertation, Columbia University, 1981.

80. Berg, Clifford L. "Career Development in a Federal Scientific Agency." Ph.D. dissertation, Harvard University, 1955.

81. Berg, Clifford L. "Lapse of Reorganization Authority." **Public Administration Review** 35 (March 1975): 195-199.

82. Berger, Harriet F. "Exclusive Recognition of Employee Organizations in the Public Service: Federal Agencies in Philadelphia and the City of Philadelphia." Ph.D. dissertation, University of Pennsylvania, 1967.

83. Berger, Raoul. **Executive Privilege.** Cambridge, MA: Harvard University Press, 1977.

84. Bergin, Thomas J. "Federal Agency Implementation of the Privacy Act of 1974." Ph.D. dissertation, American University, 1978.

85. Berkley, George E. **The Administrative Revolution.** Englewood Cliffs, NJ: Prentice-Hall, 1971.

86. Berkowitz, Edward D. "The Federal Government and the Emergence of Rehabilitation Medicine." **Historian** 43 (August 1981): 530-545.

87. Berkowitz, Edward D. "Mary E. Switzer: The Entrepreneur within the Federal Bureaucracy." **American Journal of Economics and Sociology** 39 (January 1980): 79-81.

88. Berkowitz, Edward D. and J. McQuaid. "Bureaucrats as Social Engineers: Federal Welfare Programs in Herbert Hoover's America." **American Journal of Economics and Sociology** 39 (October 1980): 321-336.

89. Berle, Adolf A. and Malcolm C. Moos. "Need to Know and the Right to Tell: Emmet John Hughes, the Ordeal of Power - A Discussion." **Political Science Quarterly** 79 (June 1964): 161-183.

90. Bernard, Hugh Y. **Public Officials: Elected and Appointed.** Dobbs Ferry, NY: Oceana Publications, 1968.

91. Bernstein, Marver H. **The Job of the Federal Executive.** Washington, DC: Brookings Institution, 1958.

92. Bernstein, Marver H. "Politics and Adjudication." **Journal of Politics** 16 (May 1954): 299-323.

93. Berstein, Samuel J. and Patrick O'Hara. **Public Administration.** New York: Harper and Row, 1979.

94. Bernsten, Elizabeth G. "Formulation and Implementation of Fair Employment Practice Policy by the Federal Government and by New York State." Ph.D. dissertation, Fordham University, 1959.

95. Bertozzi, Mark. "Oversight of the Executive Branch: A Policy Analysis of Federal Special Prosecutor Legislation." Ph.D. dissertation, State University of New York, 1980.

96. Beyer, Janice M. "Predicting How Federal Managers Perceive Criteria Used for Their Promotion." **Public Administration Review** 40 (January 1980): 55-66.

97. Beyer, Janice M. and Harrison M. Trice. "Reexamination of the Relations between Size and Various Components of Organizational Complexity." **Administrative Science Quarterly** 24 (March 1979): 48-64.

98. Bingham, Richard D. and Marcus E. Ethridge. **Reaching Decisions Is Public Policy and Administration.** New York: Longman, 1982.

99. Binkley, Wilfred E. "The Relation of the Federal Executive of the United States to the Congress of the United States." Ph.D. dissertation, Ohio State University, 1937.

100. Blachly, Frederick F. and Miriam E. Oatman. **Administrative Legislation and Adjudication.** Washington, DC: Brookings Institution, 1934.

101. Blachly, Frederick F. and Miriam E. Oatman. **Federal Regulatory Action and Control.** Washington, DC: Brookings Institution, 1940.

102. Blauvaelt, Howard. "Controlling the Federal Bureaucracy." **Chemical Engineering Progress** 74

(October 1978): 32-35.

103. Blinder, Alan S. **The Economics of Public Finance.** Washington, DC: Brookings Institution, 1974.

104. Bloch, Frank S. "The Role of Litigation in the Development of Federal Welfare Policy: A Study of Legal Challenges to State Administration of Aid to Families with Dependent Children Programs as Politic of Redistributive Policy." Ph.D. dissertation, Brandeis University, 1978.

105. Block, Herbert. "Wage Administration in the Federal Civil Service." Ph.D. dissertation, New York University, 1952.

106. Bock, Edwin. **Essays on the Case Method in Public Administration.** Syracuse, NY: Inter-University Case Program, Syracuse University, 1962.

107. Bolster, Mel H. "The Strategic Deployment of Exceptional Talent: An Account of the Career Executive Roster's Short History." **Public Administration Review** 27 (December 1967): 446-451.

108. Bolton, John R. **The Hatch Act: A Civil Libertarian Defense.** Washington, DC: American Enterprise Institute for Public Policy Research, 1976.

109. Bonafede, Dom. "Bureaucracy, Congress, and Interests See Threat in Nixon's Reorganization Plan." **National Journal** 3 (May 8, 1971): 977-986.

110. Bonafede, Dom. "The Federal Bureaucracy: An Inviting Target." **National Journal** 7 (September 13, 1975): 1308-1311.

111. Bonafede, Dom. "Winding Down the Bureaucracy." **National Journal** 3 (May 8, 1971): 977-986.

112. Bonafede, Dom and Jonathan Cottin. "Nixon in Reorganization Plan Seeks to Tighten Control of the Bureaucracy." **National Journal** 2 (March 21, 1970): 620-626.

113. Bond, A. D. "Producer Responses to the Attitudes toward Federal Price Support Programs for Potatoes." Ph.D. dissertation, Michigan State University, 1953.

114. Borcherding, Thomas E., ed. **Budgets and Bureaucrats: The Sources of Government Growth.** Durham, NC: Duke University Press, 1977.

115. Borjas, George J. "Wage Determination in the Federal Government: The Role of Constituents and Bureaucrats." **Journal of Political Economy** 88 (December 1980): 1110-1147.

116. Borjas, George J. **Wage Policy in the Federal Bureaucracy.** Washington, DC: American Enterprise Institute for Public Policy Research, 1980.

117. Borman, Walter C. and Marvin D. Dunnette. "Behavior-Based versus Trait-Oriented Performance Ratings: An Empirical Study." **Journal of Applied Psychology** 60 (October 1975): 561-565.

118. Bauer, Jospeh L. and Charles J. Christenson. **Management: Text and Cases.** Englewood Cliffs, NJ: Prentice-Hall, 1978.

119. Boyer, William W. **Bureaucracy on Trial: Policy-Making by Government Agencies.** Indianapolis: Bobbs-Merrill, 1964.

120. Bozeman, Barry. "Effect of Economic and Partisan Change on Federal Appropriations." **Western Political Quarterly** 30 (March 1977): 112-124.

121. Bozeman, Barry. **Public Management and Policy Analysis.** New York: St. Martin's Press, 1979.

122. Bradbury, William C. "Racial Discrimination in the Federal Service: A Study of the Sociology of Administration." Ph.D. dissertation, Columbia University, 1952.

123. Brenton, Albert and Ronald Wintrobe. "The Equilibrium Size of a Budget-Maximizing Bureau: A Note on Niskanen's Theory of Bureaucracy." **Journal of Political Economy** 83 (February 1975): 195-207.

124. Bresnick, David A. **Public Organizations and Policy.** Glenview, IL: Scott, Foresman, 1982.

125. Briggs, Jean. "The President Proposes, the Bureaucrats Dispose." **Forbes** 121 (June 1978): 55-57.

126. Brigman, William E. "The Executive Branch and the Independent Regulatory Agencies." **Presidential Studies Quarterly** (Spring 1981): 244-261.

127. Briscoe, Dennis R. and Gene S. Leonardson. **Experiences in Public Administration.** North Scituate, MA: Duxbury Press, 1980.

128. Britain, Gerald M. "Evaluating a Federal Experiment in Bureaucratic Reform." **Human Organization** 38 (Fall 1979): 319-324.

129. Britain, Gerald M. "Some Problems of Field Work in the Federal Bureaucracy." **Anthropological Quarterly** 52 (April 1979): 211-220.

130. Brooks, J. "Federal Telecommunications System." **Public Utilities Fortnightly** 71 (April 25, 1963): 19-24.

131. Brower, Brock. "Bureaucrats Redux." **Harper's** 254 (March 1977): 25-26.

132. Brown, David S. **Federal Contributions to Management.** New York: Praeger, 1971.

133. Brown, David S. "President and the Bureaus: Time for a Renewal of Relationships?" **Public Administration Review** 26 (September 1966): 174-182.

134. Brown, David S. "The Public Advisory Board in the Federal Government: An Administrative Analysis of Several Boards with Particular Attention to the Public Advisory Board of the Economic Cooperation Administration and the Mutual Security Program." Ph.D. dissertation, University of Notre Dame, 1956.

135. Brown, David S. "Reforming the Bureaucracy: Some Suggestions for the New President." **Public Administration Review** 37 (March 1977): 163-170.

136. Brown, David S. "Survey Finds Federal Bureaucracy Too Slow." **Public Administration Times** 4 (January 15, 1981): 12.

137. Brown, Paula. "Bureaucracy in a Government Laboratory." **Social Forces** 32 (March 1954): 259-268.

138. Brown, Roger G. "Party and Bureaucracy: From Kennedy to Reagan." **Political Science Quarterly** 97 (Summer 1982): 279-294.

139. Browne, William P. **Politics, Programs and Bureaucrats.** Port Washington, NY: Kennikat Press, 1980.

140. Brownfeld, Allan. "The Inherent Inefficiency of Government Bureaucracy." **Freeman** 27 (June 1977): 361-367.

141. Buchanan, James M. and Robert D. Tollison. **Theory of Public Choice: Political Applications of Economics.** Ann Arbor: University of Michigan Press, 1972.

142. Buchanan, James M. and Gordon Tullock. **The Calculus of Consent.** Ann Arbor: University of Michigan Press, 1962.

143. Buechner, John C. **Public Administration.** Belmont, CA: Dickenson, 1968.

144. Burch, Philip H. **The Civil War to the New Deal.** New York: Holmes and Meier, 1981.

145. Burch, Philip H. **The Federalist Years to the Civil War.** New York: Holmes and Meier, 1981.

146. Burch, Philip H. **The New Deal to the Carter Administration.** New York: Holmes and Meier, 1980.

147. Burdick, Keith H. "A Study to Develop Criteria for the Reporting of Financial Information by Contractors to Federal Agency Management on Cost-Type Government Contracts." D.B.A., University of Colorado, 1970.

148. Burger, Alvin. "Bureaucracy and Inflation: Uncle Sam Should Follow His Own Advice." **Tax Digest** 29 (1951): 221-223.

149. Burkhead, Jesse. **Government Budgeting.** New York: Wiley, 1955.

150. Burkhead, Jesse and Jerry Miner. **Public Expenditure.** New York: Aldine, 1971.

151. Byse, Clark. "Suing the Wrong Defendant in Judicial Review of Federal Administrative Action: Proposals for Reform." **Harvard Law Review** 77 (November 1963): 40-60.

152. Cacioppe, Ron and Philip Mock. "A Comparision of the Quality of Work Experience in Government and Private Organizations." **Human Relations** 37 (November 1984): 923-940.

153. Caiden, Gerald E. **Administrative Reform.** Chicago: Aldine, 1969.

154. Caiden, Gerald E. **The Dynamics of Public Administration.** New York: Holt, Rinehart and Winston, 1971.

155. Caiden, Gerald E. "Reform and the Revitalization of the American Bureaucracy." **Quarterly Journal of Administration** 13 (April/July 1979): 243-258.

156. Caldwell, Lynton K. **Man and His Environment: Policy and Administration.** New York: Harper and Row, 1975.

157. Calvert, Randall and Barry R. Weingast. "Runaway Bureaucracy and Congressional Oversight: Why Reforms Fail." **Policy Studies Review** 1 (May 1981): 557-564.

158. Carroll, James D. "The Implications of President Johnson's Memoranda of September 13 and 14, 1965, for the Funding of Academic Research by Federal Agencies: A Study of Federal-University Research Policies." Ph.D. dissertation, Syracuse University, 1967.

159. Carter, John F. **The New Dealers.** New York: Simon and Schuster, 1934.

160. Cary, William L. "Administrative Agencies and the Securities and Exchange Commission." **Law and Contemporary Problems** 29 (Summer 1964): 653-662.

161. Cayer, N. Joseph. **Public Personnel Administration in the United States.** New York: St. Martin's Press, 1975.

162. Chamberlain, John. "The Compleat Bureaucrat." **National Review** 18 (January 1966): 75-76.

163. Chamberlain, Joseph P. **The Judicial Function in Federal Administrative Agencies.** New York: Commonwealth Fund, 1942.

164. Chamberlain, William H. "Bureaucratic Blight." **Freeman** 17 (January 1967): 34-41.

165. Charlesworth, James C. **Governmental Administration.** New York: Harper, 1951.

166. Chernick, Howard A. "The Economics of Bureaucratic Behavior: An Application to the Allocation of Federal Project Grants." Ph.D. dissertation, University of Pennsylvania, 1976.

167. Chiogioji, Melvin H. "A Critical Analysis of Federal Research and Development Project Selection Methodology for Water Quality

Projects." D.B.A., George Washington University, 1972.

168. Chouchan, D. S. "Politics of Executive-Legislative Relationship in American Democracy: Conflict and Consensus on Uneasy Partnership." **Journal of Constitutional and Parliamentary Studies** 8 (April/June 1974): 141-168.

169. Christopherson, Richard. **Regulating Political Activities of Public Employees.** Chicago: Civil Service Assembly, 1954.

170. Clark, John D. "The Federal Trust Policy." Ph.D. dissertation, Johns Hopkins University, 1931.

171. Clasen, Don and James T. Jones. "Increasing Minority Representation in the Public Bureaucracies." **Bureaucrat** 2 (Summer 1973): 178-188.

172. Cleveland, Harlan. "The Case for Bureaucracy." **New York Times Magazine** (October 27, 1963): 19, 113-114.

173. Cleveland, Harlan. **The Future Executive.** New York: Harper and Row, 1972.

174. Cleveland, Harlan. "Survival in a Bureaucratic Jungle." **Report** 14 (April 5, 1956): 29-32.

175. Cohen, Harry. **The Demonic of Bureaucracy: Problems of Change in a Government Agency.** Ames: Iowa State University Press, 1965.

176. Colm, Gerhard. "Executive Office and Fiscal and Economic Policy." **Law and Contemporary Problems** 21 (Fall 1956): 710-723.

177. Colman, William G. "The Role of the Federal Government in the Design and Administration of Inter-governmental Programs." **Annals of the American Academy of Political and Social Science** 359 (May 1965): 23-34.

178. Cooper, Terry L. **The Responsible Administrator.** Port Washington, NY: Kennikat Press, 1982.

179. Corbett, D. C. "The Politics of Bureaucracy in the United States of America." **Public Administration** 32 (March 1973): 28-41.

180. Corson, John J. "Neglected Element of Political Leadership." **Personnel Administration** 34 (May

1971): 37-43.

181. Corson, John J. and Joseph P. Harris. **Public Administration in Modern Society.** New York: McGraw-Hill, 1963.

182. Corson, John J. and Paul R. Shale. **Men Near the Top.** Baltimore: Johns Hopkins University Press, 1966.

183. Coston, Dean W. "Bureaucratic Reactions to Congressional Pressures." **Bureaucrat** 2 (Fall 1973): 269-277.

184. Craft, Arnold M. "The Federal Government: An Insurer of Last Resort." D.B.A., George Washington University, 1972.

185. Crenson, Matthew A. **The Federal Machine: Beginnings of Bureaucracy in Jacksonian America.** Baltimore: Johns Hopkins University Press, 1975.

186. Crider, John. **The Bureaucrat.** Philadelphia: Lippincott, 1944.

187. Croxall, John R. "An Inquiry into Reporting of Accrued Expenditures for a Federal Agency's Grant Activities." Ph.D. dissertation, American University, 1970.

188. Cross, Jennefer. "Smoking Out the Bureaucrats." **Nation** 221 (October 1975): 306-308.

189. Curnow, Geoffrey R. "The Dimensions of Executive Work in the United States Federal Career Civil Service: A Factor Analytic Study." Ph.D. dissertation, Cornell University, 1967.

190. Dahl, Robert A. **Who Governs?** New Haven, CT: Yale University Press, 1961.

191. Dahl, Robert A. and Charles E. Lindblom. **Politics, Economics, and Welfare: Planning and Politico-Economic Systems Resolved into Basic Social Processes.** New York: Harper and Row, 1953.

192. Damon, Allan I. "Federal Bureaucracy." **American Heritage** 25 (August 1974): 65-68.

193. Danhof, Clarence H. **Government Contracting and Technological Change.** Washington, DC: Brookings Institution, 1967.

194. Daniels, Jonathan. "I Am a Bureaucrat." **Atlantic**

Monthly 173 (April 1944): 96-101.

195. David, Paul T. and Ross Pollock. **Executives for Government: Central Issues of Federal Personnel Administration.** Washington, DC: Brookings Institution, 1957.

196. Davis, James W. "Executive Roles in Technical Bureaus: A Study of Senior Executives in Five Scientific and Technical Bureau of the Federal Government." Ph.D. dissertation, University of Michigan, 1964.

197. Davis, James W. **An Introduction to Public Administration: Politics, Policy, and Bureaucracy.** New York: Free Press, 1974.

198. Davis, James W. **The National Executive Branch.** New York: Free Press, 1970.

199. Davis, James W. **Politics, Policy, and Bureaucracy.** New York: Free Press, 1974.

200. Davis, Otto A. "Towards a Predictive Theory of Government Expenditure: U.S. Domestic Appropriations." **British Journal of Political Science** 4 (October 1974): 419-452.

201. Dawson, Irving O. "New Developments and Problems in Labor Relations in the Federal Civil Service." **Rocky Mountain Social Science Journal** 11 (October 1974): 91-101.

202. Dean, Alan L. "Management of Executive Departments." **Annals of the American Academy of Political and Social Science** 466 (March 1983): 77-90.

203. Dean, Larry M. "Manning Levels, Organizational Effectiveness, and Health." **Human Relations** 32 (March 1979): 237-246.

204. Dearmont, Nelson S. "Federalist Attitudes toward Governmental Secrecy in the Age of Jefferson." **Historian** 37 (February 1975): 222-240.

205. Debeer, Anne Marie M. "Zero-Base Budgeting in the Federal Government: Attitudes of Mid-Management and Analysis of Theory Versus Practice." D.B.A., George Washington University, 1980.

206. Dellums, Ronald. "Bureaucratic Accountability Act." **Congressional Record** 119 (1973): 10044-10045.

207. Dem Kovich, Linda. "The Rewards and Frustrations of the Federal Bureaucracy." **National Journal** 11 (June 16, 1979): 998-1000.

208. Dempsey, John R. "Carter Reorganization: A Midterm Appraisal." **Public Administration Review** 39 (January 1979): 74-78.

209. Denhart, Robert B. **In the Shadow of Organization.** Lawrence: University of Kansas Press, 1981.

210. Dennard, Cleveland. "The Minority Bureaucrat." **Bureaucrat** 2 (Summer 1973): 127-130.

211. Derthick, Martha. **Between State and Nation.** Washington, DC: Brookings Institution, 1974.

212. Desrochers, Lindsay P. "Federal Government Sponsored Advocacy Programs: A Study in Public Learning." Ph.D. dissertation, University of California, 1980.

213. Deutsch, Karl W. **The Nerves of Government: Models of Political Communication and Control.** New York: Free Press, 1963.

214. Dietsch, Robert W. "The Invisible Bureaucracy." **New Republic** 164 (February 20, 1971): 19-21.

215. Dimock, Marshall E. "Administrative Law and Bureaucracy." **Annals of the American Academy of Political and Social Science** 292 (March 1954): 57-64.

216. Dimock, Marshall E. **Administrative Vitality.** New York: Harper and Row, 1959.

217. Dimock, Marshall E. **The Executive in Action.** New York: Harper and Row, 1945.

218. Dimock, Marshall E. **Law and Dynamic Administration.** New York: Praeger, 1981.

219. Dimock, Marshall E. **The New American Political Economy: A Synthesis of Politics and Economics.** New York: Harper, 1962.

220. Dimock, Marshall E. "Objectives of Governmental Reorganization." **Public Administration Review** 11 (Autumn 1951): 233-241.

221. Dimock, Marshall E. and Gladys O. Dimock. **Public Administration.** New York: Rinehart, 1983.

222. Dince, R. R. "Coping with the Civil Service." **Fortune** 97 (June 5, 1978): 132-135.

223. Ditter, J. William. "Bureaucratic Ambitions." **Congressional Record** 87 (1941): A3813-3814.

224. Divine, William R. "Second Hoover Commission Reports: An Analysis." **Public Administration Review** 15 (Fall 1959): 263-269.

225. Divine, William R. "Strengthening the Management of Federal Programs." **Public Administration Review** 11 (Spring 1951): 109-115.

226. Doctors, Samuel I. "Technology Transfer in the Federal Agency Setting: A Case Study of Federal Agency Policies and Programs Affecting the Secondary Application of Aerospace Technology." Ph.D. dissertation, Harvard University, 1969.

227. Dodd, Lawrence C. and Richard L. Schott. **Congress and the Administrative State.** New York: Wiley, 1979.

228. Dodds, Harold W. "Bureaucracy and Representative Government." **Annals of the American Academy of Political and Social Science** 189 (January 1937): 165-172.

229. Dolbeare, Kenneth M. **Political Change in the United States: A Framework for Analysis.** New York: McGraw-Hill, 1974.

230. Dolbeare, Kenneth M. **Public Policy Evaluation.** Beverly Hills, CA: Sage, 1975.

231. Douty, H. M. "Fair Comparison: The Case of the United States White-Collar Civil Service." **Economica** 32 (November 1965): 375-392.

232. Downs, Anthony. **Bureaucratic Structure and Decision Making.** Santa Monica, CA: Rand, 1966.

233. Downs, Anthony. **An Economic Theory of Democracy.** New York: Harper and Row, 1957.

234. Downs, Anthony. **Inside Bureaucracy.** Boston: Little, Brown, 1967.

235. Downs, Anthony. **A Theory of Bureaucracy.** Santa Monica, CA: Rand, 1964.

236. Drew, Elizabeth. **Politics and Money: The New Road to Corruption.** New York: Macmillan, 1983.

237. Drury, James W. "Separations of Federal Employees, 1937-1947." Ph.D. dissertation, Princeton University, 1948.

238. Dubnoff, Caren. "The Lost War on Poverty: The Dynamics of a Federal Program in an Urban Political System." Ph.D. dissertation, Columbia University, 1974.

239. Dummont, Matthew. "Down the Bureaucracy." **Trans-Action** 7 (October 1970): 10-14.

240. Dunn, Delmer D. "Differences among Public Officials in Their Reliance on the Press for Information." **Social Science Quarterly** 49 (March 1969): 829-839.

241. Durham, G. Homer. "Coordination by Special Representatives of the Chief Executive." **Public Administration Review** 8 (Summer 1948): 176-180.

242. Dvorin, Eugene P. and Robert H. Simmons. **Public Administration.** New York: Alfred, 1977.

243. Dwivedi, O. P. **Public Service Ethics.** Brussels: International Institute of Administrative Sciences, 1978.

244. Dye, Thomas R. **Understanding Public Policy.** Englewood Cliffs, NJ: Prentice-Hall, 1972.

245. Eberhardt, Larry A. "Permanent Citizen Advisory Councils on Foreign Relations in the Executive Branch: A Descriptive and Analytical Survey of Role Conceptions and Their Correlates." Ph.D. dissertation, Northwestern University, 1971.

246. Eccles, James R. **The Hatch Act and the American Bureaucracy.** New York: Vantage Press, 1981.

247. Eccles, Mary E. "Race, Sex, and Government Jobs: A Study of Affirmative Action Programs in Federal Agencies." Ph.D. dissertation, Harvard University, 1976.

248. Eckstein, Harry. **The Evaluation of Political Performances: Problems and Dimensions.** Beverly Hills, CA: Sage, 1971.

249. Eddy, William B. **Public Organization Behavior and Development.** Boston: Little, Brown, 1981.

250. Edelman, Murray. "Governmental Organization and Public Policy." **Public Administration Review** 12

(Autumn 1952): 276-283.

251. Edmunds, Sterling. **Basics of Private and Public Management.** Lexington, MA: Lexington Books, 1978.

252. Edmunds, Sterling. **The Federal Octopus: A Survey of the Destruction of Constitutional Government and of Civil and Economic Liberty in the United States and the Rise of an All-Embracing Federal Bureaucratic Despotism.** Charlottesville, VA: Michie, 1932.

253. Edmunds, Sterling. "The Growth of the Federal Bureaucratic Tyranny." **Lawyer and Banker** 26 (January/February 1933): 20-29.

254. Edwards, George C., ed. **Public Policy Implementation.** Greenwich, CT: JAI Press, 1984.

255. Ehrenberg, Ronald G. "Correlates of Underfunding of Public Sector Retirement Systems." **Economic Inquiry** 18 (July 1980): 493-500.

256. Eichner, Alfred S. and Charles M. Brecher. **Controlling Social Expenditures.** New York: Universe Books, 1979.

257. Eimicke, William B. **Public Administration in a Democratic Context.** Beverly Hills, CA: Sage, 1974.

258. Einhorn, Jessica P. "The Effect of Bureaucratic Politics on the Expropriation Policy of the Nixon Administration: 2 Case Studies, 1969-1972." Ph.D. dissertation, Princeton University, 1974.

259. Eisinger, Peter K. **Citizen Contact with Public Officials.** Madison: Institute for Research on Poverty, University of Wisconsin, 1971.

260. Eliash, Moshe. "A Government of Men: An Analysis of the Discretionary Powers Delegated to the Executive." Ph.D. dissertation, Cornell University, 1955.

261. Ellett, Joseph C. "The Federal Emergency Relief Administration: An Experiment in Financing and Administering Unemployment Relief." Ph.D. dissertation, University of Virginia, 1951.

262. Elman, Philip A. "A Note on Administrative Adjudication." **Yale Law Journal** 74 (March 1965): 652-656.

263. Emmerich, Herbert. **Essays on Federal Reorganization.** University: University of Alabama Press, 1950.

264. Emmerich, Herbert. **Federal Organization and Administrative Management.** University: University of Alabama Press, 1971.

265. Ensley, Grover W. "The Nation's Budget and the Federal Government's Budget." Ph.D. dissertation, New York University, 1947.

266. Epstein, Edward J. "Krogh File - The Politics of Law and Order." **Public Interest** 39 (Spring 1975): 99-124.

267. Esman, Milton J. "The Organization of Personnel Administration in a Sample of Federal Agencies." Ph.D. dissertation, Princeton University, 1942.

268. Estall, Robert C. "Regional Planning in the United States: An Evaluation of Experience under the 1965 Economic Development Act." **Town Plan Review** 48 (October 1977): 341-364.

269. Ethridge, Marcus E. "Legislative-Administrative Interaction as Intrusive Access: An Empirical Analysis." **Journal of Politics** 43 (May 1981): 473-492.

270. Ethridge, Marcus E. **Legislative Participation in Implementation: Policy through Politics.** New York: Praeger, 1985.

271. Fain, Tyrus G., ed. **Federal Reorganization: The Executive Branch.** New York: Bowker, 1977.

272. Fairlie, John A. **The National Administration of the United States of America.** New York: Macmillan, 1914.

273. Fanin, Paul. "The Bureaucratic Revolution." **Congressional Record** 121 (1975): 27340-27342.

274. Farago, Ladislas. **Its Your Money: Waste and Mismanagement in Government Spending.** New York: Random House, 1964.

275. Farber, Mindy. "Tales from the Public Sector: Diary of a Bureaucrat." **Policy Review** 22 (Fall 1982): 167-175.

276. Farnum, George R. "America Confronts Bureaucracy." **Law Society Journal** 7 (August 1936): 514-519.

277. Feldman, Daniel L. **Reforming Government.** New York: Morrow, 1981.

278. Fenno, Richard F. **The Power of the Purse.** Boston: Little, Brown, 1966.

279. Fenno, Richard F. **The President's Cabinet: An Analysis in the Period from Wilson to Eisenhower.** Cambridge, MA: Harvard University Press, 1959.

280. Fenno, Richard F. "President-Cabinet Relations: A Pattern and a Case Study." **American Political Science Review** 52 (June 1958): 388-405.

281. Fesler, James W. "Administrative Literature and the Second Hoover Commission Reports." **American Political Science Review** 51 (March 1957): 135-157.

282. Fesler, James W. "Federal Administrative Regions, with Special Reference to Procurement Planning Activities of the War Department." Ph.D. dissertation, Harvard University, 1935.

283. Fesler, James W. **Public Administration: Theory and Practice.** Englewood Cliffs, NJ: Prentice-Hall, 1980.

284. Finer, Herman. "Critics of Bureaucracy." **Political Science Quarterly** 60 (March 1945): 100-112.

285. Finn, Chester E. "Federal Patronage of Universities in the United States: A Rose by Many Other Names?" **Minerva** 14 (Winter 1976-1977): 496-529.

286. Fiorina, Morris P. "The Case of the Vanishing Marginals: The Bureaucracy Did It." **American Political Science Review** 71 (March 1977): 177-181.

287. Fiorina, Morris P. and Roger G. Noll. "Voters, Bureaucrats and Legislators: A Rational Choice Perspective on the Growth of Bureaucracy." **Journal of Public Economics** 9 (April 1978): 239-254.

288. Fiorina, Morris P. and Roger G. Noll. "Voters, Legislators, and Bureaucracy." **American Economic Review** 68 (May 1978): 256-263.

289. Firestone, John M. "Cyclical Behavior of Federal Receipts and Expenditures, 1879-1949." Ph.D. dissertation, Columbia University, 1955.

290. Fishel, Leslie H. "The Federal Government and History." **Wisconsin Magazine of History** 47 (Autumn 1963): 47-49.

291. Fisher, Louis. "Congress, the Executive and the Budget." **Annals of the American Academy of Political and Social Science** 411 (January 1974): 102-113.

292. Fisher, Louis. **Presidential Spending Power.** Princeton, NJ: Princeton University Press, 1975.

293. Fisher, Louis and Ronald C. Moe. "Presidential Reorganization Authority: Is It Worth the Cost?" **Political Science Quarterly** 96 (Summer 1981): 301-318.

294. Fisk, Donald M. "Productivity Trends in the Federal Government." **Monthly Labor Review** 108 (October 1985): 3-9.

295. Fitzpatrick, Dick. "Public Information Activities of Government Agencies." **Public Opinion Quarterly** 11 (Winter 1947): 530-539.

296. Fitzsimmons, Allan K. "Environmental Quality as a Theme in Federal Legislation." **Geographical Review** 70 (July 1980): 314-327.

297. Fleishman, Joel L. **Public Duties.** Cambridge, MA: Harvard University Press, 1981.

298. Fleming, Harold C. "The Federal Executive and Civil Rights: 1961-1965." **Daedalus** 94 (Fall 1965): 921-948.

299. Fletcher, Arthur A. "Random Thoughts on the Bureaucracy." **Bureaucrat** 2 (Summer 1973): 136-143.

300. Flynn, Warren R. "A Study of Alienation from Work and Perceived Support for Work Activities in the Federal Government." D.B.A., University of Colorado, 1973.

301. Foley, Fred. "Effectiveness of Federal Programs: The Politics of Bureaucracy." **Polity** 9 (1976): 220-227.

302. Fox, Douglas M. **Managing the Public's Interest.** New York: Holt, Rinehart and Winston, 1979.

303. Fox, Douglas M. "President's Proposals for Executive Reorganization: A Critique." **Public Administration** 33 (September 1973): 401-406.

304. Frank, Elke. "The Role of Bureaucracy in Transition." **Journal of Politics** 28 (November 1966): 724-753.

305. Frederickson, H. George. **New Public Administration.** University: University of Alabama Press, 1980.

306. Frederickson, H. George and Charles Wise. **Public Administration and Public Policy.** Lexington, MA: Lexington Books, 1977.

307. Freedman, James O. **Crisis and Legitimacy: The Administrative Process and American Government.** New York: Cambridge University Press, 1978.

308. Freedman, Robert. "The Inflationary Impact of Eight Federal Aid Agencies During the Year 1946-1950." Ph.D. dissertation, Yale University, 1953.

309. Freeman, John L. "The Bureaucracy in Pressure Politics." **Annals of the American Academy of Political and Social Science** 319 (September 1958): 10-19.

310. Freeman, John L. "The New Deal for Indians: A Study in Bureau-Committee Relations in American Government." Ph.D. dissertation, Princeton University, 1952.

311. Freeman, John L. **The Political Process: Executive Bureau-Legislative Committee Relations.** Garden City, NY: Doubleday, 1955.

312. Freeman, Robert A. **The Growth of American Government: A Morphology of the Welfare State.** Stanford, CA: Hoover Institution Press, 1975.

313. French, Bruce H. "Federal Government Professional Personnel Movements: A Study of College Graduates Appointed from January 1935 to April 1939." Ph.D. dissertation, University of Pennsylvania, 1947.

314. Fried, Robert C. **Performance in American Bureaucracy.** Boston: Little, Brown, 1976.

315. Friedrich, Carl J. and Taylor Gole. **Responsible Bureaucracy.** Cambridge, MA: Harvard University Press, 1932.

316. Friedrich, Carl J. **Constitutional Government and Democracy: Theory and Practice in Europe and**

America. Boston: Ginn, 1946.

317. Friedrich, Carl J. **Man and His Government: An Empirical Theory of Politics.** New York: McGraw-Hill, 1963.

318. Fritschler, A. Lee. "Bureaucracy and Democracy: The Unanswered Question." **Public Administration Review** 26 (March 1966): 69-74.

319. Fritschler, A. Lee. **Smoking and Politics: Policymaking and the Federal Bureaucracy.** Englewood Cliffs, NJ: Prentice-Hall, 1975.

320. Frolich, Norman, Joe Oppenheimer and Oran Young. **Political Leadership and Collective Goods.** Princeton, NJ: Princeton University Press, 1971.

321. Fuchs, Eliezer. "The Policy Formation Process: A Conceptual Framework for Analysis." Ph.D. dissertation, Northwestern, 1972.

322. Fucik, William C. "Challenge of Implementing Federally Assisted New Communities." **Public Administration Review** 35 (May 1975): 249-256.

323. Gaertner, Gregory H. "Federal Agencies in the Context of Transition: A Contrast between Democratic and Organizational Theories." **Public Administration Review** 43 (September/October 1983): 421-432.

324. Galbraith, John K. **Economics and the Public Purpose.** Boston: Houghton Mifflin, 1973.

325. Gallas, Nesta M. "Public Personnel Selection: A Behavioral Analysis of Current Practices." D.P.A. dissertation, University of Southern California, 1967.

326. Galper, Harvey. "The Federal Government Expenditure Process: A Case Study." Ph.D. dissertation, Yale University, 1966.

327. Gandy, Oscar H. **Beyond Agenda Setting: Information Subsidies and Public Policy.** Norwood, NJ: Ablex, 1982.

328. Garand, James C. and Donald A. Gross. "Toward a Theory of Bureaucratic Compliance with Presidential Directives." **Presidential Studies Quarterly** 12 (Spring 1982): 195-207.

329. Garson, G. David and H. Oliver Williams. **Public**

Administration. Boston: Allyn and Bacon, 1981.

330. Gartner, A. and F. Reissman. **The Emerging Service Society.** New York: Harper and Row, 1974.

331. Garwood, John D. "When Should Government Agency Operations Remain Secret?" **Public Utilities Fortnightly** 70 (August 30, 1962): 274-283.

332. Gates, Bruce L. **Social Program Administration.** Englewood Cliffs, NJ: Prentice-Hall, 1980.

333. Gates, Paul W. "Federal Land Policies in the Southern Public Land States." **Agricultural History** 53 (January 1979): 206-227.

334. Gaus, John M. **Reflections on Public Administration.** University : University of Alabama Press, 1947.

335. Gaus, John M., Leonard D. White and Marshall E. Dimock. **Frontiers of Public Administration.** Chicago: University of Chicago Press, 1936.

336. Gawthrop, Louis C. **Administrative Politics and Social Change.** New York: St. Martin's Press, 1971.

337. Gawthrop, Louis C. **The Administrative Process and Democratic Theory.** Boston: Houghton Mifflin, 1970.

338. Gawthrop, Louis C. **Bureaucratic Behavior in the Executive Branch.** New York: Free Press, 1969.

339. Gawthrop, Louis C. **Public Sector Management Systems and Ethics.** Bloomington: Indiana University Press, 1984.

340. Geekie, William J. **Why Government Fails or What's Really Wrong with the Bureaucracy.** Roslyn Heights, NY: Libra, 1976.

341. Gellhorn, Walter. **Federal Administrative Proceedings.** Baltimore: Johns Hopkins University Press, 1941.

342. Gensheimer, Cynthia F. "The Political Economy of Federal Project Grant Distribution." Ph.D. dissertation, University of California, 1979.

343. Gervasi, Frank H. **Big Government: The Meaning and Purpose of the Hoover Commission Report.** New

York: Whittlesey House, 1949.

344. Gianos, Philip L. "Scientists as Policy Advisors: The Context of Influence." **Western Political Quarterly** 27 (September 1974): 424-468.

345. Giblin, Edward J. "Organization Development: Public Sector Theory and Practice." **Public Personnel Management** 5 (March 1976): 108-109.

346. Gilbert, Charles E. and Max M. Kampelman. "Legislative Control of the Bureaucracy." **Annals of the American Academy of Political and Social Science** 292 (March 1954): 76-87.

347. Gilbert, G. Ronald, ed. **Making and Managing Policy: Formulation, Analysis, Evaluation.** New York: Dekker, 1984.

348. Gill, William A. "Sound Management and Effective Use of Computers in the Federal Government." **Computers and Automation** 14 (April 1965): 14-17.

349. Goldman, Don. "Need a Fall Guy? Blame a Bureaucrat." **Bureaucrat** 9 (Fall 1980): 7-9.

350. Goldwater, Barry M. "Bureaucrats Should Follow Laws, Not Make Them." **Congressional Record** 116 (1970): 41591-41593.

351. Goldwater, Barry M. **The Coming Breakpoint.** New York: Macmillan, 1976.

352. Goldwin, Robert A. **Bureaucrats, Policy Analysts, Statesmen: Who Leads?** Washington, DC: American Enterprise Institute for Public Policy Research, 1980.

353. Golembiewski, Robert T. **Approaches to Organizing.** Washington, DC: American Society for Public Administration, 1980.

354. Golembiewski, Robert T. **Cases in Public Management.** Chicago: Rand McNally, 1973.

355. Golembiewski, Robert T. "Organization Development in Public Agencies: Perspectives on Theory and Practice." **Public Administration Review** 29 (July 1969): 367-377.

356. Golembiewski, Robert T. **Perspectives on Public Management.** Itasca, IL: Peacock, 1968.

357. Golembiewski, Robert T. **Public Budgeting and**

Finance. Itasca, IL: Peacock, 1968.

358. Golembiewski, Robert T. and Michael Cohen. **People in Public Service.** Itasca, IL: Peacock, 1976.

359. Golembiewski, Robert T., Frank Gibson and Geoffrey Y. Carnog. **Public Administration.** Chicago: Rand McNally, 1966.

360. Goodin, Robert E. "Rational Politicians and Rational Bureaucrats in Washington and Whitehall." **Public Administration** 60 (Spring 1982): 23-41.

361. Goodin, Robert T. "The Logic of Bureaucratic Back Scratching." **Public Choice** 21 (1975): 53-67.

362. Goodnow, Frank J. **Politics and Administration.** New York: Macmillan, 1900.

363. Goodrick, M. George. "Integration vs. Decentralization in the Federal Field Service." **Public Administration Review** 9 (Autumn 1949): 272-277.

364. Goodsell, Charles T. **The Case for Bureaucracy: A Public Administration Polemic.** Chatham, NJ: Chatham House, 1985.

365. Goodsell, Charles T. "Congressional Access to Executive Information: A Problem of Legislative-Executive Relations in American National Government." Ph.D. dissertation, Harvard University, 1961.

366. Goodsell, Charles T. **The Public Encounter.** Bloomington: Indiana University Press, 1981.

367. Gordon, George J. **Public Administration in America.** New York: St. Martin's Press, 1978.

368. Gore, William J. **Administrative Decision Making.** New York: Wiley, 1964.

369. Gortner, Harold F. **Administration in the Public Sector.** New York: Wiley, 1977.

370. Gourley, Jay. "Bureaucrat's Country Club." **Washington Monthly** 8 (May 1976): 45-47.

371. Grabosky, Peter N. and David H. Rosenbloom. "Racial and Ethnic Integration in the Federal Service." **Social Science Quarterly** 56 (June 1975): 71-84.

372. Grace, J. Peter. **Burning Money: The Waste of Your Tax Dollars.** New York: Macmillan, 1984.

373. Graebner, William. "Efficiency, Security, Community: The Origins of Civil Service Retirement." **Prologue** 12 (Fall 1980): 116-133.

374. Graebner, William. "Uncle Sam Just Loves the Ladies: Sex Discrimination in the Federal Government, 1917." **Labor History** 21 (Winter 1979-1980): 75-85.

375. Graev, Lawrence G. "S. 1035 - Congress in the Vanguard: The Establishment of Rights for Federal Employees." **George Washington Law Review** 37 (October 1968): 101-131.

376. Graham, George A. "Presidency and the Executive Office of the President." **Journal of Politics** 12 (November 1950): 599-621.

377. Graham, Hugh. "Short-Circuiting the Bureaucracy in the Great Society Policy Origins in Education." **Presidential Studies Quarterly** 12 (Summer 1982): 407-420.

378. Graham, Jean C. "Merit Systems in Social Security: A Study of the Administration of the Personnel." Ph.D. dissertation, University of Chicago, 1943.

379. Graham, Otis L. "The Broker State." **Wilson Quarterly** 8 (Winter 1984): 86-97.

380. Gramlich, Edward M. "The Behavior and Adequacy of the United States Federal Budget, 1952-1964." Ph.D. dissertation, Yale University, 1965.

381. Graske, Theodore W. **Federal Reference Manual.** Washington, DC: National Law Book Company, 1939.

382. Graves, Thomas J. "IGR and the Executive Branch: The New Federalism." **Annals of the American Academy of Political and Social Science** 416 (November 1974): 40-51.

383. Graves, William B. **Public Administration in a Democratic Society.** Boston: Heath, 1950.

384. Gray, Richard G. "Freedom of Access to Government Information (A Study of the Federal Executive)." Ph.D. dissertation, University of Minnesota, 1965.

385. Green, Mark J. **The Other Government.** New York:

Norton, 1978.

386. Greene, Sheldon L. "Public Agency Distortion of Congressional Will: Federal Policy Toward Non-President Alien Labor." **George Washington Law Review** 40 (March 1972): 440-463.

387. Greenlaw, Paul S. "Legislative Riders and Federal Personnel Administration: A Case Study of the Jensen, Thomas and Whitten Amendments." Ph.D. dissertation, Syracuse University, 1955.

388. Greenwood, Royston. "Politics and Public Bureaucracies: A Reconsideration." **Policy and Politics** 6 (June 1978): 403-420.

389. Greenwood, Royston and C. R. Hinings. "Contingency Theory and Public Bureaucracies." **Policy and Politics** 5 (December 1976): 159-180.

390. Gregorian, Hrach. "Congressional-Executive Relations and Foreign Policymaking in the Post-Vietnam Period: Case Studies of Congressional Influence." Ph.D. dissertation, Brandeis University, 1981.

391. Grosenick, L. E. **The Administration of the New Federalism.** Washington, DC: American Society for Public Administration, 1973.

392. Gross, Bertram M. and Michael Springer. "A New Orientation in American Government." **Annals of the American Academy of Political and Social Science** 371 (May 1967): 1-19.

393. Grunschlag, Dov M. "Administering Federal Programs of Production Adjustment." **Agricultural History** 49 (January 1975): 131-149.

394. Guyot, James F. "Government Bureaucrats Are Different." **Public Administration Review** 22 (December 1962): 195-202.

395. Haider, Donald H. "Presidential Management Initiatives: A Ford Legacy to Executive Management Improvement." **Public Administration Review** 39 (May 1979): 248-259.

396. Hallman, H. **Administrative Decentralization and Citizen Control.** Washington, DC: Center for Governmental Studies, 1971.

397. Halperin, Morton H. **Bureaucratic Politics and Foreign Policy.** Washington, DC: Brookings

Institution, 1974.

398. Hamill, Katherine. "This Is a Bureaucrat." **Fortune** 48 (1953): 156-158.

399. Hampton, Robert E. "Civil Service Perspective." **Civil Service Journal** 15 (April 1975): 28-31.

400. Hansen, Michael G. "Management Improvement Initiatives in the Reagan Administration: Round Two." **Public Administration Review** 45 (May/June 1985): 441-446.

401. Harman, Keith A. "Compliance-Gaining Strategies as Revealed by the Contents of Selected Federal Funding Proposals." Ph.D. dissertation, University of Oklahoma, 1982.

402. Harper, Edwin, L. "The Policy-Making Role of Federal Political Executives: The Case of the Comptrollers of the Currency." Ph.D. dissertation, University of Virginia, 1968.

403. Harris, Joseph P. **Congressional Control of Administration.** Washington, DC: Brookings Institution, 1964.

404. Hartman, Robert W. **Pay and Pensions for Federal Workers.** Washington, DC: Brookings Institution, 1983.

405. Hatter, Gary M. "The Effects of the Hatch Act on the Political Participation of Federal Employees." **American Journal of Political Science** 16 (November 1972): 723-729.

406. Hattery, Lowell H. "Management of Social Science Research in the Federal Government: With Special Reference to the Division of Statistical and Historical Research, U.S. Department of Agriculture." Ph.D. dissertation, American University, 1951.

407. Haveman, Robert H. **The Economics of the Public Sector.** New York: Wiley, 1970.

408. Haveman, Robert H. and Julius Margolis. **Public Expenditures and Policy Analysis.** Chicago: Rand McNally, 1970.

409. Hawley, Claude E. and Ruth G. Weintraub. **Administrative Questions and Political Answers.** Princeton, NJ: Van Nostrand, 1966.

410. Hayford, Stephen L. "First Amendment Rights of Government Employees: A Primer for Public Officials." **Public Administration Review** 45 (January/February 1985): 241-248.

411. Hayward, Nancy and George Kuper. "National Economy and Productivity in Government." **Public Administration Review** 38 (January 1978): 2-5.

412. Heady, Ferrel. "Reorganization Act of 1949." **Public Administration Review** 9 (Summer 1949): 165-174.

413. Heady, Ferrel. "Reports of the Hoover Commission." **Review of Politics** 11 (July 1949): 355-378.

414. Heatherly, Charles L., ed. **Mandate for Leadership: Policy Management in a Conservative Administration.** Washington, DC: Heritage Foundation, 1981.

415. Hebron, Lawrence. "Why Bureaucracy Keeps Growing." **Business Week** (November 15, 1976): 23-24.

416. Heclo, Hugh. **A Government of Strangers.** Washington, DC: Brookings Institution, 1977.

417. Heclo, Hugh. "Political Executives and the Washington Bureaucracy." **Political Science Quarterly** 92 (Fall 1977): 395-424.

418. Heclo, Hugh and Lester M. Salamon. **The Illusion of Presidential Government.** Boulder, CO: Westview, 1981.

419. Heim, Peggy. "Financing the Federal Reclamation Program, 1902-1919: The Development of Repayment Policy." Ph.D. dissertation, Columbia University, 1953.

420. Heisler, William J. "Environmental Control Beliefs and the Distribution of Time among Managerial Functions." **Psychological Reports** 34 (February 1974): 33-34.

421. Heller, Deane and David Heller. **The Kennedy Cabinet: America's Men of Destiny.** Derby, CT: Monarch, 1961.

422. Helms, Jesse. "Bureaucratic Absurdities and Citizen Harassment." **Congressional Record** 122 (1976): 22589-22591.

423. Henderson, Thomas A. **Congressional Oversight of**

Executive Agencies: A Story of the House Committee on Government Operations. Gainesville: University of Florida Press, 1970.

424. Henderson, Thomas A. "The House Committee on Government Operations and Congressional Oversight of Executive Agencies." Ph.D. dissertation, Columbia University, 1968.

425. Hendricks, Henry G. "The Federal Debt, 1919-1929." Ph.D. dissertation, University of Illinois, 1930.

426. Henry, Nicholas L. **Public Administration and Public Affairs.** Englewood Cliffs, NJ: Prentice-Hall, 1975.

427. Herber, Bernard P. **Modern Public Finance.** New York: Irwin, 1976.

428. Herber, Bernard P. "The Use of Informers Rewards in Federal Tax Administration." Ph.D. dissertation, University of Washington, 1960.

429. Herman, Walter J. "Federal Debt Management: An Analysis of Its Objectives and Application from 1953 through 1962." Ph.D. dissertation, University of Florida, 1965.

430. Herring, Edward P. **Public Administration and the Public Interest.** New York: McGraw-Hill, 1936.

431. Herring, Edward P. "Social Forces and the Reorganization of the Federal Bureaucracy." **Southwestern Social Science Quarterly** 15 (December 1934): 185-200.

432. Hershey, Cary. **Protest in the Public Service.** Lexington, MA: Lexington Books, 1973.

433. Herwitz, Michael. "Strangers in a Strange Land." **Washington Monthly** 10 (March 1978): 55-61.

434. Hess, Stephen. **Organizing the Presidency.** Washington, DC: Brookings Institution, 1976.

435. Hill, John P. **The Federal Executive.** Boston: Houghton Mifflin, 1916.

436. Hill, Larry B. and F. Ted Herbert. **Essentials of Public Administration.** North Scituate, MA: Duxbury Press, 1979.

437. Hills, William G. **Conducting the Public's Business.** Norman: University of Oklahoma Press,

1973.

438. Hinsdale, Mary L. **A History of the President's Cabinet.** Ann Arbor, MI: Wahr, 1911.

439. Hirsch, Phil. "Privacy: The Problem Doesn't Alarm Bureaucrats." **Datamation** 19 (August 1973): 86-89.

440. Hobbs, Edward H. "Historical Review of Plans for Presidential Staffing." **Law and Contemporary Problems** 21 (Fall 1956): 663-687.

441. Hockett, D. F. and J. E. Kasprzak. "Uncle Sam Needs Help from Business in Cutting Office Costs." **Harvard Business Review** 52 (July 1974): 7-8.

442. Hodgson, John S. **Public Administration.** New York: McGraw-Hill, 1969.

443. Hoffman, Abraham. "The Federal Bureaucracy Meets a Superior Spokesman for Alien Deportation." **Journal of the West** 14 (October 1975): 91-106.

444. Holden, Matthew and Dennis L. Dresang. **What Government Does.** Beverly Hills, CA: Sage, 1975.

445. Holtzman, Abraham. **Legislative Liaison: Executive Leadership in Congress.** Chicago: Rand McNally, 1970.

446. Holzer, Marc. **Productivity in Public Organizations.** Port Washington, NY: Dunellen, 1975.

447. Holzer, Marc and Ellen D. Rosen. **Current Cases in Public Administration.** Monterey, CA: Duxbury Press, 1981.

448. Hoobler, James F. "Management-By-Objectives in the Department of Justice: Theoretical Constructs and Real World Problems Associated with the Evolution of a Formal Management System in a Major Federal Department." Ph.D. dissertation, University of Maryland, 1980.

449. Hook, Sidney. "Bureaucrats Are Human." **Saturday Review of Literature** 41 (May 17, 1958): 12-14, 41.

450. Hoos, Ida R. **Systems Analysis in Public Policy: A Critique.** Berkeley: University of California Press, 1983.

451. Hopkins, Raymond F. "International Rule of Domestic Bureaucracy." **International Organization** 30 (Summer 1976): 405-432.

452. Horn, Stephen. **The Cabinet and Congress.** New York: Columbia University Press, 1960.

453. Horowitz, Donald L. **The Jurocracy: Government, Lawyers, Agency Programs and Judicial Decisions.** Lexington, MA: Lexington Books, 1977.

454. Horton, Forest W. "Building Block Approach: Key to Federal Management Systems?" **Journal of Systems Management** 22 (October 1971): 38-41.

455. Horton, Forrest W. and Donald A. Marchand. **Information Management in Public Administration.** Arlington, VA: Information Resources Press, 1982.

456. Hoshovsky, Alexander G. "Work and Information Requirements of R and D Managers in Two Mission-Oriented Agencies of the Federal Government." Ph.D. dissertation, American University, 1974.

457. Hudson, James R. "Creating Accountable Public Bureaucracies." **Journal of Sociology and Social Welfare** 1 (1973): 103-105.

458. Huerta, Faye C. and Thomas A. Lane. "Participation of Women in Centers of Power." **Social Science Journal** 18 (April 1981): 71-86.

459. Hughes, Jonathan R. T. **The Governmental Habit.** New York: Basic Books, 1977.

460. Hutchens, Philip H. "Equal Employment Opportunity in the Federal Government: An Empirical Analysis." Ph.D. dissertation, American University, 1976.

461. Hyneman, Charles. **Bureaucracy in a Democracy.** New York: Harper, 1950.

462. Ickes, Harold. "Bureaucrats vs. Business Men." **New Republic** 109 (August 2, 1943): 131-133.

463. Ickes, Harold. "Ickes Defines - and Defends - the Bureaucrats." **New York Times Magazine** (January 16, 1944): 9, 45-47.

464. Ickes, Harold, Elbert Thomas and Christian Herter. "Bureaucracy in Review." **State Government** 17 (1944): 273-275.

465. Inbar, Michael. **Routine Decision-Making: The Future of Bureaucracy.** Beverly Hills, CA: Sage, 1979.

466. Ingrassia, Anthony F. "Status Report on Federal Labor-Management Relations." **Civil Service Journal** 18 (July 1977): 38-43.

467. Ippolito, Dennis S. **The Budget and National Politics.** San Francisco: Freeman, 1978.

468. Jacob, Charles E. **Leadership in the New Deal: The Administrative Challenge.** Englewood Cliffs, NJ: Prentice-Hall, 1967.

469. Jacobson, Solomon G. "Implementation of a Federal Program at the Local Level: A Critique of the Introduction of the Model Cities Planning Program in Detroit." Ph.D. dissertation, University of Michigan, 1977.

470. Jaffe, Louis L. "The Effective Limits of the Administrative Process: A Reevaluation." **Harvard Law Review** 67 (May 1954): 1105-1135.

471. Jaffe, Louis L. "The Illusion of the Ideal Administration." **Harvard Law Review** 86 (May 1973): 1183-1199.

472. Jenkins, John A. "Revolving Door Between Government and the Law Firms." **Washington Monthly** 8 (January 1977): 36-44.

473. Jochnowitz, Rose S. "The Federal Area Redevelopment Administration." Ph.D. dissertation, New York University, 1963.

474. Johnson, Herbert A. "Toward a Reappraisal of the Federal Government: 1783-1789." **American Journal of Legal History** 8 (October 1964): 314-325.

475. Johnson, Ronald W. "Organizational Adaptivity and Federal Agency Budgetary Decision-Making." Ph.D. dissertation, State University of New York, Buffalo, 1971.

476. Johnston, Janet C. "Intergovernmental Politics: Defining the Federal Role under the Comprehensive Employment and Training Act of 1973." "Ph.D. dissertation, University of Chicago, 1979.

477. Jones, Augustus J. **Law, Bureaucracy, and Politics: The Implementation of Title VI of the Civil Rights Act of 1964.** Washington, DC: University

Press of America, 1982.

478. Jones, Ralph C. "The Consolidated Return in Federal Taxation." Ph.D. dissertation, Yale University, 1929.

479. Jones, Rochelle and Peter Woll. "Carter vs. the Bureaucrats: The Interest Vested in Chaos." **Nation** 224 (March 1977): 402-404.

480. Judd, Leda R. "Federal Involvement in Health Care after 1945." **Current History** 72 (May/June 1977): 201-206, 227.

481. Junz, Alfred J. "Congressional Investigating Committees." **Social Research** 21 (Winter 1954): 379-396.

482. Kahn, Robert L., Daniel Katz and Barbara Gutek. "Bureaucratic Encounters - An Evaluation of Government Services." **Journal of Applied Behavioral Science** 12 (1976): 178-198.

483. Kahn, Robert L., Barbara Gutek, Eugenia Barton and Daniel Katz. "Americans Love Their Bureaucrats." **Psychology Today** 9 (June 1975): 110-113.

484. Kaiser, Fred M. "Congress Oversees the Bureaucracy." **Bureaucrat** 5 (October 1976): 357-366.

485. Kamlet, Mark S. and David C. Mowery. "Budgetary Side Payments and Government Growth: 1953-1968." **American Journal of Political Science** 27 (November 1983): 636-664.

486. Kammerer, Gladys M. "The Impact of the War on Federal Personnel Administration, 1939-1945." Ph.D. dissertation, University of Chicago, 1947.

487. Kampelman, Max M. "The Legislative Bureaucracy: Its Response to Political Change." **Journal of Politics** 16 (August 1954): 539-550.

488. Karl, Barry D. **Executive Reorganization and Reform in the New Deal: The Genesis of Administrative Management, 1900-1939.** Cambridge, MA: Harvard University Press, 1963.

489. Katz, Daniel, Barbara Gutek, Robert L. Kahn and Eugenia Barton. **Bureaucratic Encounters: A Pilot Study in the Evaluation of Government Services.** Ann Arbor: Institute for Social Research, Survey Research Center, University of Michigan, 1975.

490. Katz, Elihu and Brenda Danet, eds. **Bureaucracy and the Public: A Reader in Official-Client Relations.** New York: Basic Books, 1973.

491. Katz, Joan M. "The Games Bureaucrats Play: Hide and Seek under the Freedom of Information Act." **Texas Law Review** 48 (November 1970): 1261-1285.

492. Katzmann, Robert A. "Judicial Intervention and Organization Theory: Changing Bureaucratic Behavior and Policy." **Yale Law Journal** 89 (January 1980): 513-537.

493. Kaufman, Herbert. **The Administrative Behavior of Federal Bureau Chiefs.** Washington, DC: Brookings Institution, 1981.

494. Kaufman, Herbert. **Administrative Feedback: Monitoring Subordinate's Behavior.** Washington, DC: Brookings Institution, 1973.

495. Kaufman, Herbert. **Are Government Organizations Immortal?** Washington, DC: Brookings Institu-tion, 1976.

496. Kaufman, Herbert. "Fear of Bureaucracy: A Raging Pandemic." **Public Administration Review** 41 (January/February 1981): 1-9.

497. Kaufman, Herbert. **Red Tape, Its Origins, Uses and Abuses.** Washington, DC: Brookings Institution, 1977.

498. Kaulback, Frank S. "The Federal Budget: An Instrument of Fiscal Control." Ph.D. dissertation, University of Virginia, 1946.

499. Keighton, Robert L. "The Executive Privilege and the Congressional Right to Know: A Study of the Investigating Powers of Congressional Committees." Ph.D. dissertation, University of Pennsylvania, 1961.

500. Kelly, Matthew A. "Regulation of Hours of Labor of Federal Employees Including Employees of Public Contractors." Ph.D. dissertation, Princeton University, 1946.

501. Kenamond, Frederick D. "Accounting Theory and Practice, Social-Economic-Political Environment and the Federal Income Tax: Their Interrelationships Concerning Inventories." Ph.D. dissertation, University of Alabama, 1971.

502. Killingsworth, Mark R. and Cordelia W. Reimers. "Race, Ranking, Promotions, and Pay at a Federal Facility: A Logit Analysis." **Industrial and Labor Relations Review** 37 (October 1983): 92-107.

503. Kilpatrick, Franklin P. and M. Kent Jennings. **The Image of Federal Service.** Washington, DC: Brookings Institution, 1964.

504. Kilpatrick, James. "Unchained Bureaucracy Gone Berserk." **Nation's Business** 67 (November 1979): 21-22.

505. Kim, Jae T. **New Readings in American Public Administration.** Dubuque, IA: Kendall Hunt, 1980.

506. Kincheloe, Clarence L. "The Growing Relative Power of the National Executive, 1885-1920." Ph.D. dissertation, University of California, 1928.

507. Kingsley, John D. and William E. Mosher. **Public Personnel Administration.** New York: Harper, 1936.

508. Kirchheimer, Donna W. "Implementation of Federal Social Policy." Ph.D. dissertation, Columbia University, 1976.

509. Klein, Walter H. "An Analysis and Evaluation of Federal Minimum Wage Legislation with Some Suggestions for Future Policy-Making in the Field." Ph.D. dissertation, University of Pittsburgh, 1954.

510. Kleinschrod, Walter A. "Government Plods Ahead to Management Reform." **Administrative Management** 31 (December 1970): 18-21.

511. Klingner, Donald E. **Public Personnel Management.** Englewood Cliffs, NJ: Prentice-Hall, 1980.

512. Knebel, Fletcher, "Bureaucrats Are People." **Look** 21 (May 124, 1957): 77-78.

513. Knowles, David R. "Evaluating the Impact of Federal Counterrecessional Job Creation Programs within the State of Washington." Ph.D. dissertation, Washington State University, 1978.

514. Kohn, Melvin L. "Bureaucratic Man." **New Society** 18 (October 1971): 820-824.

515. Kraines, Oscar. **Congress and the Challenge of Big Government.** New York: Bookman, 1958.

516. Kramer, Fred A. **Contemporary Approaches to Public Budgeting.** Cambridge, MA: Winthrop, 1979.

517. Kramer, Fred A. **Dynamics of Public Bureaucracy.** Cambridge, MA: Winthrop, 1977.

518. Kramer, Fred A. **Perspectives on Public Bureaucracy.** Cambridge, MA: Winthrop, 1973.

519. Kranz, Harry. **The Participatory Bureaucracy: Women and Minorities in a More Representative Public Service.** Lexington, MA: Lexington Books, 1976.

520. Krasner, William. "How to Live with the Bureaucracy - and Win." **New Society** 12 (1968): 116-118.

521. Krauss, Wilma R. "Some Aspects of the Influence Process of Public Bureaucrats: An Ideal-Typic Model and Cross-Cultural Guttman Scale." **Western Political Quarterly** 25 (June 1972): 323-339.

522. Krislov, Samuel and David H. Rosenbloom. **Representative Bureaucracy and the American Political System.** New York: Praeger, 1981.

523. Krause, Leon E. "Management of the Federal Debt." Ph.D. dissertation, New York University, 1958.

524. Kull, Donald C. "Productivity Programs in the Federal Government." **Public Administration Review** 38 (January 1978): 5-8.

525. Kuruvilla, P. K. "A Comparative Study of Recruitment and Training of Higher Federal Civil Servants in Canada and India." Ph.D. dissertation, Carleton University, 1972.

526. Lacy, Alex B. "The White House Staff Bureaucracy." **Trans-Action** 6 (January 1968): 50-56.

527. Lajoie, Susan N. "Research and Analysis: An Assessment of Their Influence on Federal Welfare Policies." Ph.D. dissertation, Harvard University, 1978.

528. Lambie, Morris B. **Training for the Public Service.** Chicago: Public Administration Service, 1935.

529. Lambro, Donald. **The Federal Rathole.** New

Rochelle, NY: Arlington House, 1975.

530. Lampen, Dorothy. "Economic and Social Aspects of Federal Reclamation." Ph.D. dissertation, Johns Hopkins University, 1929.

531. Landis, James M. **The Administration Process.** New Haven, CT: Yale University Press, 1938.

532. Lane, Frederick S. **Current Issues in Public Administration.** New York: St. Martin's Press, 1978.

533. Larson, Arthur D. "Representative Bureaucracy and Administrative Responsibility: A Reassessment." **Midwest Review of Public Administration** 7 (April 1973): 79-89.

534. Larson, Arthur D. "Some Myths About the Executive Branch." **Center Magazine** 7 (September 1974): 53-55.

535. Lasson, Kenneth. **Private Lives of Public Servants** Bloomington: Indiana University Press, 1978.

536. Latham, Earl. **The Federal Field Service.** Chicago: Public Administration Service, 1947.

537. Lawhorne, Clifton O. **Defamation and Public Officials: The Evolving Law of Libel.** Carbondale: Southern Illinois University Press, 1971.

538. Lawton, Frederick J. "Role of the Administrator in the Federal Government." **Public Administration Review** 14 (Spring 1954): 112-118.

539. Learned, Henry B. **The President's Cabinet: Studies in the Origin, Formation and Structure of an American Institution.** New Haven, CT: Yale University Press, 1912.

540. Lee, Robert D. **Public Personnel Systems.** Baltimore, MD: University Park Press, 1979.

541. Lee, Robert D. and Ronald W. Johnson. **Public Budgeting Systems.** Baltimore, MD: University Park Press, 1983.

542. Lees, J. D. "Legislative Review and Bureaucratic Responsibility: The Impact of Fiscal Oversight by Congress on the American Federal Administration." **Public Administration** 45 (Winter 1967): 369-386.

543. Leighton, Alexander H. **The Governing of Men** Princeton, NJ: Princeton University Press, 1945.

544. Leigh, Robert D. "Politicians vs. Bureaucrats." **Harper's** 190 (January 1945): 97-105.

545. Leiserson, Avery. **Administrative Regulation: A Study in Representation of Interests.** Chicago: University of Chicago Press, 1942.

546. Leloup, Lance T. **Budgetary Politics.** Brunswick, OH: Kings Court Communication, 1977.

547. Leloup, Lance T. "Explaining Agency Appropriations Change, Success, and Legislative Support: A Comparative Study of Agency Budget Determination." Ph.D. dissertation, Ohio State University, 1973.

548. Lemann, Nicholas. "Why Carter Fails: Taking the Politics Out of Government." **Washington Monthly** 10 (September 1978): 12-16.

549. Lomov, Michael R. "Administrative Agency New Releases: Public Information Versus Private Injury." **George Washington Law Review** 37 (October 1968): 63-81.

550. Lepawsky, Albert. **Administration.** New York: Knopf, 1960.

551. Lerner, Max. **Public Journal: Marginal Notes on Wartime America.** New York: Viking, 1945.

552. Levine, Charles H. **Managing Human Resources.** Beverly Hills, CA: Sage, 1977.

553. Levine, Charles H. "The Federal Government in the Year 2000: Administrative Legacies of the Reagan Years." **Public Administration Review** 46 (May/June 1986): 195-206.

554. Levine, Charles H. "Unrepresentative Bureaucracy: Or Knowing What You Look Like Tells You Who You Are (and Maybe What to Do About It)." **Bureaucrat** 4 (April 1975): 90-98.

555. Levine, Robert A. **Public Planning: Failure and Redirection.** New York: Basic Books, 1972.

556. Levitar, Sar A. **Working for the Sovereign: Employee Relations in the Federal Government.** Baltimore: Johns Hopkins University Press, 1983.

557. Levy, Sidney J. "Public Image of Government Agencies." **Public Administration Review** 23 (March 1963): 25-29.

558. Lewis, Eugene. **American Politics in a Bureaucratic Age: Citizens, Constituents, Clients and Victims.** Cambridge, MA: Winthrop, 1977.

559. Lewis, Gail B. "Race, Sex, and Supervisory Authority in Federal White-collar Employment." **Public Administration Review** 46 (January/February 1986): 25-30.

560. Leys, Wayne A. R. **Ethics for Policy Decision.** Englewood Cliffs, NJ: Prentice-Hall, 1952.

561. Li, Veh-Shan. "Legal Status of the Federal Government Corporation." Ph.D. dissertation, New York University, 1949.

562. Lieberman, Jethro K. **How the Government Breaks the Law.** New York: Stein and Day, 1972.

563. Lindblom, Charles E. **The Intelligence of Democracy.** New York: Free Press, 1964.

564. Lindblom, Charles E. **The Policy Making Process.** Englewood Cliffs, NJ: Prentice-Hall, 1968.

565. Lindblom, Charles E. **Politics and Markets.** New York: Basic Books, 1977.

566. Linder, Stephen H. "Policy Formulation in Executive Branch Agencies." Ph.D. dissertation, University of Iowa, 1976.

567. Lindquist, Charles A. "The Origin and Development of the United States Commissioner System." **American Journal of Legal History** 14 (January 1970): 1-16.

568. Lindveit, Earl W. "Scientists in Government: A Background Study of the Retention of Scientific Personnel in Federal Employment." Ph.D. dissertation, American University, 1958.

569. Ling, Ta-Tseng. "The War on Poverty and the Concept of Participatory Administration." Ph.D. dissertation, University of Tennessee, 1972.

570. Long, Norton E. "Bureaucracy and Constitutionalism." **American Political Science Review** 46 (September 1952): 808-818.

571. Long, Norton E. "Power and Administration." **Public Administration Review** 9 (Autumn 1949): 257-264.

572. Lorch, Robert S. **Public Administration.** St. Paul, MN: West, 1978.

573. Loucheim, Katie. **The Making of the New Deal: The Insiders Speak.** Cambridge, MA: Harvard University Press, 1983.

574. Lowi, Theodore J. **The End of Liberalism.** New York: Norton, 1969.

575. Lowi, Theodore J. and A. Stone. **Nationalizing Government.** Beverly Hills, CA: Sage, 1979.

576. Ludlow, Louis. **America Go Bust: An Expose of the Federal Bureaucracy and Its Wasteful and Evil Tendencies.** Boston: Stratford, 1933.

577. Ludlow, Louis. "A Resolution to Curb Bureaucracy and Unconstitutional Trends of Government." **Congressional Record** 90 (1944): 4288-4289.

578. Ludtke, James B. "A Positive Program for Federal Debt Management." Ph.D. dissertation, University of Iowa, 1951.

579. Lutrin, Carl E. and Allen K. Settle. **American Public Administration.** Palo Alto, CA: Mayfield, 1985.

580. Lyden, Fremont J. "Program Change and Bureaucracy." **Public Administration Review** 28 (May/June 1968): 278-279.

581. Lyden, Fremont J. "Project Management: Beyond Bureaucracy?" **Public Administration Review** 30 (July/August 1970): 435-436.

582. Lyden, Fremont J. and E. Miller. **Public Budgeting: Program, Planning, and Evaluation.** Chicago: Rand McNally, 1969.

583. Lynn, Laurence E. **Managing the Public's Business.** New York: Basic Books, 1981.

584. Lynn, Laurence E. **The State and Human Services.** Cambridge, MA: MIT Press, 1980.

585. Lynn, Naomi B. and Richard Vaden. "Bureaucratic Response to Civil Service Reform." **Public Administration Review** 39 (July/August 1979): 333-343.

586. Lynn, Naomi B. and Richard Vaden. "Toward a Non-Sexist Personnel Opportunity Structure: The Federal Executive Bureaucracy." **Public Personnel Management** 8 (July-August 1979): 209-215.

587. Maass, Arthur. **Congress and the Common Good.** New York: Basic Books, 1983.

588. McCamy, James L. "Federal Administrative Publicity." Ph.D. dissertation, University of Chicago, 1939.

589. Macauley, William A. "Diffuse and Specific Support for the Executive Branch of Government: A Quasi-Experimental Study." Ph.D. dissertation, University of Houston, 1976.

590. McCurdy, Howard E. **Public Administration.** Menlo Park, CA: Cummings, 1977.

591. McCurdy, Howard E. "Selecting and Training Public Managers: Business Versus Public Administration." **Public Administration Review** 38 (November 1978): 571-578.

592. McFadden, Daniel. "The Revealed Preferences of a Government Bureaucracy: Empirical Evidence." **Bell Journal of Economics** 7 (Spring 1976): 55-72.

593. McFadden, Daniel. "The Revealed Preferences of a Government Bureaucracy: Theory." **Bell Journal of Economics** 6 (Autumn 1975): 401-416.

594. McGregor, Eugene B. "Education and Career Mobility among Federal Administrators: Toward the Development of a Comparative Model." Ph.D. dissertation, Syracuse University, 1969.

595. McGregor, Eugene B. "Politics and the Career Mobility of Bureaucrats." **American Political Science Review** 68 (March 1974): 18-26.

596. McGregor, Russell C. "The Allocation of Federal Expenditures: Plant Disease and Pest Control Programs in the United States Department of Agriculture." Ph.D. dissertation, University of Michigan, 1968.

597. McGuire, O. R. "Federal Administrative Decisions and Judicial Control Thereof, or, Bureaucracy under Control." **Report of the Virginia State Bar Association** 48 (1963): 301-307.

598. McKay, David. "Theory and Practice in Public Policy: The Case of the New Federalism." **Political Studies** 33 (June 1989): 181-202.

599. McKean, Roland N. **Efficiency in Government through Systems Analysis.** New York: Wiley, 1958.

600. Mackenzie, G. Calvin. **The Politics of Presidential Appointments.** New York: Free Press, 1981.

601. McKenzie, Richard B. and Hugh Macaulay. "A Bureaucratic Theory of Regulation." **Public Choice** 35 (1980): 297-314.

602. McKinley, Charles. "Federal Administrative Pathology and the Separation of Powers." **Public Administration Review** 11 (Winter 1951): 17-25.

603. McKinney, Jerome B. and Lawrence C. Howard. **Public Administration.** Oak Park, IL: Moore, 1979.

604. Macmahon, Arthur W. **Federal Administrators: A Biographical Approach to the Problem of Departmental Management.** New York: Columbia University Press, 1939.

605. MacNeil, Neil. **The Hoover Report, 1953-1955.** New York: Macmillan, 1956.

606. Macy, John W., Bruce Adams and J. Jackson Walter. **America's Unelected Government: Appointing the President's Team.** Cambridge, MA: Ballinger, 1983.

607. Madison, Christopher. "He Makes the Bureaucracy Move by Breaking the Bureaucratic Rules." **National Journal** 12 (June 7, 1980): 929-932.

608. Mailick, Sidney and Edward H. Van Ness. **Concepts and Issues in Administrative Behavior.** Englewood Cliffs, NJ: Prentice-Hall, 1962.

609. Mainzer, Lewis C. **Political Bureaucracy.** Glenview, IL: Scott, Foresman, 1973.

610. Malek, Frederic V. "Mr. Executive Goes to Washington." **Harvard Business Review** 50 (September 1972): 63-68.

611. Mann, Dean E. "Selection of Federal Political Executives." **American Political Science Review** 58 (March 1964): 81-99.

612. Mann, Dean E. and Jameson W. Doig. **The Assistant**

Secretaries: Problems and Processes of Appointment. Washington, DC: Brookings Institution, 1965.

613. Mann, Seymour Z. "Policy Formulation in the Executive Branch: The Taft-Hartley Experience." **Western Political Quarterly** 13 (September 1960): 597-608.

614. Manning, Bayless. "Congress, the Executive and Intermestic Affairs: Three Proposals." **Foreign Affairs** 55 (January 1977): 306-324.

615. Mansfield, Harvey C. "Federal Executive Reorganization: Thirty Years of Experience." **Public Administration Review** 29 (July 1969): 332-345.

616. March, James G. and Johan P. Olson. "Organizing Political Life: What Administrative Reorganization Tells Us About Government." **American Political Science Review** 77 (June 1983): 281-296.

617. March, Michael S. "Pensions for Public Employees Present Nationwide Problems." **Public Administration Review** 40 (July 1980): 382-389.

618. Marini, Frank. **Toward a New Public Administration.** Scranton, PA: Chandler, 1971.

619. Marion, David E. "Toward A Political Theory of Public Administration: The Place and Role of Federal Public Service Personnel in the American Democratic Republic." Ph.D. dissertation, Northern Illinois University, 1977.

620. Markham, William T. "Gender and Opportunity in the Federal Bureaucracy." **American Journal of Sociology** 91 (July 1985): 129-150.

621. Marks, Ellen L. **Representation in Theory, Legislatures, and Bureaucracies.** Santa Monica, CA: Rand, 1981.

622. Marshall, Eliot. "Efficiency Expert: Carter's Plan to Shake up the Bureaucracy." **New Republic** 175 (August 21, 1976): 15-17.

623. Martin, David L. "Presidential Attitudes toward the Bureaucracy: The White House Tapes." **Bureaucrat** 4 (July 1975): 223-224.

624. Martin, Roscoe C. **Public Administration and**

Democracy. Syracuse, NY: Syracuse University Press, 1965.

625. Marx, Fritz M. **The Administrative State.** Chicago: University of Chicago Press, 1957.

626. Marx, Fritz M. **Elements of Public Administration.** Englewood Cliffs, NJ: Prentice-Hall, 1946.

627. Masters, Marick F. and Leonard Bieman. "The Hatch Act and the Political Activities of Federal Employee Unions: A Need for Policy Reform." **Public Administration Review** 45 (July/August 1985): 518-526.

628. Mater, Jean. **Public Hearings, Procedures and Strategies: A Guide to Influencing Public Decisions.** Englewood Cliffs, NJ: Prentice-Hall, 1984.

629. Mathews, David. "The War on Bureaucracy." **Southern Review of Public Administration** 1 (September 1977): 247-253.

630. May, Geoffrey. "Daydreams of a Bureaucrat." **Public Administration Review** 5 (Spring 1945): 153-161.

631. May, James V. and Aaron B. Wildavsky. **The Policy Cycle.** Beverly Hills, CA: Sage, 1979.

632. Mayer, M. "World without Government." **Center Magazine** 16 (March/April 1983)" 43-58.

633. Medeiros, James A. and David E. Schmitt. **Public Bureaucracy: Values and Perspectives.** North Scituate, MA: Duxbury Press, 1977.

634. Meier, August and Elliott Rudwick. "The Rise of Segregation in the Federal Bureaucracy, 1900-1930." **Phylon** 28 (Summer 1967): 178-184.

635. Meier, Kenneth J. **Politics and the Bureaucracy: Policymaking in the Fourth Branch of Government.** North Scituate, MA: Duxbury Press, 1979.

636. Meier, Kenneth J. "Representative Bureaucracy: An Empirical Assessment." **American Political Science Review** 69 (June 1975): 526-542.

637. Meier, Kenneth J. and Lloyd G. Nigro. "Representative Bureaucracy and Policy Preferences: A Study in the Attitudes of Federal Executives." **Public Administration Review** 36 (July/August 1976): 458-469.

638. Meltsner, Arnold J. **Policy Analysts in the Bureaucracy.** Berkeley: University of California Press, 1976.

639. Menge, Edward. "Congress and Agency Appropriations: An Explanation of House Appropriations Committee Actions for Federal Agencies." Ph.D. dissertation, Ohio State University, 1973.

640. Meriam, Lewis. **Reorganization of the National Government.** Washington, DC: Brookings Institution, 1939.

641. Merriam, C. **Better Government Personnel.** New York: McGraw-Hill, 1935.

642. Merrill, Amy. "Cabinet Secretaries: What Do They Do All Day?" **Washington Monthly** 10 (February 1979): 22-28.

643. Merton, Robert K. **Reader in Bureaucracy.** New York: Free Press, 1951.

644. Methuin, Eugene H. "Why Can't Do-Nothing Bureaucrats Be Fired?" **Reader's Digest** 111 (November 1977): 119-122.

645. Meyer, Marshall W. **Change in Public Bureaucracies.** New York: Cambridge University Press, 1979.

646. Meyer, Marshall W. and Craig M. Brown. "The Process of Bureaucratization." **American Journal of Sociology** 83 (September 1977): 364-385.

647. Meyer, William J. **Public Good and Political Authority: A Pragmatic Proposal.** Port Washington, NY: Kennikat Press, 1975.

648. Meyerson, Martin and Edward C. Banfield. **Politics, Planning and the Public Interest.** New York: Free Press, 1955.

649. Michael, James R. **Working on the System.** New York: Basic Books, 1974.

650. Michelson, Stephan. "The Working Bureaucrat and the Nonworking Bureaucracy." **American Behavioral Scientist** 22 (May/June 1979): 585-608.

651. Mieszkowski, Peter and George E. Peterson, eds. **Public Sector Labor Markets.** Washington, DC: Urban Institute Press, 1981.

652. Miewald, Robert. **Public Administration.** New York:

McGraw-Hill, 1978.

653. Miewald, Robert and Michael Steinman, eds. **Problems in Administrative Reform.** Chicago: Nelson-Hall, 1984.

654. Miles, Raymond E. "Considerations for a President Bent on Reorganization." **Public Administration Review** 37 (March 1977): 155-162.

655. Milkis, Sidney M. "The New Deal, the Decline of Parties and the Administrative State." Ph.D. dissertation, University of Pennsylvania, 1981.

656. Miller, John T. "The Civil Service Commission's New Hearing Examiner Recruitment Program." **Administrative Law Review** 17 (Fall 1964): 104-109.

657. Miller, William H. "Energy: The Hottest Show in Washington." **Industry Week** 183 (September 23, 1974): 38-40.

658. Milles, Richard J. "The Role of Federal Governmental Agencies in Modern Accounting Theory and Practice." Ph.D. dissertation, St. Louis University, 1971.

659. Millett, John D. **Government and Public Administration.** New York: Holt, Rinehart and Winston, 1959.

660. Millett, John D. **Management in the Public Service.** New York: McGraw-Hill, 1954.

661. Millett, John D. **Organization for the Public Service.** Princeton, NJ: Van Nostrand, 1966.

662. Millet, John D. "Post-War Trends in Public Administration in the United States." **Journal of Politics** 11 (November 1949): 744-746.

663. Misey, Edward G. "Management Planning in the National Administration." Ph.D. dissertation, Columbia University, 1950.

664. Mitroff, Ian I. "Application of Behavioral and Philosophical Technologies to Strategic Planning: A Case Study of a Large Federal Agency." **Management Science** 24 (September 1977): 44-58.

665. Mogulof, Melvin B. "Federal Interagency Action and Inaction: The Federal Regional Council Experience." **Public Administration Review** 32

(May 1972): 232-240.

666. Monaghan, J. R. "Executive Reorganization Plan Sent to Hill." **Public Utilities Fortnightly** 87 (April 15, 1971): 36-38.

667. Moon, Marilyn L. "The Economic Welfare of the Aged: A Measure of Economic Status and an Analysis of Federal Programs." Ph.D. dissertation, University of Wisconsin, 1974.

668. Morley, Felix. "Strain on Government Ethics Increases about Every Six Months." **Nation's Business** (August 1958): 19-20.

669. Morley, Morris H. "Toward a Theory of Imperial Policymaking." **Contemporary Asia** 11 (1981): 333-350.

670. Morris, Roger. "Thomson, Moyers, and Ball: Prophets without Office." **Washington Monthly** 9 (June 1977): 45-48.

671. Morrisey, George L. **Performance Appraisals in the Public Sector: Key to Effective Supervision.** Reading, MA: Addison-Wesley, 1983.

672. Morrisey, G. Ivan. **Management by Objective and Results in the Public Sector.** Reading, MA: Addison-Wesley, 1970.

673. Morrow, Hugh. "Can We Reform Our Bureaucrats?" **Saturday Evening Post** 219 (May 10, 1947): 20-21, 116-119.

674. Morrow, William L. **Public Administration.** New York: Random House, 1975.

675. Moseley, John. "Democratic Gains from Wartime Bureaucracy." **Southwestern Social Science Quarterly** 26 (June 1945): 135-142.

676. Mosher, Frederick C. **American Public Administration: Past, Present and Future.** University: University of Alabama Press, 1975.

677. Mosher, Frederick C. **Basic Literature of American Public Administration, 1787-1950.** New York: Holmes and Meier, 1980.

678. Mosher, Frederick C., ed. **Basic Documents of American Public Administration, 1776-1950.** New York: Holmes and Meier, 1976.

679. Mosher, Frederick C. **Democracy and the Public Service.** New York: Oxford University Press, 1968.

680. Mosher, Frederick C. **Governmental Reorganizations.** Indianapolis: Bobbs-Merrill, 1967.

681. Mosher, Frederick C. **Watergate: Implications for Responsive Government.** New York: Basic Books, 1974.

682. Murphy, Charles J. V. "What's Wrong with Our Federal Bureaucracy?" **Reader's Digest** 100 (April 1972): 77-82.

683. Murphy, Thomas P. "Political Executive Roles, Policymaking and Interface with the Carter Bureaucracy." **Bureaucrat** 6 (Summer 1977): 96-127.

684. Murphy, Thomas P. **Contemporary Public Administration.** Itasca, IL: Peacock, 1980.

685. Murphy, Thomas P., Donald E. Neuchterlein and Ronald J. Stupak. **Inside the Bureaucracy: The View from the Assistant Secretary's Desk.** Boulder, CO: Westview, 1978.

686. Murray, Lawrence L. "Bureaucracy and Bipartisanship in Taxation: The Mellon Plan Revisited." **Business History Review** 52 (Summer 1978): 220-225.

687. Musgrave, Richard A. and Peggy B. Musgrave. **Public Finance in Theory and Practice.** New York: McGraw-Hill, 1973.

688. Nachmias, David. "Are Federal Bureaucrats Conservative? A Modest Test of a Popular Image." **Social Science Quarterly** 65 (December 1984): 1080-1087.

689. Nachmias, David and David H. Rosenbloom. **Bureaucratic Government USA.** New York: St. Martin's, 1980.

690. Nader, Ralph, Peter J. Petkas and Kate Blackwell. **Whistle Blowing.** New York: Bantam, 1972.

691. Nager, Glen D. "Bureaucrats and the Cost-Benefit Chameleon." **Regulation** 6 (September/October 1982): 37-46.

692. Nakamura, Robert T. and Frank Smallwood. **The**

Politics of Policy Implementation. New York: St. Martin's Press, 1980.

693. Nash, Bradley D. **A Hook in Leviathan: A Critical Interpretation of the Hoover Commission Report.** New York: Macmillan, 1950.

694. Nash, Gerald D. **Perspectives on Administration.** Berkeley: Institute of Governmental Studies, University of California, 1969.

695. Nathan, Richard P. "Administrative Presidency." **Public Interest** 44 (Summer 1976): 40-54.

696. Nathan, Richard P. **The Plot That Failed: Nixon and the Administrative Presidency.** New York: Wiley, 1975.

697. Nelson, Charles A. **Developing Responsible Public Leaders.** Dobbs Ferry, NY: Oceana, 1963.

698. Nelson, Dalmas H. **Administrative Agencies of the USA: Their Decisions and Authority.** Detroit: Wayne State University Press, 1964.

699. Nelson, Dalmas H. "Regulation of the Political Activity of Federal Employees." Ph.D. dissertation, Harvard University, 1957.

700. Nelson, Michael. "Bureaucracy: The Biggest Crisis of All." **Washington Monthly** 9 (January 1978): 51-59.

701. Nelson, Michael. "How to Break the Ties That Bind Congress to the Lobbies and Agencies." **Washington Monthly** 8 (December 1976): 36-38.

702. Nelson, Michael. "A Short, Ironic History of American National Bureaucracy." **Journal of Politics** 44 (August 1982): 747-748.

703. Neustadt, Richard E. "Approaches to Staffing the Presidency: Notes on FDR and JFK." **American Political Science Review** 57 (December 1963): 855-864.

704. Neustadt, Richard E. "Presidency and Legislation: Planning the President's Program." **American Political Science Review** 49 (December 1955): 980-1021.

705. Neustadt, Richard E. "Staffing the Presidency: Premature Notes on the New Administration." **Political Science Quarterly** 93 (Spring 1978): 1-

9, 12-14.

706. Newell, Charldean. "Bureaucratic Politics: Whither Goest Democracy?" **Political Science Reviewer** 9 (Fall 1979): 231-256.

707. Newland, Chester A. "Mid-Term Appraisal - The Reagan Presidency: Limited Government and Political Administration." **Public Administration Review** 43 (January/February 1983): 1-21.

708. Newland, Chester A. **Professional Public Executives.** Washington, DC: American Society for Public Administration, 1980.

709. Nickerson, Bee D. "Social Services: Planning and Accountability in a Federal Structure." Ph.D. dissertation, University of Delaware, 1981.

710. Niehaus, Richard J. "The Application of Computer-Assisted Multi-Level Manpower Planning Models in the Federal Government." D.B.A., George Washington University, 1972.

711. Nigro, Felix A. **Modern Public Administration.** New York: Harper and Row, 1965.

712. Nigro, Felix A. **Public Administration.** New York: Holt, Rinehart and Winston, 1951.

713. Nigro, Felix A. **Public Personnel Administration.** New York: Holt, Rinehart and Winston, 1959.

714. Nigro, Felix A. and Lloyd G. Nigro. **The New Public Personnel Administration.** Itasca, IL: Peacock, 1976.

715. Nigro, Lloyd G. and Kenneth Meier. "Bureaucracy and the People: Is the Higher Federal Service Representative?" **Bureaucrat** 4 (October 1975): 300-308.

716. Niskanen, William A. **Bureaucracy and Representative Government.** Chicago: Aldine, 1971.

717. Niskanen, William A. "Bureaucrats and Politicians." **Journal of Law and Economics** 18 (December 1975) 617-643.

718. Niskanen, William A. "Competition among Government Bureaus." **American Behavioral Scientist** 22 (May 1979): 517-524.

719. Niskanen, William A. "The Peculiar Economics of

Bureaucracy." **American Economic Review** 58 (May 1968): 293-305.

720. North, James . "My Brief Career As a Bureaucrat." **New Republic** 180 (February 3, 1979): 21-23.

721. Novick, David. **Program Budgeting.** Cambridge, MA: Harvard University Press, 1965.

722. Novogrod, Reevan J. "Theories and Practices of Staff and Line in Selected City, State, and Federal Government Departments." Ph.D. dissertation, New York University, 1966.

723. Novogrod, Reevan J., E. Dimock and Marshall Dimock. **Casebook in Public Administration.** New York: Holt, Rinehart and Winston, 1969.

724. O'Connor, James R. **The Fiscal Crisis of the State.** New York: St. Martin's Press, 1973.

725. O'Donnell, Maurice E. **Readings in Public Administration.** Boston: Houghton Mifflin, 1966.

726. Ogul, Morris S. **Congress Oversees the Bureaucracy: Studies in Legislative Supervision.** Pittsburgh: University of Pittsburgh Press, 1976.

727. O'Neil, Robert M. **The Rights of Government Employees.** New York: Avon, 1978.

728. Opotowsky, Stan. **The Kennedy Government.** New York: Dutton, 1961.

729. Oppenheimer, Joe A. "Legislators, Bureaucrats, and Locational Decisions and Beyond: Some Comments." **Public Choice** 37 (1981): 133-140.

730. Ordeshook, Kenneth A. **Political Equilibrium: A Delicate Balance.** Boston: Kluwer, 1982.

731. O'Reilly, Charles A. and Karlene H. Roberts. "Supervisor Influence and Subordinate Mobility Aspirations as Moderators of Consideration and Initiating Structure." **Journal of Applied Psychology** 63 (February 1978): 96-102.

732. Ostrom, Vincent. "Nonhierarchical Approaches to the Organization of Public Activity." **Annals of the American Academy of Political and Social Science** 466 (March 1983): 135-147.

733. Ott, David J. and Attiat F. Ott. **Federal Budget Policy.** Washington, DC: Brookings Institution,

1977.

734. Ourairatana, Arthitya. "A Study of Selected Career Executive Development Programs in the United States Federal Service: 1962-1966." Ph.D. dissertation, University of Colorado, 1968.

735. Outland, George E. "The New Personal Devil: Bureaucracy." **New Republic** 109 (October 25, 1943): 561-563.

736. Pannell, Robert C. and Gerald J. Laabs. "Construction of a Criterion-Referenced, Diagnostic Test for an Individualized Instruction Program." **Journal of Applied Psychology** 64 (June 1979): 255-261.

737. Park, Chung Soo. "Government by Contract: Its Implications for Federal Personnel Administration." Ph.D. dissertation, American University, 1965.

738. Parker, Donald F. and Lee Dyer. "Note on the Measurement of Valence Perceptions in Expectancy Theory Research." **Journal of Applied Psychology** 60 (December 1975): 761-764.

739. Pastor, Robert A. "Legislative-Executive Relations and the Politics of United States Foreign Economic Policy 1929-1976." Ph.D. dissertation, Harvard University, 1977.

740. Patterson, Bradley H. **Issues and Questions.** Washington, DC: American Society for Public Administration, 1976.

741. Patterson, Bradley H. "The White House Staff: The Bashful Bureaucracy." **Bureaucrat** 7 (Spring 1978): 81-84.

742. Pear, Richard H. "American Presidency under Eisenhower." **Political Quarterly** 28 (January 1957): 5-12.

743. Pechman, Joseph A. **Federal Tax Policy.** Washington, DC: Brookings Institution, 1966.

744. Peck, Cornelius J. "Regulation and Control of Ex Parte Communications with Administrative Agencies." **Harvard Law Review** 76 (December 1962): 233-274.

745. Pemberton, William E. **Bureaucratic Politics: Executive Reorganization during the Truman Admin-**

istration. Columbia: University of Missouri Press, 1979.

746. Pennock, James R. "Federal Unemployment Policy." Ph.D. dissertation, Harvard University, 1932.

747. Perkins, Roswell B. "The New Federal Conflict-of-Interest Law." **Harvard Law Review** 76 (April 1963): 111-169.

748. Perry, James L. and Kenneth L. Kramer. **Public Management: Public and Private Perspectives.** Palo Alto, CA: Mayfield, 1982.

749. Peters, B. Guy and Brian W. Hogwood. "In Search of the Issue-Attention Cycle." **Journal of Politics** 47 (February 1985): 238-253.

750. Peters, Charles. "Blind Ambition in the White House." **Washington Monthly** 9 (March 1977): 16-21.

751. Peters, Charles. "Bribery, Graft, and Conflicts of Interest: The Scope of Public Official." **Journal of Criminal Law and Criminology** 75 (Fall 1984): 874-892.

752. Peters, Charles. "How Carter Can Find Out What the Government Is Doing." **Washington Monthly** 8 (January 1977): 11-15.

753. Peters, Charles and Taylor Branch. **Blowing the Whistle: Dissent in Public Interest.** New York: Praeger, 1972.

754. Peters, Charles and Michael Nelson, eds. **The Culture of Bureaucracy.** New York: Holt, Rinehart and Winston, 1979.

755. Peterson, John E. and Catherine L. Spain. **Essays in Public Finance and Financial Management.** Chatham, NY: Chatham House, 1980.

756. Peterson, William, ed. **American Social Patterns: Studies of Race Relations, Popular Heroes, Union Democracy and Government Bureaucracy.** Garden City, NY: Doubleday, 1956.

757. Pfiffner, John M. **Public Administration.** New York: Ronald Press, 1935.

758. Pfiffner, John M. and Frank P. Sherwood. **Administrative Organization.** Englewood Cliffs, NJ: Prentice-Hall, 1960.

759. Pharo, Eugene. "America's Wet-Nurse Bureaucracy." **American Mercury** 41 (July 1937): 283-291.

760. Pierce, William S. **Bureaucratic Failure and Public Expenditures.** New York: Academic Press, 1981.

761. Pinney, Harvey F. "Federal Government Corporations as Instrumentalities of Government and of Administration." Ph.D. dissertation, New York University, 1937.

762. Pipe, G. Russell. "Congressional Liaison: The Executive Branch Consolidates Its Relations with Congress." **Public Administration Review** 26 (March 1966): 14-24.

763. Plumlee, John P. "Lawyers as Bureaucrats: The Impact of Legal Training in the Higher Civil Service." **Public Administration Review** 41 (March/April 1981): 220-228.

764. Polenberg, Richard. **Reorganizing Roosevelt's Government: The Controversy over Executive Reorganization, 1936-1939.** Cambridge, MA: Harvard University Press, 1966.

765. Polsby, Nelson W. "Presidential Cabinet Making: Lessons for the Political System." **Political Science Quarterly** 93 (Spring 1978): 15-25.

766. Porter, David. "Senator Carl Hatch and the Hatch Act of 1939." **New Mexico Historical Review** 48 (April 1973): 151-164.

767. Poschel, Jerome R. "A Comparative Study of Internal Techniques Used by Federal Agencies for Financing Administrative and Other Common Supporting Services." D.B.A., George Washington University, 1969.

768. Posner, Richard A. "The Behavior of Administrative Agencies." **Journal of Legal Studies** 1 (June 1972): 305-347.

769. Potter, Ralph. "Where Are the Self-Serving Bureaucrats?" **Bureaucrat** 9 (Summer 1980): 3-4.

770. Pound, Roscoe. **Administrative Law: Its Growth, Procedure and Significance.** Pittsburgh: University of Pittsburgh Press, 1942.

771. Powell, Norman J. **Personnel Administration in Government.** Englewood Cliffs, NJ: Prentice-Hall, 1956.

772. Powell, Norman J. **Responsible Public Bureaucracy in the United States.** Boston: Allyn and Bacon, 1967.

773. Pratt, James W. "Ordeal of Cordell Hull." **Review of Politics** 28 (January 1966): 76-98.

774. Presthus, Robert V. **Public Administration.** 6th ed. New York: Ronald Press, 1975.

775. Presthus, Robert V. and W. Monopoli. "Bureaucracy in the United States and Canada: Social, Attitudinal and Behavioral Variables." **International Journal of Comparative Sociology** 18 (March/June 1977): 176-190.

776. Price, Don K. **Government and Science.** New York: New York University Press, 1954.

777. Pursley, Robert D. and Neil Shortland. **Managing Government Organizations.** North Scituate, MA: Duxbury Press, 1980.

778. Raksasataya, Amara. "Executive Development in the United States: With Special Emphasis on Top Federal Career Executives." Ph.D. dissertation, Indiana University, 1960.

779. Rand, Peter. "Collecting Merit Badges: The White House Fellows." **Washington Monthly** 6 (June 1974): 47-56.

780. Randall, Raymond L. "An Evaluation of Selected Executive Development Programs for Government Officials." Ph.D. dissertation, American University, 1961.

781. Randall, Ronald. "Presidential Power versus Bureaucratic Intransigence: The Influence of the Nixon Administration on Welfare Policy." **American Political Science Review** 73 (September 1979): 795-810.

782. Rankin, Alan C. "The Administration of Federal Contract and Grant Research." D.S.S., Syracuse University, 1955.

783. Rans, Donald L. "Federal Collection of State Individual Income Taxes: An Empirical Evaluation." D.B.A., Indiana University, 1972.

784. Rather, Dan and Gary P. Gutes. **The Palace Guard.** New York: Harper and Row, 1974.

785. Ravelle, James J. "Employee Management Relations in the Federal Service: An Introduction." D.B.A., Lehigh University, 1978.

786. Raven, Bertram H. "Nixon Group." **Journal of Social Issues** 30 (1974): 297-320.

787. Ray, Jayanta K. "The American Bureaucratic Establishment." **Indian Journal of Public Administration** 21 (April/June 1975): 231-246.

788. Reagan, Michael D. **The Administration of Public Policy.** Glenview, IL: Scott, Foresman, 1969.

789. Redfield, William C. **With Congress and Cabinet.** Garden City, NY: Doubleday, 1924.

790. Redford, Emmette S. **Democracy in the Administrative State.** New York: Oxford University Press, 1969.

791. Redford, Emmette S. **Ideal and Practice in Public Administration.** University: University of Alabama Press, 1958.

792. Redford, Emmette S. **Organizing the Executive Branch: The Johnson Bureaucracy.** Chicago: University of Chicago Press, 1981.

793. Redford, Emmette S. **Public Administration and Policy Formation.** Austin: University of Texas Press, 1956.

794. Redford, Emmette S. and M. Blissert. **Organizing the Executive Branch: The Johnson Presidency.** Chicago: University of Chicago Press, 1981.

795. Reed, Leonard. "The Bureaucracy: The Cleverest Lobby of Them All." **Washington Monthly** 10 (April 1978): 49-54.

796. Reed, Leonard. "Firing a Federal Employee: The Impossible Dream." **Washington Monthly** 9 (July/August 1977): 15-25.

797. Rehfuss, John. **Public Administration as Political Process.** New York: Scribner's, 1973.

798. Reilly, Sheila A. "Disputes between Federal Agencies and Their Employees." **Chicago Bar Record** 63 (May/June 1982): 320-327.

799. Reynolds, Harry W. "Merit Controls, the Hatch Acts, and Personnel Standards in

Intergovernmental Relations." **Annals of the American Academy of Political and Social Science** 359 (May 1965): 81-93.

800. Reynolds, Mary T. **Interdepartmental Committees in the National Administration.** New York: Columbia University Press, 1939.

801. Rich, Robert F. ""An Investigation of Information Gathering and Handling in Seven Federal Bureaucracies: A Case Study of the Continuous National Survey." Ph.D. dissertation, University of Chicago, 1975.

802. Richardson, Ivan L. and Sidney Baldwin. **Public Administration.** Columbus, OH: Merrill, 1976.

803. Rigby, Ronald K. "Federal and Non-Federal Employees: A Study of Values." Ph.D. dissertation, University of Minnesota, 1973.

804. Ripley, Randall B. **Structure, Environment and Policy Actions: Exploring a Model of Policy Making.** Beverly Hills, CA: Sage, 1973.

805. Ripley, Randall B. and Grace A. Franklin. **Bureaucracy and Policy Implementation.** Homewood, IL: Dorsey, 1982.

806. Ripley, Randall B. and Grace A. Franklin. **Congress, the Bureaucracy and Public Policy.** Homewood, IL: Dorsey Press, 1976.

807. Ripley, Randall B. and Grace A. Franklin. **Policy-making in the Federal Executive Branch.** New York: Free Press, 1975.

808. Rivlin, Alice M. **Systematic Thinking for Social Action.** Washington, DC: Brookings Institution, 1971.

809. Robbins, Stephen P. **The Administrative Process.** Englewood Cliffs, NJ: Prentice-Hall, 1976.

810. Roberts, Charles W. **LBJ's Inner Circle.** New York: Delacorte Press, 1965.

811. Robinson, Glen O. and Ernest Gellhorn. **The Administrative Process.** St. Paul, MN: West, 1974.

812. Roche, George C. **America by the Throat: The Stranglehold of Federal Bureaucracy.** Hillsdale, MI: Hillsdale College Press, 1985.

813. Rockman, Bert A. "The Beliefs of American Federal Executives: Exploring the Political Culture of and Elite." Ph.D. dissertation, University of Michigan, 1974.

814. Rockman, Bert A. **Studying Elite Political Culture: Problems in Design and Interpretation.** Pittsburgh: University of Pittsburgh, 1976.

815. Rodgers, Charles S. "The Internal Allocation of Labor in a Federal Agency." Ph.D. dissertation, Brandeis University, 1978.

816. Rohr, John A. **Ethics for Bureaucrats.** New York: Dekker, 1978.

817. Romer, Thomas and Howard Rosenthal. "Bureaucrats versus Voters: On the Political Economy of Resource Allocation by Direct Democracy." **Quarterly Journal of Economics** 93 (November 1979): 563-587.

818. Romzek, Barbara S. "The Multidimensional Bureaucrat: Identities, Loyalties and Conflicts of Professional Level Federal Employees." Ph.D. dissertation, University of Texas, 1979.

819. Rose, Richard. **Managing Presidential Objectives.** New York: Free Press, 1976.

820. Rosen, Bernard. **Holding Government Bureaucracies Accountable.** New York: Praeger, 1982.

821. Rosenbaum, Allan. "Federal Management: Pathological Problems and Simple Cures." **PS** 15 (Spring 1982): 187-193.

822. Rosenbloom, David H. "Civil Service Commission's Decision to Authorize the Use of Goals and Timetables in the Federal Equal Employment Opportunity Program." **Western Political Quarterly** 26 (June 1973): 236-251.

823. Rosenbloom, David H. "Constitutional and Public Bureaucrats." **Bureaucrat** 11 (Fall 1982): 54-56.

824. Rosenbloom, David H. **Federal Service and the Constitution.** Ithaca, NY: Cornell University Press, 1971.

825. Rosenbloom, David H. "Forms of Bureaucratic Representation in the Federal Service." **Midwest Review of Public Administration** 8 (July 1974): 159-177.

826. Rosenbloom, David H. "Public Administrators' Official Immunity and the Supreme Court: Developments during the 1970s." **Public Administration Review** 40 (March 1980): 166-173.

827. Rosenbloom, David H. "The Rise of Participatory Bureaucracy and the United States Federal Service." **Chinese Journal of Administration** 24 (1975): 14-23.

828. Rosenbloom, David H. "The Size of Public Bureaucracies: An Exploratory Analysis." **State and Local Government Review** 13 (September 1981): 115-123.

829. Rosenblum, Marc J. "Federal Manpower Forecasting: An Analysis and Evaluation." Ph.D. dissertation, University of Minnesota, 1972.

830. Rosener, Judy B. "Making Bureaucracy Responsive: A Study of the Impact of Citizen Participation and Staff Recommendations on Regulatory Decision Making." **Public Administration Review** 42 (July/August 1982): 339-345.

831. Rosenthal, Stephen R. **Managing Government Operations.** Glenview, IL: Scott, Foresman, 1982.

832. Ross, Bernard H. "American Government in Crisis: An Analysis of the Executive Branch of Government during the Cuban Missile Crisis." Ph.D. dissertation, New York University, 1971.

833. Rothchild, John. "Finding the Facts Bureaucrats Hide." **Washington Monthly** 3 (January 1972): 15-27.

834. Rourke, Francis E. "Administrative Secrecy: A Congressional Dilemma." **American Political Science Review** 54 (September 1960): 684-694.

835. Rourke, Francis E. **Bureaucracy, Politics, and Public Policy.** Boston: Little, Brown, 1976.

836. Rourke, Francis E., ed. **Bureaucracy: Some Case Studies.** Washington, DC: Government Research Corporation, 1976.

837. Rourke, Francis E. "Bureaucratic Autonomy and the Public Interest." **American Behavioral Scientist** 22 (May/June 1979): 537-546.

838. Rourke, Francis E., ed. **Bureaucratic Power in**

National Policy-Making. 4th ed. Boston: Little, Brown, 1986.

839. Rourke, Francis E. "Bureaucratic Secrecy and Its Constituents." **Bureaucrat** 1 (Summer 1972): 116-121.

840. Rourke, Francis E., ed. **Reforming the Bureaucracy.** Washington, DC: Government Research Corporation, 1978.

841. Rourke, Francis E. **Secrecy and Publicity.** Baltimore, MD: Johns Hopkins University Press, 1961.

842. Rourke, Francis E. "Secrecy in American Bureaucracy." **Political Science Quarterly** 72 (December 1957): 540-564.

843. Rouse, John E. **Public Administration in American Society.** Detroit: Gale, 1980.

844. Rowat, Donald C. **Basic Issues in Public Administration.** New York: Macmillan, 1961.

845. Rubin, Irene S. "Marasmus or Recover? The Effects of Cutbacks in Federal Agencies." **Social Science Quarterly** 65 (March 1984): 74-88.

846. Rubin, Ronald I. "The Controversies over the Objectives of the United States Information Agency according to Congress, the Executive Branch, and the Agency." Ph.D. dissertation, New York University, 1965.

847. Rusbult, Caryl and David Lowery. "When Bureaucrats Get the Blues: Responses to Dissatisfaction among Federal Employees." **Journal of Applied Social Psychology** 15 (1985): 80-103.

848. Russell, Beverly and Arnold Shore. "Limitations on the Governmental Use of Social Science in the United States." **Minerva** 14 (Winter 1976-1977): 475-495.

849. Ryan, Edward J. "Management by Objectives in Perspective: A Comparative Study of Selected Federal Experience with the Fiscal Year 1975 Program." D.B.A., George Washington University, 1976.

850. Ryter, Mark. **A Whistle Blower's Guide to the Federal Bureaucracy.** Washington, DC: Institute for Policy Studies, 1977.

851. Sainsbury, Trevor. "The Internal Audit Function in a Government Department: A Field Study." Ph.D. dissertation, Carnegie-Mellon University, 1967.

852. Saltzstein, Alan, ed. **Public Employees and Policy-making.** Pacific Palisades, CA: Palisades, 1979.

853. Sanders, Jennings B. **Evolution of Executive Departments of the Continental Congress, 1774-1789.** Chapel Hill: University of North Carolina Press, 1935.

854. Sanders, John T. **The Ethical Argument against Government.** Washington, DC: University Press of America, 1980.

855. Sanzoner, John G. "The Impact of General Revenue Sharing on Federal Policy-Making Authority." Ph.D. dissertation, University of California, 1977.

856. Sarri, Rosemary C. and Yeheskel Hasenfeld, eds. **Management of Human Services.** New York: Columbia University Press, 1979.

857. Saulinier, Raymond J. "An Appraisal of Federal Fiscal Policies: 1961-1967." **Annals of the American Academy of Political and Social Science** 379 (September 1968): 63-71.

858. Savas, Emmanuel S. **Privatizing the Public Sector: How to Shrink Government.** Chatham, NJ: Chatham House, 1982.

859. Savells, Jerald. "The Americanization of the Bureaucratic Ethos." **Personnel Journal** 51 (November 1972): 835-839.

860. Sayre, Wallace S. "The Recruitment and Training of Bureaucrats in the United States." **Annals of the American Academy of Political and Social Science** 292 (March 1954): 39-44.

861. Schecter, Alan H. "Businessmen as Government Policy-Makers." **Columbia Journal of World Business** 3 (May 1968): 67-72.

862. Scher, Samuel C. "Politics of Agency Organization." **Western Political Quarterly** 15 (June 1962): 328-344.

863. Schick, Allen. **Perspectives on Budgeting.** Washington, DC: American Society for Public Administration, 1980.

864. Schinagl, Mary S. "History of Efficiency Ratings in the Federal Government." Ph.D. dissertation, University of Pennsylvania, 1962.

865. Schlesinger, James R. **Systems Analysis and the Political Process.** Santa Monica, CA: Rand, 1967.

866. Schmeckebier, Laurence F. **New Federal Organizations: An Outline of Their Structure and Function.** Washington, DC: Brookings Institution, 1934.

867. Schmid, A. Allan. **Property, Power, and Public Choice: An Inquiry into Law and Economics.** New York: Praeger, 1978.

868. Schmidt, Terry and Terry Margerum. "Working for the Feds: A Primer for Would Be Bureaucrats." **MBA** 6 (December 1972): 6-8, 52.

869. Schooler, Seward D. "Scientists and the Executive Branch: Scientific Inputs in American National Policy, 1945-1968." Ph.D. dissertation, Ohio State University, 1969.

870. Schott, Richard L. **The Bureaucratic State: The Evolution and Scope of the American Federal Bureaucracy.** Morristown, NJ: General Learning Press, 1974.

871. Schott, Richard L. and Dagmar S. Hamilton. **People, Positions and Power: The Political Appointments of Lyndon Johnson.** Chicago: University of Chicago Press, 1983.

872. Schrag, Philip and Michael Meltsner. "Class Action: A Way to Beat the Bureaucracies without Increasing Them." **Washington Monthly** 4 (November 1972): 55-61.

873. Schubert, Glendon A. **The Public Interest.** New York: Free Press, 1960.

874. Schuettinger, Robert. "Bureaucracy and Representative Government: A Review Analysis." **Midwest Review of Public Administration** 7 (January 1973): 17-22.

875. Schultze, Charles L. **The Politics and Economics of Public Spending.** Washington, DC: Brookings Institution, 1968.

876. Schultze, Charles L. **The Public Use of Private Interest.** Washington, DC: Brookings Institution, 1977.

877. Schweitzer, Glenn E. "Rights of Federal Employees Named as Alleged Discriminatory Officials." **Public Administration Review** 37 (January 1977): 58-63.

878. Scott, William G. and David K. Hart. **Organizational America.** Boston: Houghton Mifflin, 1979.

879. Seaborg, Glenn T. "Science the Humanities, and the Federal Government-Partners in Progress." **Proceedings of the American Philosophical Society** 110 (August 1966): 318-325.

880. Sebris, Robert. "Bureaucracy and Labor Relations." **Civil Service Journal** 19 (October/December 1978): 28-31.

881. Seidman, Harold. "Crisis of Confidence in Government." **Political Quarterly** 43 (January 1972): 79-88.

882. Seidman, Harold. **Politics, Position and Power.** New York: Oxford University Press, 1986.

883. Seidman, Harold. "Theory of the Autonomous Government Corporation: A Critical Appraisal." **Public Administration Review** 12 (Spring 1952): 89-96.

884. Seidman, Laurence S. "The Design of Federal Employment Programs: An Economic Analysis." Ph.D. dissertation, University of California, 1974.

885. Selznick, Philip. **Leadership in Administration.** New York: Row, Peterson, 1957.

886. Shafritz, Jay M. **Personnel Management in Government.** New York: Dekker, 1986.

887. Shafritz, Jay M. and Albert C. Hyde. **Classics of Public Administration.** Oak Park, IL: Moore, 1978.

888. Shannon, James A. "Thoughts on the Relationships between Science and Federal Programs." **American Journal of Political Science** 48 (Summer 1967): 214-223.

889. Sharkansky, Ira. "Four Agencies and an Appropriations Subcommittee: A Comparative Study of

Budget Relations." Ph.D. dissertation, University of Wisconsin, 1964.

890. Sharkansky, Ira. **Public Administration.** Chicago: Markham, 1970.

891. Sharkansky, Ira. **Public Administration: Agencies, Policies, and Politics.** San Francisco: Freeman, 1982.

892. Shaw, Albert. "Will Federal Bureaucracy Last?" **Review of Reviews** 93 (June 1936): 17-24.

893. Sheposh, John P. "Assessment by Technical Personnel of the Role of the Change Advocate." **Journal of Applied Psychology** 60 (August 1975): 483-490.

894. Shocket, Sol. "An Economic Analysis of the Problems of Federal Debt Management." Ph.D. dissertation, University of Southern California, 1962.

895. Shor, Edgar. "Public Interest Representation and the Federal Agencies." **Public Administration Review** 37 (March 1977): 131-154.

896. Short, Larry E. "Equal Employment Opportunity in the United States Federal Government." D.B.A., University of Colorado, 1971.

897. Short, Lloyd M. **The Development of National Administrative Organization in the United States.** Baltimore: Johns Hopkins University Press, 1923.

898. Shostak, Arthur. "Appeals from Discrimination in Federal Employment: A Case Study." **Social Forces** (December 1963): 174-178.

899. Shoup, Carl S. **Public Finance.** Chicago: Aldine, 1969.

900. Shull, Steven A. "A Comparative Examination of Agency Policy Response to Structural, Environmental, and Budgetary Stimuli." Ph.D. dissertation, Ohio State University, 1974.

901. Siegan, Bernard H. **Government, Regulation and the Economy.** Lexington, MA: Lexington Books, 1980.

902. Sigel, Leon V. "Official Secrecy and Informal Communication in Congressional-Bureaucratic Relations." **Political Science Quarterly** 90 (Spring 1975): 71-92.

903. Sigelman, Lee and William G. Vanderbok. "The Saving Grace? Bureaucratic Power and American Democracy." **Polity** 10 (Spring 1978): 440-447.

904. Simasthien, Panas. "The Budgetary Control of Federal Expenditures." Ph.D. dissertation, University of Illinois, 1958.

905. Simon, Herbert A. **Administrative Behavior.** New York: Macmillan, 1947.

906. Simon, Herbert A., D. Smithburg and V. Thompson. **Public Administration.** New York: Knopf, 1950.

907. Singer, James. "Changing of the Guard: Reagan's Chance to Remold the Senior Bureaucracy." **National Journal** 12 (November 1980): 2028-2031.

908. Smith, Bruce L. R. **The Dilemma of Accountability in Modern Government.** New York: St. Martin's Press, 1971.

909. Smith, Claude C. "The Budget Function in the Federal Government: A Study of the Development of Budgeting as an Operating Tool of Administrative Management." Ph.D. dissertation, Stanford University, 1948.

910. Smith, Richard D. "A Conceptual Model of Managerial Training in the Planning-Programming-Budgeting System of the Federal Government and an Evaluation of Current Training Efforts." D.B.A., University of Oklahoma, 1972.

911. Smith, Sammie L. "An Investigation of the Evolution of Last-in-First-out Inventory Costing into a Generally Accepted Accounting Principle with Emphasis on the Influence of Federal Income Tax Regulations." Ph.D. dissertation, University of Arkansas, 1972.

912. Smith, Sharon P. **Equal Pay in the Public Sector: Fact or Fantasy.** Princeton, NJ: Princeton University Press, 1977.

913. Smith, Sharon P. "Wage Differentials between Federal Government and Private Sectors Workers." Ph.D. dissertation, Rutgers University, 1974.

914. Somers, Herman M. "Coordinating the Federal Executive." Ph.D. dissertation, Harvard University, 1947.

915. Somers, Herman M. "The Federal Bureaucracy and the

Change of Administration." **American PoliticalScience Review** 48 (March 1954): 13-151.

916. South, Scott J. "Sex and Power in the Federal Bureaucracy: A Comparative Analysis of Male and Female Supervisors." **Work and Occupations** 9 (May 1982): 233-254.

917. Spiro, Herbert J. **Responsibility in Government: Theory and Practice.** New York: Van Nostrand Reinhold, 1969.

918. Spurgal, Frederick A. "A Comparative Study of the Implementation and Use of Management Information Systems in a Federal Research Agency: Factors Affecting User Acceptance." Ph.D. dissertation, Northwestern University, 1976.

919. Stahl, Oscar G. **Public Personnel Administration.** New York: Harper and Row, 1976.

920. Stafford, Samuel. "Federal Job Classification: How Much Rigidity Can the Bureaucract Stand?" **Government Executive** 4 (October 1972): 19-23.

921. Stanfield, Rochelle. "Bureaucrat Can't Count on His Old Allies." **National Journal** 13 (1981): 525-527.

922. Stanley, David T. **Changing Administrations: The 1961 and 1964 Transitions in Six Departments.** Washington, DC: Brookings Institution, 1965.

923. Stanley, David T. **The Higher Civil Service.** Washington, DC: Brookings Institution, 1964.

924. Starling, Grover. **Managing the Public Sector.** Homewood, IL: Dorsey, 1977.

925. Steelman, John R. **Science and Public Policy.** New York: Arno, 1980.

926. Steelman, John R. and H. Dewayne Kreager. "Executive Office as Administrative Coordinator." **Law and Contemporary Problems** 21 (Fall 1956): 688-709.

927. Stein, Herbert. "The Federal Budget, the Debt and Economic Stability." Ph.D. dissertation, University of Chicago, 1959.

928. Stein, Robert M. "Federal Grant-in-Aid Programs: Equalization and the Application Process." Ph.D. dissertation, University of Wisconsin, 1977.

929. Steiner, Gordon J. E. "The Disbursement of Federal Funds." Ph.D. dissertation, Fordham University, 1948.

930. Stenberg, Carl W. "American Public Administration in Three Centuries: Contemporary Public Administration: Challenge and Change." **Public Administration Review** 36 (September 1976): 505-576.

931. Sternenberg, Robert E. "A Study of Full Cost Versus Marginal Cost Pricing of Proposals to Government Agencies and Their Impact on Contract Award and Performance." Ph.D. dissertation, University of Houston, 1972.

932. Stillman, Richard J. **Public Administration.** Boston: Houghton Mifflin, 1976.

933. Stone, Alan. **Economic Regulation and the Public Interest.** Ithaca, NY: Cornell University Press, 1977.

934. Straight, Michael W. **After Long Silence.** New York: Norton, 1983.

935. Stratton, Owen S. "The Politics of Price Control: A Study of Executive-Legislative Relationships in Wartime." Ph.D. dissertation, Stanford University, 1950.

936. Stuligross, John D. "Planning by Federal Governmental Agencies in the State of Missouri." Ph.D. dissertation, University of Oklahoma, 1971.

937. Sullivan, Lawrence. **Bureaucracy Runs Amok.** Indianapolis: Bobbs-Merrill, 1944.

938. Sulzner, George T. "The Policy Process and the Uses of National Governmental Study Commissions." **Western Political Quarterly** 24 (September 1971): 438-448.

939. Summers, Hatton B. "America's Capacity for Self-Government Is Being Destroyed by Bureaucracy," **American Bar Association Journal** 30 (January 1944): 3-5.

940. Summers, Hatton B. "Don't Blame the Bureaucrats." **Reader's Digest** 43 (September 1943): 1-4.

941. Summers, Hatton B. "Our Choice-Decentralization of Government or Government by a Centralized Bureaucracy." **Congressional Record** 86 (1940): 2218-2221.

942. Sundquist, James L. "Jimmy Carter as Public Administrator: An Appraisal at Midterm." **Public Administration Review** 39 (January 1979): 3-11.

943. Sundquist, James L. "Reflections on Watergate: Lessons for Public Administration." **Public Administration Review** 34 (September 1974): 453-461.

944. Sundstrom, John W. "An Analysis and Evaluation of the Recommendations Relative to Personnel Management by the Commission on Organization of the Executive Branch of the Government." Ph.D. dissertation, American University, 1951.

945. Swiss, James E. "Implementing Federal Programs: Administrative Systems and Organizational Effectiveness." Ph.D. dissertation, Yale University, 1976.

946. Szanton, Peter. **Federal Reorganization: What Have We Learned?** Chatham, NJ: Chatham House, 1981.

947. Tanzer, Lester, ed. **The Kennedy Circle.** Washington, DC: Luce, 1961.

948. Tead, Ordway. **Democratic Administration.** New York: Association Press, 1945.

949. Teigen, Robert L. "Trends and Cycles in the Composition of the Federal Budget, 1947-78." **Policy Studies Journal** 9 (Autumn 1980): 11-19.

950. Thomas, Robert D. and Roger B. Handberg. "Congressional Budgeting for Eight Agencies, 1947-1972." **American Journal of Political Science** 18 (February 1974): 179-187.

951. Thomforde, F. H. "Controlling Administrative Sanctions." **Michigan Law Review** 74 (March 1976): 709-758.

952. Thompson, Frank J. **Classics of Public Personnel Policy.** Oak Park, IL: Moore, 1979.

953. Thurow, Lester C. "Indirect Incidence of Government Expenditures." **American Economic Review** 70 (May 1980): 82-87.

954. Tileson, Dean. "The Politics of the Federal Income Tax Reform Program." Ph.D. dissertation, Johns Hopkins University, 1978.

955. Titlow, Richard E. "Americans Import Merit:

Origins of the United States Civil Services System and the Influence of the British Model: 1865-1886." Ph.D. dissertation, American University, 1977.

956. Titus, Joyce P. "Future of Computers in the Federal Government." **Computers and Automation** 14 (May 1965): 22-25.

957. Torpey, William G. **Public Personnel Management.** New York: Van Nostrand, 1953.

958. Trees, James F. "Federal Government Financing and Its Effect on Interest Rates: 1965-1967." Ph.D. dissertation, Harvard University, 1972.

959. Truman, David B. **The Governmental Process.** New York: Knopf, 1951.

960. Tullock, Gordon. **The Politics of Bureaucracy.** Washington, DC: Public Affairs Press, 1965.

961. Ugalde, Antonio. "A Decision Model for the Study of Public Bureaucracies." **Policy Sciences** 4 (March 1973): 75-84.

962. Uveges, Joseph A. **Cases in Public Administration.** Boston: Holbrook, 1979.

963. Uveges, Joseph A., comp. **The Dimensions of Public Administration.** Boston: Holbrook Press, 1975.

964. Uveges, Joseph A. **Public Administration.** New York: Dekker, 1982.

965. Valentine, John P. "An Analysis and Evaluation of the Federal Employee Health Benefit Program." Ph.D. dissertation, George Washington University, 1965.

966. Van Riper, Paul P. **History of the United States Civil Service.** Evanston, IL: Row, Peterson, 1958.

967. Van Riper, Paul P. and Keith A. Sutherland. "The Northern Civil Service: 1861-1865." **Civil War History** 11 (December 1965): 351-369.

968. Van Sant, Edward R. "The Floating Debt of the Federal Government." Ph.D. dissertation, Johns Hopkins University, 1935.

969. Vaughn, Robert G. **Conflict-of-Interest Regulation in the Federal Executive Branch.** Lexington, MA:

Lexington Books, 1979.

970. Vieg, John A. "Democracy and Bureaucracy," **Public Administration Review** 4 (Summer 1944): 247-252.

971. Vinyard, Dale. "The Congressional Committees on Small Business: Pattern of Legislative Committee-Executive Agency Relations." **Western Political Quarterly** 21 (September 1968): 391-399.

972. Vocino, Thomas and Jack Rabin. **Contemporary Public Administration.** New York: Harcourt Brace Jovanovich, 1980.

973. Vom Baur, Francis T. **Federal Administrative Law.** Chicago: Callaghan, 1942.

974. Vosloo, Willem B. "Collective Bargaining in the United States Federal Civil Service." Ph.D. dissertation, Cornell University, 1965.

975. Waldmann, Raymond J. "Domestic Council: Innovation in Presidential Government." **Public Administration Review** 36 (May 1976): 206-208.

976. Waldo, Dwight. **The Administrative State.** New York: Ronald Press, 1948.

977. Waldo, Dwight. **Democracy, Bureaucracy and Hypocrisy.** Berkeley: Institute of Governmental Studies, University of California, 1977.

978. Waldo, Dwight. **The Enterprise of Public Administration.** Novato, CA: Chandler and Sharp, 1980.

979. Waldo, Dwight. **Ideas and Issues in Public Administration.** New York: Macmillan, 1953.

980. Waldo, Dwight. **Perspectives on Administration.** University: University of Alabama Press, 1955.

981. Waldo, Dwight. **Public Administration in a Time of Turbulence.** Scranton, PA: Chandler, 1971.

982. Waldo, Dwight. **The Study of Public Administration.** Garden City, NY: Doubleday, 1955.

983. Walk, Everett G. "Loans of Federal Agencies and Their Relationship to the Capital Market." Ph.D. dissertation, University of Pennsylvania, 1937.

984. Walker, Alvan G. "The Federal Budgetary Process: A Study in Administrative Discretion and Uncontrollable Spending." Ph.D. dissertation,

University of Georgia, 1979.

985. Walker, Harvey. **Public Administration in the United States.** New York: Farrar and Rinehart, 1937.

986. Wallace, Schuyler C. **Federal Departmentalization: A Critique of Theories of Organization.** New York: Columbia University Press, 1941.

987. Wallace, Schuyler C. **Our Governmental Machine.** New York: Knopf, 1924.

988. Walsh, Annmarie H. **The Public's Business.** Cambridge, MA: MIT Press, 1978.

989. Walton, Richard E. **Conflict and Integration in the Federal Bureaucracy.** Cambridge, MA: Fellows of Harvard College, 1971.

990. Wamsley, Gary L. and Mayer N. Zold. **The Political Economy of Public Organizations.** Lexington, MA: Heath, 1973.

991. Wanat, John A. "Bases of Budgetary Incrementalism." **American Political Science Review** 68 (September 1974): 1221-1228.

992. Wanat, John A. **Introduction to Budgeting.** North Scituate, MA: Duxbury Press, 1978.

993. Wanat, John A. "Patterns of Growth and Their Correlates in Selected Federal Agencies." Ph.D. dissertation, University of Illinois, 1972.

994. Waterman, Bernard S. "Small Business Participation in Federal Government Research and Development - The Government Perception." D.B.A., George Washington University, 1971.

995. Watson, Goodwin. "Bureaucracy in the Federal Government." **Journal of Social Issues** 1 (December 1945): 14-31.

996. Wayne, Stephen J. "Advising the President on Enrolled Legislation: Patterns of Executive Influence." **Political Science Quarterly** 94 (Summer 1979): 303-317.

997. Weber, W. and W. Weigel. "Government Bureaucracy: A Survey in Positive and Normative Theory." **Acta Economia** 24 (1980): 341-356.

998. Weidenbaum, Murray L. **The Modern Public Sector.**

New York: Basic Books, 1969.

999. Weisband, Edward. **Resignation in Protest.** New York: Grossman, 1975.

1000. Weiss, Armand B. "Development of Guidelines for the Determination of Economic Retention Stock in the Federal Government." D.B.A., George Washington University, 1971.

1001. Weiss, Carol H. and Allen H. Barton. **Making Bureaucracies Work.** Beverly Hills, CA: Sage, 1980.

1002. Wellford, Harrison. "Staffing the Presidency: An Insider's Comments." **Political Science Quarterly** 93 (Spring 1978): 10-12.

1003. Wengert, Egbert S. "The Public Relations of Selected Federal Administrative Agencies." Ph.D. dissertation, University of Wisconsin, 1937.

1004. Wetzel, James N. "The Federal Role in the Economy." **Current History** 69 (November 1975): 179-182, 196.

1005. Wheare, Kenneth. "Bureaucracy in a Democracy," **Public Administration** 29 (Summer 1951): 144-150.

1006. White, Leonard D. **Civil Service in Wartime.** Chicago: University of Chicago Press, 1945.

1007. White, Leonard D. **Introduction to the Study of Public Administration.** New York: Macmillan, 1926.

1008. White, Michael J. "A Descriptive Model of the Development of Management Science Activities in Federal Civilian Agencies: A Longitudinal, Comparative Field Study with Illustrations." Ph.D. dissertation, Northwestern University, 1974.

1009. White, Michael J. **Management Science in Federal Agencies.** Lexington, MA: Lexington Books, 1975.

1010. White, Michael J., et al. **Managing Public Systems.** North Scituate, MA: Duxbury Press, 1980.

1011. White, Orion F. "The Bureaucratic Game in the Political Arena: An Analysis of the Environment of American Bureaucracy." Ph.D. dissertation, Indiana University, 1964.

1012. Whitesel, Russel G. "The Power of Congress to Remove Federal Officers." Ph.D. dissertation, Cornell University, 1948.

1013. Whitnah, Donald R., ed. **Government Agencies.** Westport, CT: Greenwood Press, 1983.

1014. Wholey, Joseph S. **Evaluation and Effective Public Management.** Boston, MA: Little, Brown, 1982.

1015. Wholey, Joseph S. **Federal Evaluation Policy.** Washington, DC: Urban Institute, 1970.

1016. Wildavsky, Aaron B. **Budgeting.** Boston: Little, Brown, 1975.

1017. Wildavsky, Aaron B. **How to Limit Government Spending.** Berkeley: University of California Press, 1980.

1018. Wildavsky, Aaron B. **The Politics of Budgetary Process.** Boston: Little, Brown, 1964.

1019. Wildavsky, Aaron B. **Speaking Truth to Power.** Boston: Little, Brown, 1979.

1020. Willard, Joseph. "Public Relations Policies and Practices of Federal Departments and Agencies." Ph.D. dissertation, Indiana University, 1959.

1021. Williams, John D. **Public Administration: The People's Business.** Boston: Little, Brown, 1980.

1022. Williams, Walter. **Government by Agency: Lessons from the Social Program Grants-in-Aid Experience.** New York: Academic Press, 1980.

1023. Willit, Virgil. "The Federal Land Banks." Ph.D. dissertation, Ohio State University, 1930.

1024. Willoughby, William F. **Principles of Public Administration.** Baltimore: Johns Hopkins University Press, 1927.

1025. Willoughby, William F. **The Reorganization of the Administrative Branch of the National Government.** Baltimore: Johns Hopkins University Press, 1923.

1026. Wilmerding, Lucius. **Government by Merit.** New York: McGraw-Hill, 1935.

1027. Wilson, James Q. "The Bureaucracy Problem." **Public Interest** 6 (Winter 1967): 3-9.

1028. Wilson, James Q. "The Rise of the Bureaucratic State." **Public Interest** 41 (Fall 1975): 77-103.

1029. Wiltse, Charles M. "The Representative Function of Bureaucracy." **American Political Science Review** 35 (April 1941): 510-516.

1030. Winchell, T. E. and L. D. Burkett. "Cost Control in the Federal Position Classification Program." **Personnel Journal** 57 (June 1978): 314-318.

1031. Wirt, John G. **R and D Management: Methods Used by Federal Agencies.** Lexington, MA: Lexington Books, 1975.

1032. Wise, Charles R. "Liability of Federal Officials: An Analysis of Alternatives." **Public Administration Review** 45 (November 1985): 746-753.

1033. Wise, Charles R. "Suits against Federal Employees for Constitutional Violations: A Search for Reasonableness." **Public Administration Review** 45 (November/December 1985): 845-856.

1034. Woll, Peter. **American Bureaucracy.** New York: Norton, 1977.

1035. Woll, Peter. **Public Administration and Policy.** New York: Harper and Row, 1966.

1036. Woll, Peter. **Public Policy.** Cambridge, MA: Winthrop, 1974.

1037. Woll, Peter and Rochelle Jones. "Against One-Man Rule: Bureaucratic Defense in Depth." **Nation** 217 (September 1976): 229-232.

1038. Woll, Peter and Rochelle Jones. "The Bureaucracy as a Check upon the President." **Bureaucrat** 3 (April 1974): 8-20.

1039. Wolle, Celia P. "A Program of Plural Management for the Federal Government." Ph.D. dissertation, Yale University, 1957.

1040. Wooddy, Carroll H. **The Growth of the Federal Government, 1915-1932.** New York: McGraw-Hill, 1934.

1041. Wright, James D. **The Dissent of the Governed.** New York: Academic Press, 1976.

1042. Wriston, Michael J. "In Defense of Bureaucracy."

Public Administration Review 40 (March/April 1980): 179-183.

1043. Wynia, Bob L. "Federal Bureacurats' Attitudes towards a Democratic Ideology." **Public Administration Review** 34 (March/April 1974): 156-162.

1044. Wysong, Earl M. "An Analysis of the Effectiveness of Computer-Based Financial Management Systems in the Civil Agencies of the Federal Government." D.B.A., George Washington University, 1972.

1045. Yamada, Gordon T. "Improving Management Effectiveness in the Federal Government." **Public Administration Review** 32 (November 1972): 764-770.

1046. Yarwood, Dean L. **The National Administrative System.** New York: Wiley, 1971.

1047. Yarwood, Dean L. and Ben M. Enis. "Advertising and Publicity Programs in the Executive Branch of the National Government: Hustling or Helping the People?" **Public Administration Review** 42 (January/February 1982): 37-46.

1048. Yates, Douglas. **Bureaucratic Democracy: The Search for Democracy and Efficiency in American Government.** Cambridge, MA: Harvard University Press, 1982.

1049. Yessian, Mark R. "Coping within the Bureaucracy: A Way to Keep the Juices Flowing." **Bureaucrat** 7 (Summer 1978): 48-49.

1050. Young, Andrew. "Growth of Government Bureaucracy." **Crisis** 82 (December 1975): 427-430.

1051. Young, John D. "Budgetary Reform-Bureau of the Budget and PPBS." Ph.D. dissertation, American University, 1974.

1052. Young, William W. "Congressional Investigations of the Federal Administration." Ph.D. dissertation, University of California, 1956.

1053. Youngberg, Ivan G. "Federal Administration and Participatory Democracy: The Agricultural Stabilization and Conservation Services (ASCS) Farmer Committee System." Ph.D. dissertation, University of Illinois, 1971.

1054. Zink, Harold. "Government Reform in the U.S.A." **Political Quarterly** 21 (January 1950): 69-79.

1055. Zola, Joan. "Portrait of a Bureaucrat." **National Review** 19 (April 1967): 410-412.

Chapter 2.
Department of Agriculture

1056. Abrahams, Paul. "Agricultural Adjustment During the New Deal Period: The New York Milk Industry: A Case Study." **Agricultural History** 39 (April 1965): 92-101.

1057. Albertson, Dean. **Roosevelt's Farmer: Claude R. Wickard in the New Deal.** New York: Columbia University Press, 1961.

1058. Ashmen, Roy. "A Study of Collecting and Reporting Wholesale Butter Prices at Chicago by the United States Department of Agriculture, 1938-1939." Ph.D. dissertation, Northwestern University, 1950.

1059. Bailey, F. "Extension Service Fights for Survival." **Banking** 56 (December 1963): 82-83.

1060. Baker, Gladys L. "And to Act for the Secretary: Paul H. Appleby and the Department of Agriculture, 1933-1940." **Agricultural History** 45 (October 1971): 235-258.

1061. Baker, Gladys L. **The County Agent.** Chicago: University of Chicago Press, 1939.

1062. Baldwin, Sidney. "The Farm Security Administration: A Study in Politics and Administration." Ph.D. dissertation, Syracuse University, 1955.

1063. Baldwin, Sidney. **Poverty and Politics: The Rise and Decline of the Farm Security Administration.** Chapel Hill: University of North Carolina Press, 1968.

1064. Barney, Daniel R. **The Last Stand: Ralph Nader's Study Report on the National Forests.** New York: Grossman, 1974.

1065. Barrett, F. A. "Legal Aspects of Major Programs Administered by the United States Department of Agriculture." **Wyoming Law Journal** 14 (Spring 1960): 175-183.

1066. Bartley, Joseph C. "A Study of Price Control by the United States Food Administration." Ph.D. dissertation, Catholic University of America, 1922.

1067. Benedict, Murry R. "Attempts to Restrict Competition in Agriculture: The Government Programs." **American Economic Review** 44 (May 1954): 93-106.

1068. Benedict, Murry R. **Farm Policies of the United States, 1790-1950.** New York: Twentieth Century Fund, 1963.

1069. Bennet, Hugh H. "Soil Conservation in a Hungry World." **Geographical Review** 38 (April 1948): 311-317.

1070. Bernstein, Barton J. "The Clash of Interests: The Postwar Battle between the Office of Price Administration and the Department of Agriculture." **Agricultural History** 41 (January 1967): 45-58.

1071. Berry, J. M. "Consumers and the Hunger Lobby." **Proceedings of the Academy of Political Science** 34 (1982): 68-78.

1072. Bhatia, K. B. "USDA Series on Net Investment in Farm Real Estate - A Critique." **American Statistical Association Journal** 66 (September 1971): 492-495.

1073. Block, John R. "Food Safety at a Crossroad." **Food Drug Cosmetic Law Journal** 37 (January 1982): 23-25.

1074. Block, William J. **The Separation of the Farm Bureau and the Extension Service.** Urbana: University of Illinois Press, 1960.

1075. Burton, Hilary D. "User-Dependent SDI System: They Said It Could Not Be Done." **Special Libraries** 64 (December 1973): 541-545.

1076. Bowen, Becky. "Promoting Agricultural Exports: The Agricultural Trade Act of 1978 - Pub. L. No. 95-501, 92 Stat. 1685." **North Carolina Journal of International Law and Regulation** 5 (Spring 1980): 263-277.

1077. Brau, A. "Assessing Supervisory Training Needs and Evaluating Effectiveness." **Training and Development Journal** 33 (February 1979): 3-10.

1078. Butz, Earl L. "Big Brother Meddles Too Much." **Gonzaga Law Review** 20 (1984-1985): 669-682.

1079. Calkin, Homer L. "Federal Government and Agriculture - 1840-1860." **Palimpsest** 52 (December 1971): 585-591.

1080. Campbell, Christiana M. **The Farm Bureau and the New Deal.** Urbana: University of Illinois Press, 1948.

1081. Clawson, Marion. "Aging Farmers and Agricultural Policy." **American Journal of Agricultural Economics** 45 (February 1963): 13-30.

1082. Clawson, Marion. "Conserving the Soil." **Proceedings of the Academy of Political Science** 34 (1982): 89-98.

1083. Clepper, Henry. "The Forest Service Backlashed." **Forest History** 11 (January 1968): 6-15.

1084. Cochrane, Raymond C. **Measures for Progress: A History of the National Bureau of Standards.** New York: Arno, 1976.

1085. Cohen, Stanley E. "Congress Eyes US Activity in Market Research." **Advertising Age** 30 (May 18, 1959): 120-121.

1086. Connery, R. T. "Generation and Transmission Loan Policy under the Rural Electrification Act." **Denver Law Journal** 43 (Summer 1966): 269-278.

1087. Conrad, David E. **The Forgotten Farmers: The Story of Sharecroppers in the New Deal.** Urbana: University of Illinois Press, 1963.

1088. Cook, R. G. "Senator Heyburn's War Against the Forest Service." **Idaho Yesterdays** 14 (Winter 1970-1971): 12-15.

1089. Cornelius, Susan F. "An Analysis of Federal Initiatives to Assure Economic Independence for Farm Women." **Ohio Northern University Law Review** 7 (January 1980): 20-53.

1090. Crafts, Edward and Susan Schrer. "Congressional Liaison in the Forest Service." **Forest History** 16 (October 1972): 12-17.

1091. Crown, Michele F. "Improving the Labeling Process." **Food Drug Cosmetic Law Journal** 36 (May 1981): 258-269.

1092. Culhane, Paul J. **Public Lands Politics: Interest Group Influence on the Forest Service and the Bureau of Land Management.** Baltimore: Johns Hopkins University Press, 1981.

1093. Danbom, David B. "The Agricultural Extension System and the First World War." **Historian** 41 (February 1979): 315-331.

1094. Dane, Charles W. "Factors Affecting the Successful Application of PERT/CPM Systems in a Government Organization." **Interfaces** 9 (November 1979): 94-98.

1095. Davenport, Charles. "The Influence of Tax Policy on Agriculture: An Overview of the Structure Project." **Tax Notes** 10 (April 28, 1980): 603-609.

1096. Deering, Ferdie. **USDA, Manager of American Agriculture.** Norman: University of Oklahoma Press, 1945.

1097. Dethloff, Henry C. "Missouri Farmers and the New Deal: A Case Study of Farm Policy Formulation on the Local Level." **Agricultural History** 39 (July 1965): 141-146.

1098. Dinnerstein, Leonard. "The Senate's Rejection of Aubrey Williams as Rural Electrification Administrator." **Alabama Review** 2 (April 1968): 133-143.

1099. Elliot, Foster F. "Adjusting Hog Production to Market Demand in Cooperation with the Bureau of Agricultural Economics, United States Department of Agriculture." Ph.D. dissertation, University of Wisconsin, 1926.

1100. Enarson, Elaine P. **Woods-working Women: Sexual Integration in the U.S. Forest Service.** Tuscaloosa: University of Alabama Press, 1984.

1101. Fischel, William A. "Urbanization of Agricultural Land: A Review of the National Agricultural Lands Study." **Land Economics** 58 (May 1982): 236-259.

1102. Fite, Gilbert C. "Farmer Opinion and the Agricultural Adjustment Act, 1933." **Journal of American**

History 48 (March 1962): 656-673.

1103. Fite, Gilbert C. **George N. Peck and the Fight for Farm Parity.** Norman: University of Oklahoma Press, 1954.

1104. Frischknecht, Reed L. "The Administration of Farm Price and Income Support Programs, 1933-1950." Ph.D. dissertation, University of Utah, 1953.

1105. Frischknecht, Reed L. "State Extension Services and the Administration of Farm Price and Income Support Programs: A Case Study in Federal State Relations." **Western Political Quarterly** 10 (June 1957): 416-441.

1106. Frome, Michael. **The Forest Service.** New York: Praeger, 1971.

1107. Gardner, Bruce L. "Economic Analysis of the Regulation of Agriculture." **American Journal of Agricultural Economics** 61 (November 1979): 732-740.

1108. Gaus, John M. and Leon D. Wolcott. **Public Administration and the United States Department of Agriculture.** Chicago: Public Administration Service, 1940.

1109. Gelb, Leslie H. and Anthony Lake. "Less Food, More Politics." **Foreign Policy** 17 (Winter 1974-1975): 176-189.

1110. Goff, N. S. "Department of Agriculture Terminal Network." **Journal of Systems Management** 26 (August 1975): 8-10.

1111. Gower, Calvin W. "The CCC, the Forest Service, and Politics in Maine, 1933-1936." **New England Social Studies Bulletin** 30 (Spring 1973): 15-21.

1112. Hadwiger, Dan F. "Experience of Black Farmers Home Administration Local Office Chiefs." **Public Personnel Management** 2 (January 1973): 49-54.

1113. Hadwiger, Dan F. **Federal Wheat Commodity Programs.** Ames: Iowa State University Press, 1970.

1114. Hadwiger, Dan F. "Nutrition, Food Safety and Farm Policy." **Proceedings of the Academy of Political Science** 34 (1982): 79-88.

1115. Hadwiger, Dan F. "Old, the New and the Emerging United States Department of Agriculture." **Public**

Administration Review 36 (March 1976): 155-165.

1116. Hadwiger, Don F. and Ross B. Talbot. **Pressures and Protests: The Kennedy Farm Program and the Wheat Referendum of 1963.** San Francisco: Chandler, 1965.

1117. Hahn, Benjamin W. **National Forest Resource Management.** Stanford, CA: Stanford Environmental Law Society, 1978.

1118. Hall, Douglas T. and Benjamin Schneider. "Correlates of Organizational Identification as a Function of Career Pattern and Organizational Type." **Administrative Science Quarterly** 17 (September 1972): 340-350.

1119. Hall, Tom G. "The Aiken Bill, Price Supports and the Wheat Farmer in 1948." **North Dakota History** 39 (Winter 1972): 13-22, 47.

1120. Hamel, R. E. "Applicability of NEPA to Forest Service Land Use Decisions." **Idaho Law Review** 11 (Spring 1975): 113-139.

1121. Hamilton, Lawrence S. "The Federal Forest Regulation Issue." **Forest History** 9 (April 1965): 2-11.

1122. Hansen, R. G. "Sealed-Bid Versus Open Auctions: The Evidence." **Economic Inquiry** 24 (January 1986): 125-142.

1123. Hardin, Charles M. **The Politics of Agriculture.** Glencoe, IL: Free Press, 1942.

1124. Hardin, Francis S. "Economic and Political Effects of Restrictions by the Department of Agriculture on United States Foreign Trade in Agricultural Commodities." Ph.D. dissertation, University of Colorado, 1955.

1125. Harding, Thomas S. "Genesis of One Government Propaganda Mill." **Public Opinion Quarterly** 11 (Summer 1947): 227-235.

1126. Harding, Thomas S. **Two Blades of Grass, A History of Scientific Development in the U.S. Department of Agriculture.** Norman: University of Oklahoma Press, 1947.

1127. Hendrickson, Roy F. **The Personnel Program of the United States Department of Agriculture.** Chicago: Civil Service Assembly of the United

States and Canada, 1939.

1128. Herring, Edward P. G. **Public Administration and the Public Interest.** New York: McGraw-Hill, 1936.

1129. Hjort, Howard W. "Regulation and Economic Analysis in the US Department of Agriculture." **American Journal of Agricultural Economics** 61 (November 1979): 746-750.

1130. Hoffman, J. E. "Jurisdiction of the Department of Agriculture over Deceptive Trademarks." **Trademark Reporter** 57 (December 1967): 833-835.

1131. Hopkins, Raymond F. "Food Policymaking." **Academy of Political Science, Proceedings** 34 (1982): 12-24.

1132. Hoover, Roy O. "Public Law 273 Comes to Shelton: Implementing the Sustained-Yield Forest Management Act of 1944." **Journal of Forest History** 22 (April 1978): 86-101.

1133. Hushon, John D. "Joint Ventures Between Multi-nationals: Government Regulatory Aspects." **North Carolina Journal of International Law and Commercial Regulation** 6 (Spring 1981): 207-233.

1134. Johnson, William R. "National Farm Organizations and the Reshaping of Agricultural Policy in 1932." **Agricultural History** 37 (January 1963): 35-42.

1135. Kaufman, Herbert. **The Forest Ranger.** Baltimore: Johns Hopkins University Press, 1960.

1136. Keith, K. and Wayne D. Purcell. "Possible Implications of Voids in USDA Cattle Slaughter Data." **American Journal of Agricultural Economics** 58 (August 1976): 568-571.

1137. Keller, Jeanne. "Anticipating Income in Calculating Food Stamp Eligibility for Migrant Farmworker Households." **Clearinghouse Review** 13 (April 1980): 955-956.

1138. Kile, Orville M. **The Farm Bureau through Three Decades.** Baltimore: Waverly Press, 1948.

1139. Kirkendall, Richard S. "Commentary on the Thought of Henry A. Wallace." **Agricultural History** 41 (April 1967): 139-142.

1140. Kirkendall, Richard S. "Howard Tolley and Agricultural Planning in the 1930's." **Agricultural History** 39 (January 1965): 25-33.

1141. Kirschner, Don S. "Henry A. Wallace as Farm Editor." **American Quarterly** 17 (Summer 1965): 187-202.

1142. Klumpp, James F. and Roberta A. Hollihan. "Debunking the Resignation of Earl Butz: Sacrificing an Official Racist." **Quarterly Journal of Speech** 65 (February 1979): 1-11.

1143. Leduc, Thomas. "Public Policy, Private Investment, and Land Use in American Agriculture, 1825-1875." **Agricultural History** 37 (January 1963): 3-9.

1144. Leloup, Lance T. and W. B. Moreland. "Agency Strategies and Executive Review: The Hidden Politics of Budgeting." **Public Administration Review** 38 (May 1978): 232-239.

1145. LeMaster, Dennis C. **Decade of Change: The Remaking of Forest Service Statutory Authority During the 1970s.** Westport, CT: Greenwood Press, 1984

1146. Lewis, Verne B. **Budgetary Administration in the United States Department of Agriculture.** Chicago: Public Administration Service, 1941.

1147. Looney, J. W. "The Future of Government Regulation of Agriculture: Finance and Credit." **Northern Illinois University Law Review** 3 (Spring 1983): 263-277.

1148. Loughran, Patrick H. **The Morgan Case in the Supreme Court as Misinterpreted in the Practice and Opinions of the Department of Agriculture Relating to Rate-making Proceedings ....** Washington, DC: Institute for the Orderly Development of Administrative Law, 1940.

1149. Lovett, Richard A. "Role of the Forest Service in Ski Resort Development: An Economic Approach to Public Lands Management." **Ecology Law Quarterly** 10 (Fall 1983): 507-578.

1150. Lowitt, Richard. "Henry A. Wallace and the 1935 Purge in the Department of Agriculture." **Agricultural History** 53 (July 1979): 607-621.

1151. Lung, Kai Lum. "A Financial History of the United States Department of Agriculture." Ph.D. dissertation, Cornell University, 1924.

1152. Lyng, Richard. "Food." **Food Drug Cosmetic Law Journal** 37 (January 1982): 87-90.

1153. McArdle, Richard E. and Elwood R. Maunder. "Wilderness Politics: Legislation and Forest Service Policy." **Journal of Forest History** 19 (October 1975): 166-179.

1154. McCune, Wesley. **Who's Behind Our Farm Policy?** New York: Praeger, 1956.

1155. McDean, Harry C. "Federal Farm Policy and the Dust Bowl: The Half-Right Solution." **North Dakota History** 47 (Summer 11980): 20-31.

1156. McGovern, George, ed. **Agricultural Thought in the Twentieth Century.** Indianapolis: Bobbs-Merrill, 1967.

1157. McMillan, C. W. "USDA and Progress of Federal Meat Inspection." **Food Drug Cosmetic Law Journal** 37 (January 1982): 26-29.

1158. MacRae, C. D. and R. J. Struyk. "Federal Housing Administration (FHA), Tenure, Choice, and Residential Land Use." **Journal of Urban Economics** 4 (July 1977): 360-378.

1159. Maddox, James G. "The Farm Security Administration." Ph.D. dissertation, Harvard University, 1950.

1160. Marshall, E. L. "The Office of Solicitor for U. S. Department of Agriculture." **Missouri Bar Journal** 3 (April 1932): 55-59.

1161. Matteson, Robert J. M. "Public Forestry and Public Administration." Ph.D. dissertation, Harvard University, 1953.

1162. Michaelson, Pete. "USDA, DOE Promote Gasohol in Own Ways." **Solar Law Reporter** 2 (September/October 1980): 461-462.

1163. Miller, David B. "Origins and Functions of the Federal Farm Board." Ph.D. dissertation, University of Kansas, 1973.

1164. Miller, J. A. "USDA Beef Grading: A Failure in Consumer Information?" **Journal of Marketing** 40 (January 1976): 25-31.

1165. Moneeb, Essam H. "Economic and Statistical Analysis of the Impact of Two Federal

Agricultural Policy Programs on Agricultural Resource Reallocation in Ohio." Ph.D. dissertation, Ohio State University, 1964.

1166. Monhollon, Jimmie R. "The Farmers Home Administration and Agricultural Poverty in Tennessee." Ph.D. dissertation, Vanderbilt University, 1964.

1167. Moore, Ernest G. **The Agricultural Research Service.** New York: Praeger, 1967.

1168. Morgan, Robert J. **Governing Soil Conservation: Thirty Years of the New Decentralization.** Baltimore: Johns Hopkins University Press, 1965.

1169. Nelson, Lawrence J. "Oscar Johnston, the New Deal, and the Cotton Subsidy Payments Controversy, 1936-1937." **Journal of Southern History** 40 (August 1974): 399-416.

1170. North, David M. "Forest Service Sets Fleet Modernization." **Aviation Week and Space Technology** 112 (April 28, 1980): 56-58.

1171. Nourse, Edwin G. **Three Years of the Agricultural Adjustment Administration.** Washington, DC: Brookings Institution, 1937.

1172. O'Day, Carol H. "The Role of the Interventionist State in Food and Agricultural Policy." **Social Science Journal** 16 (January 1979): 1-16.

1173. Olson, Philip. "Public Policy and the Politics of Agriculture: Organization Inaction." **Rural Social** 44 (Summer 1979): 266-280.

1174. Olsson, Philip C. "Food Inspection: The Quest for Objectivity." **Food Drug Cosmetic Law Journal** 35 (March 1980): 149-159.

1175. Ostheimer, John M. **The Forest Service Meets the Public: Decision-making and Public Involvement on the Coconino National Forest.** Fort Collins, CO: Eisenhower Consortium for Western Environmental Forestry Research, 1977.

1176. Paarlberg, Don. **American Farm Policy: A Case Study of Centralized Decision Making.** New York: Wiley, 1964.

1177. Paulino, Leonardo A. and Shen Sheng Tseng. **A Comparative Study of FAO and USDA Data on Production, Area, and Trade of Major Food Staples.** Washington, DC: International Food

Policy Research Institute, 1980.

1178. Pavlick, Anthony L. "An Analysis of the Effects of Federal Farm Programs on Income of Appalachian Farmers." Ph.D. dissertation, University of Minnesota, 1963.

1179. Perkins, Van L. "The AAA and the Politics of Agriculture: Agricultural Policy Formulation in the Fall of 1933." **Agricultural History** 39 (October 1965): 220-229.

1180. Perkins, Van L. **Crisis in Agriculture: The Agricultural Adjustment Administration and the New Deal, 1933.** Berkeley: University of California Press, 1969.

1181. Pinkett, Harold T. "The Archival Product of a Century of Federal Assistance to Agriculture." **American Historical Review** 69 (April 1964): 689-706.

1182. Pinkett, Harold T. "Early Records of the U.S. Department of Agriculture." **American Archivist** 25 (October 1962): 407-416.

1183. Pisani, Donald J. "Federal Reclamation and Water Rights in Nevada." **Agricultural History** 51 (July 1977): 540-558.

1184. Polenberg, Richard. "Conservation and Reorganization: The Forest Service Lobby, 1937-1938." **Agricultural History** 39 (October 1965): 230-239.

1185. Pope, Edward V. "Extension Service Programs Affecting American Families." **Marriage and Family Living** 20 (August 1958): 270-277.

1186. Post, Robert C. **Physics, Patents, and Politics: A Biography of Charles Grafton Page.** New York: Science History Publications, 1976.

1187. Pressman, Jeffrey L. and Aaron B. Wildavsky. **Implementation.** Berkeley: University of California Press, 1984.

1188. Purcell, Wayne D. and K. E. Nelson. "Recent Changes in Beef Grades: Issues and Analysis of the Yield Grade Requirement." **American Journal of Agricultural Economics** 58 (August 1976): 475-484.

1189. Pursell, Carroll W. "The Administration of Science in the Department of Agriculture, 1933-1940." **Agricultural History** 42 (July 1968): 231-240.

1190. Rasmussen, Wayne D., ed. **Readings in the History of American Agriculture.** Urbana: University of Illinois Press, 1960.

1191. Rasmussen, Wayne D. and Gladys L. Baker. **The Department of Agriculture.** New York: Praeger, 1972.

1192. Raup, Philip M. "Agricultural Critique of the National Agricultural Lands Study." **Land Economics** 58 (May 1982): 260-274.

1193. Richards, Henry M. "Attempts by the Federal Government to Support Agricultural Prices." Ph.D. dissertation, New York University, 1951.

1194. Riggs, Robert E. "FAO and the USDA: Implications for Functionalist Learning." **Western Political Quarterly** 33 (September 1980): 314-329.

1195. Riggs, S. "USDA's Carol Foreman Speaks Out on a National Nutrition Policy." **Institutions** 82 (June 1, 1978): 15-18.

1196. Rikleen, L. S. "Animal Welfare Act: Still a Cruelty to Animals." **Boston College Environ-mental Affairs Law Review** 7 (Winter 1978): 129-145.

1197. Roberts, Ralph S. "USDA's Pioneering Performance Budget." **Public Administration Review** 20 (Spring 1960): 74-78.

1198. Robinson, Glen O. **The Forest Service: A Study in Public Land Management.** Baltimore: Johns Hopkins University Press, 1975.

1199. Robinson, Glen O. "Wilderness: The Last Frontier." **Minnesota Law Review** 59 (November 1974): 1-65.

1200. Rogers, Benjamin F. "The United States Department of Agriculture (1862-1889): A Study in Bureaucracy." Ph.D. dissertation, University of Minnesota, 1951.

1201. Rosen, G. R. "High Price of Earl Butz." **Dun's Review** 102 (October 1973): 72-75.

1202. Rosen, Jerold A. "Henry A. Wallace and American Liberal Politics, 1945-1948." **Annals of Iowa** 44 (Fall 1978): 462-474.

1203. Rosenbaum, Walter A. **The Burning of the Farm Population Estimates.**Indianapolis: Bobbs,1965.

1204. Rosenberry, Paul E. "A Proposal for Improving the United States Department of Agriculture's Cost and Return Studies." Ph.D. dissertation, Iowa State University, 1971.

1205. Salmond, John A. "Postscript to the New Deal: The Defeat of the Nomination of Aubrey W. Williams as Rural Electrification Administrator in 1945." **Journal of American History** 61 (September 1974): 417-436.

1206. Saloutos, Theodore. "Agricultural Organizations and Farm Policy in the South after World War II." **Agricultural History** 53 (January 1979): 377-404.

1207. Saloutos, Theodore. "New Deal Agricultural Policy: An Evaluation." **Journal of American History** 61 (September 1974): 394-416.

1208. Sanderson, Fred H. "Expert Opportunities for Agricultural Products: Implications for US Agricultural and Trade Policies." **Columbia Journal of World Business** 10 (Fall 1975): 15-28.

1209. Schapsmeier, Edward L. and Frederick H. Schapsmeier. "Henry A. Wallace: Agrarian Idealist or Agricultural Realist?" **Agricultural History** 41 (April 1967): 127-138.

1210. Schapsmeier, Edward L. and Frederick H. Schapsmeier. "A Prophet in Politics: The Public Career of Henry A. Wallace." **Annals of Iowa** 39 (Summer 1967): 1-21.

1211. Schapsmeier, Edward L. and Frederick H. Schapsmeier. "The Wallaces and Their Farm Paper: A Story of Agrarian Leadership." **Journalism Quarterly** 44 (Summer 1967): 289-296.

1212. Scher, H. S. "USDA: Agriculture at the Expense of Small Farmers and Farmworkers." **University of Toledo Law Review** 7 (Spring 1976): 837-862.

1213. Schiff, Ashley L. **Fire and Water: Scientific Heresy in the Forest Service.** Cambridge, MA: Harvard University Press, 1962.

1214. Schiff, Ashley L. "The United States Forest Service: Science and Administration,." Ph.D. dissertation, Harvard University, 1959.

1215. Scott, L. C. and L. B. Jones. "USDA and Wages in the Sugar Crop Industry." **Labor Law Journal** 25 (January 1974): 18-30.

1216. Scruggs, Otey M. "The Bracero Program under the Farm Security Administration, 1942-1943." **Labor History** 3 (Spring 1962): 149-168.

1217. Sellers, Ashley. "Administrative Law - The Extent to Which S.915 or H.R.4236 Would Affect the Work of the Department of Agriculutre." **George Washington Law Review** 7 (May 1939): 819-843.

1218. Sellers, Ashley. "Administrative Procedure - A Suggested Classification of Procedures of Regulatory Agencies in the United States Department of Agriculture." **Washington University Law Quarterly** 25 (April 1940): 352-398.

1219. Shands, William E., Perry R. Hagenstein and Marrisa T. Roche. **National Forest Policy: From Conflict toward Consensus.** Washington, DC: Conservation Foundation, 1979.

1220. Shepherd, Jack. **The Forest Killers: The Destruction of the American Wilderness.** New York: Weybright and Talley, 1975.

1221. Simms, D. Harper. **The Soil Conservation Service.** New York: Praeger, 1970.

1222. Skurzynski, Gloria. **Safeguarding the Land: Women at Work in Parks, Forests, and Rangelands.** New York: Harcourt Brace Jovanovich, 1981.

1223. Solkoff, Joel. **The Politics of Food.** San Francisco: Sierra Club Books, 1986.

1224. Steen, Harold K. "Grazing and the Environment: A History of Forest Service Stock-Reduction Policy." **Agricultural History** 49 (January 1975): 238-242.

1225. Steen, Harold K. **The U.S. Forest Service: A History.** Seattle: University of Washington Press, 1976.

1226. Taeuber, Conrad. "Some Aspects of the Statistics Program in the Department of Agriculture." **American Statistical Association Journal** 42 (March 1947): 41-45.

1227. Terrell, John U. **The United States Department of Agriculture.** New York: Duell, Sloan and Pearce, 1966.

1228. Tiffany, David M. "Agricultural Policy-Making in the Eisenhower Administration." Ph.D. dissertation, State University of New York, 1974.

1229. Tok, Toong Kien. "Planning, Programming and Budgeting System in U.S. Department of Agriculture, Department of Health, Education, and Welfare and National Aeronautics and Space Administration." Ph.D. dissertation, University of Pittsburgh, 1970.

1230. Tontz, Robert L. and Alex D. Angelidis. "The Farm Surplus and Tariff Reform." **Current History** 43 (August 1962): 95-102.

1231. Truman, David B. **Administrative Decentralization: A Study of the Chicago Field Offices of the United States Department of Agriculture.** Chicago: University of Chicago Press, 1940.

1232. Twight, Ben W. **Organizational Values and Political Power: The Forest Service Versus the Olympic National Forest.** University Park: Pennsylvania State University Press, 1983.

1233. Wadley, James B. "Small Farms: The USDA, Rural Communities and Urban Pressures." **Washburn Law Journal** 21 (Spring 1982): 478-514.

1234. Wanlass, William L. "The United States Department of Agriculture, A Study in Administration." Ph.D. dissertation, Johns Hopkins University, 1919.

1235. Weber, Gustavus A. **The Bureau of Standards: Its History, Activities and Organization.** Baltimore: Johns Hopkins University Press, 1925.

1236. Weber, Gustavus A. **The Patent Office: Its History, Activities and Organization.** Baltimore: Johns Hopkins University Press, 1925.

1237. White, Henry G. "Forest Regulation - A Study of Public Control of Cutting Practices on Private Forest Land in the United States." Ph.D. dissertation, University of Minnesota, 1949.

1238. Wiest, Edward. **Agricultural Organization in the United States.** New York: Arno Press, 1975.

1239. Wildavsky, Aaron B. and Arthur Hammond. "Comprehensive Versus Incremental Budgeting in the Department of Agriculture." **Administrative Science Quarterly** 10 (December 1965): 321-346.

1240. Williams, Burton J. "Trees But No Timber: Prelude to the Timber Culture Act." **Nebraska History** 53 (Spring 1972): 77-86.

1241. Williams, C. L. "Soil Conservation and Water Pollution Control: The Muddy Record of the United States Department of Agriculture." **Boston College Environmental Affairs Law Review** 7 (Summer 1979): 365-421.

1242. Wilson, Graham K. "Are Department Secretaries Really a President's Natural Enemies." **British Journal of Political Science** 7 (July 1977): 273-299.

1243. Wilson, Harold O. "Housing the Rural Poor: Why We Need the Farmers Home Administration." **Journal of Housing** 43 (July/August 1986): 159-163.

1244. Winters, Donald L. **Henry Cantwell Wallace, As Secretary of Agriculture, 1921-1924.** Urbana: University of Illinois Press, 1970.

1245. Wirfs, R. M. "Two Tools for Safety in the Woods." **Job Safety and Health** 4 (September 1976): 20-27.

1246. Yanowitch, Murry. "Protecting the Consumer." **Challenge** 20 (September 1977): 24-28.

Chapter 3.
Department of Commerce

1247. Alterman, Hyman. **Counting People: The Census in History.** New York: Harcourt Brace and World, 1969.

1248. Andrews, Don D. and Simon M. Newman. "Activities and Objectives of the Office of Research and Development in US Patent Office." **Journal of the Patent Office Society** 40 (February 1958): 79-84.

1249. Arnold, Peri E. "Great Engineer as Administrator: Herbert Hoover and Modern Bureaucracy." **Review of Politics** 42 (July 1980): 329-348.

1250. Ash, Roy L. "Reorganizing the Executive Branch for National Economic Growth." **Conference Board Record** 8 (April 1971): 7-9.

1251. Bailey, J. "Practice by Non-Lawyers before the United States Patent Office." **Federal Bar Journal** 15 (June/September 1955): 211-223.

1252. Baker, D. H. "Commerce Department Guides Exporters to Global Markets." **Industrial Development** 143 (March 1974): 12-14.

1253. Ballard, William R. "Money for the Patent Office." **Journal of the Patent Office Society** 37 (June 1955): 435-438.

1254. Banner, Donald W. "American Bar Association Address." **Journal of the Patent Office Society** 61 (September 1979): 535-543.

1255. Banner, Donald W. "Patent and Trademark Office Operations Today." **Journal of the Patent Office Society** 65 (October 1983): 586-592.

1256. Barabba, Vincent P. "World's Best Kept Secrets:

Private Data Revealed to US Government." **Commerce Today** 5 (September 1, 1975): 8-10.

1257. Barks, J. "I'm from the Government and I'm Here to Help You." **Distribution** 79 (October 1980): 99-102.

1258. Barovick, R. "Commerce's New Look at How to Expand Foreign Trade and Investment." **Business Abroad** 96 (January 1971): 9-11.

1259. Barovick, R. "Each US/FCS Post Is Unique: A Look at Manila and Hong Kong." **Business America** 5 (April 19, 1982): 3-7.

1260. Barovick, R. "Foreign Commercial Service." **Business America** 3 (October 6, 1980): 3-6.

1261. Barovick, R. "San Francisco District Office Spearheads Export Expansion." **Business America** 3 (December 15, 1980): 3-7.

1262. Barovick, R. "US Commercial Service: District Office Network Reaches Out to Exporters." **Business America** 3 (November 3, 1980): 2-6.

1263. Bartlett, Jospeh W. and Douglass N. Jones. "Managing a Cabinet Agency: Problems of Performance at Commerce." **Public Administration** 34 (January 1974): 62-70.

1264. Becker, William H. **The Dynamics of Business-Government Relations: Industry and Exports, 1893-1921.** Chicago: University of Chicago Press, 1982.

1265. Bello, J. H. and J. J. R. Talbot. "Foreign Government Subsidy Reductions: When Should the Commerce Department Take Them into Account?" **George Washington Journal of International Law and Economics** 19 (1985): 109-121.

1266. Berman, H. "History of Division 32." **Journal of the Patent Office Society** 40 (July 1958): 506-511.

1267. Billingsley, Keith R. and Delmer D. Dunn. "States and the Bureau of the Census." **State Government** 47 (Summer 1974): 180-184.

1268. Bjorge, G. H. "35 USC 103: The PTO, the Courts, and the Future." **American Patent Law Association Quarterly Journal** 5 (1977): 137-145.

1269. Bodansky, Harry. "Treasury Proposes Changes in Investigation Procedures under Antidumping Act of 1921." **International Commerce** 70 (May 18, 1964): 12-13.

1270. Bogorad, A. "Impact of the Amended Rules upon Discovery Practice before the Trademark Trial and Appeal Board." **Trademark Reporter** 66 (January/February 1976): 28-38.

1271. Bowers, E. W. and G. A. Weimer. "Chrysler Not the Only One Looking for Government Bankroll." **Iron Age** 222 (September 3, 1979): 36-39.

1272. Bradford, Amory. **Oakland's Not for Burning.** New York: McKay, 1968.

1273. Bradshaw, M. T. and M. Lechter. "Contraction of United States Merchandise Trade Surplus." **Survey of Current Business** 39 (December 1959): 11-18.

1274. Brandes, Joseph. **Herbert Hoover and Economic Diplomacy: Department of Commerce Policy, 1921-1928.** Pittsburgh: University of Pittsburgh Press, 1962.

1275. Brenner, E. J. "Current and Future Programs in the Patent Office." **Journal of the Patent Office Society** 47 (March 1965): 139-142.

1276. Brenner, E. J. "Patent Office Activities during Fiscal Year 1966 - Outlook for Fiscal Year 1967." **Journal of the Patent Office Society** 48 (August 1966): 475-479.

1277. Brink, Edward L. "Differences in the Age Distribution of Farm and Nonfarm Populations: An Analysis of Bureau of the Census Data." Ph.D. dissertation, University of Pennsylvania, 1954.

1278. Britain, Gerald M. **Bureaucracy and Innovation: An Ethnography of Policy Change.** Beverly Hills, CA: Sage, 1981.

1279. Carlson, D. L. "Best Made Disclosure Requirement in Patent Practice." **Journal of the Patent Office Society** 60 (March 1978): 171-197.

1280. Cathey, P. J. "Industry Can Make Greater Use of Commerce Field Services." **Iron Age** 186 (August 11, 1-960): 149-150.

1281. Clark, E. H. "The Past of the Patent Office." **Journal of the Patent Office Society** 14 (April

1932): 262-272.

1282. Clesner, J. M. and H. F. Clesner. "Board of Appeals of the Patent Office." **Journal of the Patent Office Society** 40 (May 1958): 298-302.

1283. Cohen, David M. "Government Troops on the Front Line: Making the Record." **Federal Rules Decisions** 94 (September 1982): 482-492.

1284. Cohen, J. "Functions, Costs, and Fees of the US Patent Office." **Idea: The Patent, Trademark, and Copyright Journal of Research and Education** 15 (Winter 1971-1972): 595-599.

1285. Cohen, J. "Location of a New Patent Office Building, Exile by Default." **Journal of the Patent Office Society** 16 (December 1964): 842-851.

1286. Connor, John T. "Evolution of Business and Government Partnership." **Iron Age** 196 (August 26, 1965): 60-63.

1287. Connor, John T. "Exporting? Here's What Your Department of Commerce Can Do for You." **Distribution Age** 654 (October 1966): 27-31.

1288. Connor, John T. "President Johnson's Message Serves as Keynote for 175th Anniversary of Patent Act of 1790." **Journal of the Patent Office Society** 47 (May 1965): 279-284.

1289. Cosimi, Ivan. "The US Export Imperative." **Florida Bar Journal** 56 (May 1982): 387-388.

1290. Crews, M. A. "Structured Patent Specifications and Imperative Need." **Journal of the Patent Office Society** 47 (September 1965): 772-775.

1291. Dam, Kenneth W. "Implementation of Import Quotas: The Case of Oil." **Journal of Law and Economics** 14 (April 1971): 1-60.

1292. Dann, C. Marshall. "What Lies Ahead for Patents?" **Journal of the Patent Office Society** 59 (September 1977): 600-608.

1293. Day, J. W. "How to Tap the United States Commerce Department." **Business Management** 39 (January 1971): 41-42.

1294. Derenberg, Walter J. "Equitable Defenses in Patent Office Proceedings." **Trade-Mark Reporter** 38 (May

1948): 495-503.

1295. Diamond, Sidney A. "View from Crystal Plaza." **Journal of the Patent Office Society** 61 (September 1979): 544-549.

1296. Dienner, John A. "Lightening the Load of the Patent Examiner." **Journal of the Patent Office Society** 47 (March 1965): 148-153.

1297. Drohan, J. F. X. "Exporting Made Easy." **Plastics World** 36 (April 1978): 62-64.

1298. Drury, R. F. "Census Computers Turn to Internal Management." **Systems** 8 (January 1967): 16-18.

1299. Eckler, A. Ross. **The Bureau of the Census.** New York: Praeger, 1972.

1300. Ewing, T. "The Great and Growing Task of the Patent Office." **Journal of the Patent Office Society** 14 (June 1932): 471-486.

1301. Federico, Bianca M. "The Patent Office Fire of 1836." **Journal of the Patent Office Society** 19 (November 1937): 804-833.

1302. Federico, Pasquale J. "The Patent Office in 1837." **Journal of the Patent Office Society** 19 (December 1937): 954-965.

1303. Federico, Pasquale J. "The Patent Office in 1839." **Journal of the Patent Office Society** 21 (October 1939): 786-794.

1304. Fernandez, F. F. "Census." **Southern California Law Review** 42 (Winter 1969): 245-262.

1305. Fishman, George S. **Project Evaluation for EDA.** Santa Monica, CA: Rand, 1966.

1306. Fox, Kenneth P. "The Census Bureau and the Cities: National Development of Urban Government in the Industrial Age: 1870-1930." Ph.D. dissertation, University of Pennsylvania, 1972.

1307. Frost, George E. "Patent Office Performance in Perspective." **Michigan Law Review** 54 (March 1956): 591-602.

1308. Gelfand, G. "Expanding the Role of the Patent Office in Determining Patent Validity: A Proposal." **Cornell Law Review** 65 (November 1979): 75-111.

1309. Goldman, Melvin R. "Interindustry Structure of the United States: A Report on the 1958 Input-Output Study." **Survey of Current Business** 44 (November 1964): 10-29.

1310. Gordon, Marvin F. "1960 Urbanized Area Program." **Annals of Association of American Geographers** 50 (September 1960): 322-324.

1311. Green, William H. "Foreign Investment in U.S. Real Estate: Analysis of the Data." **International Tax Journal** 6 (August 1980): 444-453.

1312. Harris, L. J. and Irving H. Siegel. "Attitude Survey on Patent Office Relocation." **Idea: The Patent, Trademark, and Copyright Journal of Research and Education** 8 (Fall 1964): 316-321.

1313. Hefter, Laurence T. and D. W. Hill. "Practical Guidelines for Dealing with Delays Trademark Prosecution." **Trademark Reporter** 10 (September/October 1980): 455-466.

1314. Henry, C. C. "Patent Office Aids in War and Peace." **Journal of the Patent Office Society** 26 (June 1944): 423-426.

1315. Herrmann, David. "Four Vital Services." **Journal of the Patent Office Society** 30 (January 1948): 13-50.

1316. Herrmann, David. "Sound Planning of an Examining Division." **Journal of the Patent Office Society** 30 (April 1948): 286-298.

1317. Himmelberg, Robert F. "Business, Antitrust Policy, and the Industrial Board of the Department of Commerce, 1919." **Business History Review** 42 (Spring 1968): 1-23.

1318. Hoffman, S. S. "Export-Import Gap: Role of Farm Products." **Conference Board Business Record** 16 (December 1959): 563-566.

1319. Hollomon, John H. "Role of the Department of Commerce." **Food, Drug Cosmetic Law Journal** 22 (June 1967): 327-334.

1320. Holtz, Milton E. "Agricultural Administration under the Patent Office, 1836-1862." **South Dakota History** 5 (Spring 1975): 123-149.

1321. Jacobson, M. "Comments on Proposed Fee Bill, S. 2225." **Journal of the Patent Office Society**

45 (August 1963): 644-651.

1322. Jones, E. Terrence and Donald Phares. "Formula Feedback and Central Cities: The Case of Comprehensive Employment and Training Act." **Urban Affairs Quarterly** 14 (September 1978): 31-54.

1323. Jones, Stacy V. **The Patent Office.** New York: Praeger, 1971.

1324. Kallek, Shirley. "Potential Applications of Census Bureau Economic Series in Microdata Analysis." **American Economic Review** 65 (May 1975): 257-262.

1325. Kestenbaum, Lionel. "Arab Boycott in U.S. Law: Flawed Remedies for an International Trade Restraint." **Law and Policy in International Business** 10 (1978): 769-814.

1326. Kiron, A. "New Vistas for Industry." **Journal of the Patent Office Society** 47 (September 1965): 736-741.

1327. Kleiler, Frank M. "Need Help on Foreign Trade?" **American Business** 28 (August 1958): 11-13.

1328. Knox, William T. "Special Libraries and NTIS." **Special Libraries** 67 (January 1976): 45-48.

1329. Ladd, David L. "Implementation of Recommendations on the Management Survey Report." **Journal of the Patent Office Society** 44 (September 1962): 635-641.

1330. Ladd, David L. "Patent Office - An Old Line Agency in a Modern World." **Journal of the Patent Office Society** 43 (August 1961): 515-519.

1331. Ladd, David L. "Patent Office Management Survey - Pain, Boon, or Both." **Journal of the Bar Association of the District of Columbia** 29 (August 1962): 439-446.

1332. Ladd, David L. "Remarks before the Delaware Council of Engineering Societies." **Journal of the Patent Office Society** 45 (December 1963): 799-804.

1333. Lamont, R. P. "The Patent Office." **Journal of the Patent Office Society** 14 (June 1932): 457-462.

1334. Lang, E. H. "Requirements of Rule 131 Affidavits to Antedate References Cited against Generic Chemical Claims." **Journal of the Patent Office**

Society 44 (August 1962): 551-553.

1335. Lanham, B. E. and J. Leibowitz. "Classification, Searching and Mechanization in the U.S. Patent Office." **Journal of the Patent Office Society** 40 (February 1958): 86-93.

1336. Lederer, W. "Balance of International Payments: Fourth Quarter and Year 1965." **Survey of Current Business** 46 (March 1966): 16-28.

1337. Lee, S. J. "Economic Development Administration." **Financial Executive** 46 (May 1978): 18-22.

1338. Lee, W. D. "Business Pipeline to the Consumer." **Public Relations Journal** 28 (December 1972): 8-9.

1339. Lefkowitz, S. "Recent Changes in Practice before the Trademark Trial and Appeal Board." **Trademark Reporter** 69 (September/October 1979): 479-497.

1340. Levy, Marilyn W. "Mandamus in Patent Office Proceedings." **Journal of the Patent Office Society** 18 (May 1936): 307-319.

1341. Lichtenstein, S. "BIC Unit Untangles Snags: Trade Complaints Section Experts Go to Work in Stormy Commercial Weather." **International Commerce** 71 (February 15, 1965): 10-12.

1342. Lichtenstein S. "Developing Countries: Investment Path Laid Out, BIC's Office of International Investment Provides Comprehensive Services." **International Commerce** 71 (April 5, 1965): 17-18.

1343. Lipman, Steven E. and A. S. Newman. "Attorney Discipline in the Patent and Trademark Office: Keeping Tune with the Times." **Journal of the Patent Office Society** 66 (May 1984): 252-306.

1344. Louviere, C. "Secretary of Commerce: Making a Dent in Our Trade Problems." **Nation's Business** 61 (September 1973): 30-32.

1345. Maassel, L. O. and M. E. Turowski. "PCT Implementation - Effect on Filing and Procedures." **Journal of the Patent Office Society** 59 (April 1977): 208-243.

1346. McCarthy, P. and J. F. McKenzie. "Commerce Department Regulations Governing Participation by United States Persons in Foreign Boycotts."

Vanderbilt Journal of Transnational Law 11 (Spring 1978): 193-247.

1347. McClenahen, J. S. "Can Secretary Dent Shine on His Own?" **Industry Week** 179 (October 8, 1973): 53-56.

1348. McDonnell, P. M. "New Approach to Mechanized Information Retrieval in the U.S. Patent Office." **Journal of the Patent Office Society** 50 (October 1968): 651-662.

1349. McElroy, K. P. "Passing the Patent Office Buck." **Journal of the Patent Office Society** 14 (May 1932): 404-408.

1350. McIntyre, J. C. "Effect of a Restriction Requirement in the Patent and Trademark Office on a Subsequent Double Patenting Adjudication." **American Patent Law Association Quarterly Journal** 4 (1976): 301-312.

1351. McKelvey, F. E. "Attorney Disqualification Cases in the PTO." **Journal of the Patent Office Society** 62 (October 1980): 625-643.

1352. Magnet, M. "Behind the Bad-News Census." **Fortune** 103 (February 9, 1981): 88-90.

1353. Marans, H. "Forty Years of U.S. Patent Office (1917-1956)." **Journal of the Patent Office Society** 39 (October/December 1957): 737, 818, 851.

1354. Markey, H. T. "Status of the U.S. Patent System - Sans Myth, Sans Fiction." **Journal of the Patent Office Society** 59 (March 1977): 164-174.

1355. Martin, Curtis H. **Local Economic Development: The Federal Connection.** Lexington, MA: Lexington Books, 1977.

1356. Martin, R. E. "Functions of the Office of the Solicitor of the United States Patent Office." **Journal of the Patent Office Society** 56 (January 1974): 30-59.

1357. Meister, Cary W. "Misleading Nature of the Data in the Bureau of the Census Subject Report on 1970 American Indian Population." **Indian History** 11 (December 1978): 12-19.

1358. Meller, M. L. "Reorganization - How and Why." **Journal of the Patent Office Society** 45 (June

1963): 431-442.

1359. Merna, J. E. "Current Look at the Business and Administrative Operations of the United States Patent Office." **Journal of the Patent Office Society** 46 (June 1964): 405-415.

1360. Merna, J. E. "U.S. Patent Office Finds a New Home - Crosses the Potomac to Crystal City, Virginia." **Journal of the Patent Office Society** 50 (March 1968): 191-202.

1361. Metcalf, Evan B. "Secretary Hoover and the Emergence of Macroeconomic Management." **Business History Review** 49 (Spring 1975): 60-80.

1362. Milkman, Raymond H. **Distress: Evaluating a Federal Effort.** Lexington, MA: Lexington Books, 1972.

1363. Miller, N. "Prison Industries in Transition: Private Sector or Multistate Involvements." **Federal Probation** 47 (December 1983): 24-31.

1364. Miller, W. H. and J. S. McClenahen. "Is the Commerce Department Out of It?" **Industry Week** 183 (November 25, 1974): 27-29.

1365. Mitchell, Ewing Y. **Kicked in and Kicked out of the President's Little Cabinet.** Washington, DC: Andrew Jackson Press, 1936.

1366. Mitroff, Ian I. and Richard O. Mason. **The 1980 Census, Policymaking Amid Turbulence.** Lexington, MA: Lexington Books, 1983.

1367. Mock, H. "Should the Patent Office Be Abolished?" **Journal of the Patent Office Society** 26 (January 1944): 39-48.

1368. Moore, A. E. "Possible Reorganization of Patent Office Divisions and Classes." **Journal of the Patent Office Society** 15 (September 1933): 688-692.

1369. Nolan, J. "For Larry Jobe, the Goal's the Thing." **Journal of Accountancy** 132 (December 1971): 22-24.

1370. Ooms, C. W. "The United States Patent Office and the Administrative Procedure Act." **Trade-Mark Reporter** 38 (February 1948): 149-163.

1371. Orrick, William H. "Problems Confronting the Antitrust Division." **American Bar Association**

Section on Antitrust Law 23 (1963): 71-85.

1372. Osterman, C. K. "How the United States Department of Commerce Helps Small Business." **Commercial Law Journal** 63 (July 1958): 199-211.

1373. Parker, L. F. "Current Developments at the Patent and Trademark Office." **Journal of the Patent Office Society** 60 (February 1978) 57-70.

1374. Polk, J. "How Strong Is Our Competitive Position?" **Conference Board Record** 1 (July 1964): 19-22.

1375. Pursell, Carroll W. "A Preface to Government Support of Research and Development: Research Legislation and the National Bureau of Standards, 1935-1941." **Technology and Culture** 9 (April 1968): 145-164.

1376. Rathbun, R. M. "New Inter Partes Practice." **American Patent Law Association Quarterly Journal** 5 (September 1976): 550-564.

1377. Redfield, William C. **With Congress and Cabinet.** New York: Doubleday, Page, 1934.

1378. Rice, Philip F. "An Input-Output Analysis of the American Textile Industry: A Synthesis of Several Techniques Applied to a Revision of the United States Department of Commerce 1958 Input-Output Study." Ph.D. dissertation, Clemson University, 1968.

1379. Robb, John F. "Patent Office Board of Supervisors." **Journal of the Patent Office Society** 16 (March 1934): 227-231.

1380. Rosa, M. C. "Patent Office Organization, Viewpoint and Classification." **Journal of the Patent Office Society** 31 (June 1949): 414-448.

1381. Rosenblum, J. E. "Practice before the Patent Office under Section 152 of the Atomic Energy Act and Section 305 of the National Aeronautics and Space Act." **Federal Bar Journal** 25 (Winter 1965): 74-87.

1382. Runfola, Ross T. "Herbert Hoover as Secretary of Commerce, 1921-1923: Domestic Economic Planning in the Harding Cabinet." Ph.D. dissertation, State University of New York, 1973.

1383. Schneider, P. "Consideration of U.S. Patent Office Practice in Citing Foreign References." **Journal**

of the Patent Office Society 45 (August 1963): 635-647.

1384. Searby, D. M. "Doing Business in the Mideast: The Game Is Rigged." **Harvard Business Review** 54 (January 1976): 56-64.

1385. Seidman, H. L. "Commerce's Export Programs for the 1980's." **Business America** 3 (October 20, 1980): 22-24.

1386. Siegel, Jacob S. "Estimates of Coverage of the Population by Sex, Race, and Age in the 1970 Census." **Demography** 11 (February 1974): 1-23.

1387. Siggers, P. E. "Suggestions for Improving Public Facilities in the Patent Office." **Journal of the Patent Office Society** 31 (February 1949): 126-130.

1388. Skillman, H. H. "1977 Rule Changes in Ex Parte Practice." **American Patent Law Association Quarterly Journal** 5 (1977): 194-223.

1389. Smith, C. W. "Common Burdens of Woe." **Journal of the Patent Office Society** 56 (July 1974): 414-421.

1390. Smith, O. L. "Conspiracy to Undermine Our Economy: Our Government by Legal Means?" **Magazine of Wall Street** 114 (July 11, 1964): 408-410.

1391. Solo, Robert. "Regional Building Codes Formulated and Enforced by the Federal Bureau of Standards." **Journal of Economic Issues** 15 (March 1981): 173-175.

1392. Stauffer, H. E. "Testimony for Use in Contested Cases before the Patent Office." **Journal of the Patent Office Society** 15 (August 1933): 619-629.

1393. Suplee, C. I. "Computer-Oriented Construction Management System in a Public Works Grant-in-Aid Program." **Construction Review** 17 (July 1971): 4-13.

1394. Tegtmeyer, R. D. "Fraud on the Patent and Trademark Office under Rule 56." **Journal of the Patent Office Society** 58 (September 1976): 550-564.

1395. Tew, G. E. "Patent Office Examining Corps." **Journal of the Patent Office Society** 14 (November 1932): 857-859.

1396. Travaglini, Vincent D. and J. M. Lightman. "Department of Commerce Assistance Available to United States Firms in Protection Abroad against Unfair Trade Practices." **Trademark Reporter** 55 (September 1965): 740-745.

1397. Vanek, Jaroslav. "Natural Resource Content of Foreign Trade, 1870-1955, and the Relative Abundance of Natural Resources in the United States." **Review of Economics and Statistics** 41 (May 1959): 146-153.

1398. Vazquez, P. R. "Role of the Department of Commerce in the Development of Minority Business Enterprise." **Business Lawyer** 25 (September 1969): 55-61.

1399. Voight, J. D. "The New Patent and Trademark Office Disciplinary Rules - Some Views from the Bar." **Journal of the Patent and Trademark Office Society** 67 (April 1985): 162-178.

1400. Walterscheid, E. C. "Interference Discovery." **Journal of the Patent Office Society** 58 (January 1976): 3-42.

1401. Walterscheid, E. C. and K. L. Cage. "Jurisdiction of the Patent and Trademark Office to Consider the Validity of Issued Patents." **Journal of the Patent Office Society** 61 (August 1979): 444-481.

1402. Wamsley, H. C. "Rulemaking Power of the Commissioner of Patents and Trademarks." **Journal of the Patent Office Society** 64 (September 1982): 490-530.

1403. Watson, R. C. "Patent Office - Its Place in the Executive Branch." **Journal of the Patent Office Society** 50 (March 1968): 152-164.

1404. Weaver, Suzanne. **Decision to Prosecute: Organization and Public Policy in the Antitrust Division.** Cambridge, MA: MIT Press, 1977.

1405. Whitmore, H. B. "Federal Salaries versus Patent Office Progress." **Journal of the Patent Office Society** 39 (December 1957): 878-887.

1406. Whitmore, H. B. "Patent Office Personnel Problems and Opportunities." **Journal of the Patent Office Society** 42 (September 1960): 583-592.

1407. Whitmore, H. B. "Significance of Compact Prosecution." **Journal of the Patent Office Society** 44

(November 1962): 719-725.

1408. Whitmore, H. B. "What's Got into the Office Lately?" **Journal of the Patent Office Society** 29 (December 1947): 869-894.

1409. Williams, C. D. "Transportation Regulation and the Department of Commerce." **Yale Law Journal** 62 (March 1953): 563-574.

1410. Williams, Julie L. "U.S. Regulation of Arab Boycott Practices." **Law and Policy in International Business** 10 (1978): 815-886.

1411. Wilson, Philip J. "Foreign Investment: Investment Disclosure Requirements - Amended Regulations to Implement the International Investment Survey Act of 1976, 46 Fed. Reg. 23, 225." **Harvard International Law Journal** 22 (Fall 1981): 694-697.

1412. Witthans, Fred. "Estimates of Effective Rates of Protection for United States Industries in 1967." **Review of Economics and Statistics** 55 (August 1973): 362-364.

1413. Wright, C. M. "View on Patent Litigation and on the Patent System." **Journal of the Patent Office Society** 59 (July 1977): 409-423.

1414. Wright, L. Christopher, and Elizabeth W. Stone. "Data and Information Services of the National Oceanic and Atmospheric Administration." **Special Libraries** 65 (August 1974): 311-318.

Chapter 4.
Department of Defense

1415. Adams, Gordon M. "Disarming the Military Subgovernment." **Harvard Journal on Legislation** 14 (April 1977): 459-503.

1416. Adams, Gordon M. and G. Quinn. "Politics of Defense Contracting." **Business and Society Review** 40 (Winter 1981-1982): 28-31.

1417. Anderson, R. M. "Anguish in the Defense Industry." **Harvard Business Review** 47 (November 1969): 162-164.

1418. Aron, C. "Billions for Defense Will Batter the Economy." **Business and Society Review** 33 (Spring 1980): 34-37.

1419. Art, Robert J. "Restructuring the Military-Industrial Complex: Arms Control in Institutional Perspective." **Public Policy** 22 (Fall 1974): 423-459.

1420. Art, Robert J. **The TFX Decision: McNamara and the Military.** Boston: Little, Brown, 1968.

1421. Ashton, C. L. "Claims by and against the Government Resulting from War Department Activity." **Dicta** 23 (September 1946): 196-206.

1422. Austin, Larry M. and William W. Hogan. "Optimizing the Procurement of Aviation Fuels." **Management Science** 22 (January 1976): 515-527.

1423. Bahr, Fred R. "The Expanding Role of the Department of Defense as an Instrument of Social Change." D. B. A., George Washington University, 1970.

1424. Baker, Morris H. "Productivity Management in the

Defense Supply Agency." **Public Administration Review** 32 (November 1972): 771-776.

1425. Baldwin, Hanson W. "Slow-Down in the Pentagon." **Foreign Affairs** 43 (January 1965): 262-280.

1426. Baral, Jaya K. **The Pentagon and the Making of U.S. Foreign Policy: A Case Study of Vietnam, 1960-1968.** Atlantic Highlands, NJ: Humanities Press, 1978.

1427. Barclay, Hartley W. "McNamara at Work." **Automotive Industries** 135 (December 1966): 19-21.

1428. Barger, K. C. "Scope of DCAA's Auditing Authority." **Public Contract Law Journal** 11 (November 1979): 259-268.

1429. Barrett, Archie D. **Reappraising Defense Organization: An Analysis Based on the Defense Organization Study of 1977-1980.** Washington, DC: National Defense University Press, 1983.

1430. Bartino, F. A. "Legislative Proposals from within the Department of Defense." **JAG Journal** (October 1959): 9-14.

1431. Beard, Edmund. **Developing the ICBM: A Study in Bureaucratic Politics.** New York: Columbia University Press, 1976.

1432. Beard, Paul E. "Bureaucratic Politics and Weapons Innovation: A Study of the Development of the Intercontinental Ballistic Missile." Ph.D. dissertation, Columbia University, 1973.

1433. Belohlavek, John M. "The Politics of Scandal: A Reassessment of John B. Floyd as Secretary of War, 1857-1861." **West Virginia History** 31 (April 1970): 145-160.

1434. Bennett, John J. "Department of Defense Systems Acquisition Management: Congressional Criticism and Concern." D.B.A., George Washington University, 1974.

1435. Benson, Robert S. "The Military on Capitol Hill: Prospects in the Quest for Funds." **Annals of the American Academy of Political and Social Science** 406 (March 1973): 48-58.

1436. Bergerson, Frederic A. "The Army Gets an Air Force: The Tactics and Process of Insurgent Bureaucratic Politics." Ph.D. dissertation,

Vanderbilt University, 1976.

1437. Bingham, Jonathan B. "Can Military Spending Be Controlled?" **Foreign Affairs** 48 (October 1969): 51-66.

1438. Binkin, Martin. **Shaping the Defense Civilian Work Force: Economics, Politics and National Security.** Washington, DC: Brookings Institution, 1978.

1439. Binkin, Martin. **Support Costs in the Defense Budget.** Washington, DC: Brookings Institution, 1972.

1440. Blechman, Barry M. and Edward R. Fried. "Controlling the Defense Budget." **Foreign Affairs** 54 (January 1976): 233-249.

1441. Booda, L. "Department of Defense Widens Control, Reshapes Services." **Aviation Week and Space Technology** 76 (March 12, 1962): 67-69.

1442. Boone, E. H. "Administration of Tort Claims in the War Department." **George Washington Law Review** 10 (February 1942): 473-481.

1443. Borklund, Carl W. **The Department of Defense.** New York: Praeger, 1968.

1444. Borklund, Carl W. **Men of the Pentagon, from Forrestal to McNamara.** New York: Praeger, 1966.

1445. Bower, C. M. "New Economic Barometer Needed to Measure Impact of Peacetime Defense Expenditures." **Analysts Journal** 15 (November 1959): 33-37.

1446. Bowers, E. W. and G. J. McManus. "Defense Contracts Will Prime the Pump." **Iron Age** 224 (April 15, 1981): 40-42.

1447. Boyd, R. G. "War Department Claims." **Federal Bar Journal** 6 (July 1945): 434-441.

1448. Braithwaite, T. B. "Privacy Education for Management." **Data Management** 15 (January 1979): 38-41.

1449. Brannon, E. M. "War Department Contracting During the Present Emergency." **Federal Bar Association Journal** 4 (April 1942): 275-283, 330.

1450. Brown, D. A. "Congress, DOD Pressed by New Budget Process." **Aviation Week and Space Technology** 102

(January 13, 1974): 16-17.

1451. Brown, Harold. "Department of Defense Report for Fiscal 1979." **Atlantic Community Quarterly** 16 (Spring 1978): 113-121.

1452. Brown, L. "UK/US Reciprocal Defence Audit Scheme." **Accountant** 182 (March 13, 1980): 374-376.

1453. Brownlow, C. "Arms Talks Could Prove Critical in Spurring New Defense Technology." **Aviation Week and Space Technology** 100 (March 11, 1974): 16-18.

1454. Brownlow, C. "Congress, SALT to Shape DOD Policy." **Aviation Week and Space Technology** 104 (March 15, 1976): 21-23.

1455. Brownlow, C. "Defense Boost Lays Foundation for Turnaround." **Aviation Week and Space Technology** 96 (March 13, 1972): 16-19.

1456. Brownlow, C. "Defense Hardware Lag Stressed." **Aviation Week and Space Technology** 88 (February 5, 1968): 14-17.

1457. Brownlow, C. "Drive to Modernize Forces Underscores DOD Budget." **Aviation Week and Space Technology** 98 (February 5, 1973): 13-16.

1458. Brownlow, C. "DOD Budget Seeks Force Modernization." **Aviation Week and Space Technology** 96 (January 31, 1972): 15-19.

1459. Brownlow, C. "DOD Request Represents $7.2 Billion Real Growth." **Aviation Week and Space Technology** 104 (January 26, 1976): 18-21.

1460. Brownlow, C. "DOD Sets Strong R & D Funding Defense." **Aviation Week and Space Technology** 102 (March 3, 1975): 15-17.

1461. Brownlow, C. "Pentagon Stresses Modernization of Its Strategic Tactical Forces." **Aviation Week and Space Technology** 100 (February 11, 1974): 13-16.

1462. Brownlow, C. "Study Panel Urges Sweeping Shifts in Pentagon." **Aviation Week and Space Technology** 93 (August 3, 1970): 14-16.

1463. Brownlow, C. "Support Service Fight Has $8 Billion Stake: Department of Defense Study Report Due on Transfer of Industry Contracts to Both Civil

Service and Military Personnel." **Aviation Week and Space Technology** 82 (March 22, 1965): 16-18.

1464. Brownlow, C. "US Force Modernization Needs to Stem Aerospace Employment Drop." **Aviation Week and Space Technology** 98 (March 19, 1973): 16-18.

1465. Bryant, F. "National Defense Through the Acquisition and Stockpiling of Strategic and Critical Materials." **Journal of Public Law** 16 (1967): 345-361.

1466. Burck, George E. "Guns, Butter, and Then - Some Economy." **Fortune** 72 (October 1965): 118-121.

1467. Burt, Richard. **Defense Budgeting: The British and American Cases.** London: International Institute for Strategic Studies, 1975.

1468. Butkus, A. A. "Packard: Defense on a Diet." **Dun's Review** 96 (August 1973): 10-14.

1469. Byrne, John A. "Problems of Adapting the Department of Defense Cost Effectiveness Analysis System to No-Defense Agencies." D.B.A., George Washington University, 1970.

1470. Canan, James W. **The Superwarriors: The Fantastic World of Pentagon Superweapons.** New York: Weybright and Talley, 1975.

1471. Capra, James R. "National Defense Budget and Its Economic Effects." **Federal Reserve Bank of New York Quarterly Review** 6 (Summer 1981): 21-31.

1472. Carey, William D. "Central-Field Relationships in the War Production Board." **Public Administration Review** 4 (Winter 1944): 31-42.

1473. Carlisle, Howard M. "Incentive Contracts: Management Strategy of the Department of Defense." **Public Administration Review** 24 (March 1964): 21.

1474. Carlson, Walter M. "Research Librarian in a Challenging Age." **Special Libraries** 55 (January 1964): 11-15.

1475. Carsen, Larry. "On-line System with Department of Defense." **Special Libraries** 71 (January 1980): 13-21.

1476. Carter, Sherman F. "An Analysis of the Influence of the Evolution of the Department of Defense on the Role of the Secretary of the Army: A Case

Study in Organization and Management." Ph.D. dissertation, American University, 1968.

1477. Clark, Asa A. "United States Defense Policy-Making: Comparative Theories of Budgetary Policies." Ph.D. dissertation, University of Denver, 1981.

1478. Clark, E. "More Procurement Funds Go to Defense." **Aviation Week and Space Technology** 68 (January 20, 1958): 28-30.

1479. Clayton, James L. "Fiscal Limits of the Warfare-Welfare State: Defense and Welfare Spending in the United States since 1900." **Western Political Quarterly** 29 (September 1976): 364-383.

1480. Cobb, S. "Defense Spending and Defense Voting in the House: An Empirical Study of an Aspect of the Military-Industrial Complex Thesis." **American Journal of Sociology** 82 (July 1976): 163-182.

1481. Coffman, Edward M. "The Battle against Red Tape: Business Methods of War Department General Staff 1917-18." **Military Affairs** 26 (Spring 1962): 1-10.

1482. Coleman, H. J. "Defense Funds Geared to NATO Needs." **Aviation Week and Space Technology** 108 (January 30, 1978): 18-20.

1483. Coletta, Paelo E. "The Defense Unification Battle, 1947-50: The Navy." **Prologue** 7 (Spring 1975): 6-17.

1484. Collins, Donald C. "Institutionalized Decision-Making: A Study of the Effects of Background, Career, Structural, and Functional Factors on the Decision-Making Behavior of Senior Administrators in the Department of Defense." Ph.D. dissertation, University of Iowa. 1970.

1485. Colm, Gerhard and Manuel L. Helzner. "When Will Defense Spending Begin to Hurt?" **Management Review** 47 (July 1958): 37-39.

1486. Cooper, Richard V. L. **Contract-hire Personnel in the Department of Defense.** Santa Monica, CA: Rand, 1977.

1487. Cosmas, Graham A. "From Order to Chaos: The War Department, the National Guard, and Military

Policy, 1898." **Military Affairs** 29 (Fall 1965): 105-121.

1488. Coulam, Robert F. "Importance of the Beginning: Defense Doctrine and the Development of the F-III Fighter-Bomber." **Public Policy** 23 (Winter 1975): 1-38.

1489. Covault, C. "NASA's Defense Department Industry Ties Hit." **Aviation Week and Space Technology** 108 (January 23, 1978): 27-29.

1490. Crecine, John P. **Defense Budgeting: Organizational Adaptation to External Constraints.** Santa Monica, CA: Rand, 1970.

1491. Crecine, John P. **On Resource Allocation Processes in the U.S. Department of Defense.** Ann Arbor: Institute for Public Policy Studies, 1980.

1492. Crockett, James R. "The Impact of the Evolution to Management Auditing on Personnel Requirements of Department of Defense Internal Audit Agencies." D.B.A., Mississippi State University, 1974.

1493. Cuff, Robert D. "Organizational Perspective on the Military-Industrial Complex." **Business History Review** 52 (Summer 1978): 250-267.

1494. Daleski, Richard J. **Defense Management in the 1980s: The Role of the Service Secretaries.** Washington, DC: National Defense University, 1980.

1495. Damon, Allan I. "Defense Spending." **American Heritage** 26 (February 1975): 30-32, 90-91.

1496. Dancy, Albert G. "Department of Defense Research and Development Management." **Public Administration Review** 37 (July 1977): 347-356.

1497. Dempsey, Richard A. and D. Schmude. "Occupational Impact of Defense Expenditures." **Monthly Labor Review** 94 (December 1971): 12-15.

1498. Dennison, W. F. "Management Developments in Government Resource Allocation: The Example of the Rise and Fall of PPBS." **Journal of Management Studies** 16 (October 1979): 270-282.

1499. Derrick, Bobby G. "An Inquiry into the Applicability of Basic Features of the Department of Defense (DOD) Programming System to Selected Busi-ness Firms." Ph.D. dissertation, American

University, 1972.

1500. De Rubertis, William A. "Congress, the Executive, and the Politics of Defense Budgeting: A Comparative Analysis of Fiscal 1950 and Fiscal 1963." Ph.D. dissertation, Claremont Graduate School, 1972.

1501. Dews, Edmund. **Acquisitions Policy Effectiveness: Department of Defense Experience in the 1970s.** Santa Monica, CA: Rand, 1979.

1502. Dews, Edmund. **Reform in Defense Acquisition Policies: A Different View.** Santa Monica, CA: Rand, 1983.

1503. Dinan, Daniel J. "Defense Investigative Service: Access to Criminal History Records." **Police Chief** 50 (February 1983): 20-21.

1504. Donnelly, J. R. and C. D. Taylor. "MOM and DOD: The Transportation by Air of Military Ordinary Mail for the Department of Defense." **Air Force JAG Law Review** 10 (May/June 1968): 18-29.

1505. Drake, H. B. "Major DOD Procurements at War with Reality." **Harvard Business Review** 48 (January 1970): 119-140.

1506. Drandell, M. "Composite Forecasting Methodology for Manpower Planning Utilizing Objective and Subjective Criteria." **Academy of Management Journal** 18 (September 1975): 501-519.

1507. Dunson, B. H. "Pay, Experience, and Productivity: The Government-Sector Case." **Journal of Human Resources** 20 (Winter 1985): 153-160.

1508. Durham, James A. and Benjamin Caplan. "Stabilization Planning under the National Security Act." **Law and Contemporary Problems** 19 (Autumn 1954): 477-485.

1509. Dworak, Robert J. "Economizing in Public Organizations." **Public Administration Review** 35 (March 1975): 158-165.

1510. Eastman, F. "Broader Planning Role Seen for Defense." **Aviation Week and Space Technology** 74 (January 2, 1961): 18-19.

1511. Eastman, F. "Reorganization Plan Faces Hill Battle." **Aviation Week and Space Technology** 68 (April 14, 1958): 28-30.

1512. Eastman, F. "Symington Plan Faces Stiff Opposition." **Aviation Week and Space Technology** 73 (December 12, 1960): 34-35.

1513. Ecker, Janet E. B. "National Security Protection: The Critical Technologies Approach to U.S. Export Control of High-Level Technology." **Journal of International Law and Economics** 15 (Summer 1981): 575-604.

1514. Eldred, Raymond K. **How the Defense Department Awards Contracts and Grants for Basic Research.** Atlanta: Georgia Institute of Technology, 1967.

1515. Elson, B. M. "Inflation, Demands Hike Military Avionics Funds." **Aviation Week and Space Technology** 68 (March 19, 1973): 101-103.

1516. Elswit, J. "First Hand Study: Defense Expenditures and Who Will Get the Orders." **Magazine of Wall Street** 105 (February 27, 1960): 606-609.

1517. Enthoven, Alain C. "Economic Analysis in the Department of Defense." **American Economic Review** 53 (May 1963): 413-423, 447-451.

1518. Fairlie, Henry. "Defense Spending: The Dodos and the Platypuses." **Washington Monthly** 7 (February 1976): 36-41.

1519. Fisher, Louis. "Reprogramming of Funds by the Defense Department." **Journal of Politics** 36 (February 1974): 77-102.

1520. Fitzgerald, Arthur E. **The High Priests of Waste.** New York: Norton, 1972.

1521. Foldes, Lucien. "Military Budgeting and Financial Control." **Public Administration Review** 17 (Winter 1957): 36-43.

1522. Foreman, Charles W. and Frederick P. Mertes. "Business Side of Defense Planning." **Business Horizons** 9 (Summer 1966): 27-35.

1523. Fox, Douglas M. "Congress and U.S. Military Service Budgets in the Post-War Period." **American Journal of Political Science** 15 (May 1971): 382-393.

1524. Fritchey, Clayton. "Navy We Need vs the Navy We've Got." **Washington Monthly** 9 (March 1977): 38-44.

1525. Fuchs, Edmund F. and Charles H. Hammer. "Survey of

Women's Aptitudes for Army Jobs." **Personnel Psychology** 16 (Summer 1963): 151-155.

1526. Fullbright, James W. **The Pentagon Propaganda Machine.** New York: Liverlight, 1970.

1527. Fuller, John W. "Congress and the Defense Budget: A Study of the McNamara Years." Ph.D. dissertation, Princeton University, 1972.

1528. Gallimore, D. "Legal Aspects of Funding Department of the Army Procurements." **Military Law Review** 67 (Winter 1975): 85-167.

1529. Gansler, Jacques S. "Let's Change the Way the Pentagon Does Business." **Harvard Business Review** 55 (May 1977): 109-118.

1530. Gapcynski, W. G. "Department of Defense Procurement and Use of Industrial Property." **Federal Bar Journal** 30 (Winter 1971): 39-47.

1531. Geddes, J. P. "US Aerospace Looks forward." **Interavia** 32 (July 1977): 695-702.

1532. Geelhoed, E. Bruce. **Charles E. Wilson and Controversy at the Pentagon, 1953-1975.** Detroit: Wayne State University Press, 1979.

1533. Geise, William R. "Kirby Smith's War Department, 1864: A Study of Organization and Command in the Trans-Mississippi West." **Military History of Texas and the Southwest** 15 (1979): 45-62.

1534. Gertcher, Franklin L. "An Economic Evaluation of Military Family Response to the Current Department of Defense Housing Program." Ph.D. dissertation, University of Hawaii, 1981.

1535. Glass, Robert L. "From Pascal to Pebbleman and Beyond." **Datamation** 25 (July 1979): 146-150.

1536. Goodhue, L. H. "Fair Profits from Defense Business." **Harvard Business Review** 50 (March 1972): 97-107.

1537. Goodrick, M. George. "WPB Decentralization within the Chicago Region." **Public Administration Review** (Summer 1944): 208-219.

1538. Goodyear, C. J. "Colonel J. Monroe Johnson and the Office of Defense Transportation." **I.C.C. Practitioners' Journal** 13 (November 1945): 125-127.

1539. Gordon, Max. "The Pentagon Papers: Perception and Reality." **Science and Society** 36 (Spring 1972): 78-85.

1540. Graham, J. H. "General Accounting Office and Foreign Military Sales." **Air Force Law Review** 19 (Spring 1977): 76-89.

1541. Greenberg, Edward. "Employment Impacts of Defense Expenditures and Obligations." **Review of Economics and Statistics** 49 (May 19678): 186-198.

1542. Gregory, W. H. "Defense Funding Plans Portend Banner Aerospace Sales Ahead." **Aviation Week and Space Technology** 114 (March 9, 1981): 8-9.

1543. Gregory, W. H. "Vietnam Financing Challenges Industry." **Aviation Week and Space Technology** 84 (April 11, 1966): 26-28.

1544. Griffiths, D. R. "Defense Offsets Lessen Funding Boost." **Aviation Week and Space Technology** 112 (April 7, 1980): 17-19.

1545. Griffiths, D. R. "Key Military Budget Official Urges Additions." **Aviation Week and Space Technology** 114 (January 26, 1981): 16-19.

1546. Gula, G. G. "Armed Forces' Quality Assurance." **Automotive Industries** 141 (December 1, 1969): 33-35.

1547. Guzzardi, Walter. "Mental Gap in the Defense Debate." **Fortune** 102 (September 8, 1980): 38-44.

1548. Haggerty, Helen R. "Evaluation of Mail-Order Ratings on Combat Performance of Officers." **Personnel Psychology** 12 (Winter 1959): 597-605.

1549. Hall, H. L. "Commanding Officer and Negligent Pilotage - Liability Aspects." **JAG Journal** 17 (August 1963): 123-129.

1550. Hamilton, P. B. "Civil Air Patrol: A Volunteer Civilian Auxiliary of the Air Force." **Air Force JAG Law Review** 12 (Winter 1970): 60-69.

1551. Hammond, Paul Y. "A Functional Analysis of Defense Department Decision-Making in the McNamara Administration." **American Political Science Review** 62 (March 1968): 57-69.

1552. Hammond, Paul Y. **Organizing for Defense: The**

American Military Establishment in the Twentieth Century. Princeton, NJ: Princeton University Press, 1961.

1553. Hanchett, William. "The War Department and Booth's Abduction Plot." **Lincoln Herald** 82 (Winter 1980): 499-508.

1554. Harlamor, S. W. "Defense Shifts Worry Congress." **Aviation Week and Space Technology** 108 (March 27, 1978): 16-18.

1555. Hazlewood, Leo A. "Planning for Problems in Crisis Management: An Analysis of Post-1945 Behavior in the U.S. Department of Defense." **International Studies Quarterly** 21 (March 1977): 75-106.

1556. Heise, Juergen A. **Minimum Disclosure: How the Pentagon Manipulates the News.** New York: Norton, 1979.

1557. Henry, Andrew F. "Armed Forces Unification and the Pentagon Officer." **Public Administration Review** 15 (Summer 1955): 173-180.

1558. Herold, Robert C. "The Politics of Decision Making in the Defense Establishment: A Case Study." Ph.D. dissertation, George Washington University, 1969.

1559. Hewes, James E. **From Root to McNamara: Army Organization and Administration, 1900-1963.** Washington, DC: U.S. Army Center of Military History, 1975.

1560. Hiller, J. R. and Robert D. Tollison. "Incentive Versus Cost-Plus Contracts in Defense Procurement." **Journal of Industrial Economics** 26 (March 1978): 239-248.

1561. Hinsberg, P. "Ford Was a Major Military Supplier in Both World Wars: A Pacifist Pitches in the War Effort." **Automotive News** (June 16, 1978): 238-245.

1562. Hitch, Charles J. "Plans, Programs, and Budgets in the Department of Defense." **Operations Research** 11 (January 1963): 1-17.

1563. Hitch, Charles J. "Program Budgeting." **Datamation** 13 (September 1967): 37-40.

1564. Hitch, Charles J. "Systems Approach to Decision-Making in the Department of Defense and the

University of California." **Operations Research Quarterly** 19 (April 1968): 37-45.

1565. Hitch, Charles J. and Roland N. McKean. **The Economics of Defense in the Nuclear Age.** Cambridge, MA: Harvard University Press, 1980.

1566. Hoewing, C. Lincoln. "Defense Organization: The Need for Change." **Public Administration Review** 46 (March/April 1986): 185-188.

1567. Hoffman, Lloyd H. "Defense War Gaming." **Orbis** 27 (Winter 1984): 812-822.

1568. Holt, Daniel D. "Cap Weinberger's Pentagon Revolution." **Fortune** 103 (May 18, 1981): 79-80.

1569. Holt, Daniel D. "Defense Budget for the 1980s." **Fortune** 103 (January 26, 1981): 52-54.

1570. Holtzman, F. D. "Is There a Soviet-US Military Spending Gap?" **Challenge** 23 (September/October 1980): 3-9.

1571. Huck, Susan L. M. "Carter's C.F.R. Leadership and the Military." **American Opinion** 23 (July 1980): 1-4.

1572. Huntington, Samuel P. "Defense Organization and Military Strategy." **Public Interest** 75 (Spring 1984): 20-46.

1573. Hunton, Benjamin. "The Budget of the Department of War." Ph.D. dissertation, American University, 1954.

1574. Huzar, Elias. "Reorganization for National Security." **Journal of Politics** 12 (February 1950): 128-152.

1575. Huzar, Elias. "Unification Controversy - Notes On." **Public Administration Review** 6 (Autumn 1946): 297-314.

1576. James, M. E. "Power of the Secretary of the Navy to Interpret and Delimit Boundary Descriptions of the Naval Petroleum Reserves: An Historical Perspective." **JAG Journal** 27 (Spring 1974): 439-461.

1577. Janowitz, Morris. **Sociology and the Military Establishment.** New York: Russell Sage Foundation, 1959.

1578. Jaquette, David L. **An Analytic Review of Personnel Models in the Department of Defense.** Santa Monica, CA: Rand, 1977.

1579. Johnsen, K. "Department of Defense, General Accounting Office Reach Truce on Pricing Policy." **Aviation Week and Space Technology** 83 (December 27, 1965): 68-70.

1580. Johnsen, K. "Recess Delays Defense Actions." **Aviation Week and Space Technology** 107 (August 15, 1977): 14-16.

1581. Johnsen, K. "Vinson Hits Reorganization Plan." **Aviation Week and Space Technology** 68 (April 21, 1958): 29-30.

1582. Johnson, James A. "Hypnosis As a Criminal Technique in the Department of Defense." **Air Force Law Review** 22 (Winter 1980-1981): 20-58.

1583. Kane, Francis X. "Security Is Too Important to Be Left to Computers." **Fortune** 69 (April 1964): 146-147.

1584. Kantor, Arnold. "Congress and the Defense Budget: 1960-1970." **American Political Science Review** 66 (March 1972): 129-143.

1585. Kantor, Arnold. **Defense Politics: A Budgetary Perspective.** Chicago: University of Chicago Press, 1979.

1586. Kaufmann, William W. **The McNamara Strategy.** New York: Harper and Row, 1964.

1587. Kaufmann, William W. **The 1985 Defense Budget.** Washington, DC: Brookings Institution, 1984.

1588. Keefe, Arthur J. and D. M. Lewis. "Department of Defense Patent Policy at the Cross Roads: An Argument for the Retention of Traditional Incentives." **Catholic University Law Review** 10 (January 1961): 22-33.

1589. King, Arthur T. "The Relationships between Socioeconomic Programs and the Department of the Air Force Budget: Section A (A) of the Small Business Act - The Economic Development and Public Finance Aspects of a Public Policy Program." Ph.D. dissertation, University of Colorado, 1977.

1590. Kinnard, Douglas. "James R. Schlesinger as Secretary of Defense." **United States Naval War**

College Review 32 (November/December 1979): 22-43.

1591. Kinnard, Douglas. "President Eisenhower and the Defense Budget." **Journal of Politics** 39 (August 1977): 596-623.

1592. Kinnard, Douglas. **The Secretary of Defense.** Lexington: University Press of Kentucky, 1980.

1593. Kinnear, George E. "The Effects of Department of Defense Procurement Policies on the Structure of the Defense Industry." Ph.D. dissertation, Stanford University, 1966.

1594. Kinter, William R. **Forging a New Sword: A Study of the Department of Defense.** New York: Harper, 1958.

1595. Kinter, William R. "Progress in Defense Organization." **Journal of Public Law** 9 (Spring 1960): 73-84.

1596. Klass, Philip J. "ARPA Net Aids Command, Control Tests." **Aviation Week and Space Technology** 105 (September 27, 1976): 63-67.

1597. Klass, Philip J. "Perry Cites Pentagon Accomplishments." **Aviation Week and Space Technology** 114 (January 19, 1981): 85-87.

1598. Klein, H. E. "Stakeout at the Pentagon." **Dun's Review** 79 (May 1962): 45-47.

1599. Kline, Adrian L. "Implication of Responsibility Centers for Successful Implementation of the Department of Defense Resource Management Systems." Ph.D. dissertation, Michigan State University, 1970.

1600. Kopkind, Andres. "Freezing-Out of McNamara." **New Statesman** 74 (December 1967): 751-752.

1601. Korb, Lawrence J. "Budget Process in the Department of Defense, 1947-1977: The Strength and Weaknesses of Three Systems." **Public Administration Review** 37 (July 1977): 334-346.

1602. Korb, Lawrence J. "Defense Budget Process and Defense Policy." **Armed Forces and Society** 7 (Winter 1981): 317-321.

1603. Korb, Lawrence J. "DOD Assistance in the War on Drugs." **Police Chief** 52 (October 1985): 57-58.

1604. Korb, Lawrence J. **The Rise and Fall of the Pentagon: American Defense Policies in the 1970s.** Westport, CT: Greenwood Press, 1979.

1605. Korb, Lawrence J. "Robert McNamara's Impact on the Budget Strategies of the Joint Chiefs of Staff." **Aerospace Historian** 17 (Winter 1970): 132-156.

1606. Kozicharow, E. "Overhaul of Defense Department Procurement Debated." **Aviation Week and Space Technology** 107 (October 24, 1977): 50-52.

1607. Kraar, L. "Yes, the Administration Does Have a Defense Policy of Sorts." **Fortune** 97 (June 19, 1978): 128-130.

1608. Krause, Elliott A. "Poverty, Human Resources, and the Military-Industrial Complex: Some Research Issues." **Social Science Quarterly** 50 (December 1969): 548-556.

1609. Kurth, James R. "Hand in Glove with the Pentagon: How Aerospace Contractors Keep the Lines Rolling." **MBA** 12 (June/July 1978): 46-52.

1610. Kurth, James R. "Political Economy of Weapons Procurement: The Follow-on Imperative." **American Economic Review** 62 (May 1972): 304-311.

1611. Laurance, Edward J. "Changing Role of Congress in Defense Policy-Making." **Conflict Resolution** 20 (June 1976): 213-253.

1612. Leathem, E. F. "Funding and Financing Defense Contracts." **Harvard Business Review** 36 (September 1958): 96-104.

1613. Lebow, Richard N. "Misconcepts in American Strategic Assessment." **Political Science Quarterly** 97 (Summer 19872): 187-206.

1614. Lee, Gus C. "Organization for National Security: Office of the Secretary of Defense." **Public Administration Review** 9 (Winter 1949): 43-44.

1615. Lee, Gus C. "Organization for National Security: War Council." **Public Administration Review** 9 (Spring 1949): 39.

1616. Leontief, Wassily W. "Economic Impact: Industrial and Regional, of an Arms Cut." **Review of Economics and Statistics** 47 (August 1965): 217-241.

1617. Lepkowski, Wil. "Defense Department Boosts Research Funding." **Chemical and Engineering News** 59 (April 27, 1981): 14-15.

1618. Levine, David D. "Administrative Control Techniques of the War Production Board." **Public Administration Review** 4 (Spring 1944): 89-96.

1619. Levitt, Theodore. "Cold-War Thaw." **Harvard Business Review** 38 (January 1960): 6-8.

1620. Levy, Michael E. "Federal Budget 1962 and Defense Spending." **Conference Board Business Record** 18 March 1961): 5-9.

1621. Levy, Michael E. "Guns and a Little Margarine, Too." **Across the Board** 17 (April 1980): 68-71.

1622. Lewis, Kevin N. **The Reagan Defense Budget: Prospects and Pressures.** Santa Monica, CA: Rand, 1981.

1623. Longley, Charles H. "McNamara and Military Behavior." **American Journal of Political Science** 18 (February 1974): 1-21.

1624. Lui, B. C. "Impacts of Defense Expenditures on Metropolitan Economy: A Case Study of St. Louis." **Land Economics** 47 (November 1971): 401-405.

1625. Lynch, John E. "Regional Impact of the Vietnam War." **Quarterly Review of Economics and Business** 16 (Summer 1976): 37-50.

1626. Lynn, B. B. "Auditing Contractors Compliance with Cost Accounting Standards." **Journal of Accountancy** 139 (June 1975): 60-70.

1627. Lyons, James F. "Defense Industry: Prosperity within a Recession." **Financial World** 143 (April 2, 1975): 18-21.

1628. Lyons, James F. "Resurrection of the Defense Industry." **Financial World** 140 (December 26, 1973): 6-10.

1629. MacCormick, A. "Defense Department Policy toward Former Offenders." **National Probation Association Yearbook** (1951): 1-19.

1630. McFarland, Keith D. "Secretary of War Harry Woodring: Early Career in Kansas." **Kansas History Quarterly** 39 (Summer 1973): 206-219.

1631. McGovern, George. "The Pentagon Papers - A Discussion." **Political Science Quarterly** 87 (June 1972): 173-183.

1632. McGuire, G. G. "Defense Department's Use of Discounting in the Procurement of Equipment by the Life Cycle Costing Concept." **Journal of Purchasing** 7 (August 1971): 41-55.

1633. McNallen, James B. "Models of the Budget Decision Process in the Department of Defense and the Department of the Navy." Ph.D. dissertation, New York University, 1975.

1634. Marino, Michael F. "Occupational Safety and Health Act and the Federal Workplace: Implementation of OSHA by the Departments of Defense and the Navy." **Labor Law Journal** 28 (November 1977): 707-720.

1635. Marsh, Alton K. "Inflation Estimate Plan for Defense Criticized." **Aviation Week and Space Technology** 114 (April 13, 1981): 25-27.

1636. Massey, Robert J. "Program Packages and the Program Budget in the Department of Defense." **Public Administration Review** 23 (March 1963): 30-34.

1637. May, Ernest R. "Development of Political-Military Consultation in the United States." **Political Science Quarterly** 70 (June 1955): 161-180.

1638. Melman, Seymour. **Pentagon Capitalism: The Political Economy of War.** New York: McGraw-Hill, 1970.

1639. Merritt, Steve. "An Investigation of the Potential of Centralized Computer System Selection in the Department of Defense and the Federal Government." Ph.D. dissertation, George Washington University, 1973.

1640. Meyerson, Martin. "Price of Admission into the Defense Business." **Harvard Business Review** 45 (July 1967): 111-123.

1641. Miles, Herman W. and Joan L. Sweeney. "Dialog with Defense Documentation Center." **Special Libraries** 67 (November 1976): 498-503.

1642. Miller, W. H. "Congress Mulls Limits on Defense Profits." **Industry Week** 210 (July 27, 1981): 25-27.

1643. Miller, W. H. "Pentagon Sows Seeds of Defense Productivity." **Industry Week** 210 (July 13, 1981): 48-53.

1644. Millett, John D. "Direction of Supply Activities in the War Department: An Administrative Survey." **American Political Science Review** 38 (April/June 1944): 249-265, 475-498.

1645. Millett, John D. "The War Department in World War II." **American Political Science Review** 40 (October 1946): 863-897.

1646. Monroe, Kristen R. "Economic Influences on Presidential Popularity." **Public Opinion Quarterly** 42 (Fall 1978): 360-369.

1647. Moore, C. H. and D. Button. "Auditing Implications of DOE Controls." **Journal of Accountancy** 148 (August 1979): 78-83.

1648. Morrison, E. J. "Defense Systems Management: The 375 Series." **California Management Review** 9 (Summer 1967): 17-26.

1649. Mosher, Frederick C. "Decision-Making in Defense: The Role of Organization: A Symposium." **Public Administration Review** 18 (Summer 1958): 169.

1650. Mosher, Frederick C. "Military Program Budgets: A Study of Current Concepts and Practices with Particular Reference to the Department of the Army." Ph.D. dissertation, Harvard University, 1953.

1651. Munn, A. A. "Role of Geographers in the Department of Defense." **Professional Geographer** 32 (August 1980): 361-364.

1652. Murdock, Clark A. **Defense Policy Formation: A Comparative Analysis of the McNamara Era.** Albany: State University of New York Press, 1974.

1653. Murphy, Charles J. V. "Desperate Drive to Cut Defense Spending." **Fortune** 69 (January 1964): 94-97.

1654. Murphy, Charles J. V. "Is the Defense Budget Big Enough?" **Fortune** 60 (November 1959): 144-147.

1655. Murphy, Charles J. V. "Pentagon Enters Its Era of Austerity." **Fortune** 86 (December 1972): 142-146.

1656. Mutter, Y. "Scandal at the PX: Marketers Go AWOL." **Sales and Marketing Management** 126 (March 16, 1981): 30-37.

1657. Nemerovski, H. "Defense Procurement and Proprietary Data." **Journal of the Patent Office Society** 42 (July 1960): 456-462.

1658. Nelson, Otto L. "The War Department General Staff: A Study in Organization and Administration." Ph.D. dissertation, Harvard University, 1940.

1659. Nelson, Otto L. "Wartime Developments in War Department Organization and Administration." **Public Administration Review** 5 (Winter 1945): 1-15.

1660. Newman, Steven L. "The Oppenheimer Case: A Reconsideration of the Role of the Defense Department and National Security." Ph.D. dissertation, New York University, 1977.

1661. Niven, John. "Gideon Welles and Naval Administration during the Civil War." **American Neptune** 35 (January 1975): 53-66.

1662. Normyle, W. J. "DOD Defends Aeronautic Research Policy." **Aviation Week and Space Technology** 88 (April 8, 1968): 24-25.

1663. Novick, David. "Decision Making in the Department of Defense." **Business Horizons** 15 (December 1972): 23-33.

1664. O'Brian, J. L. and M. Fleischmann. "The War Production Board Administrative Policies and Procedures." **George Washington Law Review** 13 (December 1944): 1-60.

1665. O'Brien, Thomas J. "DOD Reassigns Administration of Industrial Security." **Security Management** 24 (March 1980): 44-47.

1666. Oliver, R. P. "Employment Effects of Reduced Defense Spending." **Monthly Labor Review** 94 (December 1971): 3-11.

1667. Olson, R. E. and T. W. Scrogin. "Containerization and Military Logistics." **Journal of Maritime Law** 6 (October 1974): 119-146.

1668. O'Meara, Andrew P. "Civil-Military Conflict within the Defense Structure." **Parameters** 8 (March 1978): 85-92.

1669. Ostrom, Charles W. "Evaluating Alternative Foreign Policy Decision-Making Models: An Empirical Test between an Arms Race Model and an Organizational Politics Model." **Journal of Consulting and Clinical Psychology** 21 (June 1977): 235-266.

1670. Ostrom, Charles W. "Reactive Linkage Model of the U.S. Defense Expenditure Policy-Making Process." **American Political Science Review** 72 (September 1978): 941-954.

1671. Packard, David. "Defense Spending and the Vietnam Peace Dividend." **Conference Board Record** 8 (January 1971): 7-9.

1672. Packard, David. "Improving Weapons Acquisition: What the Defense Department Can Learn from the Private Sector." **Policy Review** 37 (Summer 1986): 11-15.

1673. Page, Harry R. "An Analysis of the Defense Procurement Program Decision Making Process." Ph.D. dissertation, American University, 1966.

1674. Palmer, Gregory. **The McNamara Strategy and the Vietnam War: Program Budgeting in the Pentagon, 1960-1968.** Westport, CT: Greenwood Press, 1978.

1675. Parker, Robert N. "National Security Issues." **Research Management** 17 (July 1974): 12-13.

1676. Peak, G. Wayne. "The War Department Manpower Board." **American Political Science Review** 40 (February 1946): 1-26.

1677. Penick, G. J. "Management Accounting and Auditing in Defense Contracting." **New York Certified Public Accountant** 36 (July 1966): 499-510.

1678. Perkins, James A. "Administration of the National Security Program." **Public Administration Review** 13 (Spring 1953): 80-86.

1679. Peroff, Kathleen A. and M. Podolak-Warren. "Does Spending on Defense Cut Spending on Health? A Time-Series Analysis of the U.S. Economy 1929-1974." **British Journal of Political Science** 9 (January 1979): 21-39.

1680. Perry, Robert M. "New Spirit of Cooperation between EPA and Other Federal Agencies." **Natural Resources Law Newsletter** 14 (Winter 1982): 1-4.

1681. Perselay, Gerald. "A Study of United States Air

Force Experience under the Federal Employee-Management Cooperation Program." D.B.A., George Washington University, 1970.

1682. Peterson, Richard S. and Charles M. Tiebout. "Measuring the Impact of Regional Defense-Space Expenditures." **Review of Economics and Statistics** 46 (November 1964): 421-428.

1683. Petrini, B. F. and Phillip D. Grub. "Product Management in High Technology Defense Industry Marketing." **California Management Review** 15 (Spring 1973): 138-146.

1684. Piekarz, Rolf. **Defense Impacts on International Payments.** Arlington, VA: Institute for Defense Analyses, 1967.

1685. Piller, Geoffrey. "DOD's Office of International Security Affairs: The Brief Ascendancy of an Advisory System." **Political Science Quarterly** 98 (Spring 1983): 59-78.

1686. Pohl, James W. "The Congress and the Secretary of War, 1915: An Instance of Political Pressure." **New Jersey History** 89 (Fall 1971): 163-170.

1687. Present, Phillip E. "Defense Contracting and Community Leadership: A Comparative Analysis." **Social Science Quarterly** 46 (December 1967): 399-410.

1688. Puritano, Vincent and Lawrence J. Korb. "Streamlining PPBS to Better Manage National Defense." **Public Administration Review** 41 (September/October 1981): 569-574.

1689. Radway, Laurence I. "The Administration of the National Defense Program: A Critique of War Production Organization before Pearl Harbor." Ph.D. dissertation, Harvard University, 1950.

1690. Ranson, Edward. "The Investigation of the War Department, 1898-99." **Historian** 34 (November 1971): 78-99.

1691. Rapoport, Daniel. "How F. Edward Herbert Shaved $46 Billion from the Defense Budget." **Washington Monthly** 8 (November 1976): 20-23.

1692. Raubitschek, J. H. "Vesting of Government Rights in DOD Financed Inventions." **Federal Bar Journal** 31 (Summer 1972): 237.

1693. Ray, Bruce A. "Defense Department Spending and Hawkish Voting in the House of Representatives." **Western Political Quarterly** 34 (September 1981): 438-446.

1694. Ray, Bruce A. "Military Committee Membership in the House of Representatives and the Allocation of Defense Department Outlays." **Western Political Quarterly** 34 (June 1981): 222-234.

1695. Raymond, Jack. **Power at the Pentagon.** New York: Harper and Row, 1964.

1696. Reagan, Michael D. "Business and Defense Services Administration, 1953-1957." **Western Political Quarterly** 14 (June 1961): 569-586.

1697. Reed, Leon S. **Military Maneuvers: An Analysis of the Interchange of Personnel between Defense Contractors and the Department of Defense.** New York: Council on Economic Priorities, 1975.

1698. Regeimbal, N. R. "Drive for Defense Spending Hike May Doom Ike's Budget Hopes." **Iron Age** 183 (January 15, 1959): 41-43.

1699. Rehfeld, Barry. "Whistle-Blowing and Pentagon Fat." **Dissent** 32 (Spring 1985): 152-154.

1700. Reich, M. "Why Carter Can't Reduce Military Spending." **Monthly Review** 29 (June 1977): 53-58.

1701. Richardson, K. L. "The Use of the General and Residual Powers under Public Law No 85-804 in the Department of Defense." **Public Contract Law Journal** 14 (October 1983): 128-157.

1702. Riddell, Thomas A. "Concentration and Inefficiency in the Defense Sector: Policy Options." **Journal of Economic Issues** 19 (June 1985): 451-461.

1703. Ries, John C. **The Management of Defense: Organization and Control of the U.S. Armed Services.** Baltimore: Johns Hopkins University Press, 1964.

1704. Roach, Ed D. "The Impact of Unionization on Personnel Policy Execution in the Department of the Army." Ph.D. dissertation, University of Texas, 1970.

1705. Robinson, C. A. "Aircraft Bid of $12 Billion Set." **Aviation Week and Space Technology** 109 (October

9, 1978): 16-18.

1706. Robinson, C. A. "Decision on C-5 Bypasses Military Leaders." **Aviation Week and Space Technology** 116 (January 25, 1982): 18-20.

1707. Robinson, C. A. "Defense Budget Cuts Weighed." **Aviation Week and Space Technology** 115 (September 7, 1981): 18-20.

1708. Robinson, C. A. "Defense Management to Change." **Aviation Week and Space Technology** 113 (December 15, 1980): 16-17.

1709. Robinson, C. A. "Defense Science Board Urges Multiyear Contracts." **Aviation Week and Space Technology** 113 (December 1, 1980): 130-133.

1710. Robinson, C. A. "Five-Year Budget Curbs Aircraft, Ship Buys." **Aviation Week and Space Technology** 111 (August 27, 1979): 12-14.

1711. Robinson, C. A. "Meddling by Congress Staff Hit." **Aviation Week and Space Technology** 107 (July 25, 1977): 14-18.

1712. Robinson, C. A. "Service Ready Fiscal 1983 Fund Bids." **Aviation Week and Space Technology** 115 (July 20, 1981): 16-18.

1713. Robinson, C. A. "Tactical Weapons Effort Slowed Two Years." **Aviation Week and Space Technology** 115 (October 26, 1981): 16-19.

1714. Robinson, C. A. "$25.2 Billion Increase Sought in Defense." **Aviation Week and Space Technology** 114 (January 19, 1981): 18-21.

1715. Robinson, C. A. "US Pushes Development of Beam Weapons." **Aviation Week and Space Technology** 109 (October 2, 1978): 14-22.

1716. Roderick, G. H. "This Is the Essence of Management Control." **Office** 51 (January 1960): 83-84.

1717. Rogers, Jimmie N. and Theodore Clevenger. "The Selling of the Pentagon: Was CBS the Fulbright Propaganda Machine." **Quarterly Journal of Speech** 57 (October 1971): 266-273.

1718. Roherty, James M. **Decisions of Robert S. McNamara: A Study of the Role of the Secretary of Defense.** Coral Gables, FL: University of Miami Press, 1970.

1719. Roos, N. J. and J. Priest. "Civilian Diversification in the Defense/Space Industry." **Research Management** 10 (November 1967): 409-424.

1720. Rosenberg, Bernard. "CIA, DIA, FBI, and 50 More!" **Dissent** 22 (Fall 1975): 311-315.

1721. Rotheim, Roy J. "Defense Budget Controversy." **Challenge** 23 (May/June 1980): 45-48.

1722. Rushford, Gregory G. "How the Defense Can Save Billions without Worrying about National Security." **Washington Monthly** 9 (March 1977): 26-30.

1723. Russett, Bruce and Donald R. DeLuca. "Don't Tread on Me: Public Opinion and Foreign Policy in the Eighties." **Political Science Quarterly** 96 (Fall 1981): 381-399.

1724. Rutledge, Donald A. "Civilian Personnel Administration in the War Department." **Public Administration Review** 7 (Winter 1947): 49-59.

1725. Ruttenberg, J. "Developments in Access to Records for Defense Contracts." **New York Certified Public Accountant** 36 (September 1966): 690-694.

1726. Ryan, Garry D. "War Department Topographical Bureau, 1831-1863: An Administrative History." Ph.D. dissertation, American University, 1968.

1727. Sabrosky, Alan N. **Military Manpower and Military Power.** Chicago: Council on Foreign Relations, 1980.

1728. Sabrosky, Alan N. "Organized Anarchies: Military Bureaucracy in the 1980s." **Journal of Applied Behavioral Science** 18 (1982): 137-153.

1729. Samuelson, P. "The Need for Reform of the Software Licensing Policy of the Department of Defense." **Jurimetrics Journal** 27 (Fall 1986): 9-64.

1730. Saragovitz, H. M. and W. G. Gapcynski. "Foreign Intellectual Property and the United States Department of Defense." **Villanova Law Review** 17 (March 1972): 605-621.

1731. Savage, V. Howard. "Interdependence of the San Antonio Economic Structure and the Defense Establishment." **Land Economics** 50 (November 1974): 374-379.

1732. Schill, Ronald L. "Buying Process in the U.S. Department of Defense." **Industrial Marketing Management** 9 (October 1980): 291-299.

1733. Schlesinger, James R. **Defense Planning and Budgeting: The Issue of Centralized Control.** Santa Monica, CA: Rand, 1968.

1734. Schlesinger, James R. **Organizational Structures and Planning.** Santa Monica, CA: Rand, 1966.

1735. Schlesinger, James R. "Testing Time for America." **Fortune** 93 (February 1976): 74-77.

1736. Schlotterbeck, Walter B. **The Role of the Department of Defense in Civil Disturbances.** Washington, DC: Industrial College of the Armed Forces, 1970.

1737. Schnurer, Eric. "Death of the Devil's Advocate." **Washington Monthly** 11 (July/August 1979): 52-54.

1738. Schratz, Paul R. **Evolution of the American Military Establishment since World War II.** Lexington, VA: George C. Marshall Research Foundation, 1978.

1739. Schulin, Robert O. "How Hard Will Missile Spending Hit Industry?" **Iron Age** 180 (November 21, 1957): 81-83.

1740. Schultze, Charles L. "Do More Dollars Mean Better Defense?" **Challenge** 24 (January/February 1982): 30-35.

1741. Seligman, D. "McNamara's Management Revolution." **Fortune** 72 (July 1965): 116-121.

1742. Shaw, B. "Office of the General Counsel of the Air Force." **Journal of Air Law** 16 (Winter 1949): 1-13.

1743. Sherman, S. P. "How Rockwell Kept the B-1 Alive." **Fortune** 104 (November 2, 1981): 106-108.

1744. Sherzer, Harvey G., M. T. Janki, and A. B. Green. "Foreign Military Sales: A Guide to the United States Bureaucracy." **Journal of International Law and Economics** 13 (1979): 545-599.

1745. Shue, R. J. and W. G. Kealy. "Military Transactions in the US Balance of Payments, 1974." **Survey of Current Business** 55 (April 1975): 56-60.

1746. Silk, Leonard S. "Defense Outlook." **Conference Board Record** 7 (July 1970): 8-11.

1747. Skeen, Carl E. "Mr. Madison's Secretary of War." **Pennsylvania Magazine of History and Biography** 100 (July 1976): 336-355.

1748. Smalter, D. J. and Rudy L. Ruggles. "Six Business Lessons from the Pentagon." **Harvard Business Review** 44 (March 1966): 64-75.

1749. Smith, H. C. "War Department Board of Contract Appeals." **Federal Bar Journal** 5 (December 1943): 74-82, 85.

1750. Snodgrass, E. H. "Judge Advocate General's Department of the Army." **Tennessee Law Review** 12 (June 1934): 261-274.

1751. Snyder, F. D. "Maximum Disclosure with Minimum Delay." **Public Relations Journal** 29 (June 1973): 26-28.

1752. Staats, Elmer B. "History of Standard No. 409." **Management Accounting** 57 (October 1975): 21-23.

1753. Stanley, Timothy W. **American Defense and National Security.** Washington, DC: Public Affairs Press, 1956.

1754. Steinberg, H. "Defense Spending: A Look below the Total." **Conference Board Business Record** 16 (May 1959): 226-228.

1755. Stennis, John C. "Illusion of Cut-Rate Defense." **Nation's Business** 60 (April 1972): 38-40.

1756. Stennis, John C. "Issues Relating to the National Defense of the United States." **Computers and Automation** 20 (November 1971): 21-23.

1757. Stephenson, J. G. "Probate Jurisdiction of the War Department." **Miami Law Quarterly** 1 (June 1947): 57-85.

1758. Stillman, Richard. "Racial Unrest in the Military: The Challenge and the Response." **Public Administration Review** 34 (May 1974): 221-229.

1759. Stockfisch, Jacob A., ed. **Planning and Forecasting in the Defense Industries.** Belmont, CA: Wadsworth, 1962.

1760. Stockfisch, Jacob A. **Plowshares into Swords:**

Managing the American Defense Establishment. New York: Mason and Lipscomb, 1973.

1761. Strange, Russell P. "Manpower and Personnel Administration in the Department of Defense." Ph.D. dissertation, University of Maryland, 1955.

1762. Swanberg, W. A. "Was the Secretary of War a Traitor?" **American Heritage** 14 (February 1963): 34-37, 96-97.

1763. Sweeney, Henry W. "Examination of Defense Contracts by the General Accounting Office." **New York Certified Public Accountant** 37 (August 1967): 609-614.

1764. Taylor, J. W. "Organizational Conflicts of Interest in Department of Defense Contracting." **Public Contract Law Journal** 14 (October 1983): 158-177.

1765. Taylor, Thayer C. "Where Will Defense Cuts Hurt Most?" **Sales Management** 93 (October 2, 1964): 29-32.

1766. Terry, Joseph G. "A Methodology for Analyzing Congressional Behavior toward Department of Defense Budget Requests." Master's thesis, Naval Postgraduate School, 1973.

1767. Tesoriere, S. A. "Taxation and National Security." **Analysts Journal** 14 (May 1958): 83-85.

1768. Thompson, Earle. "Taxation and National Defense." **Journal of Political Economy** 82 (July/August 1974): 755-782.

1769. Thompson, F. "Managing Defense Expenditures." **Proceedings of the Academy of Political Science** 35 (1985): 72-84.

1770. Tisone, A. A. "Measuring Purchasing Performance in the Defense Supply Agency." **Journal of Purchasing** 5 (November 1969): 53-76.

1771. Trainor, Richard J. "Study of Factors Leading to Changes in Cost Estimates on Selected Major Departments of Defense and National Aeronautics and Space Administration Development Systems." D.B.A., George Washington University, 1977.

1772. Tribble, William D. "Factors Influencing the Retention of Physicians in the Department of Defense." Ph.D. dissertation, University of

Texas, 1967.

1773. Wamsley, Gary L. "Contrasting Institutions of Air Force Socialization: Happenstance or Bell-wether?" **American Journal of Sociology** 78 (September 1972): 399-417.

1774. Wasko, Arthur I. "The Politics of the Pentagon Papers." **Peace and Change** 1 (Fall 1972): 1-10.

1775. Weidenbaum, Murray L. "Changing Trend in Government Spending." **Financial Analysts Journal** 24 (January 1968): 77-80.

1776. Weidenbaum, Murray L. "More Competition, Less Regulation for Defense Contractors." **Industry Week** 184 (January 13, 1975): 44-46.

1777. Weidenbaum, Murray L. "What's ahead for Defense Spending?" **Industrial Marketing** 44 (December 1959): 56-57.

1778. Weimer, Clarence D. "Defense Acquisition Policies and Contractor Responses: A Comparative Analysis of Managerial Response to Department of Defense Policies for Cost-Constrained Acquisition of Electronics Subsystems." D.B.A., George Washington University, 1975.

1779. Whittmore, Irving C. "Manpower Symposium at the 1952 Annual APA Meeting." **American Psychologist** 8 (March 1953): 119-122.

1780. Wilner, M. H. "Presidential Defense Department Appointments and the Conflict of Interest Laws." **Pennsylvania Bar Association Journal** 32 (June 1961): 335-347.

1781. Wilson, G. C. "Defense Denies Bid for NASA Programs." **Aviation Week and Space Technology** 76 (June 25, 1962): 34-35.

1782. Wilson, G. L. "Office of Defense Transportation." **I.C.C. Practitioners' Journal** 9 (June 1942): 847-856.

1783. Wilson, Samuel M. "The Development of Work Measurement System in the Department of Defense." Ph.D. dissertation, University of Pennsylvania, 1955.

1784. Winkler, Fred H. "The War Department and Disarmament, 1926-1935." **Historian** 28 (May 1966): 426-446.

1785. Winslow, John F. "How the Conglomerates Get Free Money from the Navy." **Washington Monthly** 9 (November 1977): 36-38.

1786. Winston, D. C. "Defense Bill Keyed to ABM Fight." **Aviation Week and Space Technology** 93 (July 27, 1970): 14-16.

1787. Winston, D. C. "Senate Unit Hits Soaring Costs in Reporting DOD Authorization." **Aviation Week and Space Technology** 95 (September 13, 1971): 22-23.

1788. Wolk, Herman. "The Defense Unification Battle, 1947-50: The Air Force." **Prologue** 7 (Spring 1975): 18-31.

1789. Yanarella, Ernest J. "Pentagon Decision-Making and Bureaucratic Politics in the ABM Controversy, 1955-1967." Ph.D. dissertation, University of North Carolina, 1971.

1790. Yarmolinsky, Adam. "Defense Establishment and the Domestic Economy." **Vanderbilt Law Review** 18 (June 1965): 911-924.

1791. Yarmolinsky, Adam. "Electronic Revolution in the Pentagon." **American Scholar** 35 (Spring 1966): 273-274.

1792. Yarmolinsky, Adam. "Science Policy and National Defense." **American Economic Review** 56 (May 1966): 489-493.

1793. Zambo, Leslie J. "A Cash Flow Concept of Profit for the Department of Defense." Ph.D. dissertation, University of Texas, 1981.

Chapter 5. Department of Education

1794. Amidon, Edna P. "Contributions to Family Life Education by the Office of Education." **Marriage and Family Living** 20 (August 1958): 282-288.

1795. Andrade, Ron. "Are Tribes Too Exclusive?" **American Indian Journal** 6 (July 1980): 12-13.

1796. Ashworth, Kenneth H. "Coordinating the Federal Role in Higher Education." **Educational Record** 49 (Summer 1968): 316-324.

1797. Babbidge, Homer D. and Robert M. Rosenzweig. **The Federal Interest in Higher Education.** New York: McGraw-Hill, 1962.

1798. Barkin, T. G. "Legal Implications of Office of Education Criteria for the Self-Supporting Student." **Journal of College and University Law** 2 (Spring 1975): 229-247.

1799. Burnes, Donald W. "Case Study of Federal Involvement in Education." **Academy of Political Science, Proceedings** 33 (1978): 87-98.

1800. Caliver, Ambrose. "Role of the Federal Government in the Higher Education of Negroes." **Phylon** 10 (1949): 370-380.

1801. Callahan, John J. "The Case for Full Federal Funding of Education." **Current History** 63 (August 1972): 76-79.

1802. Carter, D. "Federal Initiatives in Correctional Education." **Corrections Today** 47 (August 1985): 12-13.

1803. Cheit, Earl F. "The Benefits and Burdens of Federal Financial Assistance to Higher

Education." **American Economic Review** 67 (February 1977): 90-95.

1804. Cunningham, Thomas E. "Performance Auditing Advocated." **Public Administration Review** 19 (Fall 1959): 283-284.

1805. Diener, Thomas J. "The U.S. Office of Education: 100 Years of Service to Higher Education." **Educational Forum** 33 (May 1969): 453-466.

1806. Flynt, Ralph C. M. "U.S. Office of Education Looks at Project English." **PMLA** 78 (September 1963): 30-32.

1807. Gaal, John. "HEW's Final Policy Interpretation of Title IX and Intercollegiate Athletics." **Journal of College and University Law** 6 (Summer 1980): 345-361.

1808. Gaal, John and Louis P. DiLorenzo. "The Legality and Requirements of HEW's Proposed Policy Interpretation of Title IX and Intercollegiate Athletics." **Journal of College and University Law** 6 (Spring 1980): 161-194.

1809. Griffith, Emlyn I. "The U.S. Department of Education and the Issue of Control of Education." **Urban Lawyer** 12 (Summer 1980): 500-504.

1810. Guthrie, James W. "The Future of Federal Education Policy." **Education and Urban Society** 14 (August 1982): 511-530.

1811. Harrington, Fred H. "The Federal Government and the Future of Higher Education." **Educational Record** 44 (April 1963): 55-160.

1812. Highwater, Jamake. "Second-Class Indians." **American Indian Journal** 6 (July 1980): 6-11.

1813. Hobbs, Edward H. "President and Administration - Eisenhower." **Public Administration Review** 18 (Fall 1958): 306-313.

1814. Irish, Marian D. "Organization Man in the Presidency." **Journal of Politics** 20 (May 1958): 259-277.

1815. Jackson, Henry M. "To Forge a Strategy for Survival." **Public Administration Review** 19 (Summer 1959): 157-163.

1816. Kelley, Dean M. "State Regulations of the

Participation of Pupils of Private Schools in Title I of the Federal Aid to Education Act of 1965." **Journal of Church and State** 8 (Autumn 1966): 415-429.

1817. Kursh, Harry. **The United States Office of Education: A Century of Service.** Philadelphia: Chilton, 1965.

1818. Mansfield, Harvey C. "History, Merit, and the Politics-Administration Boundary." **Public Administration Review** 19 (Summer 1959): 186-188.

1819. Mickelsen, Allen R. "Title I of the Higher Education Act: A Case Study of Bureaucracy." Ph.D. dissertation, University of Virginia, 1969.

1820. Miles, Rufus E. "Cabinet Department of Education: An Unwise Campaign Promise or a Sound Idea?" **Public Administration Review** 39 (March 1979): 103-110.

1821. Miles, Rufus E. "Case for a Federal Department of Education." **Public Administration Review** 27 (March 1967): 1-9.

1822. Miles, Rufus E. "Orientation of Presidential Appointees." **Public Administration Review** 18 (Winter/Spring 1958): 1-6, 106-112.

1823. Morse, John F. "The Federal Government and Higher Education: General and Specific Concerns in the Years Ahead." **Education Record** 47 (Fall 1966): 429-438.

1824. Oulahan, C. "Legal Implications of Evaluation and Accreditation." **Journal of Law and Education** 7 (April 1978): 193-238.

1825. Peskin, Allan. "Short, Unhappy Life of the Federal Department of Education." **Public Administration Review** 33 (November 1973): 572-575.

1826. Radin, Beryl A. **Implementation, Change and the Federal Bureaucracy: School Desegregation Policy in HEW, 1964-1968.** New York: Teachers College Press, 1977.

1827. Schick, Frank L. "Status of Library Statistics in the United States Office of Education." **Special Libraries** 57 (March 1966): 176-178.

1828. Schick, Frank L. and H. Holzbauer. "New Special and Other Library Programs of the U.S. Office of Education." **Special Libraries** 53 (October 1962):

482-484.

1829. Seabury, Paul. "HEW and the Universities." **Commentary** 53 (February 1972): 38-44.

1830. Shurque, Michael F. "New Materials for the Teaching of English: The English Program of the USOE." **PMLA** 81 (September 1966): 3-38.

1831. Sinai, A. and E. E. Dahl. "Who Investigates Crimes against the Department of Education?" **Police Chief** 52 (May 1980): 30-32.

1832. Sky, T. "Rulemaking and the Federal Grant Process in the United States Office of Education." **Virginia Law Review** 62 (October 1976): 1017-1043.

1833. Sky, T. "Rulemaking in the Office of Education." **Administrative Law Review** 26 (Spring 1974): 129-140.

1834. Smith, G. "Education for the Natives of Alaska: The Work of the United States Bureau of Education, 1884-1931." **Journal of West** 6 (July 1967): 440-450.

1835. Stephens, David. "President Carter, the Congress, and NEA: Creating the Department of Education." **Political Science Quarterly** 98 (Winter 1983-1984): 641-663.

1836. Stewart, Joseph and Charles S. Bullock. "Implementing Equal Education Opportunity Policy: A Comparison of the Outcomes of HEW and Justice Department Efforts." **Administration and Society** 12 (February 1981): 427-447.

1837. Taylor, Arthur J. "Federal Financing of Education, 1945-1972." **Current History** 62 (June 1972): 298-301, 306.

1838. Verville, R. E. and P. S. Leyton. "Department of Education Student Financial Assistance Audit and Regulatory Proceedings: Limitations, Suspensions and Terminations." **Administrative Law Review** 36 (Winter 1984): 1-25.

1839. Weinberger, Caspar W. "Reflection on the Seventies." **Journal of College and University Law** 8 (Fall 1981): 451-461.

Chapter 6.
Department of Energy

1840. Alexander, T. "ERDA's Job Is to Throw Money at the Energy Crisis." **Fortune** 94 (July 1976): 152-156.

1841. Allott, G. L. "Crude Oil Deregulation." **Rocky Mountain Mineral Law Institute** 25 (1979): 15.1-15.15.

1842. Aman, Alfred C. "Institutionalizing the Energy Crisis: Some Structural and Procedural Lessons." **Cornell Law Review** 65 (April 1980): 491-598.

1843. Attwell, J. Evans. "Federal Energy Regulatory Commission Developments." **Oil and Gas Law Taxation Institute** (Southwestern Legal Foundation) 32 (1981): 49-82.

1844. Attwell, J. Evans. "Natural Gas and the Federal Energy Regulatory Commission: Drawbacks of Federal Natural Gas Regulation." **Tulsa Law Journal** 13 (1978): 751-770.

1845. Bachman, K. L. "Developments and Trends in DOE Enforcement." **Oil and Gas Law Taxation Institute** (Southwestern Legal Foundation) 31 (1980): 61-85.

1846. Bachman, W. A. "DOE's for First Year.." **Oil and Gas Journal** 76 (November 13, 1978): 137-150.

1847. Bachman, W. A. "DOE Takes Command of US Petroleum Testing." **Oil and Gas Journal** 75 (October 3, 1977): 47-52.

1848. Bachman, W. A. "DOE - Vast New Bureaucracy for a Big Energy Job." **Oil and Gas Journal** 75 (November 14, 1977): 119-162.

1849. Bachman, W. A. "Energy Conservation: How Much Is Possible in US?" **Oil and Gas Journal** 75 (March 21, 1977): 57-61.

1850. Bachman, W. A. "New Energy Department Shaping Up in Congress." **Oil and Gas Journal** 75 (June 13, 1977): 19-22.

1851. Bagge, Carl E. "Our Nation's March to the Sea." **Public Utilities Fortnightly** 98 (September 23, 1976): 36-39.

1852. Bardin, David J. "Role of the New Department of Energy." **National Resources Lawyer** 10 (1978): 639-654.

1853. Bardin, David J. "Role of the New Department of Energy." **Public Utilities Fortnightly** 100 (September 29, 1977): 62-65.

1854. Barnes, G. H. "Update on DOE's Oil Pricing Regulations." **Oil and Gas Law Taxation Institute** 32 (Southwestern Legal Foundation) (1981): 267-299.

1855. Bell, J. C. and K. MacKenzie. "Windfall Profit Tax and DOE Regulation: Problems in Property Definition." **Oil and Gas Law Taxation Institute** 32 (Southwestern Legal Foundation) (1981): 301-334.

1856. Bink, Barbara H. "The Federal Budget: Playing the Numbers in Washington." **Public Utilities Fortnightly** 109 (June 10, 1982): 51-54.

1857. Bodi, F. Lorraine and E. Erdheim. "Swimming Upstream: FERC's Failure to Protect Anadromous Fish." **Ecology Law Quarterly** 13 (Winter 1986): 7-49.

1858. Bradshaw, T. "My Case for National Planning." **Fortune** 95 (February 1977): 100-104.

1859. Braitman, Jackie L. **Nuclear Waste Disposal: Can Government Cope.** Santa Monica, CA: Rand, 1983.

1860. Brown, Omer F. and Warren E. Bergholz. "Nuclear Waste - The Case for Confidence in Disposal." **South Carolina Law Review** 32 (July 1981): 851-891.

1861. Byse, Clark. "Department of Energy Organization Act: Structure and Procedure." **Administrative Law Review** 30 (Spring 1978): 193-236.

1862. Cameron, James. "Huffing and Puffing at the Energy Department." **Fortune** 103 (January 26, 1981): 38-40.

1863. Cameron, James. "James Schlesinger in Dubious Battle." **Fortune** 97 (February 27, 1978): 36-40.

1864. Cantelon, Philip L. and Robert C. Williams. **Crisis Contained: The Department of Energy at Three Mile Island.** Cambridge, MA: Harvard University Press, 1982.

1865. Cheit, Ross. "The Energy Mobilization Board." **Ecology Law Quarterly** 8 (Summer 1980): 727-747.

1866. Christie, J. D. "National Energy Policy Plans." **Transportation Journal** 16 (Winter 1976): 35-40.

1867. Cicchetti, Charles J. "National Energy Policy Plans - A Critique." **Transportation Journal** 16 (Winter 1976): 41-47.

1868. Cohen, Tom. **Open for Business Only?: A Common Cause Study of the Department of Energy.** Washington, DC: Common Cause, 1979.

1869. Comstock, G. R. "FUA: The Transition of Alternate Fuels in the Industrial and Electric Utility Sectors." **Kansas Law Review** 29 (Spring 1981): 337-368.

1870. Craven, Donald B. "New Dimensions in Federal Regulation of Crude Oil and Petroleum Products under the Department of Energy." **Oil and Gas Law Taxation Institute** 29 (Southwestern Legal Foundation) (1978): 1-37.

1871. Debevoise, Thomas M. "Role of the Federal Energy Regulatory Commission in Licensing Small Hydroelectric Projects." **Vermont Law Review** 5 (Fall 1980): 279-293.

1872. Doria, Marilyn L. "Enforcement at the Federal Energy Regulatory Commission: Considerations for the Practitioner." **Energy Law Journal** 4 (1983): 39-59.

1873. Frank, Steven A. and Scott A. Spiewak. "Coal Conversion and the Clean Air Act: Help from DOE." **Public Utilities Fortnightly** 110 (August 19, 1982): 22-25.

1874. Gleichman, Ted. "Handicapped Trained to Build Collectors." **Solar Law Reporter** 2 (July/August

1980): 244-246.

1875. Glennan, Thomas K. **Policy and Program Planning in the Department of Energy.** Santa Monica, CA: Rand, 1980.

1876. Glennan, Thomas K. **The Role of Department of Energy Field Offices in the Commercialization of Energy Technologies.** Santa Monica, CA: Rand, 1979.

1877. Goodwin, Robert C. "Aspects of the Department of Energy International Legal Program." **Denver Journal of International Law and Policy** 8 (Winter 1979): 289-313.

1878. Greenberg, Judith G. "Legitimating Administrative Actions: The Experience of the Federal Energy Office, 1974." **University of Cincinnati Law Review** 51 (1982): 735-778.

1879. Hammaker, Michael K. "Ambiguous Federal Regs Should Not Be Enforced." **District Lawyer** 6 (November/December 1981): 14-19.

1880. Hammond, Paul B. "Economists, Scientists and Energy Policy: Bureaucracy and the Politics of Federal Energy Management." Ph.D. dissertation, Massachusetts Institute of Technology, 1980.

1881. Hart, Gary W. and Keith R. Glaser. "A Failure to Enact: A Review of Radioactive Waste Issues and Legislation Considered by the Ninety-Sixth Congress." **South Carolina Law Review** 32 (July 1981): 639-787.

1882. Hausman, Jerry A. "Project Independence Report: An Appraisal of U.S. Energy Needs up to 1985." **Bell Journal of Economics** 6 (Autumn 1975): 517-551.

1883. Heilman, John. "Uses of Direct and Indirect Measures: A Case Study of Program Impact in the Energy Conservation Field." **Evaluation Review** 6 (February 1982): 61-78.

1884. Henke, Michael J. "Natural Gas Liquid Pricing under DOE Regulations." **Rocky Mountain Mineral Law Institute Proceedings** 26 (1981): 857-886.

1885. Henke, Michael J. and E. G. Andersen. "Current Issues Concerning DOE Regulation of Natural Gas Liquids." **Oil and Gas Law Taxation Institute** 31 (Southwestern Legal Foundation) (1980): 27-59.

1886. Herzog, Richard B. "The Coverage of the Fuel Use Act - How to Avoid Unpleasant Surprises." **Natural Resources Lawyer** 13 (Fall 1981): 553-569.

1887. Hill, R. L. "FEA: Back from the Brink - Temporarily." **Public Utilities Fortnightly** 98 (July 29, 1976): 9-11.

1888. Hill, R. L. "Reconciling Foreign and Domestic Nuclear Energy Policies." **Public Utilities Fortnightly** 98 (November 18, 1976): 13-15.

1889. Horovitz, B. "Disgruntled Staff: A Real Crisis at DOE?" **Industry Week** 206 (July 7, 1980): 32-34.

1890. Horovitz, B. "DOE: Now You See It, Now You Don't." **Industry Week** 212 (February 8, 1982): 26-28.

1891. Hughes, J. David. "Indefinite Escalators: 1985 Does FERC Have a Stairway Down." **Energy Law Journal** 4 (1983): 189-199.

1892. Irwin, Donald P. and K. Dennis Sisk. "The Fuel Use Act and DOE's Regulations: A Utility Industry Perspective." **University of Kansas Law Review** 29 (Spring 1981): 319-336.

1893. Johnson, Jared. "Future of RSECS Hinges on Court Challenge of Shutdown Order." **Solar Law Reporter** 3 (January/February 1982): 742-743.

1894. Johnson, Jared. "Proposed RCS Changes Would Limit Auditors Solar Recommendations." **Solar Law Reporter** 3 (November/December 1981): 582-584.

1895. Johnson, R. Tenny. "National Energy Policy - The Department of Energy's Perspective." **Energy Law Journal** 3 (1982): 331-336.

1896. Journey, Drexel D. "PURPA Rate Studies: Much Ado about Technical Analysis." **Public Utilities Fortnightly** 108 (July 16, 1981): 23-27.

1897. Kennedy, Jay B. "DOE Mandates: Taking Power away from the States." **Public Utilities Fortnightly** 106 (November 6, 1980): 11-14.

1898. Kinney, G. "Love: Reluctant Regulator Tackles US Energy Policy." **Oil and Gas Journal** 71 (September 10, 1973): 39-41.

1899. Landow-Esser, J. "Department of Energy: To Be or

Not to Be?" **Federal Bar News and Journal** 29 (September/October 1982): 320-326.

1900. Lang, S. H. "DOE Organization: The Limits of Regulatory Power." **Oil and Gas Law Taxation Institute** 30 (Southwestern Legal Foundation) (1979): 119-153.

1901. Lange, Timothy. "PIFUA Compliance Study Includes Alternatives Energy Sources." **Solar Law Reporter** 2 (July/August 1980): 237-239.

1902. Lavenant, R. P. "Operator's Liability for Over-Charges in the Sale of Production." **Oil and Gas Law Taxation Institute** 31 (Southwestern Legal Foundation) (1980): 131-176.

1903. Lemann, Nicholas. "Why the Sun Will Never Set on the Federal Empire." **Washington Monthly** 8 (September 1976): 32-41.

1904. Levenson, Mark S. "Energy Law." **Annual Survey of American Law** (March 1982): 637-664.

1905. Ligon, Duke R. "Crude Oil Pricing: Current Regulations and the Shift to Decontrol." **Oil and Gas Law Taxation Institute** 31 (Southwestern Legal Foundation) (1980): 1-25.

1906. Lublin, Edward L. "Future of the Department of Energy's Coal Conversion Program." **Energy Law Journal** 2 (1981): 355-368.

1907. McClenahen, J. S. "US Making Progress on Energy, Says Richardson." **Industry Week** 190 (August 2, 1976): 26-28.

1908. Marston, P. M. and Sheila S. Hollis. "Review and Assessment of the FERC Natural Gas Enforcement Program." **Houston Law Review** 16 (July 1978): 1105-1127.

1909. Mead, Walter J. "The National Energy Program Evaluated." **Current History** 74 (July 1978): 9-12.

1910. Melton, Stephen R. "Separation of Functions at the FERC: Does the Reorganization of the Office of General Counsel Mean What It Says?" **Energy Law Journal** 5 (1984): 349-356.

1911. Michaelson, Pete. "Insurance Scarce for Windmills in Cities." **Solar Law Reporter** 2 (January/February 1981): 877-880.

1912. Miers, Sheppard F. "Windfall Profit Tax and DOE Regulations: Can the IRS Touch Up This 8 by 10 Glossy?" **Oil and Gas Tax Quarterly** 30 (June 1982): 587-608.

1913. Mighdoll, M. J. and P. D. Weisse. "We Need a National Materials Policy." **Harvard Business Review** 54 (September 1976): 143-151.

1914. Moody, Rush. "FERC Inheritance-Unresolved Problems in Producer Regulation." **Oil and Gas Law Taxation Institute** 29 (1978): 417-453.

1915. Moore, Charles A. "New Trial Program at the Federal Energy Regulatory Commission." **Energy Law Journal** 3 (1982): 337-342.

1916. Morgan, Richard G. and C. W. Garrison. "Enforcement Policies and Procedures of the Federal Energy Regulatory Commission." **Tulsa Law Journal** 15 (Spring 1980): 501-531.

1917. Morris, Joseph W. "Windfall Profits Tax: Implications of the Crude Oil Windfall Profit Tax Act of 1980 for the Federal Courts." **Federal Rules Decisions** 89 (June 1981): 467-472.

1918. Munter, P., Robert J. Koester and Thomas A. Ratcliffe. "Streamlining Department of Energy Financial Reporting." **Oil and Gas Tax Quarterly** 30 (March 1982): 544-557.

1919. Murphy, Edward E. and Mark McEnearney. "Import Price Indexes for Crude Petroleum." **Monthly Labor Review** 105 (November 1982): 29-33.

1920. Nash, Susan E. "Collecting Overcharges from the Oil Companies: The Department of Energy's Restitutionary Obligation." **Stanford Law Review** 32 (May 1980): 1039-1059.

1921. Nassikas, John N. "Regulatory Official's Assessment of the New Department of Energy." **Natural Resources Lawyer** 10 (1978): 639-654.

1922. Oosterhuis, Paul W. "The Crude Oil Windfall Profit Tax Act of 1980." **Institute on Federal Taxation** 39 (1981): 42-80.

1923. Overstreet, Lana B. and James B. Wilcom. "The Department of Energy Crude Oil Property Definition - A Controversial Concept with Critical Continuing Importance under the Windfall Profit Tax Act." **Rocky Mountain Mineral Law**

Institute Proceedings 26 (1981): 745-789.

1924. Page, Ann L. and Thomas C. Hood. "Attitude Change among Teachers in U.S. Department of Energy Educational Workshops." **Journal of Social Psychology** 115 (December 1981): 183-188.

1925. Peterson, Bruce D. "Administrative Law - Subpoena Power - Department of Energy Needs No Express Grant of Subpoena Power to Study Oil Company Fuel Sales Study Oil Company Fuel Sales Subsidization." **Notre Dame Lawyer** 56 (February 1981): 515-520.

1926. Poland, S. S. "Contrasting Administrative Procedures before the Department of Energy." **Oil and Gas Law Taxation Institute** 30 (Southwestern Legal Foundation) (1979): 97-118.

1927. Rankin, Bob. "New Department Given Wide Energy Powers." **Congressional Quarterly** 35 (July 30, 1977): 1581-1584.

1928. Regens, James L. and Robert W. Rycroft. "Administrative Discretion in Energy Policy-Making: The Exceptions and Appeals Program of the Federal Energy Administration." **Journal of Politics** 43 (August 1981): 875-888.

1929. Reitze, Arnold W. and G. L. Reitze, "Electric Vehicles Get a Boost." **Environment** 18 (December 1976): 41-42.

1930. Reitze, Arnold W. and G. L. Reitze. "Nuclear Drummer." **Environment** 18 (November 1976): 37-38.

1931. Richardson, Julia R. "Motor Gasoline: The Regulatory Web." **Urban Law Review** 3 (Winter 1980): 180-205.

1932. Rycroft, Robert W. "Bureaucratic Responsibility in the Federal Energy Administration." **Bureaucrat** 6 (Fall 1977): 19-33.

1933. Rycroft, Robert W. "Bureaucratic Performance in Energy Policy-Making: An Evaluation of Output Efficiency in the Federal Energy Administration." **Public Policy** 26 (Fall 1978): 599-627.

1934. Rycroft, Robert W. "The Federal Energy Administration: A Case Study of Energy Policy-Making." Ph.D. dissertation, University of Oklahoma, 1976.

1935. Sellers, John M. "Decontrol and Regulatory Legitimacy: The Case of the Entitlements Program." **Administrative Law Review** 37 (Summer 1985): 281-315.

1936. Sheldon, Karin P. "Nuclear Waste: The Problem Remains Unburied." **South Carolina Law Review** 32 (July 1981): 911-941.

1937. Sherman, Ann. "The Development of Synthetic Fuels." **Ecology Law Quarterly** 8 (Summer 1980): 781-789.

1938. Sherry, Edward V. "What the National Association of Manufacturers Thinks about DOE's Voluntary Guideline for a Cost-of-Service Standard." **Public Utilities Fortnightly** 107 (January 1, 1981): 42-43.

1939. Smartt, Lucien E. "Buildings' Energy Performance Standards a Growing Concern." **Public Utilities Fortnightly** 105 (March 13, 1980): 6.

1940. Smartt, Lucien E. "Home Builders Urge Restudy of Building Energy Standards." **Public Utilities Fortnightly** 105 (March 27, 1980): 6-7.

1941. Smartt, Lucien E. "Thought on the Governmental Presence in the Energy Field." **Public Utilities Fortnightly** 106 (August 28, 1980): 4-5.

1942. Smith, D. S. "Jurisdictional Transfers under the Department of Energy Act." **Oil and Gas Law Taxation Institute** 29 (1978): 375-415.

1943. Smith, Sandra L. "The Regulation of Natural Gas Liquids: An Introduction of DOE Approaches and Problems." **South Texas Law Journal** 21 (Summer 1980): 98-113.

1944. Solo, P. and M. Jendrzejczyk. "Federal Rescue for the Nuclear Establishment." **Business and Social Review** 33 (Spring 1980): 4-8.

1945. Tate, Douglass T. "Congress Gears Up for Energy-Plan Bills." **Oil and Gas Journal** 75 (May 2, 1977): 122-124.

1946. Tate, Douglass T. "Flood of Energy Law Seen from Revamped Congress." **Oil and Gas Journal** 75 (March 28, 1977): 27-29.

1947. Tynan, Vicki F. **The Wolf Guarding the Door: An Analysis of the U. S. Department of Energy**

Budget. Fairfax, VA: Institute for Ecological Policies, 1980.

1948. Velocci, T. "Department of Energy: Phoenix or Dead Duck?" **Nation's Business** 70 (February 1982): 50-52.

1949. Verleger, Philip K. "U.S. Petroleum Crisis of 1979." **Brookings Papers on Economic Activity** 2 (1979): 463-476.

1950. Vicek, Jan B. and Anita V. Spivey. "DOE Dismantlement: An Overview of the Federal Energy Reorganization Act of 1982." **Natural Resources Lawyer** 15 (1982): 457-481.

1951. Weiner, Stephen. "Science Group Disputes DOE Cost Projections for Solar Satellites." **Solar Law Reporter** 3 (September/October 1981): 385-387.

1952. Weiner, Stephen and Sherry Caloia. "DOE Proposes Rules But Opposes Funding for Wind System Grants." **Solar Law Reporter** 3 (September/October 1981): 389-390.

1953. Werner, Carol. "Low-Income Energy Programs." **Clearinghouse Review** 15 (January 1982): 810-813.

1954. Wilcox, Ron. "Conservation, Solar, Draw Support during Energy Plan Hearings." **Solar Law Reporter** 3 (July/August 1981): 189-190.

Chapter 7. Department of Health and Human Services

1955. Adams, L. J. "Cosmetic or Drug? FDA's OTC Drug Review Program Provides Some Answers and Raises New Questions." **Food Drug Cosmetic Law Journal** 35 (February 1980): 98-111.

1956. Alexander, L. A. and Thomas B. Jabine. "Access to Social Security Microdata Files for Research and Statistical Purposes." **Social Security Bulletin** 41 (August 1978): 3-17.

1957. Allera, E. J. "FDA's Combination Animal Drug Policy - Is It Feasible? Or, Should Elsie Be the Only One Getting Milked?" **Food Drug Cosmetic Law Journal** 33 (June 1978): 267-273.

1958. Allera, E. J. "FDA's Use of Guidelines, Notices of Proposed Rulemaking, and Compliance Policies as De Facto Rules: An Abuse of Discretion." **Food Drug Cosmetic Law Journal** 36 (May 1981): 270-280.

1959. Alvey, Wendy and F. Aziz. "Mortality Reporting in SSA Linked Data: Preliminary Results." **Social Security Bulletin** 42 (November 1979): 15-19.

1960. Ames, C. C. and S. C. McCracken. "Framing Regulatory Standards to Avoid Formal Adjudication: The FDA as a Case Study." **California Law Review** 64 (January 1976): 14-73.

1961. Anderson, Thomas M. "Distribution of Indian Health Care Benefits." **Golden Gate University Law Review** 11 (Spring 1981): 31-32.

1962. Austern, H. Thomas. "Congressional and Legal/Regulatory Developments under the Federal Food, Drug, and Cosmetic Act." **Food Drug Cosmetic Law Journal** 29 (December 1974): 588-

595.

1963. Babyak, Blythe. "Califano's Cigarette Campaign: All Smoke and No Fire." **Washington Monthly** 10 (July 1978): 32-36.

1964. Babcrach, Eve E. "The Food and Drug Administration Cosmetic Inspection: An Industry Approach." **Food Drug Cosmetic Law Journal** 38 (October 1983): 373-382.

1965. Banta, H. David and Stephen B. Thacker. "Policies toward Medical Technology: The Case of Electronic Fetal Monitoring." **American Journal of Public Health** 69 (September 1979): 931-935.

1966. Banta, P. M. and M. B. Hiller. "Patent Policies of the Department of Health, Education and Welfare." **Federal Bar Journal** 21 (Winter 1961): 89-98.

1967. Barkdoll, Gerald L. "Perils and Promise of Economic Analysis for Regulatory Decision-Making." **Food Drug Cosmetic Law Journal** 34 (December 1979): 625-630.

1968. Barkdoll, Gerald L. "Type III Evaluations: Consultation and Consensus." **Public Administration Review** 40 (March 1980): 174-179.

1969. Barnhart, Gilbert R. "Note on the Impact of Public Health Service Research on Poverty." **Journal of Social Issues** 21 (January 1965): 142-149.

1970. Barr, C. J. "Requiem for Pactra? The Scope of Agency Discretion to Deny an Opportunity for a Hearing under Section 701 (e)." **Food Drug Cosmetic Law Journal** 38 (October 1983): 334-348.

1971. Bauer, Theodore J. "International VD Activities of the U.S. Public Health Service." **Journal of Social Hygiene** 36 (January 1950): 35-36.

1972. Becker, R. H. "Is the Over-the-Counter Drug Review Program Still Viable?" **Food Drug Cosmetic Law Journal** 38 (October 1983): 349-354.

1973. Beers, D. O. "Litigating Formal Evidentiary Hearings at the Food and Drug Administration." **Food Drug Cosmetic Law Journal** 41 (July 1986): 306-329.

1974. Bisogni, Carole. "Food Safety Laws Eyed in Washington." **Human Ecology Forum** 13 (Summer 1982): 18-20.

1975. Bisogni, Carole. **Nutrition Council Seminar.** Geneva: New York State Agricultural Station, 1977.

1976. Bisogni, Carole. "Widening Debate over Food Additives." **Human Ecology Forum** 10 (Fall 1979): 15-18.

1977. Black, Eric. "Great Contact Lens Con." **Washington Monthly** 12 (September 1980): 23-29.

1978. Blume, Sheila B. "Changing the Federal Regulations on Confidentiality of Alcohol and Drug Abuse Patient Records: Views of Clinical Staff." **Journal of Studies on Alcohol** 42 (March 1981): 344-349.

1979. Boggan, E. C. "FDA's Combination Drug Policy." **Food Drug Cosmetic Law Journal** 30 (May 1975): 276-287.

1980. Bolster, Mel H. "The Scientist-Administrator: A Study of a Professional Specialization at the National Institutes of Health." Ph.D. dissertation, American University, 1974.

1981. Borjas, George J. "Discrimination in HEW: Is the Doctor Sick or Are the Patients Healthy?" **Journal of Law and Economics** 21 (April 1978): 97-110.

1982. Bouchard, E. F. "The Food and Drug Administrations Redbook: The Practical Implications for Business Practices." **Food Drug Cosmetic Law Journal** 39 (April 1984): 211-216.

1983. Bozeman, Barry and J. Massey. "Investing in Policy Evaluation: Some Guidelines for Skeptical Public Managers." **Public Administration Review** 42 (May/June 1982): 264-270.

1984. Brady, Rodney H. "MBO Goes to Work in the Public Sector." **Harvard Business Review** 51 (March 1973): 65-74.

1985. Brandt, Edward N. "AIDS Research: Charting New Directions." **Public Health Reports** 99 (September /October 1984): 433-435.

1986. Brandt, Edward N. "PHS Perspectives on Misconduct in Science." **Public Health Reports** 98 (March/ April 1983): 136-140.

1987. Brandt, Edward N. "Technology Assessment, a

Private-Public Partnership." **Public Health Reports** 99 (July/August 1984): 329-332.

1988. Brisson, E. L. "A Look at the Bioresearch Monitoring Program: The Agency Perspective." **Food Drug Cosmetic Law Journal** 38 (April 1983): 184-189.

1989. Broadhurst, Diane D. and B. Gross. "Model Law That Isn't." **Public Welfare** 40 (Spring 1982): 22-27.

1990. Brown, Bertram S. "American Psychiatric Education: A Review." **American Journal of Psychiatry** 134 (March 1977): 1-28.

1991. Brown, Bertram S. "Crisis in Mental Health Research." **American Journal of Psychiatry** 134 (February 1977): 113-120.

1992. Brown, Bertram S. "Drugs and Public Health: Issues and Answers." **Annals of the American Academy of Political and Social Science** 417 (January 1975): 110-119.

1993. Brown, Bertram S. "Federal Role in Mental Health." **State Government** 50 (Autumn 1977): 209-213.

1994. Brown, Lawrence D. "The Regulatory Assault." **Journal of Health Policy and Law** 7 (Fall 1982): 772-779.

1995. Burditt, George M. "Quo Vadit FDA?" **Food Drug Cosmetic Law Journal** 38 (April 1983): 87-92.

1996. Burkhauser, Richard V. and Timothy M. Smeeding. "The Net Impact of the Social Security System on the Poor." **Policy Studies Review Annual** 6 (1982): 137-156.

1997. Caldwell, Janice M. and Marshall B. Kapp. "The Rights of Nursing Home Patients: Possibilities and Limitations of Federal Regulation." **Journal of Health Politics, Policy and Law** 6 (Spring 1981): 40-48.

1998. Califano, Joseph A. **Governing America: An Insider's Report from the White House and the Cabinet.** New York: Simon and Schuster, 1981.

1999. Campbell, John R. "Twain Do Meet: Regional Conferences." **Public Administration Review** 7 (Summer 1947): 204-207.

2000. Campbell, Rita R. **Drug Lab: Federal Government**

Decision Making. Stanford, CA: Hoover Institution Press, 1976.

2001. Cannizzaro, John F. and Madelon M. Rosenfeld. "Laetrile and the FDA: A Case of Reverse Regulation." **Journal of Health Politics, Policy and Law** 3 (Summer 1978): 181-195.

2002. Cates, Jerry R. **Insuring Inequality: Administrative Leadership in Social Security, 1935-1954.** Ann Arbor: University of Michigan Press, 1983.

2003. Catrice-Lorey, Antoinette. "Social Security and Its Relations with Beneficiaries: The Problem of Bureaucracy in Social Administration." **Bulletin of the International Social Security Association** 19 (1966): 286-297.

2004. Celeste, A. C. "Inevitable FDA Inspection." **Food Drug Cosmetic Law Journal** 34 (January 1979): 32-39.

2005. Clark, Franklin D. "The Regulatory Functions of the Food and Drug Administration." **Food Drug Cosmetic Law Journal** 16 (August 1961): 500-507.

2006. Cody, W. F. "Authoritative Effect of FDA Regulations." **Business Lawyer** 24 (January 1969): 479-488.

2007. Comanor, William S. "The Drug Industry and Medical Research: The Economics of the Kefauver Committee Investigations." **Journal of Business** 39 (January 1966): 12-18.

2008. Cooper, Iver P. "FDA, the BATF, and Liquor Labeling: A Case Study of Interagency Jurisdictional Conflict." **Food Drug Cosmetic Law Journal** 34 (July 1979): 370-390.

2009. Cooper, Laura. "Goldberg's Forgotten Footnote: Is There a Due Process Right to a Hearing Prior to the Termination of Welfare Benefits When the Only Issue Raised Is a Question of Law?" **Minnesota Law Review** 64 (July 19680): 1107-1179.

2010. Cooper, R. M. "Drug Labeling and Products Liability: The Role of the Food and Drug Administration." **Food Drug Cosmetic Law Journal** 41 (July 1986): 233-240.

2011. Cribbett, James R. "Report from the Division of Pharmacology." **Food Drug Cosmetic Law Journal** 16

(December 1961): 738-743.

2012. Croft, Caroline J. and Mary K. Jolly. "A Second Look at the National Program for Runaway and Homeless Youth." **Juvenile and Family Courts Journal** 33 (August 1982): 39-45.

2013. Davis, Alan D. "Food and Drug Administration Plans and Programs." **Food Drug Cosmetic Law Journal** 21 (January 1966): 57-64.

2014. Davis, John A. **Regional Organization of the Social Security Administration: A Case Study.** New York: Columbia University Press, 1950.

2015. Davis, P. W. "An Incipient Wonder Drug Movement: DMSO and the Food and Drug Administration." **Social Problems** 32 (December 1984): 197-212.

2016. DeBell, L. E. and and D. L. Chesney. "FDA Inspection Process." **Food Drug Cosmetic Law Journal** 37 (April 1982): 244-249.

2017. DeWitt, William B. "Contributions of the U.S. Public Health Service in Tropical Medicine." **Bulletin of the New York Academy of Medicine** 44 (June 1968): 728-736.

2018. Dixon, Paul R. "Guidance and Enforcement." **Food Drug Cosmetic Law Journal** 22 (March 1967): 177-184.

2019. Docksai, M. F. "FDA Announces Oraflex Testing." **Trial** 19 (March 1973): 17-18.

2020. Docksai, M. F. "FDA Considers Depo-Provera as Contraceptive." **Trial** 19 (March 1983): 16-17.

2021. Donley, R. "Inside View of the Washington Health Scene." **American Journal of Nursing** 79 (November 1979): 1976-1949.

2022. Doolittle, Fred. "Auditing Disputes in Federal Grant Programs: The Case of AFDC." **Public Administration Review** 41 (July/August 1981): 430-436.

2023. Dorsey, R. "American Psychiatric Association and the Food and Drug Administration: An Analysis and Proposal for Action." **American Journal of Psychiatry** 135 (September 1978): 1049-1058.

2024. Doty, Pamela and Amitai Etzioni. "National Health Insurance: Mobilizing Profit for Public

Service." **Public Policy** 26 (Summer 1978): 405-413.

2025. Edwards, Charles C. "Meeting New Challenges." **Food Drug Cosmetic Law Journal** 28 (January 1973): 4-12.

2026. Eiermann, H. J. "The Food and Drug Administration's Cosmetics Inspection Program." **Food Drug Cosmetic Law Journal** 38 (January 1983): 53-57.

2027. Elengold, M. "Freedom of Information Policy at the FDA." **Food Drug Cosmetic Law Journal** 35 (November 1980): 627-632.

2028. Elson, Robert T. "In Man for the Cabinet." **Fortune** 72 (October 1965): 154-157.

2029. Farmer, Francesta. "Selling the Adams Criteria: The Response of OCR to Political Intervention in Adams v. Califano." **Howard Law Journal** 22 (1979): 417-425.

2030. Feder, Judith M. **Medicare: The Politics of Federal Hospital Insurance.** Lexington, MA: Lexington Books, 1977.

2031. Feder, Judith M. "The Social Security Administration and Medicare: The Politics of Federal Hospital Insurance." Ph.D. dissertation, Harvard University, 1977.

2032. Feldstein, Martin S. "Facing the Social Security Crisis." **Public Interest** 47 (Spring 1977): 88-100.

2033. Fine, Sam D. "Philosophy of Enforcement." **Food Drug Cosmetic Law Journal** 31 (June 1976): 324-332.

2034. Finkel, Marion J. "The Orphan Drug Act and the Federal Government's Orphan Products Development Program." **Public Health Reports** 99 (May/June 1984): 313-316.

2035. Fisk, M. "Drug Regulation Reform: To Disclose Or Not to Disclose." **Trial** 15 (March 1979): 53-55.

2036. Flannery, E. J. "Should It Be Easier or Harder to Use Unapproved Drugs and Devices." **Hastings Center Report** 16 (February 1986): 17-23.

2037. Flato, L. "SSA's Huge Systems Scheme." **Datamation** 23 (July 1977): 140-143.

2038. Fleece, Steven M. "A Review of the Child Support Enforcement Program." **Journal of Family Law** 20 (May 1982): 489-522.

2039. Flemming, Arthur S. "Industry's Stake in Social Welfare." **Duns Review** 75 (February 1960): 109-110.

2040. Folsom, Marion B. "Health, Education and Welfare: The First Decade." **Current History** 45 (August 1963): 87-91, 117.

2041. Forte, W. E. "Food and Drug Administration and the Economic Adulteration of Foods." **Food Drug Cosmetic Law Journal** 21 (October 1966): 533-552.

2042. Freedman, H. "Welfare Advocacy before HEW." **NLADA Briefcase** 35 (September 1978): 104-109.

2043. Freeman, Joseph T. "Some Notes on the History of the National Institute on Aging." **Gerontologist** 20 (October 1980): 610-614.

2044. Fritz, Dan. "Administration on Aging as an Advocate: Progress, Problems, and Prospects." **Gerontologist** 19 (April 1979): 141-150.

2045. Furman, Bess. **A Profile of the United States Public Health Service, 1798-1948.** Bethesda, MD: National Institutes of Health, 1973.

2046. Gibbs, J. N. "Federal Regulation of Food and Food Additive Biotechnology." **Administrative Law Review** 38 (Winter 1986): 1-32.

2047. Gieringer, Dale H. "The FDA's Bad Medicine: Overregulation Is Dangerous to Your Health." **Policy Review** 33 (Summer 1985): 71-73.

2048. Gilbert, Charles E. "Policy-Making in Public Welfare: The 1962 Amendments." **Political Science Quarterly** 81 (June 1966): 196-224.

2049. Gilhooley, M. "Federal Regulation of Cosmetics: An Overview." **Food Drug Cosmetic Law Journal** 33 (May 1978): 231-238.

2050. Glenna, Thomas K. **The Management of Demonstration Programs in the Department of Health and Human Services.** Santa Monica, CA: Rand, 1985.

2051. Glick, Lee E. "An Analysis of the Effect of Federal Regulatory Policies on Major Chains in Retail Food Distribution." Ph.D. dissertation,

University of Pittsburgh, 1965.

2052. Goddard, J. L. "Year in Review." **Food Drug Cosmetic Law Journal** 22 (February 1967): 92-104.

2053. Gold, Byron D. "The Role of the Federal Government in the Provision of Social Services to Older Persons." **Annals of the American Academy of Political and Social Science** 415 (September 1974): 55-69.

2054. Goldstein, E. M. "Medical Devices: Soon Federal Control." **Trial** 15 (February 1975): 68-69.

2055. Goyan, Jere E. "Future of the FDA under a New Administration." **Food Drug Cosmetic Law Journal** 36 (February 1981): 60-65.

2056. Grabowski, Henry G. **The Regulation of Pharmaceuticals: Balancing the Benefits and Risks.** Washington, DC: American Enterprise Institute for Public Policy Research, 1983.

2057. Grabowski, Henry G. and J. M. Vernon. "Consumer Protection Regulation in Ethical Drugs." **American Economic Review** 67 (February 1977): 359-364.

2058. Granick, Samuel and Morton H. Kleban. "Data File of NIMH Study of Healthy Aged Males." **Gerontologist** 17 (December 1977): 531-536.

2059. Greenberg, George D. "Governing HEW: Problems of Management and Control at the Department of Health, Education and Welfare." Ph.D. dissertation, Harvard University, 1972.

2060. Greenberg, George D. "Reorganization Reconsidered: The U.S. Public Service 1960-1973." **Public Policy** 23 (Fall 1975): 483-522.

2061. Greenberger, Marcia D. "Consumer Advocate's View of the FDA's Procedures and Practices." **Food Drug Cosmetic Law Journal** 32 (June 1977): 293-299.

2062. Greenblum, J. "Evaluating Vocational Rehabilitation Programs for the Disabled: National Long-Term Follow-Up Study." **Social Security Bulletin** 38 (October 1975): 3-12.

2063. Greene, R. J. "Informal FDA Hearings." **Food Drug Cosmetic Law Journal** 32 (August 1977): 354-360.

2064. Guttenberger, A. E. "Use of Summary Judgment by

the FDA to Avoid Formal Adjudication: In the Public Interest?" **Food Drug Cosmetic Law Journal** 36 (August 1981): 396-419.

2065. Haas, E. "An Assessment of FDA's Track Record on Issues of Consumer Protection." **Food Drug Cosmetic Law Journal** 40 (April 1985): 253-258.

2066. Hadwiger, Don F. "Nutrition, Food Safety and Farm Policy." **Academy of Political Science, Proceedings** 34 (1982): 79-88.

2067. Hallquist, Scott G. "Legal Consequences of Disposable Dialyzer Reuse." **American Journal of Law and Medicine** 8 (Spring 1982): 1-25.

2068. Halperin, Jerome A. "From Investigation to Marketplace: Moving Drugs through the System." **Food Drug Cosmetic Law Journal** 36 (April 1981): 166-174.

2069. Hamilton, Robert W. "Rulemaking on a Record by the Food and Drug Administration." **Texas Law Review** 50 (August 1972): 1132-1194.

2070. Hamilton, Robert W. **Corporations.** St. Paul, MN: West, 1986.

2071. Hamilton, Robert W. and W. W. Goodrich. "Rulemaking on a Record: A Reply to Professor Hamilton's Comments and Recommendations for Procedural Reform." **Food Drug Cosmetic Law Journal** 26 (December 1971): 627-638.

2072. Hansen, A. W. "FDA Inspection: Preparing for the Inevitable." **Food Drug Cosmetic Law Journal** 36 (December 1981): 641-646.

2073. Harlow, D. R. "FDA's OTC Drug Review: The Development and an Analysis of Some Aspects of the Procedure." **Food Drug Cosmetic Law Journal** 32 (June 1977): 248-274.

2074. Hartmann, Ernest. "L-Tryptophan: A Rational Hypnotic with Clinical Potential." **American Journal of Psychiatry** 134 (April 1977): 366-370.

2075. Harvey, John L. "Current Developments in Food and Drug Administration." **Business Lawyer** 17 (November 1961): 130-136.

2076. Harvey, John L. "Report on the Growth, Organization, Operations and Plans of the Food and Drug Administration." **Business Lawyer** 20 (November

1964): 151-157.

2077. Havender, William R. "Science and Politics of Cyclamate." **Public Interest** 71 (Spring 1983): 17-32.

2078. Havender, William R. and Kathleen A. Meister. **Does Nature Know Best?: Natural Carcinogens in American Food.** Summit, NJ: American Council on Science and Health, 1986.

2079. Hayes, A. H. "Accomplishments at FDA and a Look toward the Future." **Food Drug Cosmetic Law Journal** 38 (January 1983): 64-76.

2080. Hayes, A. H. "Food and Drug Administration's Role in the Canned Salmon Recalls of 1982." **Public Health Reports** 98 (September/October 1983): 412-415.

2081. Hayes, A. H. "Major Regulatory Challenges Confronting the FDA." **Food Drug Cosmetic Law Journal** 36 (November 1981): 565-572.

2082. Heady, Ferrel. "Reports of the Hoover Commission: Welfare and Labor." **Review of Politics** 11 (July 1949): 370-372.

2083. Hellman, Louis M. "A History and Reminiscence of the Office of the Deputy Assistant Secretary for Population Affairs, Department of Health, Education and Welfare, 1969-1977." **Bulletin of the History of Medicine** 56 (Spring 1982): 77-87.

2084. Helm, Lewis M. "HEW: Going Public." **Public Relations Journal** 30 (May 1974): 28-29.

2085. Hickman, D. H. "Advisory Committees at FDA Legal Perspective." **Food Drug Cosmetic Law Journal** 29 (July 1974): 395-408.

2086. Hoar, William P. "Joseph Califano, the $180 Billion Do Gooder." **American Opinion** 22 (February 1979): 7-10.

2087. Hochheiser, Sheldon. "The Evolution of U.S. Food Color Standards, 1913-1919." **Agricultural History** 55 (October 1981): 385-391.

2088. Hoffman, J. E. "FDA's New Forms of Public Hearing-Choosing among the Alternatives." **Food Drug Cosmetic Law Journal** 32 (July 1977): 330-339.

2089. Hornbrook, Mark C. "Medicinal Drugs: Risks and

Regulations." **Current History** 78 (May 1980): 201-205, 223-226.

2090. Hornbrook, Mark C. "Prescription Drugs: Problems for Public Policy." **Current History** 72 (May/June 1977): 215-222, 228-229.

2091. Howell, M. A. and Mark G. Ginsburg. "Evaluation of the Professional and Executive Corps of the Department of Health, Education, and Welfare." **Public Personnel Management** 2 (January 1973): 37-42.

2092. Hunter, Beatrice T. **The Mirage of Safety: Food Additives and Federal Policy.** New York: Scribner's, 1975.

2093. Hutt, Peter B. "Food and Drug Regulation in Transition." **Food Drug Cosmetic Law Journal** 35 (May 1980): 283-299.

2094. Hutt, Peter B. "Future of the Food and Drug Administration." **Food Drug Cosmetic Law Journal** 30 (December 1975): 694-705.

2095. Hyman, P. M. "What Is Happening to OTC Drugs?" **Food Drug Cosmetic Law Journal** 33 (April 1978): 203-215.

2096. Iglehart, John K. "Federal Government as Venture Capitalist: How Does It Fare?" **Milbank Memorial Fund Quarterly** 58 (Fall 1980): 656-666.

2097. Jackson, Charles O. "Muckraking and Consumer Protection: The Case of the 1938 Food, Drug and Cosmetic Act." **Pharmacy History** 13 (1971): 103-110.

2098. Janowitz, Morris. **Social Control of the Welfare State.** New York: Elsevier, 1978.

2099. Janssen, Wallace F. "Food and Drug Administration Celebrates 75 Years of Consumer Protection - An Album from the Archives." **Public Health Reports** 96 (November/December 1981): 487-494.

2100. Jeffrey, Geoffrey M. "Contributions of the U.S. Public Health Service in Tropical Medicine." **Bulletin of the New York Academy of Medicine** 44 (June 1968): 737-746.

2101. Jenkins, Roland E. "A Comparative Study of State Food and Drug Regulatory Programs." Ph.D. dissertation, Ohio State University, 1976.

2102. Johnson, M. P. and Karl Hufbauer. "Sudden Infant Death Syndrome as a Medical Research Problem since 1945." **Social Problems** 30 (October 1982): 65-81.

2103. Kahan, J. S. "Criminal Liability under the Federal Food, Drug, and Cosmetic Act - The Large Corporation Perspective." **Food Drug Cosmetic Law Journal** 36 (June 1981): 314-331.

2104. Kanig, Joseph L. "Advisory Committees: An Expanding Concept in the Field of Drug Regulation: The Perspective of a Liaison Representative." **Food Drug Cosmetic Law Journal** 29 (July 1974): 353-359.

2105. Karnavas, C. A. "Food and Drug Administration and Trademarks." **Trademark Reporter** 54 (July 1964): 492-497.

2106. Karny, G. M. "Regulation of a Genetic Engineering: Less Concern about Frankensteins But Time for Action on Commercial Production." **University of Toledo Law Review** 12 (Summer 1981): 815-868.

2107. Katz, Martin M. and Gerald L. Klerman. "Psychobiology of Depression - NIMH - Clinical Research Branch Collaborative Program." **American Journal of Psychiatry** 136 (January 1979): 49-70.

2108. Kelleher, W. A. "FDA Inspection and Restricted Devices." **Food Drug Cosmetic Law Journal** 33 (July 1978): 331-341.

2109. Kennedy, D. "FDA and the Future." **Food Drug Cosmetic Law Journal** 34 (January 1979): 13-19.

2110. Kennedy, D. "Remarks of the Commissioner of Food and Drugs." **Food Drug Cosmetic Law Journal** 32 (September 1977): 384-391.

2111. King, Richard A. "Economic Research Conference on US Food System Regulation." **American Journal of Agricultural Economics** 61 (November 1979): 836-838.

2112. Kingham, R. F. "Comments on Proposed Revisions of FDA's New Drug Regulations." **Food Drug Cosmetic Law Journal** 38 (January 1983): 58-63.

2113. Kirk, J. Kenneth. "Standard-Setting-FDA." **Food Drug Cosmetic Law Journal** 24 (August 1969): 408-412.

2114. Klerman, Gerald L. "Current Evaluation Research on Mental Health Services." **American Journal of Psychiatry** 13 (July 1974): 783-787.

2115. Kurtz, Howie. "Real Problem with the FDA." **Washington Monthly** 9 (July/August 1977): 59-62.

2116. Kushen, Allan S. "FDA: A Case Study in Administrative Legislation." **Business Lawyer** 24 (November 1968): 261-266.

2117. Land, S. J. "Current Issues Relating to FDA Regulation of New Drugs." **Food Drug Cosmetic Law Journal** 38 (January 1983): 29-34.

2118. Langan, Kenneth J. "Computer Matching Programs: A Threat to Privacy?" **Columbia Journal of Law and Social Problems** 15 (Winter 1979): 143-180.

2119. Larrick, George P. "Decision Making in the Food and Drug Administration." **Food Drug Cosmetic Law Journal** 20 (April 1965): 197-207.

2120. Lasagna, Louis. "Who Will Adopt the Orphan Drugs?" **Regulation** 3 (November/December 1979): 27-32.

2121. Laubach, Gerald D. "Federal Regulation and Pharmaceutical Innovation." **Proceedings of the Academy of Political Science** 33 (1980): 60-90.

2122. Lawer, Neil D. "Relocation of the United States Public Health Service." **Public Administration Review** 32 (January 1972): 43-48.

2123. Lebowitz, Barry D. G. "Management of Research in Aging: A Case Study in Science Policy." **Gerontologist** 19 (April 1979): 151-157.

2124. Leman, Christopher. "Patterns of Policy Development: Social Security in the United States and Canada." **Public Policy** 25 (Spring 1977): 261-291.

2125. Lepkowski, Wil. "The Saccharin Debate: Regulation and the Public Taste." **Hastings Center Report** 7 (December 1977): 5-7.

2126. Levin, Arthur. **The Satisficers.** New York: McCall, 1970.

2127. Levine, Selma M. "Separation of Functions in FDA Administrative Proceedings." **Food Drug Cosmetic Law Journal** 23 (March 1968): 132-141.

2128. Lewis, J. S. "Bupivacaine - Fatal Cardiotoxicity Caused by Obstetric Drug." **Trial** 20 (January 1984): 28-29.

2129. Linderman, T. G. "Freedom of Information - Animal Drug Regulations." **Food Drug Cosmetic Law Journal** 33 (June 1978): 274-280.

2130. Long, J. M. "Cosmetic Industry Concerns Arising from Recent FDA Activities." **Food Drug Cosmetic Law Journal** 35 (June 1980): 392-400.

2131. McFee, T. S. "There's an Asper in Your Future." **Civil Service Journal** 18 (April 1978): 28-30.

2132. McKay, F. E. "Lawyers of the FDA - Yesterday and Today." **Food Drug Cosmetic Law Journal** 30 (October 1975): 621-628.

2133. McNamara, S. H. "FDA Inspection: What You Need to Know to Protect Your Company." **Food Drug Cosmetic Law Journal** 36 (May 1981): 245-257.

2134. McNamara, S. H. "The Food and Drug Administration Over-the-Counter Drug Review - Concerns of the Cosmetic Industry." **Food Drug Cosmetic Law Journal** 38 (October 1983): 289-298.

2135. McNamara, S. H. "New Age of FDA Rule-Making." **Food Drug Cosmetic Law Journal** 31 (July 1976): 393-403.

2136. McNish, Linda C. "Federal Decentralization through Regionalization: The Case of the United States Public Health Service." Ph.D. dissertation, University of Maryland, 1975.

2137. Magar, Michele. "Medicaid Sterilization Rules Violated: Group." **American Bar Association Journal** 67 (October 1981): 1249-1255.

2138. Mamana, Joseph M. "FDA's Obligations under the 1966 Public Information Act." **Food Drug Cosmetic Law Journal** 22 (October 1967): 563-568.

2139. Manser, Marilyn E. and E. A. Fineman. "Impact of the NHSC on the Utilization of Physician Services and on Health Status in Rural Areas." **Journal of Human Resources** 18 (Fall 1983): 521-538.

2140. Mashaw, Jerry L. **Bureaucratic Justice: Managing Social Security Disability Claims.** New Haven, CT: Yale University Press, 1983.

2141. Mashaw, Jerry L. **Social Security Hearings and Appeals: A Study of the Social Security Administration Hearing System.** Lexington, MA: Lexington Books, 1978.

2142. Mason, Malcolm S. "Current Developments in Federal Grant Law." **Public Contracts Newsletter** 18 (Fall 1982): 15-18.

2143. Mason, Malcolm S. "Openness in Government: HHS Still Won't Explain." **Public Contracts Newsletter** 18 (Winter 1983): 6-8.

2144. Matarazzo, J. D. "Behavioral Health and Behavioral Medicine: Frontiers for a New Health Psychology." **American Psychologist** 35 (September 1980): 807-817.

2145. Merrill, Richard A. "FDA and Effects of Substantive Rules." **Food Drug Cosmetic Law Journal** 35 (May 1980): 270-282.

2146. Merrill, Richard A. "Risk-Benefit Decisionmaking by the Food and Drug Administration." **George Washington Law Review** 45 (August 1977): 994-1012.

2147. Meyer, Harry M. "Food and Drug Administration Responses to the Challenges of AIDS." **Public Health Reports** 98 (July/August 1983): 320-323.

2148. Meyers, Earl L. "FDA Role in the Labeling of Blood Bank Products." **Food Drug Cosmetic Law Journal** 17 (February 1962): 169-174.

2149. Michael, Jerrold M. **Swimming Pools: Disease Control through Proper Design and Operation.** Atlanta: Department of Health, Education and Welfare, 1959.

2150. Michael, Jerrold M. and Thomas R. Bender. "Fighting Smallpox on the Texas Border: An Episode from PHS's Proud Past." **Public Health Reports** 99 (November/December 1984): 579-582.

2151. Miles, Rufus E. **The Department of Health, Education and Welfare.** New York: Praeger, 1974.

2152. Mills, R. "Justice Delayed and Denied: HEW and Northern School Desegregation." **Civil Rights Digest** 7 (Fall 1974): 10-21.

2153. Mintz, Morton. **By Prescription Only.** Boston: Beacon Press, 1967.

2154. Mintz, Morton. **The Therapeutic Nightmare.** Boston: Houghton Mifflin, 1965.

2155. Moore, T. "Food Chemicals: Just a Slight Taste of Recession." **Purchasing** 93 (August 5, 1982): 50-55.

2156. Morey, R. S. "FDA Publicity against Consumer Products - Time for Statutory Revitalization?" **Business Lawyer** 30 (November 1974): 165-178.

2157. Morgareidge, Kenneth. "Getting FDA Clearance for Food Additives." **Food and Drug Cosmetic Law Journal** 19 (July 1964): 364-373.

2158. Moscorice, Ira and R. Rosenblatt. "Viability of Mid-Level Practitioners in Isolated Rural Communities." **American Journal of Public Health** 69 (May 1979): 503-505.

2159. Mullins, Nicholas C. "The Structure of an Elite: The Advisory Structure of the U.S. Public Health Service." **Social Studies** 2 (January 1972): 3-30.

2160. Mushkin, Selma J. **Services to People.** Washington, DC: Georgetown University, 1973.

2161. Musto, David F. "Whatever Happened to Community Mental Health?" **Public Interest** 39 (Spring 1975): 53-79.

2162. Neal, Harry E. **The Protectors: The Story of the Food and Drug Administration.** New York: Messner, 1968.

2163. Necheles, Thomas. "Standards of Medical Care: How Does an Innovative Medical Procedure become Accepted?" **Law, Medicine and Health Care** 10 (February 1982): 15-18.

2164. Neely, Alfred S. "FDA Inspectional Authority - Is There an Outer Limit?" **Food Drug Cosmetic Law Journal** 33 (December 1978): 710-725.

2165. Neff, Diana R. "Look-alike Drugs: Eliminating a Profitable Loophole in Existing Drug Laws." **Dickinson Law Review** 87 (Fall 1982): 155-191.

2166. Neubauer, Deane and Richard Pratt. "The Second Public Health Revolution: A Critical Appraisal." **Journal of Health Politics, Policy and Law** 6 (Summer 1981): 205-228.

2167. Nightingale, Stuart L. "Emerging Technologies and FDA Policy Formulation: The Impact of Government Regulation on Developing Drugs from New Technologies." **Food Drug Cosmetic Law Journal** 37 (April 1982): 212-221.

2168. Nightingale, Stuart L. "Laetrile: The Regulatory Challenge of an Unproven Remedy." **Public Health Reports** 99 (July/August 1984): 333-338.

2169. Norcross, M. A. "Animal Drug Control: The Challenge of Coordination - An FDA Intraagency Perspective." **Food Drug Cosmetic Law Journal** 38 (April 1983): 141-146.

2170. Norton, D. B. "Constitutionality of Warrantless Inspections by the Food and Drug Administration." **Food Drug Cosmetic Law Journal** 35 (January 1980): 25-43.

2171. O'Gara, Geoffrey. "Where Are the Children? The New Data Game at HEW." **Washington Monthly** 11 (June 1979): 35-38.

2172. Ogilvy, J. P. "Road Map to Adjudications under the Medical-Vocational Guidelines." **Trial** 19 (August 1983): 76-79.

2173. O'Keefe, Daniel F. "Legal Issues in Food Establishment Inspections." **Food Drug Cosmetic Law Journal** 33 (March 1978): 121-133.

2174. O'Keefe, Harold F. "Food and Drug Administration Industry Information Programs." **Food Drug Cosmetic Law Journal** 21 (January 1966): 52-56.

2175. Okura, K. P. "Mobilizing in Response to a Major Disaster." **Community Mental Health Journal** 11 (Summer 1975): 136-144.

2176. O'Reilly, James T. "Role of Corporate Counsel in Defense of FDA Court Actions." **Food Drug Cosmetic Law Journal** 35 (June 1980): 370-375.

2177. Ostergard, Donald R. "Potential for Paramedical Personnel in Family Planning: An Analysis Based on the Department of Health, Education, and Welfare 5-Year Plan for Family Planning Services." **American Journal of Public Health** 64 (January 1974): 27-31.

2178. Ozawa, Martha N. "Analysis of HEW's Proposals on Social Security." **Social Service Review** 54 (March 1980): 92-107.

2179. Pacht, Arline. "Adams Case: An HEW Perspective." **Howard Law Journal** 22 (1979): 427-443.

2180. Palley, Howard A. "Policy Formulation in Health: Some Considerations of Governmental Constraints on Pricing in the Health Delivery System." **American Behavioral Scientist** 17 (March/April 1974): 572-584.

2181. Peltzman, Samuel. "The Benefits and Costs of New Drug Regulation." In **Regulating New Drugs,** edited by Richard L. Landau, pp. 113-211. Chicago: Center for Policy Study, University of Chicago, 1973.

2182. Perkins, R. B. "New Federal Department of Health, Education, and Welfare." **Harvard Law School Bulletin** 5 (October 1954): 12-13.

2183. Peskoe, M. P. "Submissions and Petitions under the FDA's Procedural Regulations." **Food Drug Cosmetic Law Journal** 32 (May 1977): 216-225.

2184. Pilot, Larry R. "FDA Update." **Food Drug Cosmetic Law Journal** 32 (March 1977): 113-120.

2185. Prindle, Richard. "The Antismoking Program of the Public Health Service." **Bulletin of the New York Academy of Medicine** 44 (December 1968): 1514-1520.

2186. Radin, Beryl A. "Leaving It to the States." **Public Welfare** 40 (Summer 1982): 16-23.

2187. Rankin, Winston B. "FDA's Organization: The Reasons for Change." **Food Drug Cosmetic Law Journal** 22 (December 1967): 660-666.

2188. Rebell, Michael A. **Equality and Education: Federal Civil Rights Enforcement in the New York School System.** Princeton, NJ: Princeton University Press, 1985.

2189. Regens, James L. "Risk Assessment in the Policy-Making Process: Environmental Health and Safety Protection." **Public Administration Review** 43 (March/April 1983): 137-145.

2190. Roberts, Russell M. "Faithful Execution of the FOI Act: One Executive Branch Experience." **Public Administration Review** 39 (July 1979): 318-323.

2191. Rose, Marilyn G. "Challenging the Relocation and Closure of Inner-City Hospitals - Analysis,

Methodologies and Limitations." **Clearinghouse Review** 16 (June 19-82): 102-117.

2192. Rosenkranz, Eric J. "FDA Regulation of Environmental Contaminants after Community Nutrition Institute v. Young." **Food Drug Cosmetic Law Journal** 41 (July 1986): 330-383.

2193. Rosner, David and Gerald Markowitz. "Research for Advocacy: Federal Occupational Safety and Health Policies during the New Deal." **Journal of Social History** 18 (Spring 1985): 365-381.

2194. Rosner, George. "Criminal Liability for Deceiving the Food and Drug Administration." **Food Drug Cosmetic Law Journal** 20 (August 1965): 446-468.

2195. Rothman, David J. "Were Tuskegee and Willowbrook Studies in Nature?" **Hastings Center Report** 12 (April 1982): 5-7.

2196. Rothschild, Donald P. "FDA's Regulations - A Model for the Future?" **Food Drug Cosmetic Law Journal** 32 (August 1977): 344-353.

2197. Rothschild, Louis. "Newest Regulatory Agency in Washington." **Food Drug Cosmetic Law Journal** 33 (February 1978): 86-93.

2198. Saber, F. A. "Laetrile: Is It Really a Matter of Free Choice?" **American Journal of Public Health** 67 (September 1977): 871-872.

2199. Scarlett, T. "FDA's Regulatory Proposals for the Management of Advisory Committees." **Food Drug Cosmetic Law Journal** 30 (August 1975): 503-508.

2200. Schaefer, George F. "Limited Guardianship: Additional Protection for Mentally Disabled Research Subjects Used in Biomedical and Behavioral Research." **Forum** 16 (Spring 1981): 796-824.

2201. Schmeckebier, Laurence F. **The Public Health Service: Its History, Activities and Organization.** Baltimore: Johns Hopkins University Press, 1923.

2202. Schmidt, Alice M. "FDA - Social Trend and Regulatory Reform." **Food Drug Cosmetic Law Journal** 31 (November 1976): 605-615.

2203. Schmidt, Alice M. "FDA Today: Critics, Congress and Consumerism." **Food Drug Cosmetic Law Journal** 29 (November 1974): 575-584.

2204. Schmidt, Alice M. "Food and Drug Administration's Enforcement Policy." **Food Drug Cosmetic Law Journal** 30 (December 1975): 687-693.

2205. Schweiker, Richard S. "Strategies for Disease Prevention and Health Promotion in the Department of Health and Human Services." **Public Health Reports** 97 (May/June 1982): 196-198.

2206. Schweiker, Richard S. "Turning around the World's Third-Largest Budget: There Is No Chapter 11 for a Government Department, So Here's How Runaway Growth Was Stopped at Health and Human Services." **Directors and Boards** 7 (Fall 1982): 14-21.

2207. Shore, Warren. **Social Security: The Fraud in Your Future.** New York: Macmillan, 1975.

2208. Shupack, R. A. "Inspectional Process: A Statutory Overview." **Food Drug Cosmetic Law Journal** 33 (December 1978): 697-709.

2209. Silverglade, B. A. "The Food Drug Administration's Review of Regulations Pursuant to Cost-Benefit Requirements of Executive Order 12, 291." **Food Drug Cosmetic Law Journal** 39 (July 1984): 332-341.

2210. Skelley, Ben D. "Implementing Federal Health Manpower Distribution Policy: The Performance of the National Health Service Corps Program." Ph.D. dissertation, University of Georgia, 1980.

2211. Skitol, R. A. "Defense of a False Advertising Case." **Food Drug Cosmetic Law Journal** 33 (February 1978): 48-58.

2212. Smith, D. J. "Detention and Seizure of Imports by the Food and Drug Administration." **Food Drug Cosmetic Law Journal** 33 (December 1978): 726-733.

2213. Smith, Roland B. "An Evaluation of the Connecticut Food and Drug Commission with Special Reference to the Supervision of Drug and Cosmetic Advertising and Labeling." Ph.D. dissertation, Columbia University, 1959.

2214. Sobel, Solomon. "The Role of Epidemiology in the Regulation of Oral Contraceptives." **Public Health Reports** 99 (July/August 1984): 350-354.

2215. Spence, G. K. "FDA Trade Secret Procedures and Standards." **Food Drug Cosmetic Law Journal** 35

(June 1980): 362-369.

2216. Spiker, Earl G. and P. Gordon Stafford. "A Look at FDA's New Rules of Practice - And Problems Still Unsolved." **Food and Drug Cosmetic Law Journal** 21 (September 1966): 448-457.

2217. Spiller, R. M. "How to Handle an FDA Inspection." **Food Drug Cosmetic Law Journal** 33 (March 1978): 101-108.

2218. Stang, Alan. "Carter Socialism in Housing, Health, Education, and Public Welfare." **American Opinion** 23 (July 1980): 19-23.

2219. Stimson, R. A. "FDA's Standards Policy." **Food Drug Cosmetic Law Journal** 35 (May 1980): 300-305.

2220. Stribling, J. H. "Regulation of Food Labeling and Advertising by the Food and Drug Administration." **Food Drug Cosmetic Law Journal** 33 (January 1978): 4-11.

2221. Strosberg, Martin A. and Joseph S. Wholey. "Evaluability Assessment: From Theory to Practice in the Department of Health and Human Services." **Public Administration Review** 43 (January/February 1983): 66-71.

2222. Sturniolo, E. J. "FDA's Sterilization Compliance Program." **Food Drug Cosmetic Law Journal** 36 (September 1981): 460-468.

2223. Summerson, William H. "The Role of Scientific Research in the Food and Drug Administration." **Food Drug Cosmetic Law Journal** 20 (July 1963): 427-432.

2224. Swain, Martha. "Pat Harrison and the Social Security Act of 1935." **Southern Quarterly** 15 (October 1976): 1-14.

2225. Swanson, J. W. "How to Handle an FDA Inspection - The Investigator's View." **Food Drug Cosmetic Law Journal** 33 (March 1978): 109-115.

2226. Swiss, James E. "Establishing a Management System: The Interaction of Power Shifts and Personality under Federal MBO." **Public Administration Review** 43 (January/February 1983): 66-71.

2227. Talbot, Bernard. "Development of the National Institutes of Health Guidelines for Recombinant

DNA Research." **Public Health Reports** 98 (July/August 1983): 361-368.

2228. Talbot, Bernard. "Introduction to Recombinant FDA Research, Development and Evolution of the NIH Guidelines, and Proposed Legislation." **University of Toledo Law Review** 12 (Summer 1981): 804-814.

2229. Taylor, M. R. "Seizures and Injunctions: Their Role in FDA's Enforcement Program." **Food Drug Cosmetic Law Journal** 33 (November 1978): 596-606.

2230. Temin, Peter. "Government Actions in Times of Crisis: Lessons from the History of Drug Regulation." **Journal of Social History** 18 (Spring 1985): 433-438.

2231. Temin, Peter. "Origin of Compulsory Drug Prescriptions." **Journal of Law and Economics** 22 (April 1979): 91-105.

2232. Temin, Peter. "Technology, Regulation, and Market Structure in the Modern Pharmaceutical Industry." **Bell Journal of Economics** 10 (Autumn 1979): 429-446.

2233. Terrell, John U. **The United States Department of Health, Education and Welfare: A Story of Protecting and Preserving Human Resources.** New York: Duell, Sloan and Pearce, 1965.

2234. Thompson, Frank J. "Bureaucratic Discretion and the National Health Service Corps." **Political Science Quarterly** 97 (Fall 1982): 427-445.

2235. Thompson, Frank J. **Health Policy and the Bureaucracy.** Cambridge, MA: MIT Press, 1981.

2236. Thompson, Gary E. "Administering Social Reform in a Federal System: The Case of the Office of Civil Rights." Ph.D. dissertation, North Texas State University, 1974.

2237. Thompson, T. "Black Colleges and Health Program Development." **Crisis** 84 (November 1977): 443-445.

2238. Turner, James S. **The Chemical Feast: The Ralph Nader Study Group Report of Food Protection and the Food and Drug Administration.** New York: Grossman, 1970.

2239. Vandenbos, Gary R. and W. F. Batchelor. "Health Personnel Requirements, Service Delivery, and National Policy: A Conversation with Thomas D. Hatch." **American Psychologist** 38 (December 1983): 1360-1365.

2240. Walden, J. R. "FDA with a Capital L." **Food Drug Cosmetic Law Journal** 31 (December 1976): 649-655.

2241. Wasserman, Bruce P. "Employee High Blood Pressure Program of National Institutes of Health." **Public Health Reports** 97 (March/April 1982): 122-126.

2242. Weber, Gustavus A. **The Food, Drug and Insecticide Administration: Its History, Activities and Organization.** Baltimore: Johns Hopkins University Press, 1928.

2243. Weeda, David F. "FDA Seizure and Injunction Actions: Judicial Means of Protecting the Public Health." **Food Drug Cosmetic Law Journal** 35 (February 1980): 112-121.

2244. Wentworth, D. N. "An Evaluation of the Social Security Administration Master Beneficiary Record File and the National Death Index in the Ascertainment of Vital Status." **American Journal of Public Health** 73 (November 1983): 1270-1274.

2245. White, Catherine, "The Ability of a Bureaucracy to Respond to Public Policy as Expressed in Legislation: The Bureau of Child Welfare and the 1962 Amendments to the Social Security Act: A Case Study." D.P.A., New York University, 1973.

2246. Wilkinson, Charles B. and V. I. Reus. "Examination of the Federal Psychiatric Training Grant Peer Review Process." **American Journal of Psychiatry** 134 (June 1977): 637-641.

2247. Williams, Carla S. "FDA's Consumer Consultant Program." **Food Drug Cosmetic Law Journal** 16 (September 1961): 569-575.

2248. Williams, James R. "The Social Security Administration's Policy of Non-Acquiescence." **Northern Kentucky Law Review** 12 (1985): 253-265.

2249. Wing, Kenneth R. "The Community Service Obligation of Hill-Burton Health Facilities." **Boston College Law Review** 23 (May 1982): 577-632.

2250. Witti, Fritz P. and M. I. Goldberg. "National Institutes of Health and Research into the Acquired Immune Deficiency Syndrome." **Public Health Reports** 98 (July/August 1983): 312-318.

2251. Wlodkowski, Bonita A. "Local Response and Federal Commitment: Implementation of Section 1513 (E) of the National Health Planning and Resources Development Act of 1974." Ph.D. dissertation, Columbia University, 1980.

2252. Wolfe, Margaret R. "The Agricultural Experiment Station and Food and Drug Control: Another Look at Kentucky Progressivism, 1898-1916." **Filson Club Historical Quarterly** 49 (October 1975): 323-338.

2253. Yessian, Mark R. "The Generalist Perspective in the HEW Bureaucracy: An Account from the Field." **Public Administration Review** 40 (March/April 1980): 138-149.

2254. Yingling, G. L. "Effect of the FDA's OTC Drug Review Program on the Cosmetic Industry." **Food Drug Cosmetic Law Journal** 33 (February 1978): 78-85.

2255. Zervos, C. and Joseph V. Rodricks. "FDA 's Ban of DES in Meat Production." **American Statistician** 36 (August 1982): 278-283.

Chapter 8. Department of Housing and Urban Development

2256. Bloom, Howard S. and Susan Bloom. "Household Participation in the Section 8 Existing Housing Program: Evaluating a Multistage Selection Process." **Evaluation Review** 5 (June 1981): 325-340.

2257. Breckenfeld, G. "Bottling Control for Fannie Mae's Billions." **Fortune** 97 (January 30, 1978): 100-101.

2258. Broadhurst, Diane D. and B. Gross. "Model Law That Isn't." **Public Welfare** 40 (Spring 1982): 22-27.

2259. Bryan, Jack. "Consolidated Supply Program: HUD Brings Together Suppliers, LHA's for Mutual Benefits of Quantity Purchasing." **Journal of Housing** 33 (August 1976): 365-367.

2260. Burkhardt, R. "Aviation on the Ground." **Airline Management and Marketing** 1 (November 1969): 77-78.

2261. Bylsma, Michael S. "Is the U.S. Committed to Fair Housing? Enforcement of the Fair Housing Act Remains a Crucial Problem." **Catholic University Law Review** 29 (Spring 1980): 641-668.

2262. Calhoun, Sally J. "Attacking the Rent Supplement Program: HUD's Attempt to Achieve Economic Mixture among Tenants." **Urban Law Annual** 19 (1980): 255-267.

2263. Cannon, M. C. "TPP Turns Around a Problem Project in St. Paul." **Journal of Housing** 36 (March 1979): 146-147.

2264. Case, Fred E. "Fiscal Aspects of Federal Urban Housing Programs." Ph.D. dissertation, Indiana University, 1951.

2265. Chickadel, Veronica. "NAHRO TPP Services Program Reports First Year Accomplishments, Plans for Second Year Activities." **Journal of Housing** 33 (December 1976): 551-553.

2266. Clark, Gordon L. **Interregional Migration, National Policy and Social Justice.** Totowa, NJ: Rowan and Allanheld, 1983.

2267. Colarulli, Guy C. "The Relationship between Housing Policy and Interest Groups: Federal Housing Policy and the Poor." Ph.D. dissertation, American University, 1977.

2268. Cooper, Aileen. "HUD Realigns Area Offices as Accommodation to Housing and Community Development Act of 1974." **Journal of Housing** 32 (January 1975): 15-18.

2269. Coven, Irving J. "Section 8 Existing Housing Program: How Worcester Makes It Work: What Its Success Has Been." **Journal of Housing** 34 (February 1977): 84-87.

2270. Cowan, Mark. "Two Groups Lodge Impoundment Suit over Solar Bank Funds." **Solar Law Reporter** 3 (January/February 1982): 741-742.

2271. Daniel, Edwin C. "What's the Best Way to Handle Foreclosed Properties? HUD Seeks the Answer as the Default and Foreclosure Figures Climb." **Journal of Housing** 32 (July 1975): 323-326.

2272. De Hancock, Tila M. "Urban Problems: International Perspective Can Strengthen and Aid Local Approaches." **Journal of Housing** 38 (March 1981): 148-151.

2273. Dommel, Paul R. "Social Targeting in Community Development." **Political Science Quarterly** 95 (Fall 1980): 465-478.

2274. Doyle, Gerard F. and James D. Backman. "Debarment after Gonzalez v. Freeman." **Public Contract Newsletter** 16 (March 1981): 2-5.

2275. Evans, Alice F. "NAHRO Member Arthur F. Evans, Executive Director, San Francisco Redevelopment Agency, Addresses Open Letter to the Secretary of Housing and Urban Development." **Journal of Housing** 32 (November 1975): 502-503.

2276. Ewers, Joseph R. "Federal Housing Programs, 1960-

1970." Ph.D. dissertation, Indiana University, 1960.

2277. Fisher, Robert M. "Economic Aspects of the Federal Low-Rent Public Housing Program under the United States Housing Act of 1937, as Amended." Ph.D. dissertation, Columbia University, 1958.

2278. Fost, Norman. "Putting Hospitals on Notice." **Hastings Center Report** 12 (August 1982): 5-8.

2279. Fraser, Stephen A. "Citizen Participation in Decision-Making by Federal Agencies: Selective Service System, Bureau of Land Management, Office of Economic Opportunity, Department of Housing and Urban Development." Ph.D. dissertation, Johns Hopkins University, 1969.

2280. Frieden, Bernard J. "Housing Allowances: An Experiment That Worked." **Public Interest** 59 (Spring 1980): 15-35.

2281. Fuerst, J. and R. Williams. "How to Destroy a Good Housing Program." **Social Policy** 13 (Spring 1983): 56-58.

2282. Gazzolo, Dorothy. "H. R. Crawford Looks back on Year as HUD Assistant Secretary for Housing Management." **Journal of Housing** 32 (February 1974): 66-68.

2283. Gifford, K. Dun. "Department of Housing and Urban Development." **Historical Preservation** 18 (November/December 1966): 234-241.

2284. Gilbert, Neil and Harry Specht. "Picking Winners: Federal Discretion and Local Experience as Bases for Planning Grant Allocation." **Public Administration Review** 34 (November 1974): 565-574.

2285. Gleichman, Ted. "U.S. Judge Rejects State's Demand for HUD Solar Standards." **Solar Law Reporter** 3 (May/June 1981): 5-6.

2286. Greenlees, J. W. "Sample Truncation in FHA Data: Implications for Home Purchase Indexes." **Southern Economic Journal** 48 (April 1982): 917-931.

2287. Harris, Patricia R. "New Look at HUD." **Black Scholar** 9 (October 1977): 15-21.

2288. Herzog, T. N. "How HUD Constructs a Survivorship

Schedule." **Mortgage Banker** 41 (May 1981): 55-58.

2289. Horn, Harold E. "HUD Will Face Challenging Task." **Public Management** 48 (January 1966): 1-3.

2290. Howell, Pamela J. "Court Asked to Halt Conversion to Separate Metering in HUD Housing." **Solar Law Reporter** 3 (November/December 1981): 587-588.

2291. Huegy, Charles W. "Commercial Bank Holdings of Mortgages Insured by the Federal Housing Administration." Ph.D. dissertation, Indiana University, 1968.

2292. Humphrey, Hubert H. "To Aid the Small City." **National Civic Review** 50 (December 1961): 582-586.

2293. Ink, Dwight A. "Department of Housing and Urban Development - Building a New Federal Department." **Law and Contemporary Problems** 32 (Summer 1967): 375-388.

2294. Ink, Dwight A. "Establishing the New Department of Housing and Urban Development." **Public Administration Review** 27 (September 1967): 224-228.

2295. Jackson, Byran O. "The Linkage between Implementation Processes and Policy Outcomes: An Analysis of HUD's Administrative Agency Experiment." Ph.D. dissertation, University of Michigan, 1982.

2296. Jackson, Kenneth T. "Federal Subsidy and the Suburban Dream: The First Quarter-Century of Government Intervention in the Housing Market." **Records of the Columbia Historical Society** 50 (1980): 421-451.

2297. Jackson, Kenneth T. "Race, Ethnicity, and Real Estate Appraisal: The Home Owners Loan Corporation and the Federal Housing Administration." **Journal of Urban History** 6 (August 1980): 419-452.

2298. Jackson, S. C. "HUD Projects Spruce up Small Towns to Stem Rural Exodus." **Industrial Development** 138 (July 1969): 16-18.

2299. Khadduri, Jill and Raymond J. Struyk. "Improving Section 8 Rental Assistance: Translating Evaluation into Policy." **Evaluation Review** 5 (April 1981): 189-206.

2300. Kramer, Douglas J. "Protecting the Urban Environment from the Federal Government." **Urban Affairs Quarterly** 9 (March 1974): 359-368.

2301. Krechter, R. G. "LS-MFD: Land Sales Mean Full Disclosure." **Real Property, Probate and Trust Journal** 4 (Spring 1969): 1-5.

2302. Krooth, David and Jeffrey G. Spragens. "The Interest Assistance Programs - A Successful Approach of Housing Problems." **George Washington Law Review** 39 (May 1971): 789-817.

2303. Landrieu, Moon and Jane L. McGrew. "HUD: The Federal Catalyst for Urban Revitalization." **Tulane Law Review** 55 (April 1981): 637-650.

2304. Lazin, Frederick A. "Federal Low-Income Housing Assistance Programs and Racial Segregation: Leased Public Housing." **Public Policy** 24 (Summer 1976): 337-360.

2305. LeGates, Richard T. **Can the Federal Welfare Bureaucracies Control Their Programs: The Case of HUD and Urban Renewal.** Berkeley: Institute of Urban and Regional Development, University of California, 1972.

2306. Lentz, Peggy A. "High-Priority Research Areas in HUD's Office of Policy Development and Research." **Professional Geographer** 32 (May 1980): 205-208.

2307. Levin, Larry. "Defining the Relevant Area in Section 8 Site Selection." **Urban Law Annual** 19 (1980): 303-318.

2308. Levine, George D. "Administration of Federal Housing Policy by an Area Office of the Department of Housing and Urban Development: A Case Study." **Connecticut Bar Journal** 48 (September 1974): 279-304.

2309. Loomis, D. O. "HUD Secretary Pierce: In the GOP Tradition." **Housing** 59 (February 1981): 9-10.

2310. Lynn, James T. and D. O. Meeker. "HUD Secretary Lynn Tell NAHRO Members Like It Is." **Journal of Housing** 31 (March 1974): 113-119.

2311. Macey, John P. **Publicly Provided and Assisted Housing in the U.S.A.: Report on HUD's Housing Management Policies and Programs.** Washington, DC: Urban Institute, 1972.

2312. McClaughry, J. "Troubled Dream: The Life and Times of Section 235 of the National Housing Act." **Loyola University Law Journal** (Chicago) 6 (Winter 1975): 1-45.

2313. McFarland, M. Carter. **Federal Government and Urban Problems: HUD: Successes, Failures, and the Fate of Our Cities.** Boulder, CO: Westview, 1978.

2314. McFarlin, Emma D. and Thomas Vitek. "The Graduated Payment Mortgage: A Huge Success in HUD's Region IX." **Federal Home Loan Bank Board Journal** 13 (January 1980): 14-17.

2315. McGrew, Jane L. and M. Landrieu. "HUD: The Federal Catalyst for Urban Revitalization." **Tulane Law Review** 55 (April 1981): 637-650.

2316. McGrew, Jane L. and John C. Bates. "Code Enforcement: The Federal Role." **Urban Lawyer** 14 (Winter 1982): 1-29.

2317. McKay, Nan. "Section 8 Is Working Well in Dakota County." **Journal of Housing** 33 (June 1976): 272-273.

2318. Maffin, Robert W. "Behind the Fiscal Year 1975 Budget of the USA." **Journal of Housing** 31 (February 1974): 57-65.

2319. Mara, Gerald and David Engel. "Institutional Barriers to Solar Energy: Early HUD Demonstration Experiences." **Solar Law Reporter** 1 (March/April 1980): 1094-1117.

2320. Mitchell, Helen. "Missouri Reports Year's Developments in Section 8/Section 515 Rural Program through Areawide Authorities." **Journal of Housing** 33 (December 1976): 541-543.

2321. Mitchell, Helen. "Section 8, Farmers Home Administration Programs Combined to Provide Rural Housing in Missouri." **Journal of Housing** 32 (November 1975): 494-498.

2322. Murray, Michael P. "An Econometric Analysis of Benefits to Tenants in Alternative Federal Housing Programs." Ph.D. dissertation, Iowa State University, 1974.

2323. Nathan, Richard P. and P. R. Dommel. "Federal-Local Relations under Block Grants." **Political Science Quarterly** 93 (Fall 1978): 421-442.

2324. Nenno, Mary K. "HUD 1977 Fiscal Year Budget." **Journal of Housing** 33 (February 1976): 71-77.

2325. Nenno, Mary K. "1980 HUD Budget Proposal Reflects the President's Lean Look but Would Sustain Existing Programs." **Journal of Housing** 36 (April 1979): 191-196.

2326. Nenno, Mary K. "President's HUD Budget: A Blueprint for the Future." **Journal of Housing** 39 (March/April 1982): 43-50.

2327. Nenno, Mary K. "Reagan's Plans for HUD: More than Shortterm Cuts." **Journal of Housing** 43 (May/June 1986): 95-100.

2328. Nye, P. "Interview with Geno Borani: America Has Cultural Indigestion, Says a Neighborhood Priest Turned Assistant Secretary." **Nation's Cities** 16 (February 1978): 5-8.

2329. Olson, Edgar O. and William J. Reeder. "Does HUD Pay Too Much for Section 8 Existing Housing?" **Land Economics** 57 (May 1981): 243-251.

2330. Ormiston, George. "Management Innovations for Indian Housing: HUD Demonstration Program Seeks to Provide Training, Assistance." **Journal of Housing** 34 (July 1977): 293-295.

2331. Padgett, John F. "Hierarchy and Ecological Control in Federal Budgetary Decision Making." **American Journal of Sociology** 87 (July 1981): 75-129.

2332. Patterson, Richard J. "Federal Regulation of the Real Estate Settlement (Closing) Process: HUD's Report to Congress." **Real Property, Probate and Trust Journal** 16 (Winter 1981): 806-818.

2333. Petty, Ann E. "Rising Housing Costs Are Due Partly to Government Controls, According to HUD Task Force Report." **Journal of Housing** 35 (August 1978): 412-413.

2334. Plott, Charles R. "Some Organizational Influence on Urban Renewal Decisions." **American Economic Review** 58 (May 1968): 306-321, 332-340.

2335. Polikoff, A. "On Gautreaux." **Center Magazine** 9 (September 1976): 28-29.

2336. Proctor, Mary. "Keys to Section 8 Success Provided by Award-Winning PHA's." **Journal of Housing** 34 (January 1977): 28-29.

2337. Radin, Beryl A. "Leaving It to the States." **Public Welfare** 40 (Summer 1982): 16-23.

2338. Rasch, Ruth L. "Federal Housing Policy: Its Aims and Its Accomplishments." Ph.D. dissertation, Johns Hopkins University, 1962.

2339. Reichley, A. James. "George Romney Is Running Hard at HUD." **Fortune** 82 (December 1970): 100-103.

2340. Rivlin, Alice M. **The Planning, Programming, and Budgeting System in the Department of Health, Education, and Welfare: Some Lessons from Experience.** Washington, DC: Brookings Institution, 1969.

2341. Robinson, J. W. "11th Chair: The Role of FHA in the New Department of Housing and Urban Development." **Title News** 45 (January 1966): 2-4.

2342. Rosenberry, Katharine. "The Effect of the Endangered Species Act on Housing Construction." **Hastings Law Journal** 33 (January 1982): 551-582.

2343. Rosenthal, Donald B. "Neighborhood Strategy Areas: HUD's New Initiative in Neighborhood Revitalization." **Journal of Housing** 35 (March 1978): 120-121.

2344. Ross, I. "Carla Hills Gives the Woman's Touch a Brand-New Meaning." **Fortune** 92 (December 1975): 120-123.

2345. Saltman, Juliet. "Housing Discrimination: Policy Research, Methods and Results." **Annals of the American Academy of Political and Social Science** 441 (January 1979): 186-196.

2346. Sanders, Barrett. "Condominium Legal Requirements of the Secondary Mortgage Market." **Florida Bar Journal** 55 (November 1981): 733-735.

2347. Schweiker, Richard S. "Strategies for Disease Prevention and Health Promotion in the Department of Health and Human Services." **Public Health Reports** 97 (May/June 1982): 196-198.

2348. Shalala, Donna E. "Using Financial Management to Avert Financial Crisis." **Governmental Finance** 8 (December 1979): 17-21.

2349. Silverman, Edward C. "Federal and HUD Budgets for Fiscal Year 1976: An Analysis." **Journal of**

Housing 32 (March 1975): 107-111.

2350. Skinner, Allene J. "Women Consumers, Women Professionals: Their Roles and Problems in Housing and Community Development Are Concerns of Special HUD Office." **Journal of Housing** 35 (May 1978): 228-230.

2351. Smartt, John M. "CDBG Independent Audit: What to Expect: How to Maximize Benefits." **Journal of Housing** 34 (April 1977): 177-179.

2352. Strange, G. L. "HUD Registrations: The Good, the Bad, and the Merely Bureaucratic." **Industrial Development and Manufacturer's Record** 144 (September/October 1975): 16-18.

2353. Thornton, Allan F. "The Economic Impact of Federal Housing Administration Insurance Programs." Ph.D. dissertation, American University, 1965.

2354. Topping, Mark B. "The Emergence of Federal Public Housing: Atlanta's Techwood Project." **American Journal of Economics and Sociology** 32 (October 1973): 379-386.

2355. Trautman, L. "HUD Audit Guide: Its History, Its Purpose and Its Requirements." **Mortgage Banker** 38 (February 1978): 51-56.

2356. Trend, M. G. "On the Reconciliation of Qualitative and Quantitative Analyses: A Case Study." **Human Organization** 37 (Winter 1978): 345-355.

2357. Warren, Charles R. and L. R. Aronson. "Sharing Management Capacity: Is There a Federal Responsibility?" **Public Administration Review** 41 (May/June 1981): 381-387.

2358. Washburn, Robert M. "The Role of Tax Syndications in Housing: A Policy Perspective." **Urban Law and Policy** 5 (March 1982): 1-22.

2359. Welfeld, Irving H. "Courts and Desegregated Housing: The Meaning of the Gautreaux Case." **Public Interest** 45 (Fall 1976): 123-135.

2360. Wheaton, William L. C. "The Evolution of Federal Housing Programs." Ph.D. dissertation, University of Chicago, 1954.

2361. Wheaton, William L. C. "New Cabinet Post?" **National Civic Review** 48 (December 1959): 574-578.

2362. Whitney, Scott C. "Standing and Remedies Available to the Department of Housing and Urban Development under the Interstate Land Sales Full Disclosure Act." **George Mason University Law Review** 6 (Fall 1983): 171-221.

2363. Wilcox, Ron. "HUD Requires Energy Statement from Developers." **Solar Law Reporter** 2 (March/April 1981): 1034-1039.

2364. Willman, John B. **The Department of Housing and Urban Development.** New York: Praeger, 1967.

Chapter 9.
Department of the Interior

2365. Abbott, Carl. "The Active Force: Enos A. Mills and the National Park Movement." **Colorado Magazine** 56 (Winter/Spring 1979): 56-73.

2366. Adams, David W. "Schooling the Hopi: Federal Indian Policy Writ Small, 1887-1917." **Pacific Historical Review** 48 (August 1979): 335-356.

2367. Alexander, Thomas G. **A Clash of Interests: Interior Department and Mountain West, 1863-96.** Provo, UT: Brigham Young University Press, 1977.

2368. Armbrust, M. "Court Liberally Interprets Secretary's Authority to Use Bidding Methods under OCS Act." **Natural Resources Law Newsletter** 14 (Winter 1982): 18-21.

2369. Bachman, W. A. "Interior's Policy Decisions Tilted toward Environment." **Oil and Gas Journal** 76 (April 3, 1978): 33-38.

2370. Bailey, Kenneth R. "Development of Surface Mine Legislation 1939-1967." **West Virginian History** 30 (April 1969): 525-529.

2371. Barsh, Russel L. "BIA Reorganization Follies of 1978: A Lesson in Bureaucratic Self-Defense." **American Indian Law Review** 7 (1979): 1-50.

2372. Barsh, Russel L. "The Red Man in the American Wonderland." **Human Rights** 11 (Winter 1984): 14-17.

2373. Berkman, Richard L. and W. Kip Viscusi. **Damming the West: Ralph Nader's Study Group Report on the Bureau of Reclamation.** New York: Grossman, 1973.

2374. Blume, Paul R. "An Evaluation of Institutional Vocational Training Received by American Indians through the Muskogee, Oklahoma Area Office of the Bureau of Indian Affairs." Ph.D. dissertation, Oklahoma State University, 1968.

2375. Boender, Debra R. "Termination and the Administration of Glenn L. Emmons as Commissioner of Indian Affairs, 1953-1961." **New Mexico Historical Review** 54 (October 1979): 287-304.

2376. Bradley, D. M. and Helen M. Ingram. "Science vs. the Grass Roots: Representation in the Bureau of Land Management." **National Resources Journal** 26 (Summer 1986): 439-518.

2377. Bradley, Jared W. "William C. C. Claiborne, the Old Southwest and the Development of American Indian Policy." **Tennessee Historical Quarterly** 33 (Fall 1974): 265-278.

2378. Bruce, Sammy D. "The Civil War and the Five Civilized Tribes - A Study in Federal-Indian Relations." Ph.D. dissertation, University of Oklahoma, 1970.

2379. Brockman, C. Frank. "Park Naturalists and the Evolution of National Park Service Interpretation through World War II." **Journal of Family History** 22 (January 1978): 24-43.

2380. Butler, Raymond V. "The Bureau of Indian Affairs: Activities since 1945." **Annals of the American Academy of Political and Social Science** 436 (March 1978): 50-60.

2381. Carleton, William G. "Government's Historic Role in Conservation." **Current History** 58 (June 1970): 321-327.

2382. Carmony, Donald F. and Francis P. Prucha, eds. "A Memorandum of Lewis Cass Concerning a System for the Regulation of Indian Affairs." **Wisconsin Magazine of History** 52 (Autumn 1968): 35-50.

2383. Cart, Theodore W. "New Deal for Wildlife: A Perspective on Federal Conservation Policy, 1933-1940." **Pacific Northwest Quarterly** 63 (July 1972): 113-120.

2384. Clawson, Marion. **The Bureau of Land Management.** New York: Praeger, 1971.

2385. Coan, Charles F. "The Federal Indian Policy in the

Pacific Northwest, 1849-1870." Ph.D. dissertation, University of California, 1920.

2386. Coggins, George C. "Livestock Grazing on the Public Lands: Lessons from the Failure of Official Conservation." **Gonzaga Law Review** 20 (1984-1985): 749-772.

2387. Colfer, Carold J. P. "Bureaucrats, Budgets, and the BIA: Segmented Opposition in a Residential School." **Human Organization** 34 (Summer 1975): 149-156.

2388. Cunnea, Patricia E. "Water Resources Policy Formation in the Appropriations Process: Congress and the Bureau of Reclamation." Ph.D. dissertation, University of Chicago, 1963.

2389. Danziger, Edmund J. **Indians and Bureaucrats: Administering the Reservation Policy during the Civil War.** Urbana: University of Illinois Press, 1974.

2390. Daugherty, J. B. "District Court's Approval of Bob Marshall Withdrawal Upstaged by Watt's Proposed Wilderness Legislation." **Environmental Law Reporter** 12 (March 1982): 10023-10027.

2391. Davis, Edward. "History of Federal Relations with the Five Civilized Tribes of Indians since 1865." Ph.D. dissertation, University of Texas, 1935.

2392. Delia, Donald J. "The Argument over Civilian or Military Indian Control, 1865-1880." **Historian** 24 (February 1962): 207-225.

2393. Deloria, Vine. "The Bureau of Indian Affairs: My Brother's Keeper." **Art in America** (July/August 1972): 110-126.

2394. DeMontigny, Lionel H. "The Bureaucratic Game and a Proposed Indian Ploy." **Indian Historian** 8 (Fall 1975): 25-30.

2395. Duncan, Thomas H. "Oil Shale Mining Claims: Alternatives for Resolution of an Ancient Problem." **Land and Water Law Review** 17 (Winter 1982): 1-41.

2396. Ellis, Richard N. "General John Pope and the Development of Federal Indian Policy, 1862-1886." Ph.D. dissertation, University of Colorado, 1967.

2397. Ellison, William H. "The Federal Indian Policy in

California, 1846-1860." Ph.D. dissertation, University of California, 1919.

2398. Embree, John F. "Indian Bureau and Self-Government." **Human Organization** 8 (Spring 1949): 11-14.

2399. Everhart, William C. **The National Park Service.** New York: Praeger, 1972.

2400. Fitzgerald, E. A. "Secretary of Interior v. California: Should Continental Shelf Lease Sales Be Subject to Consistency Review?" **Boston College Environmental Affairs Law Review** 12 (Spring 1985): 425-471.

2401. Foresta, Ronald A. **America's National Parks and Their Keepers.** Baltimore: Johns Hopkins University Press, 1984.

2402. Frishberg, N., M. Hickey and J. R. Kleiler. "Effect of the Federal Land Policy and Management Act on Adjudication Procedures in the Department of the Interior and Judicial Review of Adjudication Decisions." **Arizona Law Review** 21 (1979): 541-584.

2403. Galliard, Frye. "The Indians and the Bureaucrats." **Progressive** 37 (January 1973): 37-42.

2404. Garrison, Lemuel A. **The Making of a Ranger: Forty Years with the National Parks.** Salt Lake City, UT: Howe Brothers, 1983.

2405. Gastile, George P. "Federal Indian Policy and the Sustained Enclave: An Anthropological Perspective." **Human Organization** 33 (Fall 1974): 219-228.

2406. Goldman-Carter, J. "Federal Conservation of Threatened Species: By Administrative Discretion or by Legislative Standard?" **Boston College Environmental Affairs Law Review** 11 (Winter 1983): 63-104.

2407. Gray, Kenneth L. "The Public Policy Process and the National Park Service." Ph.D. dissertation, 1976.

2408. Grundlach, James H. "Migration, Labor Mobility, and Relocation Assistance: The Case of the American Indian." **Social Service Review** 51 (September 1977): 464-473.

2409. Hall, George R. "Conservation as a Public Policy Goal." **Yale Review** 51 (March 1962): 400-413.

2410. Hampton, Harold D. "Opposition to National Parks." **Journal of Forest History** 25 (January 1981): 36-45.

2411. Harmon, George D. "The Federal, Financial, and Economic Administration of Indian Affairs, 1789-1850." Ph.D. dissertation, University of Pennsylvania, 1930.

2412. Hart, Eugene D. "The Field Organization of the Bureau of Land Management." Ph.D. dissertation, American University, 1958.

2413. Hartzog, George B. "The National Park Service." **Historical Preservation** 18 (November/December 1966): 226-233.

2414. Hebal, John J. "Field Administration of the Bureau of Indian Affairs in Minnesota and Wisconsin." Ph.D. dissertation, University of Minnesota, 1959.

2415. Hebal, John J. "Generalist versus Specialist in the Bureau of Indian Affairs." **Public Administration Review** 21 (Winter 1961): 16-22.

2416. Hennigh, Lawrence. "Negative Stereotyping Structural Contributions in a BIA Community." **Human Organization** 34 (Fall 1975): 263-268.

2417. Henning, Daniel H. "National Park Wildlife Management Policy: A Field Administration and Political Study at Rocky Mountain National Park." D.S.S., Syracuse University, 1965.

2418. Hickel, Walter J. "The U.S. Department of the Interior and the Economic Geology of the West." **Journal of the West** 10 (January 1971): 129-132.

2419. Hill, Edward E. **The Office of Indian Affairs.** New York: Clearwater, 1974.

2420. Hoffman, Abraham. "Origins of a Controversy: The U.S. Reclamation Service and the Owens Galley-Los Angeles Dispute." **Arizona and the West** 19 (Winter 1977): 333-346.

2421. Hofsommer, Donovan L. "William Palmer Dole, Commissioner of Indian Affairs, 1861-1865." **Lincoln Herald** 75 (Fall 1973): 97-114.

2422. Infanger, Carlton A. "Economic Significance of Federal Ownership of Bureau of Land Management Administered Land on Selected Montana County Incomes." Ph.D. dissertation, Montana State University, 1964.

2423. Jackson, Curtis E. **A History of the Bureau of Indian Affairs and Its Activities among the Indians.** San Francisco: R and E Research Associates, 1977.

2424. Johnson, James P. "Drafting the NRA Code of Fair Competition for the Bituminous Coal Industry." **Journal of American History** 53 (December 1966): 521-541.

2425. Johnson, R. N. and Gary D. Libecap. "Agency Costs and the Assignment of Property Rights: The Case of Southwestern Indian Reservations." **Southern Economic Journal** 47 (October 1980): 332-347.

2426. Johnston, M. A. "Federal Relations with the Great Sioux Indians of South Dakota, 1887-1933." Ph.D. dissertation, Catholic University of America, 1949.

2427. Kelly, Lawrence C. **The Assault on Assimilation: John Collier and the Origins of Indian Reform Policy.** Albuquerque: University of New Mexico Press, 1983.

2428. Kelly, Lawrence C. "Choosing the New Deal Indian Commissioner: Ickes vs. Collier." **New Mexico Historical Review** 49 (October 1974): 269-288.

2429. Kelly, Lawrence C. "The Indian Reorganization Act: The Dream and the Reality." **Pacific Historical Review** 44 (August 1975): 291-312.

2430. Kinney, G. T. "Hickel Firing Mires Interior Actions." **Oil and Gas Journal** 68 (December 7, 1970): 36-38.

2431. Kinney, G. T. "How New Federal Oil Team Shapes Up." **Oil and Gas Journal** 67 (March 31, 1969): 38-40.

2432. Kirwan, Betty J. "Application of the Clean Air Act to Petroleum Operations on the Outer Continental Shelf." **Natural Resource Lawyer** 13 (Summer 1980): 411-419.

2433. Klein, Robert. "Scalping the Indians." **Policy Review** 19 (Winter 1982): 152-154.

2434. Kvasnicka, Robert M. and Herman J. Viola, eds. **The Commissioners of Indian Affairs, 1824-1977.** Lincoln: University of Nebraska Press, 1979.

2435. Lawson, Michael L. "How the Bureau of Indian Affairs Discourages Historical Research." **Indian History** 10 (Fall 1977): 25-27.

2436. Lear, Linda J. "The Aggressive Progressive: The Political Career of Harold L. Ickes, 1874-1933." Ph.D. dissertation, George Washington University, 1974.

2437. Lear, Linda J. "Harold L. Ickes and the Oil Crisis of the First Hundred Days." **Mid-America** 63 (January 1981): 3-17.

2438. Leonard, Charles B. "The Federal Indian Policy in the San Joaquin Valley, Its Application and Results." Ph.D. dissertation, University of California, 1927.

2439. Libecap, Gary D. **Locking up the Range: Federal Land Controls and Grazing.** Cambridge, MA: Ballinger, 1981.

2440. Littlefield, Daniel F. and Lonnie E. Underhill. "The Cherokee Agency Reserve, 1828-1866." **Arkansas Historical Quarterly** 31 (Summer 1972): 166-180.

2441. Littlefield, Daniel F. and Lonnie E. Underhill. "Negro Marshals in the Indian Territory." **Journal of Negro History** 56 (April 1971): 77-87.

2442. Lukaczer, Moses. **The Federal Buy Indian Program: Promise versus Performance.** Reseda, CA: Mojave Books, 1976.

2443. Lynxwiler, John "Organization and Impact of Inspector Discretion in a Regulatory Bureaucracy." **Social Problems** 30 (April 1983): 25-36.

2444. McCarty, R. L. "View of the Decision-Making Process within the Department of the Interior." **Administrative Law Review** 19 (March 1967): 147-159.

2445. McDermott, John E. "Expanded Offshore Leasing and the Mandates of NEPA." **Natural Resources Lawyer** 10 (1977): 531-553.

2446. Martone, Rosalie. "The U.S. and the Betrayal of

Indian Water Rights." **Indian Historian** 7 (Summer 1974): 3-11.

2447. Mason, Alpheus T. **Bureaucracy Convicts Itself: The Ballinger-Pinchot Controversy of 1910.** New York: Viking Press, 1941.

2448. Menzel, Donald C. and Terry D. Edgmon. "The Struggle to Implement a National Surface Mining Policy." **Publius** 10 (Winter 1980): 81-91.

2449. Morton, Rogers C. B. "View from Interior." **Public Relations Journal** 30 (July 1974): 14-17.

2450. Moulton, Gary E. "John Ross and W. P. Dole: A Case Study of Lincoln's Indian Policy." **Journal of the West** 12 (July 1973): 414-423.

2451. Myer, D. S. "Indian Administration: Problems and Goals." **Social Service Review** 27 (June 1953): 193-200.

2452. Myers, Henry R. "Federal Decisionmaking and the Trans-Alaska Pipeline." **Ecology Law Quarterly** 4 (Fall 1975): 915-961.

2453. Nelson, Robert A. and Joseph F. Sheley. "Current BIA Influence on Indian Self-Determination: A Criminal Justice Planning Illustration." **Social Science Journal** 19 (July 1982): 73-85.

2454. Nickeson, Steve. "Structure of the Bureau of Indian Affairs." **Law and Contemporary Problems** 40 (Winter 1976): 61-76.

2455. Officer, James E. "Bureau of Indian Affairs since 1945: An Assessment." **Annals of the American Academy of Political and Social Science** 436 (March 1978): 61-72.

2456. Paulsen, David F. "An Approach to Organizational Analysis: A Case Study of the Bureau of Land Management." Ph.D. dissertation, University of Washington, 1966.

2457. Paulson, Howard W. "Federal Indian Policy and the Dakota Indians: 1800-1840." **South Dakota History** 3 (Summer 1973): 25-309.

2458. Penick, James L. **Progressive Politics and Conservation: The Ballinger-Pinchot Affair.** Chicago: University of Chicago Press, 1968.

2459. Phillips, J. H. "In Washington, the Policy-Makers

Fret and Sweat." **National Wildlife** 15 (August 1977): 12-13.

2460. Philip, Kenneth R. **John Collier's Crusade for Indian Reform, 1920-1954.** Tuscon: University of Arizona Press, 1977.

2461. Philip, Kenneth R. "John Collier and the Indians of the Americas: The Dream and the Reality." **Prologue** 11 (Spring 1979): 5-21.

2462. Pope, W. C. and E. R. Nocolai. "In Case of Accident - Call a Computer." **Journal of Systems Management** 23 (September 1972): 34-37.

2463. Powell, Fred W. **The Bureau of Mines: Its History, Activities and Organization.** New York: Appleton, 1922.

2464. Prucha, Francis P. "Books on American Indian Policy: A Half-Decade of Important Work, 1970-1975." **Journal of American History** 63 (December 1976): 658-669.

2465. Quetone, Allen C. "Indian Self-Determination - The Human Factor." **Public Administration Review** 44 (November/December 1984): 533-538.

2466. Reed, Nathaniel P. and Dennis Drabelle. **The United States Fish and Wildlife Service.** Boulder, CO: Westview Press, 1984.

2467. Reeve, Frank D. "The Federal Indian Policy in New Mexico, 1858-1880." Ph.D. dissertation, University of Texas, 1937.

2468. Richardson, Elmo R. "Federal Park Policy in Utah: The Escalante National Monument Controversy of 1935-1940." **Utah Historical Quarterly** 33 (Spring 1965): 109-133.

2469. Richardson, Elmo R. "Interior Secretary as Conservation Villain: The Notorious Case of Douglas Giveaway McKay." **Pacific Historical Review** 41 (August 1972): 333-345.

2470. Robinson, Michael C. **Water for the West: The Bureau of Reclamation, 1902-1977.** Chicago: Public Works Historical Society, 1979.

2471. Sady, Emil J. "Department of the Interior and Pacific Island Administration." **Public Administration Review** 10 (Winter 1950): 13-19.

2472. Sager, Daniel D. "Planning-Programming-Budgeting and the Bureau of Mines: An Evaluation of Planned Change in Organizational Behavior." Ph.D. dissertation, University of Washington, 1970.

2473. Satz, Ronald N. "Federal Indian Policy, 1829-1849." Ph.D. dissertation, University of Maryland, 1972.

2474. Schmeckebier, Laurence F. **The Office of Indian Affairs: Its History, Activities and Organization.** Baltimore: Johns Hopkins University Press, 1927.

2475. Schmid, R. L. "Notation Rule - Doctrine of Sovereign Impunity of the Department of the Interior." **Utah Law Review** 7 (Fall 1960): 171-188.

2476. Schrader, Robert F. "The Indian Arts and Crafts Board: An Aspect of New Deal Indian Policy." Ph.D. dissertation, Marquette University, 1981.

2477. Schusky, Ernest L. "Development by Grantsmanship: Economic Planning on the Lower Brulo Sioux Reservation." **Human Organization** 34 (Fall 1975): 227-236.

2478. Sedacca, Sandra. **Who Minding the Store?" A Common Cause Guide to the Top Officials at the Department of the Interior.** Washington, DC: Common Cause, 1981.

2479. Shankland, Robert. **Steve Mather of the National Parks.** New York: Knopf, 1951.

2480. Shapiro, David L. "Statistical Appraisal of the Economic Efficiency of Trinity River Division of the Central Valley Project of the United States Bureau of Reclamation." Ph.D. dissertation, University of California, 1966.

2481. Sievers, Michael A. "Malfeasance of Indirection? Administration of the California Indian Superintendency's Business Affairs." **Southern California Quarterly** 56 (Fall 1974): 273-294.

2482. Sink, D. "Making the Indian Child Welfare Act Work: Missing Social and Governmental Linkages." **Phylon** 43 (December 1982): 360-367.

2483. Smith, Burton M. "The Politics of Allotment: The Flathead Indian Reservation as a Test Case."

Pacific Northwest Quarterly 70 (July 1979): 131-140.

2484. Stahl, Rose M. **The Ballinger-Pinchot Controversy.** Northampton, MA: Department of History, Smith College, 1926.

2485. Sterling, Everett W. "The Indian Reservation System." **Montana Magazine of Western History** 14 (April 1964): 92-100.

2486. Strauss, Peter L. "Mining Claims on Public Lands: A Study of Interior Department Procedures." **Utah Law Review** 18 (Summer 1974): 185-271.

2487. Strauss, Peter L. "Rules, Adjudications, and Other Sources of Law in an Executive Department: Reflections on the Interior Department's Administration of the Mining Law." **Columbia Law Review** 74 (November 1974): 1231-1275.

2488. Stuart, Paul. **The Indian Office: Growth and Development of an American Institution, 1865-1900.** Ann Arbor, MI: UMI Research Press, 1979.

2489. Sturges, D. R. "Administrative and Judicial Review of Interior Department Decisions." **Rocky Mountain Mineral Law Institute** 31 (1985): 1-60.

2490. Swain, Donald C. "The Bureau of Reclamation and the New Deal, 1933-1940." **Pacific Northwest Quarterly** 61 (July 1970): 137-146.

2491. Swain, Donald C. "The Founding of the National Park Service." **American West** 6 (September 1969): 6-9.

2492. Swain, Donald C. "The National Park Service and the New Deal, 1933-1940." **Pacific Historical Review** 41 (August 1972): 312-332.

2493. Swain, Donald C. "The Passage of the National Park Service Act of 1916." **Wisconsin Magazine of History** 50 (Autumn 1966): 4-17.

2494. Swain, Donald C. **Wilderness Defender: Horace M. Albright and Conservation.** Chicago: University of Chicago Press, 1970.

2495. Symons, Craig. "The Failure of America's Indian Policy on the Southwestern Frontier, 1785-1793." **Tennessee Historical Quarterly** 35 (Spring 1976): 29-45.

2496. Szasz, Margaret G. "Indian Reform in a Decade of Prosperity." **Montana Magazine of Western History** 20 (January 1970): 16-27.

2497. Taylor, Theodore W. **The Bureau of Indian Affairs.** Boulder, CO: Westview Press, 1984.

2498. Taylor, Theodore W. "The Regional Organization of the Bureau of Indian Affairs." Ph.D. dissertation, Harvard University, 1960.

2499. Terry, Newell B. "Collective Bargaining in the U.S. Department of the Interior." **Public Administration Review** 22 (Winter 1962): 19-23.

2500. Trani, Eugene P. "Hubert Work and the Department of the Interior, 1923-28." **Pacific Northwest Quarterly** 61 (January 1970): 31-40.

2501. Trulove, William T. "Economics of Paternalism: Federal Policy and the Klamath Indians." Ph.D. dissertation, University of Oregon, 1973.

2502. Turner, Alvin O. "Financial Relations between the United States and the Cherokee Nation, 1830-1870." **Journal of the West** 12 (July 1973): 372-385.

2503. Unrau, William E. "The Civilian as Indian Agent: Villain or Victim?" **Western Historical Quarterly** 3 (October 1972): 405-420.

2504. Unrau, William E. "Indian Agent vs. the Army: Some Background Notes on the Kiowa-Comanche Treaty of 1865." **Kansas Historical Quarterly** 30 (Summer 1964): 129-152.

2505. Vivian, James and Jean H. Vivian. "Congressional Indian Policy during the War for Independence: The Northern Department." **Maryland Magazine of Genealogy** 63 (September 1968): 241-274.

2506. Warner, William E. **The Bureau of Reclamation.** New York: Praeger, 1973.

2507. Watson, John L. "The Federal Coal Follies - A New Program Ends (Begins) a Decade of Anxiety?" **Denver Law Journal** 58 (Winter 1980): 65-140.

2508. Wengert, Norman and John C. Honey. "Program Planning in the U.S. Department of the Interior, 1946-1953." **Public Administration Review** 14 (Summer 1954): 193-201.

2509. Wheatley, R. "BLM Rejects Big Batch of Sale 59 Bids." **Oil and Gas Journal** 80 (January 4, 1982): 74-76.

2510. Wicks, Gary J. "Coal Leasing Program: Department of the Interior." **Tulsa Law Journal** 13 (1978): 664-670.

2511. Winfrey, William S. "Developments under the Surface Mining Control and Reclamation Act of 1977." **West Virginia Law Review** 82 (Summer 1980): 1277-1345.

2512. Wirth, Conrad L. **Parks, Politics and the People.** Norman: University of Oklahoma Press, 1980.

Chapter 10.
Department of Justice

2513. Andewelt, R. B. "Organization and Operation of the Antitrust Division." **Antitrust Law Journal** 54 (1985): 71-83.

2514. Anenson, J. V. "FBI's First 75 Years." **FBI Law Enforcement Bulletin** 52 (July 1983): 2-11.

2515. Appleson, Gail. "Justice Department, FDA Study Firm's Report on Drug." **American Bar Association Journal** 67 (November 1981): 1443.

2516. Aragon, Ellen W. "The Factory Raid: An Unconstitutional Act?" **Southern California Law Review** 56 (January 1983): 605-645.

2517. Arnold, Thurman W. "Antitrust Activities of the Department of Justice." **Oregon Law Review** 19 (December 1939): 22-31.

2518. Ashman, Allan. "Freedom of Information ... Judges' Conduct." **American Bar Association Journal** 66 (August 1980): 1004-1011.

2519. Baker, Donald I. "Antitrust in the Sunshine." **St. Louis University Law Journal** 21 (1977): 347-357.

2520. Baker, Donald I. "Past As Prologue." **American Bar Association Antitrust Law Journal** 46 (Spring 1977): 544-552.

2521. Baker, Donald I. "To Indict or Not to Indict: Prosecutorial Discretion in Sherman Act Enforcement." **Cornell Law Review** 63 (March 1978): 405-418.

2522. Baker, Howard H. "Proposed Judicially Appointed Independent Office of Public Attorney: Some Constitutional Objections and an Alternative."

Southwestern Law Journal 29 (Fall 1975): 671-683.

2523. Barnett, E. William. "Interview with William F. Baxter: Assistant Attorney General: Antitrust Division." **Antitrust Law Journal** 50 (Winter 1982): 23-40.

2524. Barovick, R. "International Antitrust - Washington Style." **Business Abroad** 95 (September 1970): 9-11.

2525. Baxter, Nevins D. and S. Shah. "Department of Justice Competitive Factors Reports." **Banking Law Journal** 101 (November/December 1984): 692-703.

2526. Baxter, William F. "Separation of Powers, Prosecutorial Discretion, and the Common Law Nature of Antitrust Law." **Texas Law Review** 60 (April 1982): 661-703.

2527. Beck, Leland E. "Administrative Law of Criminal Prosecution: The Development of Prosecutorial Policy." **American University Law Review** 27 (Winter 1978): 310-380.

2528. Belknap, Michael R. "Above the Law and Beyond Its Reach: O'Reilly and Theoharis on FBI Intelligence Operations." **American Bar Foundation Research Journal** (Winter 1985): 201-215.

2529. Bell, Griffin B. "Attorney General: The Federal Government's Chief Lawyer and Chief Litigator: Or One Among Many." **Fordham Law Review** 46 (May 1978): 1049-1070.

2530. Bell, Griffin B. "Improving the Justice System." **Trial** 13 (November 1977): 22-25.

2531. Berger, Raoul. **Government by Judiciary.** Cambridge, MA: Harvard University Press, 1977.

2532. Bickel, D. R. "The Antitrust Division's Adoption of a Chicago School Economic Policy Calls for Some Reorganization: But Is the Division's New Policy Here to Stay?" **Houston Law Review** 20 (July 1983): 1083-1127.

2533. Bicks, Robert A. "Department of Justice and Private Treble Damage Actions." **Antitrust Bulletin** 4 (January/February 1959): 5.

2534. Biddle, F. "The Department of Justice - The War Effort." **West Virginia Bar Association** 59 (1943): 130-139.

2535. Biddle, F. "Resume of Remarks about the Department." **Vermont Bar Association Journal** 36 (1942): 42-47.

2536. Boe, K. S. "Paraquat Eradication: Legal Means for a Prudent Policy?" **Boston College Environmental Affairs Law Review** 12 (Spring 1985): 491-526.

2537. Bork, Robert H. "Problems and Pleasures of Being Solicitor General." **American Bar Association Antitrust Law Journal** 42 (1973): 701-706.

2538. Bransdorfer, S. C. "Justice Department Lawyers: The Attorney General's Honor Program." **American Bar Association Journal** 45 (January 1959): 58-63.

2539. Bratter, H. "Antitrust Division and Banking." **Banking** 62 (July 1969): 48-49.

2540. Breit, William and Kenneth C. Elzinga. "Antitrust Penalties and Attitudes toward Risk: An Economic Analysis." **Harvard Law Review** 86 (February 1973): 693-713.

2541. Brill, Steven. "Report Card on William French Smith." **American Lawyer** 4 (July 1982): 28-35.

2542. Brown, R. G. **Illegal Practices of the Department of Justice.** New York: Arno Press, 1969.

2543. Brownstein, Ronald. "Big Is Beautiful." **Student Lawyer** 10 (October 1981): 10.

2544. Bruck, Connie. "Springing the Haitians." **American Lawyer** 4 (September 1982): 35-40.

2545. Bullock, Charles S. "Justice Department and School Desegregation: The Importance of Developing Trust." **Journal of Politics** 39 (November 1977): 1036-1044.

2546. Burger, Warren E. "Office of the United States Attorney General." **Labor Law Journal** 2 (October 1954): 124-133.

2547. Burns, Malcolm R. "The Competitive Effects of Trust-Busting: A Portfolio Analysis." **Journal of Political Economy** 85 (August 1977): 717-740.

2548. Caldwell, D. D. "Department of Justice Building." **Federal Bar Association Journal** 1 (September 1931): 24-27, 30.

2549. Caldwell, D. D. "Reorganization of the Federal Legal Service." **Federal Bar Association Journal** 1 (October 1933): 31-32, 69-70.

2550. Carlson, J. A. "It Can Happen in Centerville, USA: Nuclear Extortion." **FBI Law Enforcement Bulletin** 54 (September 1985): 1-4.

2551. Carlson, Norman A. "Federal Bureau of Prisons." **Federal Rules Decisions** 75 (October 1977): 413-421.

2552. Carlson, Norman A. "Federal Prison System: Forty-five Years of Change." **Federal Probation** 39 (June 1975): 37-42.

2553. Carr, Robert K. **Federal Protection of Civil Rights: Quest for a Sword.** Ithaca, NY: Cornell University Press, 1947.

2554. Carr, Ronald G. "Some Reflections on Vertical Restraints." **University of Toledo Law Review** 13 (Spring 1982): 587-594.

2555. Carter, William A. "Commercial Banking and the Antitrust Laws." **Antitrust Bulletin** 1 (January/April 1966): 141-180.

2556. Cavanaugh, Francis P. "Immigration Restriction at Work Today: A Study of the Administration of Immigration Restriction by the United States." Ph.D. dissertation, Catholic University of America, 1928.

2557. Clark, Tom C. "Your Attorney General's Office." **Virginia State Bar Association** 57 (1946): 351-357.

2558. Clearwaters, K. I. "Department of Justice Enforcement Policies with Respect to Business Practices in an Inflation and Shortage Economy - Trying to Keep up with the Game." **Antitrust Law Symposium** (1975): 49-67.

2559. Clynch, Edward J. "Law Enforcement Assistance Administration Block Grants: Policy Analysis." Ph.D. dissertation, Purdue University, 1975.

2560. Coan, Blair. **The Red Web: An Underground Political History of the United States from 1918**

to the Present Time, Showing How Close the Government Is to Collapse, and Told in an Understandable Way. Boston: Western Isands, 1969.

2561. Collie, Marvin K. "Probing Look at Justice Department's Policy of Removing Taxpayer's Counsel-Witness." **Journal of Taxation** 43 (September 1975): 171-173.

2562. Collins, Frederick L. **The FBI in War and Peace.** New York: Putnam's, 1943.

2563. Colwell, William L. and J. W. Koletar. "Performance Measurement for Criminal Justice - The FBI Experience." **Journal of Police Science and Administration** 12 (June 1984): 146-156.

2564. Comegys, Walter B. "Business Reviews by the Antitrust Division." **Conference Board Record** 11 (March 1974): 22-27.

2565. Comegys, Walter B. "Quo Vadis: Case Selection by the Antitrust Division of the Department of Justice." **American Bar Association Antitrust Law Journal** 46 (Spring 1977): 563-574.

2566. Connell, Gerald A. "View from the Department of Justice." **Antitrust Bulletin** 22 (Summer 1977): 259-265.

2567. Cook, Fred J. **The FBI Nobody Knows.** New York: Macmillan, 1964.

2568. Costantino, Mark A., V. A. Cannavo and A. Goldstein. "Drug Courier Profiles and Airport Stops: Is the Sky the Limit?" **Western New England Law Review** 3 (Fall 1980): 175-198.

2569. Craver, T. F. "On the Road to Regulation." **Conference Board Record** 12 (October 1975): 20-26.

2570. Crosby, R. W. "Antitrust Policy Winds Shift: With Appointment of New Antitrust Chief in Department of Justice." **Iron Age** 192 (July 43, 1963): 58-59.

2571. Cummings, Homer S. **Federal Justice: Chapters in the History of Justice and the Federal Executive.** New York: Macmillan, 1935.

2572. Cummings, Homer S. "New Home of the Department of Justice." **Federal Bar Association Journal** 12 (November 1934): 73-74, 113.

2573. Cummings, Homer S. **Selected Papers of Homer Cummings, Attorney General of the United States, 1933-1939.** Edited by Carl B. Swisher. New York: Scribner's, 1939.

2574. Cummings, Homer S. and Carl McFarland. **Federal Justice: Chapters in the History of Justice and the Federal Executive.** New York: Macmillan, 1937.

2575. Deniel, A. T. "United States Department of Justice." **North Carolina Law Review** 8 (April 1930): 340-344.

2576. Davidow, Joel. "Competition, Trade and the Antitrust Division: 1981." **Northwestern Journal of International Law and Business** 2 (Fall 1980): 300-316.

2577. Davids, James A. "DEA Administrative Inspections: Authority and Practical Applications." **Food Drug Cosmetic Law Journal** 36 (May 1981): 229-244.

2578. Davis, J. C. "Investigations by the Department of Justice - As Seen by the Potential Defendant." **American Bar Association Section of Antitrust Law** 29 (1965): 54-61.

2579. Day, Sherman R. "People Make the Difference." **Federal Probation** 44 (September 1980): 40-44.

2580. Days, Drew S. "Vindicating Civil Rights in Changing Times." **Yale Law Journal** 93 (May 1984): 990-994.

2581. Deak, Frank. "Police Apprenticeship Programs." **FBI Law Enforcement Bulletin** 55 (September 1986): 6-8.

2582. DeFronzo, J. "Climate and Crime: Tests of an FBI Assumption." **Environment and Behavior** 16 (March 1984): 185-210.

2583. Demaris, Ovid. **The Director: An Oral Biography of J. Edgar Hoover.** New York: Harper's Magazine Press, 1975.

2584. Depue, Roger L. "American Response to an Era of Violence." **FBI Law Enforcement Bulletin** 55 (December 1986): 2-5.

2585. Devins, N. "Closing the Classroom Door on Civil Rights." **Human Rights** 11 (Winter 1984): 26-29.

2586. Dinkins, Carol E. and James D. Santini. "Remarks at ABA Annual Meeting: August 11, 1981." **Natural Resources Law Newsletter** 14 (Spring 1982): 17-21.

2587. Diplock, Kenneth. "Antitrust and Judicial Process." **Journal of Law and Economics** 7 (October 1964): 27-44.

2588. Doerfer, Gordon L. "The Limits on Trade Secret Law Imposed by Federal Patent and Antitrust Supremacy." **Harvard Law Review** 80 (May 1967): 1432-1467.

2589. Donavan, Leslie. "Justice Department's Prosecution Guidelines of Little Value to State and Local Prosecutors." **Journal of Criminal Law and Criminology** 72 (Fall 1981): 955-992.

2590. Dunne, Gerald T. "Potential Competition - Fantasy Compounded." **Banking Law Journal** 99 (September 1982): 675-683.

2591. Edwards, Steven M. "Proposed Revisions of the Justice Department's Merger Guidelines." **Columbia Law Review** 81 (December 1981): 1543-1581.

2592. Eizenstat, Stuart E. "White House and Justice Department after Watergate." **American Bar Association Journal** 68 (February 1982): 175-177.

2593. Elliff, John T. "The Attorney General's Guidelines for FBI Investigations." **Cornell Law Review** 69 (April 1984): 785-815.

2594. Elliff, John T. **Crime, Dissent and the Attorney General: The Justice Department in the 1960s.** Beverly Hills, CA: Sage, 1971.

2595. Elliff, John T. **The Reform of FBI Intelligence Operations.** Princeton, NJ: Princeton University Press, 1979.

2596. Elman, Philip. "Antitrust Enforcement: Retrospect and Prospect." **American Bar Association Journal** 53 (July 1967): 609-612.

2597. Fahy, Charles. "The Office of the Solicitor General." **American Bar Association Journal** 28 (January 1942): 20-22.

2598. Farnum, George R. "Department of Justice of the United States." **Law Society Journal** 1 (November

1929): 9-18.

2599. Favretto, Richard J. "Settlement of Government and Private Cases: The Antitrust Division." **Antitrust Law Journal** 50 (Winter 1982): 7-15.

2600. Feeley, Malcolm and Austin D. Sarat. **The Policy Dilemma: Federal Crime Policy and the Law Enforcement Assistance Administration.** Minneapolis: University of Minnesota Press, 1980.

2601. Fish, Peter G. "The Politics of Judicial Administration: Transfer of the Federal Probation System." **Western Political Quarterly** 23 (December 1970): 769-784.

2602. Floherty, John J. **Inside the FBI.** Philadelphia: Lippincott, 1943.

2603. Foust, James D. "U.S. Bankers vs. the Department of Justice: The 1966 Amendment to the Bank Merger Act, Banking Structure, and Regulation." **Revue Internationale de L'Histoire de la Banque** 9 (1974): 80-106.

2604. Fox, A. W. "Dedication of New Home of Department of Justice." **American Bar Association Journal** 20 (November 1934): 724-729.

2605. Freeman, L. A. and A. F. Ettinger. "A Plaintiff's View of the Justice Department's Vertical Restraints Guidelines." **Antitrust Law Journal** 54 (1985): 345-361.

2606. Fricano, John C. "How Trade Associations and Trade Association Executives Can Limit Their Exposure to Antitrust Division Discovery Procedures." **Antitrust Bulletin** 22 (Summer 1977): 365-385.

2607. Friedman, S. B. "Narcotic Addict Rehabilitation Act: Its Impact on Federal Prisons." **Contemporary Drug Problems** 11 (Spring 1982): 101-111.

2608. Garcia, Peter. "Disseminating Criminal Justice Information to the U. S. Office of Personnel Management." **Police Chief** 49 (October 1982): 50-53.

2609. Garrow, David J. **The FBI and Martin Luther King.** New York: Norton, 1981.

2610. Gaswirth, Mitchell M. "Reformulating Seizures - Airport Drug Stops and the Fourth Amendment." **California Law Review** 69 (September 1981): 1486-

1512.

2611. Gentry, M. "Five Years Later, It's Judge Webster's FBI." **Police Magazine** 6 (March 1983): 26-33.

2612. Gentry, M. "Who's Who in the Reagan Justice Department." **Police Magazine** 5 (January 1982): 38-39.

2613. Georges, W. C. "Foreign Corrupt Practices Act Review Procedure: A Quest for Clarity." **Cornell International Law Journal** 14 (Winter 1981): 57-93.

2614. Gettinger, Stephen H. "Power Struggle over Federal Parole." **Correction Magazine** 8 (April 1982): 41-43.

2615. Glasheen, Leah. "Crime and Politics." **Security Management** 26 (January 1982): 66-68.

2616. Gleeson, G. A. "The United States Attorney's Office." **Pennsylvania Bar Association Quarterly** 13 (April 1942): 190-195.

2617. Golden, Olive H. "Administration of the Attorney-General's List of Subversive Organizations: The Case of the Workers Party-Independent Socialist League." Ph.D. dissertation, University of Chicago, 1963.

2618. Goldstein, E. M. "Tax Division Is Concerned Only with Litigation: Does Not Initiate Tax Legislation." **Hennepin Lawyer** 28 (January 1960): 51.

2619. Goldstein, Robert J. "The FBI and American Politics Textbooks." **PS** 18 (Spring 1985): 237-246.

2620. Goodman, Oscar R. "Antitrust and Competitive Issues in U.S. Banking Structure." **Journal of Finance** 26 (May 1971): 615-646, 650-651.

2621. Goodrich, Edgar J. "On the Selection and Keeping of Apples: Some Observations on the Tax Scandals." **American Bar Association Journal** 38 (June 1952): 479-482.

2622. Gordon, C. "Powers and Responsibilities of Immigration Officers." **American Bar Association Journal** 59 (January 1973): 64.

2623. Graham, Fred P. **The Alias Program.** Boston: Little, Brown, 1977.

2624. Green, Mark J. **The Closed Enterprise System: Ralph**

Nader's Study Group on Antitrust Enforcement. New York: Grossman, 1972.

2625. Greenberg, J. "Civil Rights Enforcement Activity of the Department of Justice." **Black Law Journal** 8 (Spring 1983): 60-67.

2626. Greenwald, R. F. "C R S: Dispute Resolution through Mediation." **American Bar Association Journal** 64 (August 1978): 1250-1254.

2627. Griffin, Joseph P. "Problems Raised by Various Types of Restrictive Clauses." **Antitrust Law Journal** 50 (Summer 1982): 499-513.

2628. Guzzardi, Walter. "Search for Sanity in Antitrust." **Fortune** 97 (January 30, 1978): 72-75.

2629. Habicht, F. H. "Justice Cracks Down on Environmental Crimes." **EPA Journal** 10 (March 1984): 16-17.

2630. Hall, R. H. and K. R. Feinberg. "Debate over a National Institute of Justice: Why NIJ Should Be Separate from the Justice Department: Why NIJ Should Be Kept within the Justice Department." **Judicature** 62 (December/January 1979): 296-309.

2631. Harris, Richard. **Justice: The Crisis of Law, Order and Freedom in America.** New York: Dutton, 1970.

2632. Harrison, Lowell H. "Attorney General John Breckinridge." **Filson Club Historical Quarterly** 36 (October 1962): 319-327.

2633. Harrison, Lowell H. "John Breckinridge and the Jefferson Administration." **Rocky Mountain Social Science Journal** 4 (October 1967): 83-91.

2634. Harrison, Lowell H. "John C. Breckinridge: Nationalist, Confederate, Kentuckian." **Filson Club Historical Quarterly** 47 (April 1973): 125-144.

2635. Henderson, Douglas B. and John F. Hornick. "Justice Department Antitrust Guide Concerning Research Joint Ventures." **Licensing Law and Business Reporter** 5 (July/August 1982): 13-20.

2636. Hensler, David J. and Walter A. Smith. "Asset Valuation: The Multibillion-Dollar Controversy in the AT&T Case." **Public Utilities Fortnightly** 109 (May 27, 1982): 13-18.

2637. Hershberger, G. L. "Development of the Federal Prison System." **Federal Probation** 43 (December 1979): 13-23.

2638. Hing, Bill O. "Estoppel in Immigration Proceedings - New Life from Akbarin and Miranda." **San Diego Law Review** 20 (December 1982): 11-36.

2639. Hofstadter, Richard. "Antitrust in America." **Commentary** 38 (August 1964): 47-53.

2640. Hohl, Donald and Michael G. Wenk. "Current U.S. Immigration Legislation: Analysis and Comment." **International Migration Review** 5 (Fall 1971): 339-356.

2641. Holmes, Allen C. "Panel Discussion Interview with John Shenefield, Assistant Attorney General, Antitrust Division." **Antitrust Law Journal** 48 (Spring 1980): 637-655.

2642. Hoobler, James F. "Management-by-Objectives in the Department of Justice: Theoretical Constructs and Real World Problems Associated with the Evolution of a Formal Management System in a Federal Justice Department." Ph.D. dissertation, University of Maryland, 1981.

2643. Hoover, J. Edgar. "Work of the Division of Investigation, United States Department of Justice." **Tennessee Law Review** 13 (April 1935): 149-157.

2644. Hurwitz, Gerald S. "Motions Practice before the Board of Immigration Appeals." **San Diego Law Review** 20 (December 1982): 79-95.

2645. Huston, Luther A. **The Department of Justice.** New York: Praeger, 1967.

2646. Irons, Peter H. "Fighting Fair: Zechariah Chafee, Jr., the Department of Justice, and the Trial at the Harvard Club." **Harvard Law Review** 94 (April 1981): 1205-1236.

2647. Jackson, R. H. "Interest of the Department of Justice in Section 77B." **Corporation Reorganization** 2 (May 1936): 405-407.

2648. Jaffe, Louis L. "The Judicial Enforcement of Administrative Orders." **Harvard Law Review** 76 (March 1963): 865-928.

2649. Janus, Michael G. "Security and Custody: Monitoring the Federal Bureau of Prisons' Classification System." **Federal Probation** 50 (March 1986): 35-43.

2650. Joffe, Robert D. "Guidelines - Past, Present and Future." **Antitrust Law Journal** 50 (Spring 1982): 187-204.

2651. Johns, C. H. "Interstate Commerce Commission and the Department of Justice." **George Washington Law Review** 31 (October 1962): 242.

2652. Jones, Clifford A. "Antitrust and Patent Licensing Problems: Are the Nine No-Nos the Nine Maybes?" **Oklahoma Bar Journal** 53 (June 26, 1982): 1568-1571.

2653. Joseph, Marc W. and Timothy W. Mountz. "The Justice Department Merger Guidelines: Impact on Horizontal Mergers between Commercial Banks." **Kentucky Law Journal** 72 (1983-1984): 505-547.

2654. Josephson, Ellen. "Commentary: The Equal Access to Justice Act." **Clearinghouse Review** 15 (April 1982): 1021-1023.

2655. Kalodner, A. B. "Consent Decrees as an Antitrust Enforcement Device." **Antitrust Bulletin** 23 (Summer 1978): 277-337.

2656. Karacki. L. "Class of '63: Career Patterns of Federal Prison Correctional Officers Who Entered Service during 1963." **Federal Probation** 46 (September 1982): 49-53.

2657. Katsh, Salem M. and Daniel R. Barney. "The Proposed AT&T Consent Decree: A Preliminary Analysis." **Media Law Notes** 9 (April 1982): 2-5.

2658. Kauper, Thomas E. "Antitrust - A Form of Regulation." **Regulation** 2 (September/October 1978): 54-57.

2659. Kauper, Thomas E. "Antitrust Enforcement from the Inside." **American Bar Association Antitrust Law Journal** 45 (Spring 1976): 154-162.

2660. Kauper, Thomas E. "Competition Policy and the Institutions of Antitrust." **South Dakota Law Review** 23 (Winter 1978): 1-29.

2661. Kauper, Thomas E. "Department of Justice: Antitrust Perspective." **University of Pittsburgh Law Review** 36 (April 1975): 667-675.

2662. Kauper, Thomas E. "The Role of Economic Analysis in the Antitrust Division Before and After the Establishment of the Economic Policy Office: A Lawyer's View." **Antitrust Bulletin** 29 (Spring 1984): 111-132.

2663. Kennedy, Edward M. "The Immigration Act of 1965." **Annals of the American Academy of Political and Social Science** 367 (September 1966): 137-149.

2664. Kennedy, Robert F. **The Pursuit of Justice.** New York: Harper and Row, 1964.

2665. Key, Sewall. "Legal Work of the Federal Government." **Virginia Law Review** 25 (December 1938): 165-201.

2666. Kirkpatrick, Wallace W. "Antitrust Enforcement in the Seventies." **Catholic University Law Review** 30 (Spring 1981): 431-481.

2667. Klawiter, Donald. "Practical Tools in Understanding Antitrust Division Policies and Procedures." **Antitrust Newsletter** 3 (Winter 1981): 1-5.

2668. Koenig, B. E. "Acoustic Gunshot Analysis: The Kennedy Assassination and Beyond." **FBI Law Enforcement Bulletin** 52 (November 1983): 1-9.

2669. Kovaleff, Theodore P. **Business and Government during the Eisenhower Administration: A Study of the Antitrust Policy of the Antitrust Division of the Justice Department.** Athens: Ohio University Press, 1980.

2670. Kramer, Victor H. "Antitrust Today: The Baxterization of the Sherman and Clayton Acts." **Wisconsin Law Review** (November/December 1981): 1287-1302.

2671. Langeluttig, Albert G. **The Department of Justice in the United States.** Baltimore: Johns Hopkins University Press, 1927.

2672. Lansing, D., J. B. Bogan and L. Karacki. "Unit Management: Implementing a Different Correctional Approach." **Federal Probation** 41 (March 1977): 43-49.

2673. Lawn, John C. "The DEA's Role in the Prevention of Drug Trafficking and Abuse." **Police Chief** 52 (October 1985): 31-32.

2674. Le Blanc, Robert E. "Department of Justice and Trademarks." **Trademark Reporter** 54 (July 1964): 511-517.

2675. Lee, Ronald E. "Lawyering in the Supreme Court: The Role of the Solicitor General." **Supreme Court Historical Society Yearbook** (1985): 15-21.

2676. Levi, Edward H. "Justice Department: Some Thoughts on Its Past, Present and Future." **Illinois Bar Journal** 64 (December 1975): 216-225.

2677. Levi, Edward H. "New Approach to Justice." **Pennsylvania Bar Association Quarterly** 46 (October 1975): 404-416.

2678. Levin, A. Leo. "Research in Judicial Administration: The Federal Experience." **New York Law School Law Review** 26 (Winter 1981): 237-262.

2679. Levinson, M. R. "Corrections Training: Beyond Bar Tapping." **Corrections Magazine** 8 (December 1982): 40-47.

2680. Levinson, R. B. and G. L. Ingram. "Security Designation/Custody Classification: Fourth (and Final) Stage." **Corrections Today** 45 (December 1983): 36-39.

2681. Liedquist, Robert E. "Recent Developments in Regional Enforcement of the Antitrust Laws." **Antitrust Law Symposium** (1975): 38-48.

2682. Lipsky, Abbott B. "Current Antitrust Division Views on Patent Licensing Practices." **Antitrust Law Journal** 50 (Summer 1982): 515-524.

2683. Litvack, Sanford M. "Government Antitrust Policy: Theory Versus Practice and the Role of Antitrust Division." **Texas Law Review** 60 (April 1982): 649-660.

2684. Litvack, Sanford M. "Remarks." **Antitrust Law Symposium** (1980): 97-104.

2685. Litvack, Sanford M. "Remarks." **Antitrust Law Symposium** (1981): 163-172.

2686. Litvack, Sanford M. "Report from the Antitrust Division." **Antitrust Law Journal** 49 (Summer 1981): 1073-1078.

2687. Locke, H. P. "Tax Division - Department of Justice." **Taxes** 25 (April 1947): 305-312.

2688. Locke, H. P. "Tax Division of the Department of Justice: Its Function and Operation." **American Bar Association Journal** 30 (June 1944): 319-325, 363-366.

2689. Loevinger, Lee. "Antitrust Is Pro-Business." **Fortune** 66 (August 1962): 96-97.

2690. Loevinger, Lee. "How to Deal with the Antitrust Division." **New York Law Forum** 9 (March 1963): 64.

2691. Lore, Martin M. and Lawrence Goldfein. "Freedom of Information Act Shields Justice Department Attorneys' Memos from Disclosure." **Journal of Taxation** 56 (February 1982): 125-133.

2692. Lowenthal, Max. **The Federal Bureau of Investigation.** New York: Sloane, 1950.

2693. Ludd, Steven O. "Administrative Discretion and the Immigration and Naturalization Service: To Review or Not to Review?" **Thurgood Marshall Law Review** 8 (Fall 1982): 65-86.

2694. McChesney, K. "Law Enforcement Recruiting: Strategies for the 1980's." **FBI Law Enforcement Bulletin** 55 (January 1986): 11-18.

2695. McCree, Wade H. "Improving the Administration of Justice: The Solicitor General's Perspective." **Pennsylvania Bar Association Quarterly** 48 (October 1977): 502-508.

2696. McCree, Wade H. "Solicitor General and His Client." **Washington University Law Quarterly** 59 (1981): 337-341.

2697. McDermott, Beatrice S. **Government Regulation of Business Including Antitrust Information Sources: A Comprehensive Annotated Bibliography of Works Pertaining to the Antitrust Division, Department of Justices and to the Major Regulatory Agencies of the Federal Government.** Detroit: Gale, 1967.

2698. McGranery, J. P. "The Department of Justice and the War." **Pennsylvania Bar Association Quarterly** 16 (October 1944): 23-29.

2699. McKavitt, M. A. "The Library of the Department of Justice." **Law Library Journal** 32 (September

1939): 271-277.

2700. Mangan, R. J. "Exploiting the Financial Aspects of Major Drug Investigations." **FBI Law Enforcement Bulletin** 53 (November 1984): 13-15.

2701. Margolick, David. "Baxter at Antitrust: Can the Professor Succeed on Brains Alone?" **American Lawyer** 3 (July 1981): 25-30.

2702. Markowitz, Gerald. "How Not to Write History: A Critique of Radosh and Milton's The Rosenberg File: Review Article." **Science and Society** 48 (Spring 1984): 74-89.

2703. Marco, Anthony. "Due Process Jeopardized by New Polygraph Policy." **American Lawyer** 2 (September 1980): 32-39.

2704. Martin, Leroy. "Chicago's Drug Enforcement Administration Task Force." **Police Chief** 51 (February 1984): 22-23.

2705. Mass, Stuart. "The Dilemma of the Intimidated Witness in Federal Organized Crime Prosecutions: Choosing Among the Fear of Reprisals, the Contempt Powers of the Court, and the Witness Protection Program." **Fordham Law Review** 50 (March 1982): 582-610.

2706. Maughan, J. "What's Ahead in Antitrust." **Dun's Review** (December 1961): 34-36.

2707. Meador, Daniel J. "Role of the Justice Department in Maintaining an Effective Judiciary." **Annals of the American Academy of Political and Social Science** 462 (July 1982): 136-151.

2708. Meadows, E. "Bold Departures in Antitrust." **Fortune** 104 (October 5, 1981): 180-182.

2709. Mendel, S. M. "Vertical Restraints Guidelines: A Synthesis of Prevailing Antitrust Standards or a Further Erosion of Antitrust Enforcement?" **Chicago Bar Record** 66 (May/June 1985): 314-318.

2710. Menninger, W. Walter. "Bureau of Prisons and the Public Health Service: A Partnership." **Federal Probation** 44 (September 1980): 45-48.

2711. Meyers, H. B. "Professor Turner's Turn at Antitrust." **Fortune** 72 (September 1965): 168-171.

2712. Mickum, George B. and Carol A. Rhees. "Federal Class Action Reform: A Response to the Proposed Legislation." **Kentucky Law Journal** 69 (Fall 1980-1981): 799-826.

2713. Middleton, Martha. "U.S. Civil Rights Policy Attacked and Defended." **American Bar Association Journal** 68 (October 1982): 1205-1214.

2714. Miscamble, Wilson D. "Thurman Arnold Goes to Washington: A Look at Antitrust Policy in the Later New Deal." **Business History Review** 56 (Spring 1982): 1-15.

2715. Mitchell, W. D. "Department of Justice." **New York County Law Association Year Book** (1929): 301-309.

2716. Moeller, H. G. "Footnotes on the History of a Correctional Organization: The Federal Bureau of Prisons (1930-1980)." **Federal Probation** 44 (September 1980): 37-40.

2717. Monroe, L. J. and M. L. Mullen. "FBI and DEA Join Forces in the Drug Training Effort." **FBI Law Enforcement Bulletin** 55 (May 1986): 2-6.

2718. Morgenfeld, Irving R. "Antitrust and the Oligopoly Problem: Intellectual Pygmies at the Enforcement Agencies?" **Antitrust Law and Economics Review** 9 (1977): 15-30.

2719. Morris, J. W. "Work of the Tax Division of the Department of Justice." **Tax Magazine** 15 (September 1937): 524-526.

2720. Moskowitz, Milton R. "McDonnell Douglas Makes Peace with the Feds: Political Connections Helped Get McDonnell Douglas in Bribery Trouble, and Political Connections Helped Bail the Company Out." **Business and Society Review** (Winter 1982): 24-27.

2721. Motomura, Hiroshi. "Preclearance under Section Five of the Voting Rights Act." **North Carolina Law Review** 61 (January 1983): 189-246.

2722. Munves, James. **The FBI and the CIA: Secret Agents in American Democracy.** New York: Harcourt, Brace Jovanovich, 1975.

2723. Murch, R. S. "The FBI Serology: Services, Policies, and Procedures." **FBI Law Enforcement Bulletin** 54 (March 1985): 15-21.

2724. Murphy, James J. "Antitrust Enforcement Policy under the Reagan Administration." **Journal of the Missouri Bar** 37 (October/November 1981): 471-474.

2725. Nanes, Allan S. "The Federal Role in Criminal Investigation Procedures." **Current History** 53 (August 1967): 107-110.

2726. Nannes, J. M. "What to Expect When the Department of Justice Calls." **I.C.C. Practitioners Journal** 50 (September/October 1983): 646-652.

2727. Navasky, Victor S. **Kennedy Justice.** New York: Atheneum, 1971.

2728. Nealon, Rita W. "Opinion Function of the Federal Attorney General." **New York University Law Quarterly Review** 25 (October 1950): 825-843.

2729. Nelson, Jack and Ronald J. Ostrow. **The FBI and the Berrigans: The Making of a Conspiracy.** New York: Coward, McCann and Geoghegan, 1972.

2730. Neudorfer, C. D. "Fingerprint Automation: Progress in the FBI's Identification Division." **FBI Law Enforcement Bulletin** 55 (March 1986): 2-8.

2731. Norman, D. L. "The Strange Career of the Civil Rights Division's Commitment to Brown." **Yale Law Journal** 93 (May 1984): 983-989.

2732. Nye, Stephen. "View from the Defense Bar." **Antitrust Bulletin** 22 (Summer 1977): 267-272.

2733. O'Connor, K. "Amicus Curiae Role of the U.S. Solicitor General in Supreme Court Litigation." **Judicature** 66 (December/January 1983): 256-264.

2734. Ollestad, Norman. **Inside the FBI.** New York: Stuart, 1967.

2735. O'Reilly, Kenneth. **Hoover and the Un-Americans: The FBI, HUAC and the Red Menace.** Philadelphia: Temple University Press, 1983.

2736. Orrick, William H. "Profile of an Antitrust Enforcement Program." **Antitrust Law Symposium** (1964): 11-23.

2737. Overstreet, Harry A. **The FBI in Our Open Society.** New York: Norton, 1969.

2738. Perkins, Cathy, ed. **Cointelpro: The FBI's Secret**

War on Political Freedom. New York: Pathfinder Press, 1975.

2739. Phillips, Robert G. "FBI Surveys State and Local Law Enforcement Training Needs." **Police Chief** 53 (July 1986): 18-19.

2740. Pickholz, Marvin G. "Expanding World of Parallel Proceedings." **Temple Law Quarterly** 53 (1980): 1100-1133.

2741. Pogue, R. A., H. M. Reasoner, J. H. Shenefield and R. A. Whiting. "60 Minutes with J. Paul McGrath Assistant Attorney General, Antitrust Division." **Antitrust Law Journal** 54 (1985): 131-152.

2742. Poveda, T. G. "FBI and Domestic Intelligence: Technocratic or Public Relations Triumph?" **Crime and Delinquency** 28 (April 1982): 194-210.

2743. Powers, Richard G. **G-men, Hoover's FBI in American Popular Culture.** Carbondale: Southern Illinois University Press, 1983.

2744. Quade, Vicki. "Justice Department Loses Loan Bias Case." **American Bar Association Journal** 68 (February 1982): 139-147.

2745. Quade, Vicki. "New Merger Guidelines Get Mixed Reviews." **American Bar Association Journal** 68 (October 1982): 1211-1218.

2746. Rabin, Robert L. "Agency Criminal Referrals in the Federal System: An Empirical Study of Prosecutorial Discretion." **Stanford Law Review** 24 (June 1972): 1036-1045.

2747. Rathbun, E. A. "Interstate Identification Index." **FBI Law Enforcement Bulletin** 54 (January 1985): 14-17.

2748. Reeves, B. "How the Antitrust Division Can Use Its New Powers to Obtain Statistical Records and Testimony from Trade Associations and Trade Association Executives." **Antitrust Bulletin** 22 (Summer 1977): 355-363.

2749. Rehnquist, William H. "Old Order Changeth: The Department of Justice under John Mitchell." **Arizona Law Review** 12 (Summer 1970): 251-263.

2750. Reynolds, W. B. "Justice Department Policies on Equal Employment and Affirmative Action." **New York University Conference on Labor** 35 (1982):

443-453.

2751. Reynolds, W. B. "Justice Department's Enforcement of Title VII." **Labor Law Journal** 34 (May 1983): 259-265.

2752. Richardson, Elliot L. "Building a New Confidence." **New York State Bar Journal** 45 (November 1973): 455-459.

2753. Richardson, Elliot L. "New Approach to Justice." **Pennsylvania Bar Association Quarterly** 44 (October 1973): 587-593.

2754. Roberts, Maurice A. "Board of Immigration Appeals: A Critical Appraisal." **San Diego Law Review** 15 (December 1977): 29-44.

2755. Roberts, Neil E. "The Department of Justice and Regulation of the One-Bank Holding Company." **Bankers Magazine** 154 (Autumn 1971): 58-63.

2756. Rogovin, M. "Reorganizing Politics out of the Department of Justice." **American Bar Association Journal** 64 (June 1978): 855-858.

2757. Roll, David L. "Dual Enforcement of the Antitrust Laws by the Department of Justice and the FTC: The Liaison Procedure." **Business Lawyer** 31 (July 1976): 2075-2085.

2758. Rose, D. L. "Role of the Justice Department in Antidiscrimination Enforcement." **Public Utilities Fortnightly** 92 (September 13, 1973): 85-87.

2759. Rosen, G. R. "Big Antitrust Crackdown." **Dun's Review** 101 (May 1973): 56-59.

2760. Rosenberg, Maurice, Peter F. Rient and Thomas D. Rowe. "Expenses: The Roadblock to Justice: A Detailed Plan for Making Litigation Affordable." **Judges Journal** 20 (Summer 1981): 16-21.

2761. Rosenblum, S. M. and M. L. Silverstein. "Investigations under Landrum-Griffin." **Georgetown Law Journal** 49 (Winter 1960): 257-264.

2762. Rosenthal, Douglas E. "Antitrust Perspective." **Journal of International Law and Economics** 12 (1978): 263-268.

2763. Rosenthal, Douglas E. and B. H. Flowe. "New Approach to U.S. Enforcement of Antitrust Laws against Foreign Cartels." **North Carolina Journal**

of International Law and Commercial Regulation 6 (Winter 1980): 81-99.

2764. Rosenthal, Douglas E. and T. E. Sheldon. "Section 337: A View from Two Within the Department of Justice." **Georgia Journal of International and Comparative Law** 8 (Winter 1978): 47-64.

2765. Rosoff, L. E. "Reorganization Plan No. 1 under Title VII." **Labor Law Journal** 30 (May 1979): 268-280.

2766. Ross, A. C. "Role of the Justice Department in School Desegregation." **Howard Law Journal** 19 (Winter 1975): 64-70.

2767. Ross-Skinner, J. "Antitrust Tensions with Europe." **Dun's Review** 111 (May 1978): 101-104.

2768. Ruben, George. "Minority Attorneys at Justice Charge Bias." **Monthly Labor Review** 103 (May 1980): 57-58.

2769. Rudnick, Edward. "The Immigration and Naturalization Service and the Administration of the Naturalization and Citizenship Laws." **International Migration Review** 5 (Winter 1971): 420-435.

2770. Sacher, S. J. "ERISA Litigation." **New York University Conference on Labor** 30 (1977): 257-273.

2771. Sagle, R. F. "To Insure that Justice Is Done." **Student Lawyer** 4 (October 1958): 13-17.

2772. Saloschin, Robert L. "Work of the Freedom of Information Committee of the Department of Justice." **Public Utilities Fortnightly** 86 (September 24, 1970): 75-77.

2773. Sargent, J. G. "Department of Justice." **Vermont Bar Association** 24 (1930): 94-120.

2774. Schlesinger, Steven R. "Programs of the Bureau of Justice Statistics." **PS** 18 (Spring 1985): 298-302.

2775. Schmidt, R. M. "Current Department of Justice Criminal Income Tax Policies." **Taxes** 38 (April 1960): 293-302.

2776. Schneider, Mark W. "Criminal Enforcement of Federal Water Pollution Laws in an Era of Deregulation." **Journal of Criminal Law and Criminology**

73 (Summer 1982): 642-674.

2777. Schott, Joseph L. **No Left Turns.** New York: Praeger, 1975.

2778. Schweinhaut, H. A. "The Civil Liberties Section of the Department of Justice." **Bill of Rights Review** 1 (Spring 1941): 206-216.

2779. Segal, William. **Law, The Science of Inefficiency.** New York: Macmillan, 1952.

2780. Seki, H. S. "Justice Department's New Antitrust Guide for International Operations - A Summary and Evaluation." **Business Lawyer** 32 (July 1977): 1633-1656.

2781. Selig, J. L. "The Reagan Justice Department and Civil Rights: What Went Wrong." **University of Illinois Law Review** (1985): 785-835.

2782. Sellers, D. "Legal Services for Congress." **American Bar Association Bar Journal** 63 (December 1977): 1728-1731.

2783. Serrill, Michael S. "Violent World of the Cocaine Cowboys." **Police Magazine** 5 (November 1982): 10-14.

2784. Shenefield, John H. "Computers, Communications, and Antitrust: Some Current Myths and Realities." **Computers and People** 27 (May 1978): 14-17.

2785. Shenefield, John H. "Disclosure of Antitrust Violations and Prosecutorial Discretion." **American Bar Association Antitrust Law Journal** 48 (May 1979): 463-470.

2786. Shenefield, John H. "The Disclosure of Antitrust Violations and Prosecutorial Discretion." **Antitrust Law Journal** 48 (Winter 1980): 463-470.

2787. Shine, R. "Enforcement of the FCPA by the Department of Justice." **Syracuse Journal of International Law and Commerce** 9 (Fall 1982): 283-300.

2788. Simon, David R. and Stanley L. Swart. "The Justice Department Focuses on White-Collar Crime: Promises and Pitfalls." **Crime and Delinquency** 30 (January 1984): 107-119.

2789. Sims, J. "Criminal and Civil Antitrust Litigation: A Prosecutor's Perspective." **American Bar Asso-**

ciation Antitrust Law Journal 46 (Summer 1977): 690-696.

2790. Sims, J. "Inedible Tallow, the Maximum Charges Rule, and Other Fables: Motor Carrier Regulation by the ICC." **Transportation Law Journal** 10 (1978): 55-66.

2791. Singarella, Maureen A. "Internal Justice Department Policy (Eighth Circuit Survey)." **Creighton Law Review** 13 (Summer 1980): 1292-1294.

2792. Sloan, Judy B. "Antitrust: Shared Information between the FTC and the Department of Justice." **Brigham Young University Law Review** (1979): 883-910.

2793. Smartt, Lucien E. "Implications of the Consent Decree for Telephone Company Investors." **Public Utilities Fortnightly** 109 (March 18, 1982): 6-8.

2794. Smith, Edward A. "Persecution Abroad as Grounds for Withholding Deportation: The Standard of Proof and the Role of the Courts." **Fordham International Law Journal** 6 (Winter 1982): 100-120.

2795. Smith, R. A. "What Antitrust Means under Mr. Bicks." **Fortune** 61 (March 1960): 120-123.

2796. Smith, S. A. "View from the Solicitor General's Office: Procedures in Appealing Lower Court Decisions and Settlement Possibilities." **New York University Institute on Federal Taxation** 35 (1977): 355-372.

2797. Sorrentino, Frank M. "Bureaucratic Ideology: The Study of the Federal Bureau of Investigation." Ph.D. dissertation, New York University, 1978.

2798. Spangler, Susan E. "Snatching Legislative Power: The Justice Department's Refusal to Enforce in the Parental Kidnaping Prevention Act." **Journal of Criminal Law and Criminology** 73 (Fall 1982): 1176-1203.

2799. Sperber, Philip. "Controversial U.S. Guidelines in International Licensing." **Patent and Trademark Review** 78 (July/August 1980): 291-296.

2800. Steinhouse, Carl L. "A Practical Approach to Representation of a Client During a Federal Antitrust Grand Jury Investigation." **Cleveland**

State Law Review 29 (Winter 1980): 97-107.

2801. Stillman, Richard H. "The Bureaucracy Problem at DOI." **Public Administration Review** 36 (July/August 1976): 429-439.

2802. Sullivan, William C. **The Bureau: My Thirty Years in Hoover's FBI.** New York: Norton, 1979.

2803. Swanson, R. D. "FBI Firearms Instructor Program for Police." **FBI Law Enforcement Bulletin** 53 (December 1984): 1-8.

2804. Swisher, Carl B. "Federal Organization of Legal Functions." **American Political Science Review** 33 (December 1939): 973-1000.

2805. Tannenbaum, Fredric D. and Michael O. Hurst. "The AT&T Agreement: Reorganization of the Telecommunications Industry and Conflicts with Illinois Law." **Journal of Maritime Law and Commerce** 15 (Summer 1982): 563-590.

2806. Terrell, John U. **The United States Department of Justice: A Story of Crime, Courts, and Counterspies.** New York: Duell, Sloan, and Pearce, 1965.

2807. Theoharis, Athan G. **Beyond the Hiss Case: The FBI, Congress and the Cold War.** Philadelphia: Temple University Press, 1982.

2808. Theoharis, Athan G. "Bureaucrats above the Law: Double-Entry Intelligence Files." **Nation** 225 (October 1977): 393-397.

2809. Theoharis, Athan G. "The FBI and the American Legion Contact Program, 1940-1966." **Political Science Quarterly** 100 (Summer 1985): 271-286.

2810. Theoharis, Athan G. "FBI Surveillance: Past and Present." **Cornell Law Review** 69 (April 1984): 883-894.

2811. Theoharis, Athan G. **Spying on Americans: Political Surveillance from Hoover to the Huston Plan.** Philadelphia: Temple University Press, 1978.

2812. Timberg, S. "Justice Department Guide for International Operations: International Antitrust Enforcement in the Year 1978." **Journal of the Patent Office Society** 60 (October 1978): 636-660.

2813. Torres, Isaias D. "Misconduct by Immigration Officers: Excluding Evidence in Deportation Hearings." **Houston Journal of International Law** 5 (Spring 1983): 243-286.

2814. Toto, Francis K. "Drug Courier Profile Stops and the Fourth Amendment: Is the Supreme Court's Case of Confusion in Its Terminal Stage?" **Suffolk University Law Review** 15 (April 1981): 217-260.

2815. Tucker, Edward. "DEA Airport Search and Seizure. United States v. Mendenhall 100 S. Ct. 1870 (1980)." **New England Law Review** 16 (Summer 1981): 597-615.

2816. Tully, Andrew. **Inside the FBI: From the Files of the Federal Bureau of Investigation and Independent Sources.** New York: McGraw-Hill, 1980.

2817. Turner, William W. **Hoover's FBI: The Men and the Myth.** Los Angeles: Sherbourne Press, 1970.

2818. Ungar, Sanford J. **FBI.** Boston: Little, Brown, 1976.

2819. Vinson, Fred M. "Federal Law Enforcement." **Current History** 53 (July 1967): 15-22.

2820. Vitiello, M. "The Ethics of Brilab." **Howard Law Journal** 27 (1984): 905-927.

2821. Vocci, Francis J. "Drug Enforcement Administration: Scheduling Policy and Classification." **Food Drug Cosmetic Law Journal** 35 (December 1980): 691-697.

2822. Walter, L. M. "Proposed Transfer of Various Agencies to the Executive Department." **I. C. C. Practitioners' Journal** 12 (June 1945): 893-898.

2823. Walters, Johnnie M. "Role of the Department of Justice in Tax Litigation." **South Carolina Law Review** 23 (1971): 193-207.

2824. Wang, Diane and Cindy Jaquith. **FBI vs. Women.** New York: Pathfinder Press, 1977.

2825. Ward, Peter C. "Anti-trust Debate." **Res Gestae** 25 (September 1981): 469-470.

2826. Ward, Peter C. "New Merger Guidelines." **Res**

Gestae 26 (August 1982): 85-87.

2827. Warren, Boulton, F. R. "Merger Policy and Enforcement at the Antitrust Division: The Economist's View." **Antitrust Law Journal** 54 (1985): 109-115.

2828. Washington, G. T. "World's Largest Law Office: Department of Justice and Its Postwar Tasks." **California State Bar** (1949): 66-73.

2829. Waters, Gola E. "An Analysis of Labor Relations in the Public Sector with Special Emphasis on the Implementation of Executive Order 10988 by the Federal Bureau of Prisons." Ph.D. dissertation, Southern Illinois University, 1970.

2830. Walters, Pat and Stephen Gillers, eds. **Investigating the FBI.** Garden City, NY: Doubleday, 1973.

2831. Weaver, Suzanne. **Decision to Prosecute: Organization and Public Policy in the Antitrust Division.** Cambridge, MA: MIT Press, 1977.

2832. Webster, William H. "The FBI's New Role in Drug Trafficking Investigations." **Police Chief** 52 (October 1985): 55-56.

2833. Webster, William H. "Second General Assembly Address." **Police Chief** 52 (March 1985): 26-27.

2834. Webster, William H. "Second General Session Address." **Police Chief** 51 (March 1984): 26-31.

2835. Weiner, Edward C. "In Search of International Evidence: A Lawyer's Guide through the United States Department of Justice." **Notre Dame Law Review** 58 (October 1982): 60-83.

2836. Weiss, J. R. "What to Do When the Department of Justice Calls." **I. C. C. Practitioners Journal** 51 (September/October 1983): 641-645.

2837. Welch, Neil J. and David W. Marston. **Inside Hoover's FBI: The Top Field Chief Reports.** Garden City, NY: Doubleday, 1984.

2838. Wellford, Charles F. "The Federal Justice Research Program." **Law and Policy Quarterly** 2 (October 1980): 504-509.

2839. Wenk, Michael. "Reflections on Current United States Immigration Policy." **International Migration Review** 4 (Spring 1970): 93-98.

2840. Wetlaufer, Gerald and Douglas Rosenthal. "Notes on the New Merger Guidelines." **Mergers and Acquisitions** 17 (Summer 1982): 18-20.

2841. Whitehead, Don. **The FBI Story: A Report to the the People.** New York: Random House, 1956.

2842. Willborn, S. L. "Public Sector Pattern or Practice Enforcement under Reorganization Plan No. 1 of 1978." **Labor Law Journal** 31 (January 1980): 27-36.

2843. Wilson, James Q. **The Investigators: Managing the FBI and Narcotics Agents.** New York: Basic Books, 1978.

2844. Windrem, Robert. "Prosecutor Goes after Wall Street Journal Reporter." **American Lawyer** 2 (January 1980): 14-18.

2845. Winter, Bill. "Probing the Probers: Does Abscam Go Too Far?" **American Bar Association Journal** 68 (November 1982): 1347-1350.

2846. Witham, Donald C. and D. T. Mitchell. "Higher Performance through Organization Development." **FBI Law Enforcement Bulletin** 54 (February 1985): 7-11.

2847. Wolvovitz, B. and J. Lobel. "The Enforcement of Civil Rights Statutes: The Reagan Administration's Record." **Black Law Journal** 9 (Winter 1986): 252-262.

2848. Wright, Richard O. **Whose FBI?** LaSalle, IL: Open Court, 1974.

2849. Zimmerman, Edwin M. "New Directions in Department of Justice Enforcement Policy." **Antitrust Law Journal** 51 (Spring 1982): 93-122.

Chapter 11. Department of Labor

2850. Adams, Leonard P. **The Public Employment Service in Transition, 1933-1968: Evolution of Placement Service into a Manpower Agency.** Ithaca, NY: State School of Industrial and Labor Relations, Cornell University, 1969.

2851. Allen, Gary. "Growing Resistance by Small Business." **American Opinion** 20 (May 1977): 31-33.

2852. Attman, J. M. "Implementing a Civil Rights Injunction: A Case Study of NAACP v. Brennan." **Columbia Law Review** 78 (May 1978): 739-770.

2853. Anderson, Sarah F. "The Employment Initiatives Program." **Clearinghouse Review** 14 (May 1980): 33-35.

2854. Angrisani, Albert. "Role of the States in Revitalizing the Economy." **Labor Law Journal** 32 (May 1981): 259-264.

2855. Appleson, Gail. "Affirmative Action under Attack: Labor Department, Congressmen Take Aim." **American Bar Association Journal** 67 (June 1981): 697-698.

2856. Arden, J. Lea. "Cotton Textiles and the Federal Child Labor Act of 1916." **Labor History** 16 (Fall 1975): 485-494.

2857. Arthur, Henry B. "Wholesale-Price Work of the United States Bureau of Labor Statistics." Ph.D. dissertation, Harvard University, 1935.

2858. Ashford, Nicholas A. **Crisis in the Workplace: Occupational Disease and Injury.** Cambridge, MA: MIT Press, 1976.

2859. Atkinson, Raymond C. **Public Employment Service in the United States.** Chicago: Public Administration Service, 1968.

2860. Auchter, T. G. "OSHA: A Year Later." **Labor Law Journal** 33 (April 1982): 195-201.

2861. Babson, Roger W. **Recent Labor Progress, with Special Reference to the Work of the Federal Government under James J. Davis, Secretary of Labor, as Outlined in the Annual Reports of the Department of Labor.** New York: Revell, 1924.

2862. Babson, Roger W. **W. B. Wilson and the Department of Labor.** New York: Brentano's, 1919.

2863. Babson, Roger W. **Washington and the Depression, Including the Career of W. N. Doak.** New York: Harper, 1932.

2864. Bailey, Stephen K. **Congress Makes a Law: The Story behind the Employment Act of 1946.** New York: Columbia University Press, 1950.

2865. Baird, V. C. "Industrial Union Department, AFL-CIO v. American Petroleum Institute: Limiting OSHA's Authority to Regulate Workplace Carcinogens under the Occupational Safety and Health Act." **Boston College Environmental Affairs Law Review** 9 (Summer 1981-1982): 623-685.

2866. Balfe, Richard. "Charles P. Neill and the United States Bureau of Labor: A Study in Progressive Economics, Social Work and Public Administration." Ph.D. dissertation, University of Notre Dame, 1956.

2867. Bangser, Paul M. "Inherent Role for Cost-Benefit Analysis in Judicial Review of Agency Decisions: A New Perspective on OSHA Rulemaking." **Boston College Environmental Affairs Law Review** 10 (September 1982): 365-443.

2868. Baram, Michael S. "The Right to Know and the Duty to Disclose Hazard Information." **American Journal of Public Health** 74 (April 1984): 385-390.

2869. Bartel, Ann P. and L. G. Thomas. "Direct and Indirect Effects of Regulation: A New Look at OSHA's Impact." **Journal of Law and Economics** 28 (April 1985): 1-25.

2870. Bayer, Ronald. "Women, Work and Reproductive

Hazards." **Hastings Center Report** 12 (October 1982): 14-19.

2871. Benson, H. W. "Union Democracy, the Department of Labor and the Sadlowski Campaign." **Dissent** 24 (Fall 1977): 455-464.

2872. Berkowitz, Monroe. "Occupational Safety and Health." **Annals of the American Academy of Political and Social Science** 443 (May 1979): 41-53.

2873. Bernhardt, Joshua. **The Division of Conciliation Service: Its History, Activities, and Organization.** Baltimore: Johns Hopkins University Press, 1923.

2874. Blum, Albert A. "Labor and the Federal Government: 1850-1933." **Current History** 48 (June 1965): 328-333, 364.

2875. Bookbinder, Hyman H. "Budget Hysteria." **American Federationist** 64 (May 1957): 11-12.

2876. Bornstein, Leon. "Marshall Becomes Secretary of Labor." **Monthly Labor Review** 100 (March 1977): 79-80.

2877. Braeman, John. "Albert J. Beveridge and the First National Child Labor Bill." **Indiana Magazine of History** 60 (March 1964): 1-36.

2878. Braverman, Burt A. "Panel Discussion: Litigation to Defend Secrets." **Administrative Law Review** 34 (Spring 1982): 189-206.

2879. Breen, Vincent I. **The United States Conciliation Service.** Washington, DC: Catholic University of America Press, 1943.

2880. Bregger, John E. "Labor Force Data from the CPS to Undergo Revision in January 1983." **Monthly Labor Review** 105 (November 1982): 3-7.

2881. Brennan, P. J. "Goals of the Labor Department." **Labor Law Journal** 24 (September 1973): 587-591.

2882. Brown, Richard D. "Bold DOL Move Threatens Cities' Sovereignty." **Current Municipal Problems** 7 (Winter 1981): 274-277.

2883. Burdetsky, B. "Marshall Plan to Meet New Needs." **Worklife** 2 (August 1977): 18-24.

2884. Burkhardt, F. X. "ERISA Problems and Programs." **Labor Law Journal** 28 (December 1977): 747-751.

2885. Burns, Arthur F. "Some Reflections on the Employment Act." **Political Science Quarterly** 77 (December 1962): 481-504.

2886. Calavita, K. "Demise of the Occupational Safety and Health Administration: A Case Study in Symbolic Action." **Social Problems** 30 (April 1983): 437-448.

2887. Cassell, Frank H. "Immigration and the Department of Labor." **Annals of the American Academy of Political and Social Science** 367 (September 1966): 105-114.

2888. Cassell, Frank H. **The Public Employment Service: Organization in Change.** Ann Arbor, MI: Academic Publications, 1968.

2889. Chadwick, William J. "Implementation of ERISA: Progress Made by the Department of Labor." **Labor Law Journal** 28 (February 1977): 67-76.

2890. Chapple, Joseph M. **Our Time: A Biography of James Davis.** Boston: Chapple, 1928.

2891. Clague, Ewen. **The Bureau of Labor Statistics.** New York: Praeger, 1968.

2892. Cleary, T. F. "Some Aspects of Agency Review of Initial Decisions of Administrative Law Judges." **Labor Law Journal** 31 (September 1980): 531-538.

2893. Cobus, Jose A. "Method to Estimate the Bureau of Labor Statistics Family Budgets for All Standard Metropolitan Statistical Areas." **Social Science Quarterly** 59 (December 1978): 546-552.

2894. Coleman, Francis T. **The New, New Reagan National Labor Relations Board and Outlook for the Future.** Washington, DC: Federal Bar Association, 1987.

2895. Coleman, Francis T. and Maurice Baskin. "Financial Disclosure under the Labor Management Reporting and Disclosure Act: A Growing Problem for Labor Lawyers." **American Bar Association Journal** 67 (February 1981): 182-185.

2896. Connolly, William L. "Standards and Labor." **American Federationist** 55 (March 1948): 22-24.

2897. Cowan, M. D. "Regulatory Reform: An OSHA Case

Study." **Labor Law Journal** 33 (December 1982): 763-770.

2898. Craft, James A. "Federal Influence in Manpower Programming: An Analysis of Recent Initiatives." **Labor Law Journal** 29 (March 1977): 168-177.

2899. Cruikshank, Nelson H. "They're Spending Your Money." **American Federationist** 62 (May 1955): 7-9.

2900. Cuff, Robert D. "The Politics of Labor Administration during World War I." **Labor History** 21 (Fall 1980): 546-569.

2901. Curran, William J. "Occupational Safety and Health: Unconstitutional Searches." **American Journal of Public Health** 67 (July 1977): 684-685.

2902. Curtis, John E. and William L. Veseley. "The Impact of the ADEA Amendments on Pension Plans: Can Anybody Here Play This Game?" **Journal of Pension Planning and Compliance** 7 (March 1981): 83-95.

2903. Delury, Bernard E. "To Improve and Protect Employment Standards: A Legal and Moral Responsibility." **Labor Law Journal** 25 (February 1974): 67-73.

2904. Docksai, M. F. "OSHA Proposed Grain-Elevator Rule Draws Labor's Fire." **Trial** 20 (March 1984): 8-9.

2905. Docksai, M. F. "OSHA Published Worker Right to Know Standard." **Trial** 20 (January 1984): 8-9.

2906. Donadio, R. E. "OSHA Criteria for Laboratory Proficiency in Blood Lead Analysis." **American Journal of Public Health** 72 (April 1982): 404-405.

2907. Donovan, Raymond J. "Effective Administration of ERISA." **Labor Law Journal** 33 (March 1982): 131-136.

2908. Donovan, Raymond J. "To Protect and Promote the Interests of the American Worker." **Labor Law Journal** 32 (April 1981): 195-202.

2909. Early, John F. "Improving the Measurement of Producer Price Change." **Monthly Labor Review** 101 (April 1978): 7-15.

2910. Early, John F. and P. O. Flaim. "Statistical Characteristics of Major BLS Series." **Monthly Labor Review** 97 (July 1974): 48-52.

2911. Ernst, Philip R. "The Appropriate Unit for Collective Bargaining under Federal Labor Legislation." Ph.D. dissertation, New York University, 1973.

2912. Feitshans, I. L. "Hazardous Substances in the Workplace: How Much Does the Employee Have the Right to Know." **Detroit College of Law Review** (Fall 1985): 697-720.

2913. Felt, Jeremy P. "The Child Labor Provisions of the Fair Labor Standards Act." **Labor History** 11 (Fall 1970): 467-481.

2914. Flanders, Ralph E. "Administering the Employment Act the First Year." **Public Administration Review** 7 (Autumn 1947): 221-227.

2915. Fragomen, Austin T. "DOL Amends Labor Certifications." **International Migration Review** 15 (Fall 1981): 551-555.

2916. Gallardo, Lloyd L. "An Evaluation of United States Department of Labor Policy Regarding Wages Paid Mexican Nationals: Michigan Pickles, A Case Study." Ph.D. dissertation, University of California, 1962.

2917. Gengarelly, W. A. "Secretary of Labor William B. Wilson and the Red Scare, 1919-1920." **Pennsylvania History** 47 (October 1980): 310-330.

2918. Gilbert, Hilda K. "The United States Department of Labor in the New Deal Period." Ph.D. dissertation, University of Wisconsin, 1943.

2919. Gill, W. J. "Losing the Unemployment Numbers Game." **Nation's Business** 62 (October 1974): 42-44.

2920. Goldberg, Joseph P. "Frances Perkins, Isador Lubin, and the Bureau of Labor Statistics." **Monthly Labor Review** 103 (April 1980): 22-30.

2921. Goldberg, Joseph P. "Labor-Management since World War II." **Current History** 48 (June 1965): 346-352, 366.

2922. Goldberg, Joseph P. and W. T. Moye. "Centennial View: The AFL and a National BLS: Labor's Role

Is Crystallized." **Monthly Labor Review** 105 (March 1982): 21-29.

2923. Gordon, Robert. "Joey, Marisa, and Monsieur Kita at the Swimming Pool Summit." **Washington Monthly** 12 (December 1980): 46-52.

2924. Green, William. "Our Nation's Labor Policy." **American Federationist** 53 (July 1946): 18.

2925. Green, William. "Real Department of Labor." **American Federationist** 53 (June 1946): 19.

2926. Grossman, Jonathan P. **The Department of Labor.** New York: Praeger, 1973.

2927. Grossman, Jonathan P. "Black Studies in the Department of Labor 1897-1907." **Monthly Labor Review** 97 (June 1974): 17-27.

2928. Grossman, Jonathan P. "Origin of the US Department of Labor." **Monthly Labor Review** 96 (March 1973): 2-7.

2929. Grossman, Jonathan P. "People's Department." **Worklife** 1 (August 1976): 23-30.

2930. Grossman, Jonathan P. and J. MacLaury. "Creation of the Bureau of Labor Statistics." **Monthly Labor Review** 98 (February 1975): 25-31.

2931. Guzda, Henry P. "Frances Perkins Interest in a New Deal for Blacks." **Monthly Labor Review** 103 (April 1980): 31-35.

2932. Guzda, Henry P. "Labor Department's First Program to Assist Black Workers." **Monthly Labor Review** 105 (June 1982): 39-44.

2933. Haber, William and David H. Krueger. **The Role of the United States Employment Service in a Changing Economy.** Kalamazoo, MI: Upjohn Institute for Employment Research, 1964.

2934. Hall, Ronald and Gerald V. Barrett. "Payday for Patients: Federal Guidelines or a Job-Sample Approach?" **American Psychologist** 32 (July 1977): 586-588.

2935. Hargrove, Ervin C. "The Bureaucratic Politics of Evaluation: A Case Study of the Department of Labor." **Public Administration Review** 40 (March/April 1980): 150-159.

2936. Harper, Michael C. "The Exercise of Executive Discretion: A Study of a Regional Office of the Department of Labor." **Administrative Law Review** 34 (Fall 1982): 559-592.

2937. Harter, Philip J. "In Search of OSHA." **Regulation** 1 (September/October 1977): 33-39.

2938. Hoar, William P. "How Government Creates Unemployment." **American Opinion** 20 (December 1977): 11-18.

2939. Hodgson, James D. "Federal Programs and Industrial Relations." **Labor Law Journal** 21 (August 1970): 518-522.

2940. Hogan, Roscoe B. "FTCA: Recovering for Injuries Caused by Negligent OSHA Inspections." **Trial** 18 (October 1982): 82-85.

2941. Hughes, J. S. "The Economic Consequences of the OSHA Cotton Dust Standards: An Analysis of Stock Price Behavior." **Journal of Law and Economics** 29 (April 1986): 29-59.

2942. Hulsey, S. "CETA Links with the Wild Kingdom." **Worklife** 2 (June 1977): 27-30.

2943. Johnson, Mark S. "U.S. Import and Export Price Indexes Show Declines during First Half." **Monthly Labor Review** 106 (January 1983): 17-24.

2944. Kaiser, Philip. "Labor and Foreign Affairs." **American Federationist** 58 (April 1951): 20-23.

2945. Kanninen, Toiro O. "New Dimensions in BLS Wage Survey Work." **Monthly Labor Review** 82 (October 1959): 1081-1084.

2946. Katz, A. "Evaluating Contributions of the Employment Service to Applicant Earnings." **Labor Law Journal** 28 (August 1977): 472-478.

2947. Kaufman, K. A. "How Will Labor Department Handle Future Problems?" **Iron Age** 202 (December 26, 1968): 27-28.

2948. Kelman, Steven. **Regulating America, Regulating Sweden: A Comparative Study of Occupational Safety and Health Policy.** Cambridge, MA: MIT Press, 1981.

2949. King, William L. **Industry and Humanity.** Boston: Houghton Mifflin, 1918.

2950. Kleinsorge, Paul L. and Robert E. Smith. "Compulsory Arbitration: A Broad View." **Current**

History 49 (August 1965): 97-105, 118.

2951. Knickerbocker, Daniel C. "Prohibited Transactions Excises after Reorganization: Ticking Time Bomb or Just a Dud?" **Tax Lawyer** 34 (Fall 1980): 147-186.

2952. Kroll, Arthur H. and Yale D. Tauber. "Fiduciary Responsibility and Prohibited Transactions under ERISA." **Real Property Probate and Trust Journal** 14 (Winter 1979): 657-682.

2953. Lamale, Helen H. "Bureau of Labor Statistics Relating to Family Living." **Marriage and Family Living** 20 (August 1958): 253-256.

2954. Lanoff, I. D. "DOL - Evolution of ERISA Role." **Pension World** 16 (January 1980): 46-49.

2955. Lapomarda, Vincent A. "Maurice Joseph Tobin, 1901-1953: A Political Profile and an Edition of Selected Public Papers." Ph.D. dissertation, Boston University, 1968.

2956. Lave, Lester B. "Lessons from Benzene." **American Statistician** 36 (August 1982): 260-261.

2957. Leiby, James. **Carroll Wright and Labor Reform: The Origin of Labor Statistics.** Cambridge, MA: Harvard University Press, 1960.

2958. Levine, Louis. "The Older Disabled Worker." **Current Medicine** 27 (May 1980): 5-6.

2959. Levine, M. J. "Meeting Compliance Review Standards: The Problem of Federal Contractors." **Labor Law Journal** 28 (October 1977): 632-640.

2960. Levitan, Sar A. and Garth L. Mangum. **Federal Training and Work Programs in the Sixties.** Ann Arbor: Institute of Labor and Industrial Relations, University of Michigan, 1969.

2961. Levin, Michael. "Politics and Polarity - The Limits of OSHA Reform." **Regulation** 3 (November/December 1979): 33-39.

2962. Leyser, Barbara. "DOL Tests New Employment and Training Program for Welfare Population." **Clearinghouse Review** 14 (May 1980): 27-30.

2963. Linden, F. "Geography of the Market Basket." **Across the Board** 13 (October 1976): 28-31.

2964. Litwin, Edward. "Live-at-Work Jobs." **Immigration Journal** 5 (March /April 1982): 17-19.

2965. Livernash, Edward R. **Collective Bargaining in the Basic Steel Industry: A Study of the Public Interest and the Role of Government.** Washington, DC: Department of Labor, 1961.

2966. Lombardi, John. **Labor's Voice in the Cabinet: A History of the Department of Labor from Its Origins to 1921.** New York: Columbia University Press, 1942.

2967. Lovell, M. C. "Least-Squartes Seasonally Adjusted Unemployment Data." **Brookings Papers on Economic Activity** 1 (1976): 225-237, 239-243.

2968. Lovell, Malcolm R. "New Directions for OFCCP." **Labor Law Journal** 32 (December 1981): 763-769.

2969. Lubove, Roy. "Workmen's Compensation and the Prerogatives of Voluntarism." **Labor History** 8 (Fall 1967): 254-279.

2970. McAdams, Alan K. **Power and Politics in Labor Legislation.** New York: Columbia University Press, 1964.

2971. McAhren, Robert W. "Making the Nation Safe for Childhood: A History of the Movement for Federal Regulation of Child Labor, 1900-1938." Ph.D. dissertation, University of Texas, 1967.

2972. McCaffrey, David P. "Assessment of OSHA's Recent Effects on Injury Rates." **Journal of Human Resources** 18 (Winter 1983): 130-146.

2973. McCaffrey, David P. "Decentralizing Occupational Health and Safety Regulation: An Evaluation of the Foundation and Prospects." **California Western Law Review** 21 (Fall 1984): 101-127.

2974. McCafferty, J. J. "Early Warning System: Can It Help Cure Labor's Ills?" **Iron Age** 191 (March 21, 1963): 43-44.

2975. McGarity, Thomas O. "The New OSHA Rules and the Worker's Right to Know." **Hastings Center Report** 14 (August 1984): 38-45.

2976. MacLaury, J. "Selection of the First US Commissioner of Labor." **Monthly Labor Review** 98 (April 1975): 16-19.

2977. Mallino, David L. **Occupational Safety and Health: A Policy Analysis.** Washington, DC: Government Research Corporation, 1973.

2978. Mangum, Garth L. **The Emergence of Manpower Policy.** New York: Holt, Rinehart, and Winston, 1969.

2979. Mangum, Garth L. **MDTA: Foundation of Federal Manpower Policy.** Baltimore: Johns Hopkins University Press, 1968.

2980. Marshall, Alpheus T. "The Federal Government and Labor Legislation." Ph.D. dissertation, University of Virginia, 1934.

2981. Mendeloff, John. **Regulating Safety: An Economic and Political Analysis of Occupational Safety and Health Policy.** Cambridge, MA: MIT Press, 1979.

2982. Miller, James C. "Is Organized Labor Rational in Supporting OSHA?" **Southern Economic Journal** 50 (January 1984): 881-885.

2983. Mills, N. "Brown-Lung Cotton-Mill Blues." **Dissent** 26 (Winter 1978): 8-11.

2984. Mintz, Benjamin W. "Role of the Department of Labor under OSHA." **New York University Conference on Labor** 27 (1974): 239-256.

2985. Mitchell, Daniel J. B. "Furor over Working Children and the Bureau of Labor." **Monthly Labor Review** 98 (October 1975): 34-36.

2986. Mitchell, James P. "Federal-State Cooperation for Labor Standards and Security." **State Government** 28 (October 1955): 227-230.

2987. Mobley, T. C. "Use of BLS Survey Data in Wage Setting at GPO." **Monthly Labor Review** 93 (April 1970): 66-68.

2988. Moore, Geoffrey H. "Long-Range Program Objectives for BLS." **Monthly Labor Review** 92 (October 1969): 3-6.

2989. Moran, Robert D. "Oversight of Penalty Increases and Adjudicatory Function under the Occupational Safety and Health Act of 1970." **Federal Bar Journal** 33 (Spring 1974): 138-148.

2990. Moran, Robert D. "Research and the Wage and Hour Division." **Monthly Labor Review** 93 (March 1970): 49-50.

2991. Morgenfeld, Irving R. "Antitrust and the Oligopoly Problem: Intellectual Pygmies at the Enforcement Agencies?" **Antitrust Law and Economics Review** 9 (1977): 15-30.

2992. Morse, David A. "Labor and American Foreign Policy." **Industrial and Labor Relations Review** 1 (October 1947): 18-28.

2993. Murphy, H. C. "Coming up to BAT." **Worklife** 2 (August 1977): 6-12.

2994. Nathan,Richard P. **Jobs and Civil Rights: The Role of the Federal Government in Promoting Equal Opportunity in Employment and Training.** Washington, DC: U.S. Government Printing Office, 1969.

2995. Nichols, Albert L. and R. Zeckhauser. "Government Comes to the Workplace: An Assessment of OSHA." **Public Interest** 49 (Fall 1977): 39-69.

2996. North, David S. **Alien Workers: A Study of the Labor Certification Program.** Washington, DC: Transcentury, 1971.

2997. Northcutt, Poppy. "Computing Reasonable Attorney's Fees: The Copeland v. Marshall Trilogy." **Housing Law Review** 19 (January 1982): 339-350.

2998. Norwood, Janet L. "One Hundred Years of the Bureau of Labor Statistics." **Monthly Labor Review** 108 (July 1985): 3-6.

2999. Northstein, Gary Z. "Dealing with a Changed Regulatory Climate: OSHA under the Auchter Administration." **Employee Relations Law Journal** 8 (Winter 1982-1983): 407-431.

3000. Oppenheimer, Carol and Patricia Ramsey. "Putting the Employment Service to Work: New Strategies for Hard Times." **Clearinghouse Review** 14 (June 1980): 273-301.

3001. Orlofsky, J. "Fourth Amendment Administration Searches and Seizures." **Journal of Criminal Law and Criminology** 69 (Winter 1978): 552-562.

3002. Patten, Thomas H. "Personnel Administration and the Proposed Commerce-Labor Merger." **Personnel Journal** 47 (January 1968): 23-31.

3003. Perlo, Victor. "False Claim of Declining Productivity and Its Political Use." **Science and Society** 46 (Fall 1982): 284-327.

3004. Pettus, Beryl E. "OSHA Inspection Costs, Compliance Costs and Other Outcomes: The First Decade." **Policy Studies Review** 1 (May 1982): 596-614.

3005. Plewes, Thomas J. "Better Measures of Service Employment Goal of Bureau Survey Redesign." **Monthly Labor Review** 105 (November 1982): 7-17.

3006. Pomper, Gerald. "Labor Legislation: The Revision of Taft-Hartley in 1953-1954." **Labor History** 6 (Spring 1965): 143-158.

3007. Richards, E. P. "OSHA Regulations: Access to Employer-Held Medical Information." **Trial** 16 (November 1980): 8-9.

3008. Richardson, Karen L. "The Application of the Service Contract Act to ADP Service Contracts: A Classic Case in Overregulation." **Public Contract Newsletter** 17 (January 1982): 3-9.

3009. Roberts, Keith. "Antitrust Problems in the Newspaper Industry." **Harvard Law Review** 82 (December 1968): 319-366.

3010. Root, Norman and D. McCaffrey. "Providing More Information on Work Injury and Illness." **Monthly Labor Review** 101 (April 1978): 16-21.

3011. Rosner, David and G. Markowitz. "Research for Advocacy: Federal Occupational Safety and Health Policies during the New Deal." **Journal of Social History** 18 (Spring 1985): 365-381.

3012. Rothstein, Joan L. "The Government of the United States and the Young Child: A Study of Federal Child Care Legislation between 1935-1971." Ph.D. dissertation, University of Maryland, 1979.

3013. Rothstein, Mark A. "Substantive and Procedural Obstacles to OSHA Rulemaking: Reproductive Hazards as an Example." **Boston College Environmental Affairs Law Review** 12 (Summer 1985): 627-700.

3014. Rourke, Francis E. **Intergovernmental Relations in Employment Security.** Minneapolis: University of Minnesota Press, 1952.

3015. Rourke, Francis E. "Reorganization of the Labor Department." Ph.D. dissertation, University of Minnesota, 1952.

3016. Ruben, George. "Government Unveils Plan to Control Carcinogens." **Monthly Labor Review** 103 (March 1980): 56-57.

3017. Ruben, George. "Serious Violations Target of Mine Safety Agency." **Monthly Labor Review** 105 (October 1982): 47-48.

3018. Rubin, Edwin R. and M. A. Mancini. "Overview of the Labor Certification Requirement for Intending Immigrants." **San Diego Law Review** 14 (December 1976): 76-110.

3019. Ruttenberg, Ruth. **Occupational Safety and Health in the Chemical Industry.** 2nd ed. New York: Council on Economic Priorities, 1981.

3020. Ruttenberg, Stanley H. and Jocelyn Gutchess. **The Federal-State Employment Service: A Critique.** Baltimore: Johns Hopkins University Press, 1970.

3021. Ryan, T. T. "Impact of Regulatory Reform on the Federal Contract Compliance Program." **Federal Bar News and Journal** 40 (September 1981): 188-190.

3022. Sand, Robert H. "Back to Basics: Reporting Illnesses and Injuries." **Employee Relations Law Journal** 5 (Spring 1980): 582-586.

3023. Scherer, Frederic M. "Sunlight and Antitrust: Discovering Each Industry's Inner Economic Logic." **Antitrust Law and Economics Review** 9 (1977): 41-53.

3024. Schmalensee, Richard. "Antitrust and the New Industrial Economics." **American Economic Review** 72 (May 1982): 24-28.

3025. Schneider, S. M. "Unprotected Minority: Employers and Civil Rights Compliance." **Labor Law Journal** 29 (January 1978): 3-8.

3026. Schultz, George P. "Use of Labor Statistics in National Decision Making." **Monthly Labor Review** 92 (November 1969): 48-50.

3027. Shabecoff, A. "Working for the Consumer." **Worklife** 1 (September 1976): 2-5.

3028. Sheifer, V. J. "New Measures of Wage-Rate Change." **Monthly Labor Review** 97 (December 1974): 10-15.

3029. Shientag, Bernard L. "The Department of Labor and

the State." **American Labor Legal Review** 28 (June 1938): 87-90.

3030. Shor, Edgar L. "The Role of the Secretary of Labor." Ph.D. dissertation, University of Chicago, 1954.

3031. Shrug, Elton P. "On the Road with the Antitrusts' Phoenix: '84 Is Coming!" **Antitrust Law and Economics Review** 13 (1981): 101-117.

3032. Shultz, Paul T. and Kathryn A. Jennings. "Suspension of Benefits during Employment: More Problems for Employers." **Employee Relations Law Journal** 7 (Autumn 1981): 293-302.

3033. Siegel, M. S. "OSHA Lists Stricter Standards for Underground Work Sites." **Trial** 19 (October 1983): 8-9.

3034. Singhal, H. K. "Labor Certification under Revised Regulations." **Southern California Law Review** 51 (July 1978): 823-843.

3035. Stevenson, G. "Interview with New Assistant Secretary." **Worklife** 2 (June 1977): 2-9.

3036. Stevenson, G. "Ray Marshall, from Professor to Labor Secretary." **Worklife** 2 (April 1977): 2-5.

3037. Stevenson, G. "Sponsors Were Primed for New Public Jobs." **Worklife** 2 (July 1977): 9-12.

3038. Stotland, Victor G. "New Computer System Improves Display of Statistical Tables." **Monthly Labor Review** 101 (March 1978): 45-47.

3039. Stuart, W. J. "Computer Editing of Survey Data: Five Years of Experience in Bureau of Labor Statistics Manpower Surveys." **American Statistical Association Journal** 61 (June 1966): 375-383.

3040. Swanson, Steven M. "Quantitative Risk Assessment in Light of the Benzene Decision." **American Statistician** 36 (August 1982): 262-263.

3041. Szasz, Andrew. "The Reversal of Federal Policy toward Worker Safety and Health." **Science and Society** 50 (Spring 1986): 25-51.

3042. Terrell, John U. **The United States Department of Labor: A Story of Workers, Unions, and the Economy.**. New York: Meredith Press, 1968.

3043. Thomas, W. A. "Supreme Court Review of the OSHA Benzene Standard." **American Statistician** 36 (August 1982): 264-265.

3044. Thompson, Frank J. "Deregulation by the Bureaucracy: OSHA and the Augean Quest for Error Correction." **Public Administration Review** 42 (May/June 1982): 202-212.

3045. Tincher, William R. "Practical Aspects of Conducting Antitrust Proceedings: Post Hearing." **Antitrust Bulletin** 4 (September/October 1959): 683-691.

3046. Tobin, Maurice J. "Department of Labor: Its Past Services and Future Program." **American Federationist** 56 (November 1949): 24-26.

3047. Tringali, Joseph F. "Redemption through Exemption: Unemployment Insurance and Sectarian Schools." **New York University Law Review** 55 (May 1980): 242-270.

3048. Usery, W. J. "New Perspective: The US Department of Labor and the Law." **Labor Law Journal** 27 (November 1976): 667-669.

3049. Valeo, R. and M. J. Walker. "Jobs for Indians Who Don't Want Handouts." **Worklife** 2 (June 1977): 19-22.

3050. Viscusi, W. Kip. "Impact of Occupational Safety and Health Regulation." **Bell Journal of Economics** 10 (Spring 1979): 117-140.

3051. Wadlaw, E. "How DOL Helps Handicapped Workers." **Worklife** 2 (May 1977): 7-13.

3052. Walker, Roger W. "The AFL and Child-Labor Legislation: An Exercise in Frustration." **Labor History** 11 (Summer 1970): 323-340.

3053. Weber, Arnold R. "The Role of the U.S. Department of Labor in Immigration." **International Migration Review** 4 (Summer 1970): 31-46.

3054. Weber, Sophie. **How OSHA Enforces the Law: A Case Study.** New York: INFORM, 1981.

3055. Weinstein, James. "Big Business and the Origins of Workmen's Compensation." **Labor History** 8 (Spring 1967): 156-174.

3056. Weintraub, Richard M. "DOL Changes Rules Governing

Reporting for Employee-Benefit Plans." **Trusts and Estates** 120 (April 1981): 40-43.

3057. White, A. P. "Organization and Functions of the United States Department of Labor." **Chicago Bar Record** 57 (September/October 1975): 84-87.

3058. Wilhelm, Clarke L. "William B. Wilson: The First Secretary of Labor." Ph.D. dissertation, Johns Hopkins University, 1967.

3059. Wilson, Robert A. "Barriers to Trustbusting: Efficiency Myths and Timid Trustbusters." **Antitrust Law and Economics Review** 9 (1977): 19-39.

3060. Wines, Michael. "Regulation Writing in Washington: Making Days Stretch into Years, A 1978 Law to Help Displaced Airline Workers, Which the Labor Department Has Still Not Implemented, Illustrates How Congress Does Not Always Have the Last Word." **National Journal** 14 (November 13, 1982): 1937-1940.

3061. Wirtz, Willard W. "U.S. Department of the Labor - The Worker's Agency." **American Federationist** 70 (February 1963): 3-6.

3062. Wirtz, Willard W. **Labor and the Public Interest.** New York: Harper and Row, 1964.

3063. Wise, Kenneth T. "The Effects of OSHA Regulations on the U.S. Lead Industry: An Economic Impact and Econometric Modeling Analysis." Ph.D. dissertation, Massachusetts Institute of Technology, 1979.

3064. Wyant, Dennis R. "Employment Services for Veterans." **Labor Law Journal** 31 (April 1980): 195-199.

3065. Yandle, Bruce. "Social Regulation Controversy: The Cotton Dust Standard." **Social Science Quarterly** 63 (March 1982): 58-69.

3066. Yellowitz, Irwin. "The Origins of Unemployment Reform in the United States." **Labor History** 9 (Fall 1968): 338-360.

3067. Young, Dudley E. and S. Goldstein. "BLS Employment Series and Manufacturing Reporting Practices." **Monthly Labor Review** 80 (November 1957): 1367-1371.

Chapter 12.
Department of State

3068. Abrams, E. "Human Rights in the Reagan Administration: Four Perspectives." **Federal Bar News and Journal** 31 (May 1984): 202-204.

3069. Acheson, Dean. "The Eclipse of the State Department." **Foreign Affairs** 49 (July 1971): 593-606.

3070. Allen, George V. "The Utility of a Trained and Permanent Foreign Service." **Foreign Service Journal** 31 (March 1954): 20-23, 49-50.

3071. Alvarez, David J. "The Department of State and the Abortive Papal Mission to China, August 1918." **Catholic Historical Review** 62 (July 1976): 455-463.

3072. Andrews, Russell O. **The Re-Americanization of Foreign Service Officers.** Syracuse, NY: Inter-University Case Program, 1970.

3073. Angel, Juvenal L. **Careers in the Diplomatic Service.** 4th ed. New York: World Trade Academy Press, 1961.

3074. Anthony, William H. "Public Diplomacy and the Nixon Doctrine, Reaction by Foreign and American Media and the U.S. Information Agency's Role." Ph.D. dissertation, George Washington University, 1976.

3075. Armstrong, Willis C. "The Trade Policy Crisis." **Foreign Service Journal** 48 (November 1971): 14-18.

3076. Attwood, William. "The Labyrinth in Foggy Bottom: A Critique of the State Department." **Atlantic** 219 (February 1967): 45-50.

3077. Atwater, Elton. "The American Foreign Service since 1939." **American Journal of International Law** 41 (January 1947): 73-102.

3078. Atwater, Elton. **Examinations for the American Foreign Service.** Washington, DC: Digest Press, 1936.

3079. Bacchus, William I. "Foreign Affairs Officials: Professionals without Professions." **Public Administration Review** 37 (November/December 1977): 641-650.

3080. Bacchus, William I. **Foreign Policy and the Bureaucratic Process: The State Department's Country Director System.** Princeton, NJ: Princeton University Press, 1974.

3081. Bahti, James H. "Personnel Integration in the Foreign Service." Ph.D. dissertation, University of Michigan, 1959.

3082. Bailie, Robert. "The UNESCO Relations Staff of the Department of State: A Study of Agency Response to Public and Private Pressures." Ph.D. dissertation, University of Pittsburgh, 1964.

3083. Baldwin, C. F. "Dog's Life in the Foreign Service." **Virginia Quarterly Review** 55 (Autumn 1979): 716-723.

3084. Ball, George W. "The New Diplomacy." **Department of State Bulletin** 52 (June 1965): 1042-1048.

3085. Ball, Harris H. "An Examination of the Major Efforts for Organizational Effectiveness in the Department of State from 1924 to 1971." Master's thesis, George Washington University, 1971.

3086. Baram, Philip J. **The Department of State in the Middle East, 1919-1945.** Philadelphia: University of Pennsylvania Press, 1978.

3087. Baram, Phillip J. "Undermining the British: Department of State Policies in Egypt and the Suez Canal before and during World War II." **Historian** 40 (August 1978): 631-649.

3088. Barnes, William and John H. Morgan. **The Foreign Service of the United States: Origins, Development, and Functions.** Washington, DC: U. S. Government Printing Office, 1961.

3089. Barron, Bryton. **Inside the State Department: A**

Candid Appraisal of the Bureaucracy. New York: Comet, 1956.

3090. Barron, Bryton. **The State Department: Blunders or Treason?** Springfield, VA: Crestwood, 1965.

3091. Barron, Bryton. **The Untouchable State Department.** Springfield, VA: Crestwood, 1962.

3092. Bean, Elizabeth A. "Down in Generation Gap: The Junior Foreign Service Officer Looks at the System." **Annals of the American Academy of Political and Social Science** 380 (November 1968): 76-81.

3093. Beaulac, Willard L. **Career Diplomat: A Career in the Foreign Service of the United States.** New York: Macmillan, 1964.

3094. Beaulac, Willard L. "Technical Cooperation as an Instrument of Foreign Policy - No Substitute for Traditional Diplomacy." **Department of State Bulletin** 32 (June 1955): 964-969.

3095. Beaulac, Willard L. "U. S. Diplomacy in a Changing World." **Department of State Bulletin** 33 (August 1955): 335-338.

3096. Becker, Joseph D. "The State Department White List and Diplomatic Immunity." **American Journal of International Law** 47 (October 1953): 704-706.

3097. Beichman, Arnold. **The "Other" State Department : The United States Mission to the United Nations - Its Role in the Making of Foreign Policy.** New York: Basic Books, 1967.

3098. Belmont, Perry. "Ambassadorial Rank for Ministers." **Current History** 29 (January 1929): 629-632.

3099. Bemis, Samuel F., ed. **The American Secretaries of State and Their Diplomacy.** New York: Knopf, 1927-1929.

3100. Bendiner, Robert. **The Riddle of the State Department.** New York: Farrar and Rinehart, 1941.

3101. Bergman, Helen A. **The Communications System of the United States Department of State as It Pertains to the Foreign Service.** Minneapolis: University of Minnesota, 1948.

3102. Bess, Demaree C. "Why Americans Hate the State

Department." **Saturday Evening Post** (August 1950): 77-78, 80, 83.

3103. Bilder, Richard B. "The Office of the Legal Adviser: The State Department Lawyer and Foreign Affairs." **American Journal of International Law** 56 (July 1962): 633-684.

3104. Blair, William D. "Communication: The Weak Link in Our Foreign Relations." **Department of State Bulletin** 63 (November 1970): 580-586.

3105. Blair, William D. "Department Discusses National Security Information System." **Department of State Bulletin** 66 (April 1972): 523-525.

3106. Blaney, Harry C. "Global Challenges and the Fudge Factory." **Foreign Service Journal** 51 (September 1974): 13-14, 26.

3107. Bloomfield, Lincoln P. "The Department of State and the United Nations." **International Organization** 4 (August 1950): 400-411.

3108. Bohlen, Charles E. "The Foreign Service and the Panorama of Change." **Department of State Bulletin** 44 (June 1961): 964-969.

3109. Bolles, Blair. "Reorganization of the State Department." **Foreign Policy Reports** 23 (August 1947): 134-143.

3110. Bolles, Blair and O. K. D. Ringwood. "Modern Functions and Tasks of the State Department." **Foreign Policy Reports** 23 (August 1947): 144.

3111. Bowie, Robert R. "Planning in the Department." **Foreign Service Journal** 38 (March 1961): 20-24.

3112. Bowles, Chester. "A Balance Sheet on U.S. Foreign Policy." **Department of State Bulletin** 46 (February 1962): 252-258.

3113. Bowles, Chester. "Total Diplomacy." **Department of State Bulletin** 46 (April 1962): 677-678.

3114. Bowling, John W. "How We Do Our Thing: Crisis Management." **Foreign Service Journal** 47 (May 1970): 19-21.

3115. Bowling, John W. "How We Do Our Thing: Innovation." **Foreign Service Journal** 47 (October 1970): 25-27, 55-56.

3116. Bowling, John W. "How We Do Our Thing: Policy Formulation." **Foreign Service Journal** 47 (January 1970): 19-22, 48.

3117. Briggs, Ellis O. **Farewell to Foggy Bottom: The Recollections of a Career Diplomat.** New York: McKay, 1964.

3118. Briggs, Ellis O. "The Sad State of the Department of State: The Hog-Tied Ambassador." **Esquire** (September 1963): 100-101.

3119. Brown, Ben H. "Congress and the Department of State." **Annals of the American Academy of Political and Social Science** 289 (September 1953): 100-107.

3120. Brown, MacAlister. "The Demise of State Department Public Opinion Polls: A Study in Legislative Oversight." **Midwest Journal of Political Science** 5 (February 1961): 1-17.

3121. Bruce, Diana A. "The Office of Congressional Relations of the Department of State, 1959-1960." Master's thesis, University of California, 1961.

3122. Burke, Lee H. **The Department of State's Congressional Relations Office.** Washington, DC: U.S. Department of State, Office of the Historian, 1977.

3123. Burke, Lee H. **Homes of the Department of State, 1774-1976: The Buildings Occupied by the Department of State and Its Predecessors.** Washington, DC: Historical Office, U.S. Department of State, 1977.

3124. Cabot, John M. "Understanding Our Foreign Service." **Department of State Bulletin** 30 (March 1954): 353-358.

3125. Calkin, Homer L. **Women in the Department of State: Their Role in American Foreign Affairs.** 2nd ed. Washington, DC: U. S. Government Printing Office, 1978.

3126. Campbell, John F. **The Foreign Affairs Fudge Factory.** New York: Basic Books, 1971.

3127. Cantrell, William A. "Culture Shock and the Foreign Service Child." **Foreign Service Journal** 51 (December 1974): 4, 6, 8, 28-29.

3128. Cardozo, Michael H. **iplomats in International Co-**

operation: Stepchildren of the Foreign Service. Ithaca, NY: Cornell University Press, 1962.

3129. Carpenter, W. B. "The Equipment of American Students for Foreign Service." **Annals of the American Academy of Political and Social Science** 122 (November 1925): 124-130.

3130. Carr, Wilbur J. "American Consular Service." **American Journal of International Law** 1 (October 1917): 891-913.

3131. Carroll, P. W. "Viewing 48 Years in the Department of State: An Interview with Bertha S. Rodrick." **Department of State Bulletin** 21 (November 1949): 741-744.

3132. Carter, Kent C. "Development of the Foreign Service Inspection System." **Foreign Service Journal** 51 (January 1974): 18-20, 25.

3133. Casey, William J. "The Economic Role of the State Department." **Department of State Bulletin** 68 (June 1973): 849-852.

3134. Charlick, Carl. "Diplomatic Caretaker." **Foreign Service Journal** 32 (October 1955): 20-23, 40, 42.

3135. Childs, James R. **American Foreign Service.** New York: Holt, 1948.

3136. Chittick, William O. "The Domestic Information Activities of the Department of State." Ph.D. dissertation, Johns Hopkins University, 1964.

3137. Chittick, William O. **State Department, Press, and Pressure Groups: A Role Analysis.** New York: Wiley, 1970.

3138. Chittick, William O. "State Department - Press Antagonism: Opinion Versus Policy-Making Needs?" **Journal of Politics** 31 (August 1969): 756-771.

3139. Chomsky, Noam. **The Washington Connection and Third World Fascism.** Boston: South End Press, 1979.

3140. Chu, Francis Yu-Ou. "The American Department of State and Foreign Service." Ph.D. dissertation, University of Wisconsin, 1936.

3141. Chu, Yung-Chao. "A History of the Hull Trade Program, 1934-1939." Ph.D. dissertation, Columbia University, 1957.

3142. Churchill, Malcolm. "What Happened to the Career Foreign Service?" **Foreign Service Journal** 47 (December 1970): 38, 50-52.

3143. Cigrand, Bernard J. **Story of the Great Seal of the United States, or History of American Emblems.** Chicago: Cameron, Amberg, 1903.

3144. Cleveland, Harlan. "View from the Diplomatic Tightrope." **Department of State Bulletin** 46 (May 1962): 803-808.

3145. Clubb, O. Edmund. "The National Security and Our Foreign Service." **Nation** (December 1954): 544-547.

3146. Clubb, O. Edmund. "Security Risks: National Security and the State Department." **Foreign Service Journal** 50 (December 1973): 13-15.

3147. Cochran, William P. "A Diplomat's Moments of Truth." **Foreign Service Journal** 30 (September 1953): 23, 62.

3148. Cohen, E. M. "Rank Injustice: The Case for Semiautomatic Promotion of Middle Grade Officers." **Foreign Service Journal** 49 (August 1972): 17-91, 27-28.

3149. Colegrove, Kenneth. "Expansion of the Publications of the Department of State." **American Political Science Review** 23 (February 1929): 69-77.

3150. Coletta, Paolo E. "Secretary of State William Jennings Bryan and Deserving Democrats." **Mid-America** 48 (April 1966): 75-98.

3151. Colligan, Francis J. **The In-Service Training of Cultural Relations Officers: An Outline Guide.** Washington, DC: U. S. Government Printing Office, 1949.

3152. Collins, Michael. "Communicating about Foreign Policy." **Department of State Bulletin** 62 (March 1970): 393-396.

3153. Cooper, Joseph D. "Decision-Making and the Action Process in the Department of State." Ph.D. dissertation, American University, 1951.

3154. Coulter, Eliot B. "Visa Work of the Department of State and the Foreign Service." **Department of State Bulletin** 21 (October 1949): 523-535.

3155. Coulter, Eliot B. "Visa Work of the Department of State and the Foreign Service." **Department of State Bulletin** 28 (February 1953): 195-203.

3156. Crane, Katharine. **Mr. Carr of State: Forty Seven Years in the Department of State.** New York: St. Martin's Press, 1960.

3157. Cunningham, John E. "Are We Administering Away Our Effectiveness?" **Foreign Service Journal** 36 (February 1959): 19-21.

3158. Curran, R. T. "The State Department's Revolution in Executive Management." **Foreign Service Journal** 49 (October 1972): 4, 6, 8, 10, 12.

3159. Current, Richard N. **Secretary Stimson: A Study in Statecraft.** New Brunswick, NJ: Rutgers University Press, 1954.

3160. Daniels, Roger. "William Jennings Bryan and the Japanese." **Southern California Quarterly** 48 (Fall 1966): 227-240.

3161. David, Joan. **Inside the State Department: How It Works at Home and Abroad.** New York: Manhattan, 1952.

3162. Davis, David. "Bureaucratic Exchange in Policy Formulation: The State Department's Relations with Three Domestic Agencies in the Foreign Affairs Arena." Ph.D. dissertation, Johns Hopkins University, 1971.

3163. Davis, Nathaniel P. "Accelerating Promotion." **Foreign Service Journal** 51 (October 1974): 16-17, 57.

3164. Davis, Nathaniel P. **Few Dull Moments: A Foreign Service Career.** Philadelphia: Dunlap, 1967.

3165. DeConde, Alexander. **The American Secretary of State: An Interpretation.** New York: Praeger, 1962.

3166. Delaney, Robert F. **Your Future in the Foreign Service.** New York: Richards Rosen, 1961.

3167. Denby, James O. "Suggestions for Improving the Foreign Service and Its Administration to Meet Its War and Postwar Responsibilities." **Foreign Service Journal** 22 (February/July 1945): 7-10, 12-15, 14-16, 14-17, 12-14, 13-15.

3168. Dougall, Richardson and Richard S. Patterson. "The Numbering of the Secretaries of State." **Department of State Bulletin** 41 (July 1959): 80-82.

3169. Dubin, Martin D. "Elihu Root and the Advocacy of a League of Nations, 1914-1917." **Western Political Quarterly** 19 (September 1966): 439-455.

3170. Duke, Angier B. "Perspectives in Protocol." **Department of State Bulletin** 44 (March 1961): 414-418.

3171. Duke, Angier B. "Protocol and Peacekeeping." **Department of State Bulletin** 51 (November 1964): 736-739.

3172. Duke, Angier B. "Protocol and the Conduct of Foreign Affairs." **Department of State Bulletin** 49 (November 1963): 700-704.

3173. Dulles, John F. "The Role of Negotiation." **Department of State Bulletin** 38 (February 1958): 159-168.

3174. Edel, Wilbur. "The State Department, the Public and the United Nations Concept, 1939-1945." Ph.D. dissertation, Columbia University, 1951.

3175. Egan, Clifford L. "Pressure Groups, the Department of State, and the Abrogation of the Russian-American Treaty of 1832." **Proceedings of the American Philosophical Society** 115 (August 1971): 328-334.

3176. Elder, Robert E. "A Career Service for USIA?" **Foreign Service Journal** 33 (February 1956): 26-27, 40, 42, 44.

3177. Elder, Robert E. **The Policy Machine: The Department of State and American Foreign Policy.** Toronto: Burns and MacEachern, 1960.

3178. Elder, Robert E. "Public Studies Division of the Department of State: Public Opinion Analysts in the Formulation and Conduct of American Foreign Policy." **Western Political Quarterly** 10 (December 1957): 783-792.

3179. Ellison, William J. "Paul Robeson and the State Department." **Crisis** 84 (May 1977): 184-189.

3180. Epernay, Mark. "The Sad State of the Department of State: Part II. The Hog-Wild Machine." **Esquire**

(September 1963): 102-103, 151-153.

3181. Esterline, John H. and Robert B. Black. **Inside Foreign Policy: The Department of State Political System and Its Subsystems.** Palo Alto, CA: Mayfield, 1975.

3182. Estes, Thomas S. and E. Allen Lightner. **The Department of State.** New York: Praeger, 1976.

3183. Estes, Thomas S. "Executive and Administrative Assignments for FSO's." **Foreign Service Journal** 29 (March 1952): 26, 48.

3184. Etzold, Thomas H. "Understanding Consular Diplomacy." **Foreign Service Journal** 52 (March 1975): 10-12.

3185. Evans, A. E. "Reorganization of the American Foreign Service." **International Affairs** 24 (April 1948): 206-217.

3186. Felix, David. "Three Suggestions for Strengthening the Foreign Service." **Foreign Service Journal** 32 (December 1955): 30-31, 42-45.

3187. Fielder, Frances and Godfrey Harris. **The Quest for Foreign Affairs Officers - Their Recruitment and Selection.** New York: Carnegie Endowment, 1966.

3188. Finch, George A. "Enlargement of the Publications of the Department of State." **American Journal of International Law** 22 (July 1928): 629-632.

3189. Finch, George A. "Present Interest in Foreign Affairs and the State Department's Publication Facilities." **American Journal of International Law** 23 (January 1929): 121-137.

3190. Fisher, Glen H. "The Foreign Service Officer." **Annals of the American Academy of Political and Social Science** 368 (November 1966): 71-82.

3191. Fiszman, Joseph R. "Development of Administrative Roles: The Labor Attache Program of the U.S. Foreign Service." **Public Administration Review** 25 (September 1965): 203-212.

3192. Fitzpatrick, Dick. "Telling the World about America." **Public Opinion Quarterly** 10 (Winter 1946): 582-592.

3193. Fosdick, Dorothy. "For the Foreign Service - Help Wanted." **New York Times Magazine** (November 20,

1955): 13, 65-69.

3194. Frankel, Charles R. **High on Foggy Bottom: An Outsider's Inside View of the Government.** New York: Harper and Row, 1968.

3195. Garnham, David. "Attitude and Personality Patterns of United States Foreign Service Officers." **American Journal of Political Science** 18 (August 1974): 525-547.

3196. Garnham, David. "Foreign Service Elitism and US Foreign Affairs." **Public Administration Review** 35 (January 1975): 44-51.

3197. Garnham, David. "State Department Rigidity: Testing a Hypothetical Hypothesis." **International Studies Quarterly** 18 (March 1974): 31-39.

3198. Gauss, Clarence E. **A Notarial Manual for Consular Officers.** Washington, DC: U.S. Government Printing Office, 1921.

3199. Gerber, William. **The Department of State of the United States.** Washington, DC: U.S. Government Printing Office, 1942.

3200. Gimlin, Hoyt. "State Department and Policy Making." **Editorial Research Reports** 1 (June 1969): 467-484.

3201. Glassman, Jon D. "The Foreign Service Officer: Observer or Advocate?" **Foreign Service Journal** 47 (May 1970): 29-30, 45.

3202. Gordon, J. C. "Diplomatic Immunity." **Foreign Service Journal** 29 (January 1952): 23, 46-47.

3203. Gormly, James L. "Secretary of State James F. Byrnes, An Initial British Evaluation." **South Carolina Historical Magazine** 79 (July 1978): 198-205.

3204. Graebner, Norman A., ed. **An Uncertain Tradition: American Secretaries of State in the Twentieth Century.** New York: McGraw-Hill, 1961.

3205. Graves, Harold N. "State Department - New Model." **Reporter** 1 (November 1949): 27-29.

3206. Greenberg, Myron A. "The Secretary of State and Secretarial Belief Systems: An Inquiry into the Relationship between Knowledge and Action." Ph.D. dissertation, University of Cincinnati,

1979.

3207. Grew, Joseph C. "Ambassador Grew on the American Foreign Service." **Foreign Service Journal** 13 (December 1936): 649, 694, 696.

3208. Gross, Ernest A. "Operation of the Legal Adviser's Office." **American Journal of International Law** 43 (January 1949): 122-127.

3209. Gustafson, Milton O. "Archival Implications of State Department Recordkeeping." **Prologue** 7 (Spring 1975): 36-38.

3210. Gustafson, Milton O. "State Department Records in the National Archives: A Profile." **Prologue** 2 (Winter 1970): 175-180.

3211. Hackworth, Green H. "Legal Work in the Department of State." **Georgetown Law Journal** 20 (May 1932): 411-426.

3212. Hall, Harold E. "The Job of Economic Reporting." **Foreign Service Journal** 32 (April 1955): 24-25, 46-47.

3213. Halle, Louis J. "Policy Making and the Career Service." **Foreign Service Journal** 30 (September 1953): 31, 48, 50.

3214. Halle, Louis J. "Significance of the Institute of Inter-American Affairs in the Conduct of U. S. Foreign Policy." **Department of State Bulletin** 18 (May 1948): 659-662.

3215. Hannah, Norman B. "Craftsmanship and Responsibility: A Restatement of the Generalist-Specialist Problem." **Foreign Service Journal** 39 (April 1962): 21-24.

3216. Hanson, Simon G. "Success of the International Coffee Agreement: How the State Department Deceived the Congress." **Inter-American Economic Affairs** 21 (Autumn 1967): 55-79.

3217. Harr, John E. **The Anatomy of the Foreign Service: A Statistical Profile.** New York: Carnegie Endowment, 1965.

3218. Harr, John E. **The Development of Careers in the Foreign Service.** New York: Carnegie Endowment, 1965.

3219. Harr, John E. "The Issue of Competence in the State

Department." **International Studies Quarterly** 14 (March 1970): 95-101.

3220. Harr, John E. **The Professional Diplomat.** Princeton, NJ: Princeton University Press, 1969.

3221. Healey, Maryanne F. "Witness, Participant, and Chronicler: The Role of Herbert Feis as Economic Adviser to the State Department, 1931-1943." Ph.D. dissertation, Georgetown University, 1973.

3222. Heller, David. **Paths of Diplomacy: America's Secretaries of State.** Philadelphia: Lippincott, 1967.

3223. Henderson, Loy. "The Foreign Service as a Career." **Department of State Bulletin** 32 (April 1955): 635-640.

3224. Henderson, Loy. "The Foreign Service - First Line of Defense." **Department of State Bulletin** 32 (May 1955): 849-853.

3225. Herring, Hubert C. "The Department of State." **Harper's Magazine** (February 1937): 225-238.

3226. Herter, Christian A. "Department Recommends Senate Approval of Mutual Security Treaty with Japan." **Department of State Bulletin** (June 1960): 1029-1032.

3227. Herter, Christian A. "New Dimensions in Diplomacy." **Department of State Bulletin** 37 (November 1957): 831-834.

3228. Herter, Christian A. "Role of the Department of State in the National Policy Machinery." **Department of State Bulletin** 43 (July 1960): 3-7.

3229. Herter, Christian A. "Secretary Herter Reports to Foreign Relations Committee on Events at Paris." **Department of State Bulletin** 42 (June 1960): 947-955.

3230. Hickman, Martin B. and N. Hollander. "Undergraduate Origin as a Factor in Elite Recruitment and Mobility: The Foreign Service - A Case Study." **Western Political Quarterly** 19 (June 1966): 337-353.

3231. Hill, Norman L. **Mr. Secretary of State.** New York: Random House, 1963.

3232. Hilton, Ralph. **Worldwide Mission: The Story of**

the United States Foreign Service. New York: World, 1970.

3233. Hinckley, Frank E. **American Consular Jurisdiction in the Orient.** Washington, DC: Lowdermilk, 1906.

3234. Hoffman, Ralph N. "Latin American Diplomacy: The Role of the Assistant Secretary of State, 1957-1969." Ph.D. dissertation, Syracuse University, 1969.

3235. Holdridge, John H. "Department of State, US Policy towards Southeast Asia." **Journal of Contemporary Asia** 11 (1981): 515-519.

3236. Hollander, Neal A. and Martin B. Hickman. "Undergraduate Origin as a Factor in Elite Recruitment and Mobility: The Foreign Service - A Case Study." **Western Political Quarterly** 19 (June 1966): 337-353.

3237. Holloway, J. K. "The Role of the Services in Support of Foreign Policy." **United States Naval Institute Proceedings** 102 (May 1976): 66-81.

3238. Holzheimer, Hermann. "Protocol as a Function of Foreign Policy." **Aussenpolitik** 27 (1976): 349-360.

3239. Hopkins, Frank S. "Training Responsibilities in the Department of State." **Public Administration Review** 8 (Spring 1948): 119-125.

3240. Hudson, Manley D. "An Annual Report by the Secretary of State, a Suggestion." **American Journal of International Law** 22 (July 1928): 624-629.

3241. Hulen, Bertram D. **Inside the Department of State.** New York: McGraw Hill, 1939.

3242. Hunt, Gaillard. **The American Passport: Its History and a Digest of Laws, Rulings, and Regulations Government Its Issuance by the Department of State.** Washington, DC: U.S. Government Printing Office, 1898.

3243. Hunt, Gaillard. **The Department of State of the United States: Its History and Functions.** New Haven, CT: Yale University Press, 1914.

3244. Hunt, Gaillard. **The History of the Seal of the United States.** Washington, DC: U.S. Government Printing Office, 1909.

3245. Hunt, Gaillard. **The Seal of the United States: How It Was Developed and Adopted.** Washington, DC: U.S. Department of State, 1892.

3246. Ilchman, Warren F. **ProfessionalDiplomacy in the United States, 1779-1939: A Study in Administrative History.** Chicago: University of Chicago Press, 1961.

3247. Jablon, Howard. "The State Department and Collective Security, 1933-34." **Historian** 33 (February 1971): 248-263.

3248. Jackson, Henry M., ed. **The Secretary of State and the Ambassador: Jackson Subcommittee Papers on the Conduct of American Foreign Policy.** New York: Praeger, 1966.

3249. James, Elizabeth M. "State Department Adaptation to Independent Africa, 1952-1962: A Study in Thought and Practice." Ph.D. dissertation, George Washington University, 1969.

3250. Johnson, Emory R. "The Early History of the United States Consular Service, 1776-1792." **Political Science Quarterly** 13 (March 1898): 19-40.

3251. Johnson, N. T. "Functions and Activities of the Department of State." **Constitutional Review** 12 (April 1928): 84-94.

3252. Johnson, Richard A. "A Proposal for Reorganizing the High Command of the Department of State." **Foreign Service Journal** 48 (October 1971): 19-20, 38.

3253. Johnson, R. C. "Recruitment and Training for the Foreign Service of the United States." **India Quarterly** 11 (October/December 1955): 376-381.

3254. Jones, Arthur G. **The Evolution of Personnel Systems for U. S. Foreign Affairs: A History of Reform Efforts.** New York: Carnegie Endowment, 1964.

3255. Jones, Chester L. **The Consular Service of the United States: Its History and Activities.** Philadelphia: University of Pennsylvania, 1906.

3256. Jones, R. L. "America's First Consular Convention." **Southwestern Social Science Quarterly** 13 (December 1932): 250-263.

3257. Kennan, George F. "The Needs of the Foreign

Service." In **The Public Service and University Education,** edited by Joseph E. McClean, pp. 1-97. Princeton, NJ: Princeton University Press, 1949.

3258. Kennan, George F. "Planning in the Department." **Foreign Service Journal** 38 (March 1961): 20-24.

3259. Kennedy, Aubrey L. "Reorganization of the Foreign Service." **Quarterly Review** 566 (October 1945): 387-413.

3260. Keogh, James. "Information and Modern Diplomacy." **Department of State Bulletin** 70 (January 1974): 57-63.

3261. Ketzel, Clifford P. "Exchange of Persons and American Foreign Policy: The Foreign Leader Program of the Department of State." Ph.D. dissertation, University of California, 1955.

3262. Kissinger, Henry A. "Secretary Kissinger Announces New Steps for Improvement of Department's Resource Allocation and Personnel Systems." **Department of State Bulletin** 73 (July 1975): 85-90.

3263. Knight, Jonathan. "On the Secretary of State's Relations with Congress: Resources, Skills, and Issues." Ph.D. dissertation, Columbia University, 1969.

3264. Knight, Jonathan. "The State Department Budget, 1933-1965: A Research Note." **American Journal of Political Science** 12 (November 1968): 587-598.

3265. Krogh, Peter F. "The State Department at Home." **Annals of the American Academy of Political and Social Science** 380 (November 1968): 118-124.

3266. Kryza, E. Gregory and William E. Knight. "Management in the Foreign Service." **Foreign Service Journal** 52 (March 1975): 16-18.

3267. Kuhn, Arnold J. "The State Department's Presentation to the American People of American-Soviet Relations, 1945-1947." Ph.D. dissertation, University of Chicago, 1950.

3268. Kuhn, Arthur K. "The Administrative Procedure Act and the State Department." **American Journal of International Law** 40 (October 1949): 784-786.

3269. Kurzban, Ira J. "Restructuring the Asylum Process." **South Dakota Law Review** 19 (Winter 1981): 91-117.

3270. Kux, Dennis and Michael Burner. "The German and American Foreign Service." **Foreign Service Journal** 50 (January 1973): 15-16, 20.

3271. Lacy, William S. B. "Usefulness of Classical Diplomacy." **Department of State Bulletin** 38 (March 1958): 326-327.

3272. Lafeber, Walter. "Kissinger and Acheson: The Secretary of State and the Cold War." **Political Science Quarterly** 92 (Summer 1977): 189-197.

3273. Lander, E. T. "The Great Seal of the United States." **Magazine of American History** 29 (May/June 1893): 471-491.

3274. Langer, John D. "The Formulation of American Aid Policy toward the Soviet Union, 1940-1943: The Hopkins Shop and the Department of State." Ph.D. dissertation, Yale University, 1975.

3275. Laves, Walter H. C. and Francis O. Wilcox. "The Reorganization of the Department of State." **American Political Science Review** 38 (April 1944): 289-301.

3276. Laves, Walter H. C. and Francis O. Wilcox. "The State Department Continues Its Reorganization." **American Political Science Review** 39 (April 1945): 309-317.

3277. Lavine, David. **Outposts of Adventure: The Story of the Foreign Service.** Garden City, NY: Doubleday, 1966.

3278. Lay, Tracy H. **The Foreign Service of the United States.** New York: Prentice-Hall, 1925.

3279. Leacacos, John P. **Fires in the In-Basket: The ABC's of the State Department.** Cleveland: World, 1968.

3280. Lee, D. E. "State Department and Foreign Policy." **Proceedings of the American Academy of Political and Social Science** 25 (May 1952): 100-108.

3281. Lee, Luke T. **Consular Law and Practice.** New York: Praeger, 1961.

3282. Lee, Robert E. "Education for the New Diplomacy." **Department of State Bulletin** 48 (March 1963): 423-427.

3283. Lenderking, William R. "Dissent, Disloyalty, and Foreign Service Finkism." **Foreign Service Journal** 51 (May 1974): 13-15.

3284. Lent, Ernest S. **The Recall or Withholding of U. S. Ambassadors to Influence Other Governments or Express Disapproval of Their Actions: Some Specific Cases.** Washington, DC: U. S. Library of Congress, 1969.

3285. Leonidov, A. "Twilight of the Gods: The Glory and Decline of the State Department." **New Times** 39 (September 1960): 9-12.

3286. Leopold, Richard W. "The Foreign Relations Series: A Centennial Estimate." **Journal of American History** 49 (March 1963): 595-612.

3287. Leopold, Richard W. "The Foreign Relations Series Revisited: One Hundred Plus Ten." **Journal of American History** 59 (March 1973): 935-957.

3288. Lichman, Warren F. **Professional Diplomacy in the United States, 1779-1939: A Study in Administrative History.** Chicago: University of Chicago Press, 1961.

3289. Lindsay, Franklin A. "Program Planning: The Missing Element." **Foreign Affairs** 39 (January 1961): 279-290.

3290. Linehan, Patrick E. **The Foreign Service Personnel System: An Organizational Analysis.** Boulder, CO: Westview, 1976.

3291. Lisagor, Peter and Marguerite Higgins. **Overtime in Heaven: Adventures in the Foreign Service.** Garden City, NY: Doubleday, 1964.

3292. Little, Douglas J. "Twenty Years of Turmoil: ITT, The State Department, and Spain, 1924-1944." **Business History Review** 53 (Winter 1979): 449-472.

3293. Loss, Richard A. "Secretary of State Dean Acheson as Political Executive: Administrator of Personnel Security." **Public Administration Review** 34 (July 1974): 352-358.

3294. Lossing, Benson J. "The Great Seal of the United States." **Harper's New Monthly Magazine** (July 1856): 178-186.

3295. Lovler, R. "Room at the Top of Foggy Bottom?" **Perspectives** 13 (Winter 1982): 42-48.

3296. Lowenfeld, Abraham F. "Act of State and Department of State: First National City Bank v. Banco Nacional de Cuba." **American Journal of International Law** 66 (October 1972): 795-814.

3297. Luce, Clare B. "The Ambassadorial Issue: Professional or Amateur?" **Foreign Affairs** 36 (October 1957): 105-121.

3298. Ludden, Howard R. "The International Information Program of the United States: State Department Years, 1945-1953." Ph.D. dissertation, Princeton University, 1966.

3299. Ludwig, Ernest. **Consular Treaty Rights and Comments on the "Most Favored Nation" Clause.** Akron, OH: New Werner, 1913.

3300. McCamy, James L. "Administration of Foreign Affairs in the United States." **World Politics** 7 (January 1955): 315-325.

3301. McCamy, James L. and Alessandro Corrandini. "The People of the State Department and the Foreign Service." **American Political Science Review** 47 (December 1954): 1067-1082.

3302. McCleod, Scott. "Security in the Department of State." **Department of State Bulletin** 30 (March 1954): 469-472.

3303. McGhee, George C. "The Changing Role of the American Ambassador." **Department of State Bulletin** 46 (June 1962): 1007-1011.

3304. McKibbin, Carroll R. "The Career Structure and Success in the U.S. Foreign Service." Ph.D. dissertation, University of Kansas, 1968.

3305. McLellan, David S. "The Operational Code Approach to the Study of Political Leaders: Dean Acheson's Philosophical and Instrumental Beliefs." **Canadian Journal of Political Science** 4 (March 1971): 52-75.

3306. McNair, Clare H. "Women in the Foreign Service." **Foreign Service Journal** 22 (June 1945): 30-31, 46.

3307. Macomber, William B. "Change in Foggy Bottom: An Anniversary Report on Management Reform and

Modernization in the Department of State." **Department of State Bulletin** 66 (February 1972): 206-212.

3308. Macomber, William B. "Department Discusses Grievance Procedures for the Foreign Service." **Department of State Bulletin** 67 (October 1972): 505-515.

3309. Macomber, William B. "Diplomacy for the Seventies: A Program of Management Reform for the Department of State." **Department of State Bulletin** 63 (December 1970): 775-793.

3310. Macomber, William B. "Management Strategy: A Program for the Seventies." **Department of State Bulletin** 62 (February 1970): 130-141.

3311. Madar, Daniel R. "Foreign Policy Planning: Its Practice and Problems in the U. S. Department of State." Ph.D. dissertation, University of Toronto, 1974.

3312. Madar, Daniel R. "Patronage, Position and Policy Planning: S/P and Secretary Kissinger." **Journal of Politics** 42 (November 1980): 1066-1084.

3313. Maddox, William P. "The Foreign Service in Transition." **Foreign Affairs** 25 (January 1947): 303-313.

3314. Maddox, William P. "Foreign Service Institute of the U. S. Department of State." **Higher Education** 4 (October 1947): 37-40.

3315. Maechling, Charles. "Our Foreign Affairs Establishment: The Need for Reform." **Virginia Quarterly Review** 45 (Spring 1969): 193-210.

3316. Maqubane, Bernard. "What Is Kissinger Up to in Southern Africa?" **Freedomways** 16 (1976): 162-171.

3317. Manning, Robert J. "Policy and People." **Department of State Bulletin** 49 (October 1963): 639-644.

3318. Marrow, Alfred J. **Making Waves in Foggy Bottom: How a New and More Scientific Approach Changed the Management at the State Department.** Washington, DC: NTL Institute, 1974.

3319. Marrow, Alfred J. "Managerial Revolution in the State Department." **Personnel** 43 (November 1966):

8-18.

3320. Martin, James V. "The Quiet Revolution in the Foreign Service." **Foreign Service Journal** 37 (February 1960): 19-22.

3321. Marx, Walter J. "The Consular Service of the United States." **Department of State Bulletin** 33 (September 1955): 447-448, 450-454.

3322. Mashberg, Michael. "Documents Concerning the American State Department and the Stateless European Jews, 1942-1944." **Jewish Social Studies** 39 (Winter/Spring 1977): 163-182.

3323. May, Ernest R. "Development of Political-Military Consultation in the United States." **Political Science Quarterly** 70 (June 1955): 161-180.

3324. Mead, Lawrence M. "Foreign Service Reform: A View from HEW." **Foreign Service Journal** 52 (October 1975): 21-24.

3325. Mendershausen, Horst. "The Diplomat's National and Transnational Commitments." **Foreign Service Journal** 47 (February 1970): 20-22, 31-33.

3326. Mennis, Bernard. **American Foreign Policy Officials: Who Are They and What Are They?** Columbus: Ohio State University Press, 1971.

3327. Merchant, Livinston T. "Diplomacy and the Modern World." **Department of State Bulletin** 43 (November 1960): 707-713.

3328. Messer, Robert L. "Paths Not Taken: The United States Department of State and Alternatives to Containment, 1945-1946." **Diplomatic History** 1 (Fall 1977): 297-320.

3329. Metzger, Stanley D. "State Department's Role in the Judicial Administration of the Act of State Doctrine." **American Journal of International Law** 66 (January 1972): 94-101.

3330. Michael, William H. **History of the Department of State of the United States: Its Functions and Duties together with Biographies of Its Present Officers and Secretaries from the Beginning.** Washington, DC: U. S. Government Printing Office, 1901.

3331. Miller, August C. "The New State Department." **American Journal of International Law** 33 (July

1939): 500-518.

3332. Millett, Richard. "The State Department's Navy: A History of the Special Service Squadron, 1920-1940." **American Neptune** 35 (April 1975): 118-138.

3333. Milner, Cooper. "The Public Life of Cordell Hull, 1907-1924." Ph.D. dissertation, Vanderbilt University, 1960.

3334. Modelski, George A. "The Foreign Ministers as a World Elite." **Peace Research Society Papers** 14 (1970): 31-46.

3335. Modelski, George A. "The World's Foreign Ministers: A Political Elite." **Journal of Conflict Resolution** 14 (June 1970): 135-176.

3336. Monroe, Elizabeth. "John Foster Dulles and the Middle East: Appraisal of the Late Secretary of State's Accomplishments." **Western World** 2 (August 1959): 41-44.

3337. Moore, J. N. "Role of the State Department in Judicial Proceedings." **Fordham Law Review** 31 (December 1962): 277-283.

3338. Morgenstern, Oskar. "Decision Theory and the State Department." **Foreign Service Journal** 37 (December 1960): 19-22.

3339. Morris, Roger. "Clientism in the Foreign Service." **Foreign Service Journal** 51 (February 1974): 24-26, 30-31.

3340. Moser, Martin W. "The Personnel System of the Foreign Service of the United States." Ph.D. dissertation, University of Maryland, 1952.

3341. Mosher, Frederick C. "Personnel Management in Foreign Affairs." **Public Personnel Review** 12 (October 1951): 175-186.

3342. Mosher, Frederick C. "Some Observations about Foreign Service Reform: Famous First Words." **Public Administration Review** 29 (November/December 1969): 600-610.

3343. Moss, Ambler H. "The Foreign Service Illusion." **Foreign Service Journal** 49 (June 1972): 6, 8, 10, 12.

3344. Moss, Kenneth B. "Bureaucrat as Diplomat: George

S. Messersmith and the State Department's Approach to War, 1933-1941." Ph.D. dissertation, University of Minnesota, 1978.

3345. Murphy, Edmund. "Extra Curricular Diplomacy." **Foreign Service Journal** 33 (January 1956): 22-24, 48, 50.

3346. Murphy, George H. **Digest of Circular Instructions to Consular Officers.** Washington, DC: U. S. Government Printing Office, 1904-1906.

3347. Murphy, Robert D. "The Interrelationship of Military Power and Foreign Policy." **Department of State Bulletin** 31 (August 1954): 291-294.

3348. Murphy, Robert D. "What Is Past Is Prologue." **Department of State Bulletin** 41 (December 1959): 898-902.

3349. Myers, Denys P. and Charles F. Ransom. "Reorganization of the State Department." **American Journal of International Law** 31 (October 1937): 713-720.

3350. Nash, Marian L. "Contemporary Practice of the United States Relating to International Law." **American Journal of International Law** 14 (January 1980): 158-183.

3351. Neal, Harry E. **Your Career in Foreign Service.** New York: Messner, 1965.

3352. Nelson, Otto L. **Report on the Organization of the Department of State.** Washington, DC: U. S. Department of State, 1946.

3353. Newcomer, James R. "Acheson, Dulles, and Rusk: Information, Coherence and Organization in the Department of State." Ph.D. dissertation, Stanford University, 1976.

3354. Ninkovich, Frank. "The Currents of Cultural Diplomacy: Art and the State Department, 1938-1947." **Diplomatic History** 1 (Summer 1977): 215-238.

3355. Norton, Henry K. "Foreign Office Organization." **Annals of the American Academy of Political and Social Science** 143 (May 1929): 1-83.

3356. Osborne, John. "Is the State Department Manageable?" **Fortune** (March 1957): 110-112, 267-268, 270, 272, 276, 278.

3357. Osborne, John. "What's the U. S. Foreign Service Worth?" **Fortune** (May 1957): 154-159, 238, 241-242, 244, 247.

3358. Outland, John W. "Decision-Maker and the Scholar: Who Reads Whom?" **International Lawyer** 4 (October 1970): 859-866.

3359. Outland, John W. "Law and the Lawyer in the State Department's Administration of Foreign Policy." Ph.D. dissertation, Syracuse University, 1970.

3360. Parr, W. Grant. "The State Department and Germany." **American-German Review** 30 (February/March 1964): 4-7.

3361. Paterson, Thomas G. "American Businessmen and Consular Service Reform, 1890's to 1906." **Business History Review** 40 (Spring 1966): 77-97.

3362. Patterson, Jefferson. **Diplomatic Duty and Diversion.** Cambridge, MA: Riverside, 1956.

3363. Patterson, Richard S. and Richardson Dougall. **The Eagle and the Shield: A History of the Great Seal of the United States.** Washington, DC: U.S. Government Printing Office, 1976.

3364. Patterson, Richard S. "The Seal of the Department of State." **Department of State Bulletin** 21 (December 1949): 894-896.

3365. Perkins, Edward J. "The Priorities Policy Group: A Case Study of the Institutionalization of a Policy Linkage and Resource Allocation Mechanism in the Department of State." D.P.A., University of Southern California, 1978.

3366. Perlmutter, Oscar. W. "Acheson and the Diplomacy of World War II." **Western Political Quarterly** 14 (December 1961): 896-911.

3367. Perry, Jack. "The Present Challenge to the Foreign Service." **Foreign Service Journal** 51 (October 1974): 18-20.

3368. Peters, C. Brooks. "Why Not a Foreign Service Career?" **Reader's Digest** (October 1956): 118-120.

3369. Peurifoy, John E. "The Department of State: A Reflection of U. S. Leadership." **Department of State Bulletin** 21 (October 1949): 671-674.

3370. Peurifoy, John E. "Reflection of United States Leadership - The Department of State." **Department of State Bulletin** 21 (October 1949): 671-674.

3371. Phillips, Howard J. "The United States Diplomatic Establishment in the Critical Period, 1783-1797." Ph.D. dissertation, University of Notre Dame, 1968.

3372. Pletcher, David M. "Inter-America Trade in the Early 1870's - A State Department Survey." **Americas** 33 (April 1977): 593-612.

3373. Plischke, Elmer. **United States Diplomats and Their Missions: A Profile of American Diplomatic Emissaries since 1778.** Washington, DC: American Enterprise Institute for Public Policy Research, 1975.

3374. Plischke, Elmer. "United States Diplomats since 1778: Bicentennial Review and Future Projection." **World Affairs** 138 (Winter 1975-1976): 205-218.

3375. Potter, Pitman B. "Rigid versus Adjustable Techniques in Diplomacy." **American Journal of International Law** 45 (October 1951): 721-723.

3376. Preston, R. K. "Asylum Adjudications: Do State Department Advisory Opinions Violate Refugees' Rights and U. S. International Obligations?" **Maryland Law Review** 45 (1986): 91-140.

3377. Price, Don K., ed. **The Secretary of State.** Englewood Cliffs, NJ: Prentice-Hall, 1960.

3378. Pringle, Robert. "Creeping Irrelevance at Foggy Bottom." **Foreign Policy** 29 (Winter 1977-1978): 128-139.

3379. Pritt, Denis N. **The State Department and the Cold War.** New York: International Publishers, 1948.

3380. Pruitt, Dean G. **Problem Solving in the Department of State.** Denver: University of Denver, 1964-1965.

3381. Puente, Julius I. **The Foreign Consul: His Juridical Status in the United States.** Chicago: B. J. Smith, 1926.

3382. Reed, Theodore L. "Organizational Change in the American Foreign Service, 1925-1965: The Utility of Cohort Analysis." **American Sociological Review** 43 (June 1978): 404-421.

3383. Regala, Roberta. **The Trends in Modern Diplomatic Practice.** Dobbs Ferry, NY: Oceana, 1959.

3384. Richardson, Elliot L. "The Office of the Under Secretary for Western Hemisphere Affairs." **Department of State Bulletin** 62 (April 1970): 498-499.

3385. Rigert, Joseph C. "The Office of the Assistant Secretary of State for Congressional Relations: A Study of an Aspect of Executive-Legislative Relations in the Formulation of Foreign Policy." Master's thesis, Georgetown University, 1959.

3386. Rindern, Robert W. and S. I. Nadler. **Life and Love in the Foreign Service.** Washington, DC: Foreign Service Journal, 1969.

3387. Ritchie, John A. "The Consular Function: The Stepchild of United States Foreign Policy Administration." Ph.D. dissertation, Southern Illinois University, 1969.

3388. Robertson, Charles L. "The American Secretary of State: A Study of the Office under Henry L. Stimson and Cordell Hull." Ph.D. dissertation, Princeton University, 1959.

3389. Robinson, James A. "Process Satisfaction and Policy Approval in State Department-Congressional Relations." **American Journal of Sociology** 67 (November 1961): 278-283.

3390. Rockman, Bert A. "America's Departments of State: Irregular and Regular Syndromes of Policy Making." **American Political Science Review** 75 (December 1981): 911-927.

3391. Rogers, William P. "Growing Ties between Science and Foreign Policy." **Department of State Bulletin** 64 (June 1971): 766-768.

3392. Rogers, William P. "The New Foreign Service and the Job of Modern Diplomacy." **Department of State Bulletin** 65 (December 1971): 675-676.

3393. Rogers, William P. "U. S. Foreign Policy in a Technological Age." **Department of State Bulletin** 64 (February 1971): 198-202.

3394. Rogers, William P. "U. S. Foreign Policy, 1969-70: A Report of the Secretary of State." **Department** of **State Bulletin** 64 (April 1971): 465-477.

3395. Rogers, William P. "U. S. Policy toward Latin America: A Official Statement." **Revista Interamericana Review** 2 (Fall 1972): 263-271.

3396. Rostow, Walt W. "The Planning of Foreign Policy." **Department of State Newsletter** 38 (June 1964): 3-5, 45.

3397. Roudybush, Franklin. **An Analysis of the Educational Background and Experience of U. S. Foreign Service Officers.** Washington, DC: George Washington University Press, 1944.

3398. Roy, William G. "Process of Bureaucratization in the U. S. State Department and the Vesting of Economic Interests, 1886-1905." **Administrative Science Quarterly** 26 (September 1981): 419-433.

3399. Rublin, Barry M. **Secrets of State.** New York: Oxford University Press, 1985.

3400. Rubottom, Roy R. **The People Who Wage the Peace: An Account of the History and Mission of the Foreign Service.** Washington, DC: U.S. Government Printing Office, 1958.

3401. Rusk, Dean. "The Anatomy of Foreign Policy Decisions." **Department of State Bulletin** 52 (September 1965): 502-509.

3402. Rusk, Dean. "Basic Issues Underlying the Present Crisis." **Department of State Bulletin** 47 (December 1962): 867-873.

3403. Rusk, Dean. "Building the Frontiers of Freedom." **Department of State Bulletin** 44 (June 1961): 947-955.

3404. Rusk, Dean. "The Formulation of Foreign Policy." **Department of State Bulletin** 44 (March 1961): 395-399.

3405. Rusk, Dean. "A Fresh Look at the Formulation of Foreign Policy." **Department of State Bulletin** 44 (March 1961): 395-399.

3406. Rusk, Dean. "Methods of Diplomacy." **Department of State Bulletin** 45 (August 1961): 287-288.

3407. Rusk, Dean. "Old-Fashioned Diplomacy." **Department of State Bulletin** 44 (April 1961): 287-288.

3408. Rusk, Dean. "The Realities of Foreign Policy." **Department of State Bulletin** 46 (March 1962): 487-494.

3409. Rusk, Dean. "Secretary of State Cites Value of Privacy in Use of Diplomatic Channel." **Department of State Bulletin** 46 (February 1961): 214.

3410. Rusk, Dean. "Views of Dean Rusk - Next Secretary of State." **U.S. News and World Report** 49 (December 26, 1960): 64-70.

3411. Russell, C. Allyn. "William Jennings Bryan: Statesman - Fundamentalist." **Journal of Presbyterian History** 53 (Summer 1975): 93-119.

3412. Sakell, Achilles N. **Career in the Foreign Service.** New York: Balck, 1962.

3413. Saltzman, Charles E. "Progress Report on the Wriston Committee Recommendations." **Foreign Service Journal** 32 (January 1955): 18-21, 42.

3414. Saltzman, Charles E. "The Reorganization of the American Foreign Service." **Department of State Bulletin** 31 (September 1954): 436-444.

3415. Schick, Alan. "Passports - Revocation - Implicit Congressional Approval of Passport Revocation." **Suffolk International Law Journal** 6 (Spring 1982): 197-207.

3416. Schulzinger, Robert D. **The Making of the Diplomatic Mind: The Training, Outlook, and Style of United States Foreign Service Officers, 1908-1931.** Middletown, CT: Wesleyan University Press, 1975.

3417. Schwartz, Abba P. "The Role of the State Department in the Administration and Enforcement of the New Immigration Law." **Annals of the American Academy of Political and Social Science** 367 (September 1966): 93-104.

3418. Schweid, B. "Interview with Secretary of State Cyrus R. Vance, February 3, 1977." **Atlantic Community Quarterly** 15 (Spring 1977): 112-121.

3419. Scott, Andrew M. "The Department of State: Formal Organization and Informal Culture." **International Studies Quarterly** 13 (Spring 1969): 1-18.

3420. Scott, Andrew M. "Environmental Change and Organizational Adaptation: The Problem of the State

Department." **Foreign Service Journal** 47 (June 1970): 25-27, 63.

3421. Scribner, Robert L. "The Diplomacy of William L. Marcy, Secretary of State, 1853-1857." Ph.D. dissertation, University of Virginia, 1949.

3422. Semmel, Andrew K. "Some Correlates of Attitudes of Multilateral Diplomacy in the U.S. Department of State." **International Studies Quarterly** 20 (June 1976): 301-324.

3423. Shade, Chloris. **Foreign Service.** 2nd ed. Chicago: Morgan, Dillon, 1940.

3424. Sheppard, Eli T. **American Consular Service.** Berkeley: University of California Press, 1901.

3425. Shoup, Laurence H. "Shaping the National Interest: The Council on Foreign Relations, the Department of State, and the Origins of the Postwar World, 1939-1943." Ph.D. dissertation, Northwestern University, 1974.

3426. Simmons, John F. "How We Work with Other Nations." **Department of State Bulletin** 33 (July 1955): 91-94.

3427. Simpson, Smith. **Anatomy of the State Department.** Boston: Beacon Press, 1967.

3428. Simpson, Smith. **The Crisis in the American Diplomacy: A Shot Across the Bow of the State Department.** North Quincy, MA: Christopher, 1979.

3429. Simpson, Smith. "Perceptives of Reform: The Era of Wilbur Carr." **Foreign Service Journal** 48 (August 1971): 17-19, 41.

3430. Simpson, Smith. "Perspectives of Reform: The Post-Carr Period." **Foreign Service Journal** 48 (September 1971): 21-25.

3431. Simpson, Smith. "Reform from Within: The Importance of Attitudes." **Foreign Service Journal** 47 (May 1970): 33-34, 47.

3432. Snyder, Charles K. "The Department of State and the Congress: A Study of the Effect of Foreign Policies of Positive Internationalism and Membership in the United Nations on Organization and Procedure." Ph.D. dissertation, Cornell University, 1953.

3433. Spaulding, E. Wilder. **Ambassadors Ordinary and Extraordinary.** Washington, DC: Public Affairs Press, 1961.

3434. Spaulding, E. Wilder and George Blue. **The Department of State of the United States.** Washington, DC: U. S. Government Printing Office, 1936.

3435. Spiers, Ronald I. "International Security Affairs and the Department of State." **Department of State Bulletin** 66 (April 1972): 591-597.

3436. Stassen, Glen H. "Individual Preference versus Role-Constraint in Policy-Making: Senatorial Response to Secretaries Acheson and Dulles." **World Politics** 25 (October 1972): 96-119.

3437. Stearns, Monteagle. "Democratic Diplomacy and the Role of Propaganda." **Foreign Service Journal** 30 (October 1953): 24, 25, 62-64.

3438. Steiner, Zara S. **Present Problems of the Foreign Service.** Princeton, NJ: Center of International Studies, Princeton University, 1961.

3439. Steiner, Zara S. **The State Department and the Foreign Service: The Wriston Report - Four Years Later.** Princeton, NJ: Center of International Studies, Princeton University, 1958.

3440. Stempel, John D. "Policy Decision Making in the Department of State: The Vietnamese Problem, 1961-1965." Ph.D. dissertation, University of California, 1965.

3441. Stern, Thomas. "Management: A New Look." **Foreign Service Journal** 49 (March 1972): 14-15.

3442. Stettinius, Edward R. "Reorganization of the Office of the Foreign Service." **Department of State Bulletin** 12 (April 1945): 777-784.

3443. Stevenson, Adlai E. "Science, Diplomacy, and Peace." **Department of State Bulletin** 45 (September 1961): 402-407.

3444. Stewart, Irvin. "Congress, the Foreign Service, and Department of State: Personal Problems." **American Political Science Review** 24 (May 1930): 355-366.

3445. Stillman, Edmund. "Dean Rusk: In the American Grain." **Commentary** 45 (May 1968): 31-37.

3446. Stowell, Ellery C. "The Ban on Alien Marriages in the Foreign Service." **American Journal of International Law** 31 (January 1937): 91-94.

3447. Stowell, Ellery C. **Consular Cases and Opinions.** Washington, DC: Byrne, 1909.

3448. Stowell, Ellery C. "Cramping Our Foreign Service." **American Journal of International Law** 29 (April 1935): 314-317.

3449. Stowell, Ellery C. **The Economic Adviser of the Department of State.** Washington, DC: Digest Press, 1935.

3450. Stowell, Ellery C. "Examinations for the American Foreign Service." **American Journal of International Law** 24 (July 1930): 577-581.

3451. Stowell, Ellery C. "Home Service of the Department of State." **American Journal of International Law** 35 (October 1941): 668-671.

3452. Stowell, Ellery C. **The Legal Adviser of the Department of State.** Washington, DC: Digest Press, 1936.

3453. Stowell, Ellery C. "The Moses-Linthicum Act on the Foreign Service." **American Journal of International Law** 25 (July 1931): 516-520.

3454. Stowell, Ellery C. "Reforms in the State Department and Foreign Service." **American Journal of International Law** 22 (July 1928): 606-610.

3455. Strobel, Edward H. **Mr. Blaine and His Foreign Policy: An Examination of the Most Important Dispatches While Secretary of State.** Boston: Hall, 1884.

3456. Stuart, Graham H. **American Diplomatic and Consular Practice.** 2nd ed. New York: Appleton-Century-Crofts, 1952.

3457. Stuart, Graham H. "A Better Foreign Service." **Current History** 21 (September 1951): 148-150.

3458. Stuart, Graham H. **The Department of State: A History of Its Organization, Procedure, and Personnel.** New York: Macmillan, 1949.

3459. Stuart, Graham H. "A Streamlined State Department." **Current History** 18 (February 1950): 71-75.

3460. Studnicky, Lawrence J. "Constitutional Law: Authority of Secretary of State to Revoke Passports." **Harvard International Law Journal** 22 (Winter 1981): 187-194.

3461. Stupak, Ronald J. "Dean Acheson: The Secretary of State as a Policy-Maker." Ph.D. dissertation, Ohio State University, 1967.

3462. Stupak, Ronald J. **The Shaping of Foreign Policy: The Role of the Secretary of State as Seen by Dean Acheson.** New York: Odyssey, 1969.

3463. Stupak, Ronald J. and David S. McLellan. "The Bankruptcy of Super-Activism and the Resurgence of Diplomacy and the Department of State." **Foreign Service Journal** 52 (April 1975): 23-28.

3464. Sylvester, John. "Will Candor Survive the Leaking Ship of State?" **Foreign Service Journal** 52 (June 1975): 15-16, 32.

3465. Taylor, Maxwell, D. "New System for Coping with Our Overseas Problems." **Foreign Service Journal** 43 (May 1966): 34-36.

3466. Terrell, John U. **The United States Department of State: A Story of Diplomats, Embassies and Foreign Policy.** New York: Duell, Sloan, and Pearce, 1964.

3467. Tessendorf, K. C. "Mr. Secretary, May We Have Your Remittance, Please?" **Foreign Service Journal** 47 (August 1970): 39-41.

3468. Thayer, Robert H. "Cultural Diplomacy and the Development of Mutual Understanding." **Department of State Bulletin** 41 (August 1959): 310-316.

3469. Thomson, I. L. "Flights Abroad and the Role of the Department of State." **Journal of Air Law and Commerce** 9 (April 1938): 220-250.

3470. Timberg, S. "Wanted: Administrative Safeguards for the Protection of the Individual in International Economic Regulation." **Administrative Law Review** 17 (Winter/Spring 1965): 159-167.

3471. Tracy, Thomas M. "Automation and the Foreign Service." **Foreign Service Journal** 48 (February 1971): 21-22.

3472. Utley, Jonathan G. "The Department of State and the Far East, 1937-1941: A Study of the Ideas

Behind Its Diplomacy." Ph.D. dissertation, University of Illinois, 1970.

3473. Utley, Jonathan G. "Upstairs, Downstairs at Foggy Bottom: Oil Exports and Japan, 1940-41." **Prologue** 8 (Spring 1976): 17-28.

3474. Vallance, William R. "Some Legal Problems Arising in the Department of State Not Involving Foreign Relations." **Federal Bar Association Journal** 1 (March 1933): 49-54.

3475. Van Dusen, Henry P., ed. **The Spiritual Legacy of John Foster Dulles.** Philadelphia: Westminster, 1960.

3476. Van Dyne, Frederick. **Our Foreign Service: The "ABC" of American Diplomacy.** Rochester, NY: Lawyers Cooperative, 1909.

3477. Villard, Henry S. **Affairs at State.** New York: Crowell, 1965.

3478. Vivian, James F. "The Commercial Bureau of American Republics, 1894-1902: The Advertising Policy, the State Department, and the Governance of the International Union." **Proceedings of the American Philosophical Society** 118 (December 1974): 555-566.

3479. Vloyantes, John P. "Edward R. Stetinius, Jr. as Secretary of State." Ph.D. dissertation, University of Utah, 1954.

3480. Vogelsang, Sandy. "Feminism in Foggy Bottom: Man's World, Woman's Place?" **Foreign Service Journal** 49 (August 1972): 4, 6, 8, 10-11.

3481. Walker, Lannon. "Our Foreign Affairs Machinery: Time for an Overhaul." **Foreign Affairs** 47 (January 1969): 309-320.

3482. Walther, Regis. **Orientations and Behavioral Styles of Foreign Service Officers.** New York: Carnegie Endowment, 1965.

3483. Ward, Paul V. "Performance Evaluation: The Annual Inventory." **Foreign Service Journal** 51 (October 1974): 29-31, 52.

3484. Warshawsky, Howard. "The Department of State and Human Rights Policy: A Case Study of the Human Rights Bureau." **World Affairs** 142 (Winter 1980): 188-215.

3485. Warwick, Donald P. "Bureaucratization in the Government Agency: The Case of the U. S. State Department." **Sociological Inquiry** 44 (Spring 1974): 75-92.

3486. Warwick, Donald P. "Performance Appraisal and Promotions in the Foreign Service." **Foreign Service Journal** 47 (July 1970): 37-41, 45.

3487. Warwick, Donald P. **A Theory of Public Bureaucracy: Politics, Personality, and Organization in the State Department.** Cambridge, MA: Harvard University Press, 1975.

3488. Watt, David C. "Henry Kissinger: An Interim Judgement." **Political Quarterly** 48 (January 1977): 3-13.

3489. Webb, James E. "Department of State." **Air Affairs** 3 (Autumn 1949): 34-43.

3490. Webb, James E. "U. S. Organization for the Conduct of Foreign Affairs." **Department of State Bulletin** 24 (February 1951): 273-276.

3491. Weil, Martin. **A Pretty Good Club: The Founding Fathers of the U. S. Foreign Service.** New York: Norton, 1978.

3492. Welch, Holmes. "The Real Life of the Foreign Service Officer." **Harper's Magazine** (March 1962): 82-85.

3493. Werking, Richard H. **The Master Architects: Building the United States Foreign Service, 1890-1913.** Lexington: University of Kentucky Press, 1978.

3494. Werking, Richard H. "Selling the Foreign Service: Bureaucratic Rivalry and Foreign-Trade Promotion, 1903-1912." **Pacific Historical Review** 45 (May 1976): 185-207.

3495. West, Rachel. **The Department of State on the Eve of World War I.** Athens: University of Georgia Press, 1978.

3496. Wiley, Marshall W. **Developing a Strategy of Organizational Change for the Department of State.** Santa Monica, CA: Rand, 1969.

3497. Wilkinson, Vernon L. "Department of State: Its Functions, Its History, and Its Operation." Ph.D. dissertation, American University, 1933.

3498. Williams, Carman C. "The Wasted Resource: Foreign Service Wives." **Foreign Service Journal** 52 (May 1975): 6-7, 20-21.

3499. Willis, Davis K. **The State Department.** Boston: Christian Science Publishing Society, 1968.

3500. Winham, Gilbert R. and H. E. Bovis. "Agreement and Breakdown in Negotiation: Report on a State Department Training Simulation." **Journal of Peace Research** 15 (1978): 285-303.

3501. Winham, Gilbert R. and H. E. Bovis. "Distribution of Benefits in Negotiation: Report on a State Department Training Simulation." **Journal of Conflict Resolution** 23 (September 1979): 408-424.

3502. Woodward, Clark H. "Relations between the Navy and the Foreign Service." **American Journal of International Law** 33 (April 1939): 283-291.

3503. Woodward, Stanley. "Protocol: What It Is and What It Does." **Department of State Bulletin** 21 (October 1949): 501-503.

3504. Woolsey, L. H. "The Legal Adviser of the Department of State." **American Journal of International Law** 26 (January 1932): 124-126.

3505. Wright, Q. "Publications of the Department of State." **Iowa Law Review** 19 (January 1934): 301-311.

3506. Wriston, Henry M. "The Secretary of State Abroad." **Foreign Affairs** 34 (July 1956): 523-541.

3507. Wriston, Henry M. "Young Men and the Foreign Service." **Foreign Affairs** 33 (October 1954): 28-42.

3508. Wynne, C. "Publications of the Department of State." **Federal Bar Association Journal** 2 (November 1934): 103-108.

3509. Yardley, Edward. "Identification Pass System for the Department of State." **Foreign Service Journal** 18 (October 1941): 554-555.

3510. Zorthian, Barry. "A Press Relations Doctrine for the Foreign Service." **Foreign Service Journal** 48 (February 1971): 20-23, 55-56.

Chapter 13.
Department of Transportation

3511. Adams, R. B. "Input-Output Program for the Department of Transportation." **Transportation Journal** 8 (Winter 1968): 45-52.

3512. Agnew, B. "Key Men at the New Department of Transportation." **Fleet Owner** 62 (May 1967): 69-75.

3513. Asher, J. "New Faces, New Questions on the Transit Scene." **Railway Age** 166 (April 7, 1969): 14-18.

3514. Barsness, Richard W. "Policy Challenges and Objectives of the Department of Transportation." **Quarterly Review of Economics and Business** 9 (Spring 1969): 63-76.

3515. Baughcum, Marshal A. "The Federal Highway Program: A Case Study in Fiscal Federalism." Ph.D. dissertation, University of North Carolina, 1976.

3516. Beggs, James M. "New Look and the New Outlook at DOT." **I.C.C. Practitioners' Journal** 36 (September/October 1969): 1960-1973.

3517. Boyd, Alan S. "Role and Impact of Federal Research in High-Speed Ground Transportation." **Public Utilities Fortnightly** 78 (September 15, 1966): 78-81.

3518. Boyd, Alan S. "Transportation Dilemma." **Virginia Law Review** 54 (April 1968): 428-439.

3519. Boyd, D. E. "Airworthiness Directives: Evidentiary Value in Aviation Litigation." **Trial** 22 (August 1986): 59-64.

3520. Brinegar, Claude S. "View from Transportation." **Public Relations Journal** 30 (July 1974): 22-24.

3521. Brown, Anthony E. "The Politics of Deregulating the Civil Aviation Industry." Ph.D. dissertation, University of Tennessee, 1982.

3522. Burkhardt, Robert. **The Federal Aviation Administration.** New York: Praeger, 1967.

3523. Callahan, J. M. "DOT's Think Tank Ponders Auto's beyond '85." **Automotive Industries** 158 (March 1978): 46-50.

3524. Cervero, Robert. "Revitalizing Urban Transit - More Money or Less Regulation?" **Regulation** 8 (May/June 1984): 36-42.

3525. Christensen, Laurits R. and Michael W. Tretheway. "Airline Productivity under Deregulation." **Regulation** 6 (November/December 1982): 25-28.

3526. Coupal, J. R. "Managers and Transportation." **Public Management** 57 (October 1975): 12-13.

3527. Davis, F. W. "Local Participation: The Key to Preserving Adequate Railroad Services." **Michigan State University Business Topics** 24 (Winter 1976): 40-46.

3528. Davis, Grant M. "Analysis of the Propriety of Transferring Car Service Functions to the U. S. Department of Transportation." **I.C.C. Practitioners' Journal** 37 (May/June 1970): 554-567.

3529. Davis, Grant M. **The Department of Transportation.** Lexington, MA: Heath, 1970.

3530. Davis, Grant M. "Department of Transportation's Organizational Futility." **Public Utilities Fortnightly** 87 (May 27, 1971): 29-33.

3531. Davis, Grant M. "Evaluation of the Propriety of Establishing One Consolidated Transportation Regulatory Commission." **I.C.C. Practitioners' Journal** 38 (July/August 1971): 726-732.

3532. Davis, Grant M. "Modifications in the Identifying Characteristics of Several Federal Transportation Activities." **Transportation Journal** 9 (Summer 1970): 5-15.

3533. Davison, Charles M. "Transportation Regulation: How Much? How Long?" **Virginia Law Review** 50 (January 1964): 5-22.

3534. Dearing, Charles L. and Winfred Owen. **National Transportation Policy.** Washington, DC: Brookings Institution, 1949.

3535. Dole, Elisabeth H. "Second General Session Address." **Police Chief** 51 (March 1984): 32-34.

3536. Dombroff, Mark A. and C. Hatfield. "Documentation for Aircraft Accident Litigation: How and Where to Obtain Accident Reports." **Trial** 20 (August 1984): 70-74.

3537. Donahue, Harry J. "The Politics of Administrative Reorganization in the Federal Government: A Study of the Formation of the Department of Transportation." Ph.D. dissertation, American University, 1968.

3538. Duncan, Carson S. **A National Transportation Policy.** New York: Appleton-Century, 1936.

3539. Frederick, John H. **Commercial Air Transportation.** 4th ed. Homewood, IL: Irwin, 1955.

3540. Gellman, Aaron J. "Effect of Regulation on Aircraft Choice." Ph.D. dissertation, Massachusetts Institute of Technology, 1968.

3541. Giemza, Raymond A. "Credibility Factor: North Carolina's Approach to Radar Training and Certification." **Police Chief** 50 (January 1983): 38-41.

3542. Giglio, Sheila B. "Transportation of Spent Nuclear Fuel: The Need for a Flexible Regulatory System." **Boston College Environmental Affairs Law Review** 12 (Fall 1985): 50-101.

3543. Gliddon, Reverdy T. "Administrative Regulation of Commercial Air Transport." Ph.D. dissertation, University of Texas, 1958.

3544. Graham, J. D. "NHTSA and Passive Restraints: A Case of Arbitrary and Capricious Deregulation." **Administrative Law Review** 35 (Spring 1983): 193-252.

3545. Halaby, Najeeb E. "Dispute between the FAA and PATCO: Conflicting Views." **Journal of Air Law and Commerce** 47 (Winter 1982): 275-280.

3546. Hamilton, J. Scott. "Administrative Practice in Aviation Medical Proceedings." **Emory Law Journal** 26 (Summer 1977): 565-588.

3547. Hamilton, J. Scott. "Appellate Practice in Air Safety Proceedings." **Southwestern University Law Review** 10 (1978): 247-266.

3548. Henzey, W. V. "Struggle for Independence." **Airline Management and Marketing** 2 (April 1970): 18-19.

3549. Herrin, Glen W. "The Applicability of Generally Accepted Accounting Principles to a Regulated Industry: Air Transportation." Ph.D. dissertation, University of Alabama, 1965.

3550. Hill, C. E. and M. A. Borenstein. "Airline Passenger Safety: Two Studies in FAA Dalliance." **Trial** 14 (August 1978): 36-39.

3551. Holden, Robert T. "Rehabilitative Sanctions for Drunk Driving: An Experimental Evaluation." **Journal of Research in Crime and Delinquency** 20 (January 1983): 55-72.

3552. Holley, Steven L. "The Relationship between Federal Standards and Litigation in the Control of Automobile Design." **New York University Law Review** 57 (October 1982): 804-847.

3553. Howe, J. "Airworthiness: The Government's Role." **Forum** 17 (Winter 1982): 645-655.

3554. Jones, R. H. and John D. Tew. "Evidentiary Aspects of NTSB Proceedings." **Federal Bar News and Journal** 29 (June 1982): 292-295.

3555. Kovarik, J. A. "Procedures before the Federal Aviation Administration." **Journal of Air Law and Commerce** 42 (Winter 1976): 11-37.

3556. Lanigan, J. A. "Department of Transportation Act: Goals and Results." **Administrative Law Review** 19 (May 1967): 263-275.

3557. Larsen, Paul B. "United States Department of Transportation: A Symposium." **Journal of Air Law** 33 (Spring 1967): 221-239.

3558. Leiser, R. "United Front Opposes Transfer of CAB's Bureau of Safety to Department of Transportation." **American Aviation** 30 (June 1966): 24-26.

3559. Levy, Sidney J. "Investigating Aircraft Accidents The Role of the Federal Government." **New York State Bar Journal** 44 (August 1972): 311-326.

3560. Locklin, Philip D. **Economics of Transportation.** 5th ed. Homewood, IL: Irwin, 1960.

3561. McKenry, E. B. "Department of Transportation Act of 1966." **American Business Law Journal** 4 (Winter 1966): 279-287.

3562. Marshall, J. "Automobile Industry and the Department of Transportation: Striving for Practicable Solutions." **Detroit College Law Review** (Spring 1982): 81-95.

3563. Marten, Bradley M. "Regulation of the Transportation of Hazardous Materials: A Critique and Proposal." **Harvard Environmental Law Review** 5 (Summer 1981): 345-376.

3564. Mehley, R. A. and W. L. Slover. "Motor Carriers and DOT." **I.C.C. Practitioners' Journal** 36 (November/December 1968): 1111-1122.

3565. Meyer, John R. **The Economics of Competition in the Transportation Industries.** Cambridge, MA: Harvard University Press, 1960.

3566. Moulton, Harold G. **American Transportation Problems.** Washington, DC: Brookings Institution, 1933.

3567. Nelson, J. C. "Critique of DOT Transport Policy." **Transportation Journal** 11 (Spring 1972): 5-22.

3568. Norton, H. S. "Department of Transportation, A Study of Organizational Futility." **Public Utilities Fortnightly** 78 (December 22, 1966): 19-25.

3569. Nupp, Byron L. "Transportation Policy Formation in the Federal Government, 1948-1960: A Test of an Administrative Theory." Ph.D. dissertation, American University, 1965.

3570. Obrzut, John J. "Urban Transit Searches for the Middle Track." **Iron Age** 218 (September 20, 1976): 39-43.

3571. O'Connor, William E. "The American Executive Departments as Successors to the Civil Aeronautics Board: The Potential Impact on International Airline Service." **Air Law** 7 (Summer 1982): 138-145.

3572. Olsson, J. P. "Planning for Growth." **I.C.C. Practitioners' Journal** 37 (September/October

1970): 949-958.

3573. Phillips, Charles F. **The Economics of Regulation: Theory and Practice in the Transportation and Public Utility Industries.** Homewood, IL: Irwin, 1969.

3574. Rabin, Yale. "Federal Urban Transportation Policy and the Highway Planning Process in Metropolitan Areas." **Annals of the American Academy of Political and Social Science** 451 (September 1980): 21-35.

3575. Rhoads, Steven E. **Policy Analysis in the Federal Aviation Administration.** Lexington, MA: Lexington Books, 1974.

3576. Rosenbloom, S. "Federal Policies to Increase the Mobility of the Elderly and the Handicapped." **American Planning Association Journal** 48 (Summer 1982): 335-350.

3577. Ryther, Philip I. **Who's Watching the Airways? The Dangerous Games of the FAA.** Garden City, NY: Doubleday, 1972.

3578. Schmerer, Henry M. "Unreviewability of Emergency Orders of the Federal Aviation Agency - The Concept of Preventive Administrative Proceedings." **University of Miami Law Review** 17 (Spring 1963): 348-370.

3579. Schuler, R. D. "Effects of the Transportation Act of 1966." **Administrative Law Review** 19 (July 1967): 384-398.

3580. Schultz, Richard J. "Federalism, Bureaucracy and Public Policy: A Case Study of the Making of Transportation Policy." Ph.D. dissertation, New York University, 1976.

3581. Slover, William L. "Department of Transportation." **I.C.C. Practitioners' Journal** 47 (March/April 1980): 331-334.

3582. Slover, William L. "Department of Transportation: D. C. Circuit Slams NHTSA's Crash Protection Decision: D.C. Circuit Rules Against PATCO: DOT Submits Comments in Coal Rate Guidelines Case." **I.C.C. Practitioners' Journal** 49 (July/August 1982): 540-542.

3583. Slover, William L. "DOT Seeks Supreme Court Entry into Controversy over Crash Protection

Standards." **I.C.C. Practitioners' Journal** 50 (November/December 1982): 94-95.

3584. Slover, William L. "FHWA Seeks Modification of Commercial Driver Qualification Rules." **I.C.C. Practitioners' Journal** 50 (November/December 1982): 96-104.

3585. Smerk, George M. "The Federal Role in Urban Transportation." Ph.D. dissertation, Indiana University, 1963.

3586. Smith, Lawrence B. "FAA Punitive Certificate Sanctions: The Emperor Wears No Clothes: Or How Do You Punish a Propeller?" **Transportation Law Journal** 14 (Winter 1985): 59-100.

3587. Smith, Richard A. "Aircraft Financing and the Government: The Federal Aviation Administration's Loan Guarantee Program." **New England Law Review** 17 (1981-1982): 807-843.

3588. Stich, Rodney. **The Unfriendly Skies: An Aviation Watergate.** Alamo, CA: Diablo Western Press, 1978.

3589. Swart, B. "Is He the Program's Key Man? Interview with A. S. Boyd." **Fleet Owner** 61 (April 1966): 94-100.

3590. Taff, Charles A. **Commercial Motor Transportation.** 3rd ed. Homewood, IL: Irwin, 1961.

3591. Tuggle, K. H. "Washington Report." **I.C.C. Practitioners' Journal** 35 (March/April 1968): 412-424.

3592. Voas, Robert B. and W. A. Layfield. "Creating General Deterrence: Can Passive Sensing of Alcohol Help?" **Police Chief** 50 (August 1983): 56-61.

3593. Whitney, Scott C. "Integrity of Agency Judicial Process under the Federal Aviation Act: The Special Problem Posed by International Airline Route Awards." **William and Mary Law Review** 14 (Summer 1973): 787-815.

3594. Wilson, G. C. "Congress Fears Creation of Czar in Transportation Department Legislation." **Aviation Week and Space Technology** 84 (April 11, 1966): 43-45.

3595. Wytze, Gorter. **United States Shipping Policy.** New York: Harper and Brother, 1956.

Chapter 14.
Department of the Treasury

3596. Aland, Robert H. "Can IRS Use Section 482 to Allocate Income Which Cannot Be Earned under Applicable Law?" **Journal of Taxation** 52 (April 1980): 220-223.

3597. Aland, Robert H. "Treasury Report on Tax Havens - A Response." **Taxes** 59 (December 1981): 993-1030.

3598. Alexander, D. C. "Commissioner Responds to Criticisms of IRS." **Tax Adviser** 5 (July 1974): 390-395.

3599. Alexander, D. C. "New IRS Procedures for Handling Joint Committee Cases." **Tax Adviser** 5 (August 1974): 481-483.

3600. Alexander, D. C. and S. R. Boshkov. "Internal Revenue Service's Ability to Dispose of Cases: General Techniques (Regulations, Rulings, and the Like)." **University of Southern California Tax Institute** 31 (1979): 1037-1072.

3601. Alpern, A. F. "Staggered Tax Filing Dates: An Idea Whose Time Has Come?" **Journal of Accountancy** 141 (April 1976): 49-51.

3602. Alvord, Ellsworth C. "Treasury Regulations and the Wilshire Oil Case." **Columbia Law Review** 40 (February 1940): 252-266.

3603. Anderson, K. E. and S. B. Wolfe. "The Ruling Process: A Tool Not to Be Overlooked in Tax Planning." **Tax Adviser** 16 (October 1985): 600-602.

3604. Anglea, Berneice A. "New Disclosure Policies of the Internal Revenue Service." **Los Angeles Bar**

Bulletin 48 (July 1973): 344-351.

3605. Ansley, N. "United States Secret Service - An Administrative History." **Journal of Criminal Law** 47 (May/June 1956): 93-97.

3606. Armstrong, A. A. "Decentralization of the Bureau of Internal Revenue." **Taxes** 19 (February 1941): 90-102.

3607. Asbill, M. "Freedom of Information and the IRS." **Oil and Gas Law Taxation Institute** (Southwestern Legal Foundation) 25 (1974): 487-528.

3608. Bacon, D. W. "Ethical Considerations in Federal Tax Administration." **Taxes** 41 (February 1963): 74-79.

3609. Bacon, D. W. "How IRS Views the Practitioners' Role in Its Criminal Enforcement Program." **Journal of Taxation** 34 (April 1971): 198-201.

3610. Bacon, D. W. "Large Case Program: How the New Coordinated Examination by IRS Works." **Journal of Taxation** 27 (November 1967): 308-310.

3611. Bacon, D. W. "New Changes Taking Place in the Office of International Operations." **Journal of Taxation** 22 (June 1965): 361-376.

3612. Bacon, D. W. "Ten Tax Audit Areas That Practitioners Are Asking About." **Tulane Tax Institute** 23 (1974): 297-323.

3613. Bailin, L. "How the IRS Intelligence Unit Attacks and Builds up a Net Worth Case." **Journal of Taxation** 13 (July 1960): 17-21.

3614. Baker, G. A. "Present IRS Position on Rulings: Changes in Procedures Still Forthcoming." **Journal of Taxation** 17 (August 1962): 114-117.

3615. Balter, Harry G. "How the Office of International Operations Enforces U. S. Taxes in Foreign Countries." **Journal of Taxation** 22 (June 1965): 356-360.

3616. Balter, Harry G. "Relief from Abuse of Administrative Discretion." **Marquette Law Review** 46 (Fall 1962): 176-187.

3617. Banks, L. "Economy under New Management." **Fortune** 71 (May 1965): 96-99.

3618. Barnes, J. P. "Inquisitorial Powers of the Federal

Government Relating to Taxes." **Taxes** 28 (December 1950): 1211-1219.

3619. Barron, Dean J. "Current Tax Issues in the Mid-Atlantic Region of the Internal Revenue Service." **Taxes** 47 (February 1969): 85-91.

3620. Barron, Dean J. "How We Audit from Magnetic Tapes." **Taxes** 40 (February 1962): 83-92.

3621. Barron, Dean J. "IRS Expands Audit Enforcement Activities in Attempt to Reduce Noncompliance." **Journal of Taxation** 18 (May 1963): 304-306.

3622. Bartolini, A. L. "Responding to the IRS Eleven Questions Investigations: Where Practitioners Stand." **Journal of Taxation** 48 (January 1978): 16-20.

3623. Behrsin, A. J. "What Is the IRS Position on Exemptions for Business Development Organizations?" **Journal of Taxation** 48 (January 1978): 48-50.

3624. Bellas, C. L. "Dual Track Career System within the Internal Revenue Service." **Personnel Administration and Public Personnel Review** 1 (September 1972): 4-8.

3625. Bernick, Daniel. "Treasury Announces Forthcoming Regs at Chicago Conference." **Tax Notes** 17 (November 1, 1982): 407-409.

3626. Best, J. S. "Practice before Field Offices of the Bureau of Internal Revenue." **Wisconsin Law Review** (May 1947): 307-320.

3627. Bierman, Jacquin D. "Introduction to the Problems Facing Bureau of Internal Revenue Administration Today." **Institute of Federal Taxation** 7 (1949): 271-281.

3628. Bittker, Boris I. "Treasury Authority to Issue the Proposed Asset Depreciation Range System Regulations." **Taxes** 49 (May 1971): 265-274.

3629. Black, S. H. "Freedom of Information Act and the Internal Revenue Service." **New York University Institute on Federal Taxation** 33 (1975): 683-706.

3630. Black, S. H. "How to Obtain a Ruling on Leveraged Lease Property and Avoid the Limited-Use Rules." **Journal of Taxation** 46 (June 1977): 354-357.

3631. Bloom, Gilbert D. and S. W. Sweet. "How IRS Uses Continuity of Interest to Raise New Problems in Reorganizations." **Journal of Taxation** 45 (September 1976): 130-138.

3632. Bloom, Robert. "Hearing Procedures of the Office of the Comptroller of the Currency." **Law and Contemporary Problems** 31 (August 1966): 723-732.

3633. Bolton, Philip P. "A Few Good Words for the IRS." **Trusts and Estates** 121 (December 1982): 4-5.

3634. Boner, Marian O. "Internal Revenue Service: A Microcosm of Government." **Texas Law Review** 36 (June 1958): 779-788.

3635. Bowe, William J. "Privacy Act of 1974: How It Affects Taxpayers, Practitioners and the IRS." **Journal of Taxation** 45 (August 1976): 74-77.

3636. Boxleitner, L. A. "What Every Tax Man Should Know about Circular 230." **Taxes** 37 (February 1959): 105-116.

3637. Bratter, H. "Treasury Building - A National Landmark." **Bankers Monthly** 89 (December 1972): 30-32.

3638. Bray, J. M. and D. J. Curtain. "IRS Power to Summons Handwriting : Analyzing the Supreme Court's Euge Decision." **Journal of Taxation** 52 (May 1980): 290-292.

3639. Brockhouse, J. D. "IRS Is Taking a Practical Line in Enforcing Compliance with Return Preparer Regs." **Journal of Taxation** 51 (September 1979): 172-176.

3640. Brown, Melissa. "Treasury Opposes Thor, LIFO, and IDB Liberalizations." **Tax Notes** 13 (October 5, 1981): 779-780.

3641. Brown, Melissa. "Treasury Supports Net Savings Concept with Interest Deduction Phaseout." **Tax Notes** 15 (May 17, 1982): 588-589.

3642. Bruchey, Stuart. "Alexander Hamilton and the State Banks, 1789-1795." **William and Mary Quarterly** 27 (July 1970): 347-378.

3643. Buchanan, Paul C. "OD Strategy at the IRS." **Personnel** 56 (March 1979): 44-52.

3644. Burroughs, J. D. "How Broad Is the IRS' Authority

to Investigate Your Clients' Tax Returns and Records?" **Journal of Taxation** 23 (November 1965): 308-314.

3645. Burroughs, J. D. "Use of the Administrative Summons in Federal Tax Investigations." **Villanova Law Review** 9 (Spring 1964): 371-387.

3646. Calkins, H. "How Does the Practicing Attorney Cope with the Ability and Inability of the Internal Revenue Service to Dispose of Cases?" **Southern California Tax Institute** 31 (1979): 1085-1111.

3647. Camp, W. B. "Comptroller of the Currency: A Report from Washington." **Business Lawyer** 23 (November 1967): 67-78.

3648. Cantrall, A. M. "Activities of the Chief Counsel of the Internal Revenue Service." **American Bar Association Section of Mineral and Natural Resources Law** (1958): 16-19.

3649. Cantrall, A. M. "Activities of the Office of the Chief Counsel." **Taxes** 36 (December 1958): 853-858.

3650. Cantrall, A. M. "What Chief Counsel Expects of the Practitioner." **Taxes** 38 (May 1960): 379-386.

3651. Caplin, Mortimer M. "Commissioner's Reply: Reasonable Tax Administration and Current Policies of IRS." **Journal of Taxation** 20 (February 1964): 110-117.

3652. Caplin, Mortimer M. "IRS, Racketeers, and White Collar Crime." **American Bar Association Journal** 62 (July 1976): 865-867.

3653. Caplin, Mortimer M. "New Directions in Tax Administration." **Tulane Tax Institute** 11 (1962): 1-16.

3654. Caplin, Mortimer M. "Pressing Tax Problems of the Day." **Tennessee Law Review** (Fall 1964): 21-35.

3655. Caplin, Mortimer M. "Role of the Commissioner." **University of Southern California School of Law Tax Institute** 14 (1962): 1-11.

3656. Caplin, Mortimer M. "Should the Service Be Permitted to Reach Accountants' Tax Accrual Workpapers?" **Journal of Taxation** 51 (October 1979): 194-200.

3657. Caplin, Mortimer M. "Taxpayer Rulings Policy of the Internal Revenue Service: A Statement of Principles." **New York University Institute on Federal Taxation** 20 (1962): 1-13.

3658. Carles, T. S. "Special Agent's Manual Gives Insight into IRS Procedures for Tax Fraud Audits." **Journal of Taxation** 43 (November 1975): 290-295.

3659. Carlock, J. K. "Managing the Treasury's Cash: Then and Now." **Banking** 61 (July 1968): 63-64.

3660. Carpenter, R. B. "How to Set up a Cash-Option Profit-Sharing Plan That Satisfies IRS Requirements." **Journal of Taxation** 35 (August 1971): 122-124.

3661. Carson, E. A. "Customs History and Records of Trade and Shipping." **Mariner's Mirror** 58 (November 1972): 447-462.

3662. Carter, M. E. "Decentralization of the Bureau of Internal Revenue." **Taxes** 17 (July 1939): 403-404.

3663. Chapoton, John E. "Treasury Asks Halt to Hearing on Two Treaties." **Tax Notes** 13 (September 1981): 645-651.

3664. Chegwidden, Cynthia S. "Justice and OMB Agree on Paperwork Reduction Rules: Treasury's Comments Reflect Tempered Concern." **Tax Notes** 17 (November 15, 1982): 563-564.

3665. Chegwidden, Cynthia S. "Treasury Supports Tax Retaliation against Canada." **Tax Notes** 15 (May 24, 1982): 692-693.

3666. Chommie, John C. **The Internal Revenue Service.** New York: Praeger, 1970.

3667. Circuit, R. K. "What You Have Always Wanted to Know About the IRS But Were Afraid to Ask." **Taxes** 51 (July 1973): 389-397.

3668. Cochran, Howe P. "Associated Patentees: A Loophole Made by IRS Policy or Want of It." **Journal of Taxation** 11 (December 1959): 358-361.

3669. Cohen, S. S. "Chief Counsel's Office." **Taxes** 42 (March 1964): 191-194.

3670. Cohen, S. S. "Current Developments in the Chief

Counsel's Office." **Taxes** 42 (October 1964): 663-672.

3671. Cohen, S. S. "Internal Revenue Service Today." **Taxes** 45 (May 1967): 317-323.

3672. Cohen, S. S. "Planning and Research: Its Evolution and Role in the Internal Revenue Service." **William and Mary Law Review** 9 (Summer 1968): 922-933.

3673. Cohen, Edwin S. "Role of the Treasury Department in the Federal Tax Legislative Process." **National Tax Journal** 32 (September 1979): 256-260.

3674. Coletta, Paolo E. "William Jennings Bryan and Currency and Banking Reform." **Nebraska History** 45 (March 1964): 31-58.

3675. Cook, M. B. "The IRS and the Secret Agent." **University of Florida Law Review** 35 (1983): 765-797.

3676. Cooper, Iver P. "FDA, the DATF, and Liquor Labeling: A Case Study of Interagency Jurisdictional Conflict." **Food and Drug Cosmetic Law Journal** 34 (July 1979): 370-390.

3677. Corey, W. S. "Letter Rulings to Apply or Not to Apply." **New York University Institute on Federal Taxation** 34 (1976): 787-828.

3678. Cox, C. R. "IRS Holds Seminar to Acquaint Tax Men with Automatic Data Processing." **Journal of Taxation** 15 (December 1961): 349-350.

3679. Crockett, Joseph P. **The Federal Tax System of the United States: A Survey of Law and Administration.** New York: Columbia University Press, 1955.

3680. Culligan, C. R. "CPA Practitioner and the Appellate Division." **New York Certified Public Accountant** 28 (October 1958): 713-719.

3681. Culverhouse, H. F. "Defending Criminal Tax Trials: Discovery Strategy." **Trial** 18 (May 1982): 52-55.

3682. Culverhouse, H. F. "Settlement Procedures before Bureau of Internal Revenue." **Alabama Lawyer** 11 (October 1980): 420-428.

3683. Dam, Kenneth W. "Trademarks, Price Discrimination

and the Bureau of Customs." **Journal of Law and Economics** 7 (October 1964): 45-52.

3684. Dobrzensky, Milton W. "IRS Ought to Support Assessments by Written Findings of Law and Fact." **Journal of Taxation** 11 (November 1959): 296-298.

3685. Donaldson, J. B. "New Law May End Privilege on IRS Records, Agent's Testimony, in Civil Tax Litigation." **Journal of Taxation** 10 (January 1959): 38-40.

3686. Donnelly, T. J. "How Regional Counsel Uses His New Authority to Settle Tax Court Cases." **Journal of Taxation** 10 (February 1959): 76-78.

3687. Doris, Lillian, ed. **The American Way in Taxation: Internal Revenue, 1862-1963.** Englewood Cliffs, NJ: Prentice-Hall, 1963.

3688. Dwan, Ralph H. "Administrative Review of Judicial Decisions - Treasury Practice." **Columbia Law Review** 46 (July 1946): 581-599.

3689. Dykes, W. T. F. "Two Recent Letter Rulings Define IRS Position on Tax-Free Break Up of PCs: What Can Be Done." **Journal of Taxation** 50 (February 1979): 92-97.

3690. Edgmon, Terry D. and Donald C. Menzel. "The Regulation of Coal Surface Mining in a Federal System." **Natural Resources Journal** 21 (April 1981): 245-265.

3691. Egan, John W. "Internal Revenue Service and Corporate Slush Funds: Some Fifth Amendment Problems." **Journal of Criminal Law and Criminology** 69 (Spring 1978): 59-74.

3692. Eggleston, Dale. "Debt-Equity Distinction: Another Approach under New Treasury Regulations." **Oil and Gas Tax Quarterly** 30 (September 1981): 1-39.

3693. Ellentuck, Albert B. "How and When to Use the Advance Ruling in Planning Tax Transactions." **Journal of Taxation** 21 (July 1964): 52-56.

3694. El-Sayeh, Hamed A. "The United States Treasury Department's Views on Legislation Affecting Income Tax Administration Since 1932." Ph.D. dissertation, University of Kentucky, 1950.

3695. Emory, M. "Private Rulings: What May Practitioners

Expect from the New Procedure?" **Journal of Taxation** 47 (December 1977): 322-328.

3696. Engquist, E. J. "Improved Statistics Resulting from the Automatic Data Processing System." **Taxes** 41 (January 1963): 39-44.

3697. Erbacher, P. J. "Should IRS Be Bound by Its Own Procedural Rules in Civil Tax Cases?" **Journal of Taxation** 37 (July 1972): 42-44.

3698. Erickson, A. G. "Increasing Federal-State Exchange of Tax Data Strengthens IRS Enforcement Program." **Journal of Taxation** 20 (April 1964): 243-244.

3699. Farioletti, M. "Some Results from First Year's Audit Control Program of Bureau of Internal Revenue." **National Tax Journal** 5 (March 1952): 65-78.

3700. Farrar, L. D. "The BIR Training School." **Taxes** 25 (March 1947): 232-239.

3701. Feig, F. H. and A. R. Knox. "Reorganization of the Internal Revenue Bureau." **Hennepin Lawyer** 21 (December 1952): 35-42.

3702. Field, Thomas F. "Firms Mull Innovative Leases as Treasury Amends Regs." **Tax Notes** 13 (November 16, 1981): 1215-1216.

3703. Flynn, J. J. "IRS Integrated Data Retrieval System - Present and Future." **CPA Journal** 43 (November 1973): 944-945.

3704. Forbes, Malcolm S. "What Manner of Man Is C. Douglas Dillon?" **Forbes** 90 (July 15, 1962): 9-10.

3705. Forster, Joel M. "IRS Disclosure Policies and Practices." **Journal of Accountancy** 139 (April 1975): 81-84.

3706. Fox, C. I. "Office of International Operations: What It Does and How It Functions." **Journal of Taxation** 22 (March 1965): 162-164.

3707. Fox, Guy H. "Regulation of Banking by the Comptroller of the Currency." Ph.D. dissertation, University of Texas, 1949.

3708. Frank, B. H. "IRS Takes Harsh Position on Exempting Condominium and Homeowner's Associations." **Journal of Taxation** 44 (May 1976): 306-309.

3709. Franklin, L. I. "Practice before Treasury Department." **Michigan State Bar Journal** 5 (April 1926): 185-186.

3710. Franklin, R. J. "New IRS Procedures for Change in Accounting Period Increase Need for Advance Planning." **Journal of Taxation** 20 (April 1964): 194-198.

3711. Franklin, Robert S. "Tax Havens - Problems with Continued Use." **Institute on Federal Taxation** 40 (1982): 33-55.

3712. Freeman, H. A. and N. D. Freeman. "Achieving a Good Settlement with the IRS: A Guide for the Negotiator." **Journal of Taxation** 11 (August 1959): 93-95.

3713. Fry, C. L. and C. P. Harper. "Treasury Deposits in Monetary Studies." **Review of Business and Economic Research** 14 (Winter 1978-1979): 78-82.

3714. Fuchs, R. S. and D. B. Ellis. "Title VII: Relationship and Effect on the National Labor Relations Board." **Boston College Industrial and Commercial Law Review** 7 (Spring 1966): 575-584.

3715. Fuchs, R. S. and H. M. Kelleher. "Back-Pay Remedy of the National Labor Relations Board." **Boston College Industrial and Commercial Law Review** 9 (Summer 1968): 829.

3716. Fuller, James P. "International Operations and Proposed Sec. 385 Regs." **Tax Executive** 32 (July 1980): 280-288.

3717. Fuller, James P. "Service Asserts Civil Fraud in Section 482 Intercompany Pricing Decision." **Journal of Taxation** 45 (November 1976): 282-285.

3718. Gaines, Tilford C. **Techniques of Treasury Debt Management.** New York: Free Press, 1962.

3719. Garbis, Marvin J. "Improving the Procedural System under Which Tax Controversies Are Resolved." **Journal of Taxation** 33 (November 1970): 278.

3720. Gentry, M. "Gun and Liquor Lobbies Put AIF Plan in Limbo." **Police Magazine** 5 (July 1982): 40-41.

3721. Gentry, M. "Post-mortem on the AFT: Powerful Enemies, Few Friends." **Police Magazine** 5 (March 1982): 28-31.

3722. Gerhart, Peter M. "Judicial Review of Customs Service Actions." **Law and Policy in International Business** 9 (1977): 1101-1189.

3723. Gilbert, Abby L. "The Comptroller of the Currency and the Freedman's Savings Bank." **Journal of Negro History** 57 (April 1972): 125-143.

3724. Glade, L. "Treasury Department and Its Procedures." **Tulane Law Review** 23 (June 1949): 513-518.

3725. Gould, Frank J. "The New Debt-Equity Treasury Regulations under Section 385." **Practical Lawyer** 28 (June 1, 1982): 33-50.

3726. Granger, Clive W. J. and D. Orr. "Infinite Variance and Research Strategy in Time Series Analysis." **American Statistical Association Journal** 67 (June 1972): 275-285.

3727. Gray, A. L. "Brouhaha in the Old Treasury." **Bankers Magazine** 157 (Summer 1974): 80-87.

3728. Gray, A. L. "Ghost of Andrew Mellon." **Bankers Magazine** 158 (Spring 1975): 51-54.

3729. Gray, A. L. "Saxon Chronicle." **Bankers Magazine** 156 (Summer 1973): 51-53.

3730. Green, William H. "Analysis of the 1981 Treasury Report on DISC." **International Tax Journal** 7 (June 1981): 333-352.

3731. Gregory, J. F. "Requirements for Enrollment to Practice before the Treasury Department of the United States and Practice and Procedure before the Bureau of Internal Revenue." **Kentucky State Bar Journal** 10 (December 1945): 51-64.

3732. Greif, J. "Analysis of Treasury Proposals on Fringe Benefits: Are They Rules of the Future?" **Journal of Taxation** 45 (August 1976): 96-101.

3733. Greiner, Larry E. "Putting Judgement Back into Decisions." **Harvard Business Review** 48 (March 1970): 59-67.

3734. Grosse, H. D. "Fresh Approach to Bank Examinations." **Bankers Magazine** 161 (May 1978): 39-42.

3735. Hald, Earl C. "Monetary Aspects of Changes in Treasury Cash Balances." **Southern Economic Journal** 22 (April 1956): 448-456.

3736. Hall, C. B. "Revised Regulatory Examinations and Their Impact on the Lending Function." **Journal of Commercial Bank Lending** 59 (September 1976): 30-37.

3737. Hall, C. B. "Update: Changes in the Loan Examination and Reporting Process." **Journal of Commercial Bank Lending** 59 (December 1976): 34-42.

3738. Halstead, Harry M. "New Internal Revenue System: What Automatic Data Processing Means to Taxpayers." **Taxes** 40 (August 1962): 632-641.

3739. Hanlon, J. F. "Maintaining an Effective IRS Examination Program - A Positive Approach." **Tax Adviser** 4 (November 1973): 644-649.

3740. Hansen, George. **To Harass Our People: The Story of the IRS.** Washington, DC: Positive Publications, 1980.

3741. Harding, B. M. "New Directions: Automation and Integrity." **Taxes** 40 (February 1962): 79-82.

3742. Harless, Donald S. "Recent Rulings Affect Allocation and Apportionment." **International Tax Journal** 7 (August 1981): 461-465.

3743. Harless, R. F. "How the IRS Evaluates and Promotes Revenue Agents." **Tax Adviser** 4 (June 1973): 324.

3744. Harrar, W. H. "Collusive State Decree: A Nullity in Determining Federal Tax Consequences?" **Journal of Taxation** 21 (December 1964): 372-375.

3745. Harris, S. M. and R. E. Warner. "Fifth Circuit Reaffirms Distaste for IRS Misrepresentation." **Taxes** 56 (January 1978): 28-36.

3746. Harstad, Paul F. and Thomas F. Field. "Most Treasury Reports on Tax Issues Are Late or Overdue." **Tax Notes** 14 (February 22, 1982): 488-489.

3747. Hauser, C. C. "Current Problems in the Office of the Chief Counsel." **Tulane Tax Institute** 12 (1963): 1-9.

3748. Heinz, S. M. "IRS Successful in Attacking Family Trust Arrangements." **Trusts and Estates** 120 (July 1981): 37-41.

3749. Hertzog, R. P. "Settlement of Tax Disputes and Litigation Policy in Tax Cases." **Taxes** 42 (September 1964): 555-559.

3750. Hertzog, R. P. "Three Steps Recently Taken by Chief Counsel to Cope with Increasing Tax Litigation." **Journal of Taxation** 10 (May 1959): 295-298.

3751. Hill, T. "Problems and Interests of the Treasury Department in Corporate Reorganization." **Corporate Reorganization** 2 (June 1936): 464-468.

3752. Hobbet, Richard D. and J. B. Donaldson. "Practitioner's Guide to Making a Good Settlement within the IRS." **Journal of Taxation** 15 (October 1961): 230-235.

3753. Hohenstein, Henry J. **The IRS Conspiracy.** Los Angeles: Nash, 1974.

3754. Holden, James P. "Evolving Standards of Professional Responsibility in Federal Tax Practice: The Circular 230 Amendments and Related Matters." **Institute on Federal Taxation** 40 (1982): 14-38.

3755. Holden, Justin S. "Some Thoughts on the Administration of the Federal Tax System." **Rhode Island Bar Journal** 31 (November 1982): 13-15.

3756. Holmes, Alan R. and S. E. Pardee. "Treasury and Federal Reserve Foreign Exchange Operations." **Federal Reserve Bulletin** 63 (March 1977): 200-221.

3757. Holzman, Robert S. "How Far Can You Trust a Revenue Agent?" **Taxes** 44 (January 1966): 37-42.

3758. Hope, W. E. "Recent Accomplishments of the Treasury." **National Income Tax Magazine** 8 (August 1930): 300-302.

3759. Horvits, Jerome S. and H. L. Tallichet. "Examination of the IRS's Voluntary Disclosure Policy." **Tax Adviser** 11 (September 1980): 545-550.

3760. Hultman, K. E. and G. Cunningham. "Focusing on Interpersonal Relations Training at the Internal Revenue Service: Preparing Employees for Upward Mobility." **Training and Development Journal** 32 (September 1978): 10-14.

3761. Hunter, M. S. "Practice before the Internal Revenue Service." **D.C. Bar Journal** 34 (March 1967): 24-31.

3762. Hynd, Alan. **The Giant Killers.** New York: R. M. McBride, 1945.

3763. Jackson, R. H. "Changes in Treasury Tax Policy." **Tax Magazine** 12 (July 1934): 342-345, 382-383.

3764. Jensen, H. L. and J. S. Horvits. "How to Get Access to Inside IRS Records." **Practical Accountant** 14 (January 1981): 65-70.

3765. Johnson, Gore G. **The Treasury and Monetary Policy, 1933-1938.** Cambridge, MA: Harvard University Press, 1939.

3766. Johnson, H. P. "Triple-Entry Bookkeeping: An Answer to Internal Revenue Service Automatic Data Processing." **Taxes** 41 (March 1963): 168-174.

3767. Jones, D. H. "Sweeping Changes in the Comptroller's Office." **Bankers Magazine** 159 (Autumn 1976): 55-61.

3768. Kaminsky, M. "Judicial Review of Procedures in the Internal Revenue Service." **Taxes** 36 (March 1958): 172-176.

3769. Kannry, G. S. "How to Mitigate the Impact of New Regs. on Exempt Organization's Advertising Income." **Journal of Taxation** 45 (November 1976): 304-308.

3770. Kaplan, Richard L. "Critical Examination of the Treasury Department's Report on the Arab Boycott." **University of Illinois Law Review** (1983): 23-26.

3771. Kaplan, Richard L. and Lowell D. Yoder. "New Variations on an Old Enigma: The Treasury Department's Debt-Equity Regulations." **University of Illinois Law Review** (Summer 1981): 567-623.

3772. Karasyk, J. "Advice from an Ex-Special Agent." **CPA Journal** 48 (November 1978): 83-85.

3773. Kazinetz, S. "Looking in on Privacy." **Financial Executive** 44 (January 1976): 6-7.

3774. Kent, A. H. "Treasury Tax Problems." **Tax Magazine** 12 (October 1934): 527-530, 560, 562.

3775. Kinley, David. **The History, Organization and Influence of the Independent Treasury of the United States.** New York: Crowell, 1893.

3776. Klotz, A. H. "Protecting the Right to Protest." **Taxes** 43 (March 1965): 165-167.

3777. Knickerbocker, Daniel C. "Prohibited Transactions Excises after Reorganization: Ticking Time Bomb or Just a Dud?" **Tax Lawyer** 34 (Fall 1980): 147-186.

3778. Knox, A. R. "Practice before the United States Treasury Department." **Minnesota Law Review** 24 (December 1939): 55-64.

3779. Korner, J. G. "Recent Cases Highlight Broad Powers of Service to Examine Taxpayer's Records." **Journal of Taxation** 34 (April 1971): 194-198.

3780. Krane, Howard G. "Public Hearings for Private Rulings: A Dissent." **Taxes** 50 (March 1972): 160-165.

3781. Kreysa, F. J. "Laboratory Support Criminal Enforcement at Treasury's Bureau of Alcohol, Tobacco and Firearms." **Journal of Police Science and Administration** 5 (June 1977): 223-226.

3782. Kurtz, Jerome. "Commissioner's Remarks on Abusive Tax Shelter Issues." **Taxes** 55 (December 1977): 774-778.

3783. Kurtz, Jerome. "Luncheon Address: The State of Tax Administration." **Southern California Tax Institute** 30 (1978): 885-897.

3784. Lane, Bruce S. and J. Ritholz. "Regional Filing: The Dog and His Tails." **American Bar Association Section of Taxation Bulletin** 20 (April 1967): 105-113.

3785. Latham, D. "Current Federal Tax Developments." **New York Certified Public Accountant** 30 (December 1960): 820-828.

3786. Latham, D. "Observations and Aims of a New Commissioner." **Taxes** 37 (December 1959): 1061-1067.

3787. Latham, D. "Responsibility of the Internal Revenue Service." **University of Southern California School of Law Tax Institute** (1960): 1-14.

3788. Latham, D. "What Is Good Government Tax Practice." **New York University Institute on Federal Taxation**

22 (1964): 1-8.

3789. Lehrfeld, William J. and G. D. Webster. "Administration by the IRS of Non-Profit Organization Tax Matters." **Tax Lawyer** 21 (Spring 1968): 591-607.

3790. Link, David T. "Reports and Information Retrieval Activity: A Legal Information System in the Internal Revenue Service." **Taxes** 43 (April 1965): 231-240.

3791. Link, David T. "RIRA - A Legal Information System in the Internal Revenue Service." **Taxes** 43 (April 1965): 231-244.

3792. Lipton, Paul P. and R. A. Petrie. "Subpoena Powers of the Internal Revenue Service." **Tulane Tax Institute** 13 (1964): 108-114.

3793. Littleton, J. W. S. "Practical Effects of New Procedures for Obtaining Rulings - An Insider's Viewpoint." **Tulane Tax Institute** 19 (1970): 289-297.

3794. Lourie, G. B. and A. R. Cutler. "Tax Fraud - A Reappraisal." **Boston University Law Review** 29 (January 1949): 79-97.

3795. Love, Robert A. "Federal Financing: A Study of the Methods Employed by the Treasury in Its Borrowing Operations." Ph.D. dissertation, Columbia University, 1931.

3796. Lovett, J. E. "Treasury Tax and Loan Accounts and Federal Reserve Open Market Operations." **Federal Reserve Bank of New York Quarterly Review** 3 (Summer 1978): 41-46.

3797. Lubick, Donald C. "Aspects of Legislative Persuasion: Treasury Department." **National Tax Journal** 32 (September 1979): 284-288.

3798. Lucia, J. L. "Allan Sproul and the Treasury-Federal Reserve Accord, 1951." **History of Political Economy** 15 (Spring 1983): 106-121.

3799. Lurie, Alvin D. "Charities Begin at the IRS: The Forms and Substance of Their Regulation." **Tax Adviser** 9 (September 1978): 536-544.

3800. Lynch, J. A. "Nontaxpayer Suits: Seeking Injunctive and Declaratory Relief against IRS Administrative Action." **Akron Law Review** 12 (Summer

1978): 1-54.

3801. McCulloch, H. "Suggestions of the Comptroller to Managers of National Banks." **Bankers Magazine** 150 (Autumn 1967): 59-61.

3802. McGuire, O. R. "Legislative or Executive Control over Accounting for Federal Funds." **Illinois Law Review** 20 (January 1926): 455-474.

3803. McNamar, T. "Treasury Encourages Support for Deregulation Bill." **Trusts and Estates** 121 (March 1982): 53-56.

3804. Mahon, R. T. "Limitations on the Commissioner: Power to Audit, to Summon, to Assess, Remedies Available to the Taxpayer." **New York University Institute on Federal Taxation** 24 (1966): 1-16.

3805. Malloy, Michael P. "Embargo Programs of the United States Treasury Department." **Columbia Journal of Transnational Law** 20 (1981): 485-516.

3806. Malloy, Michael P. "The Impact of U. S. Control of Foreign Assets on Refugees and Expatriates." **Michigan Yearbook of International Legal Studies** (1982): 399-420.

3807. Malzeke, H. F. "Current IRS Procedure for Issuing Rulings in Reorganization Cases: How It Operates." **Journal of Taxation** 26 (May 1967): 290-293.

3808. Mandel, G. "Brookhaven Internal Revenue Service Center." **CPA Journal** 46 (March 1976): 21-24.

3809. Marrs, Aubrey R. "Procedure in Practice before the Bureau of Internal Revenue." **University of Cincinnati Law Review** 19 (November 1950): 460-480.

3810. Mason, Bernard. "Alexander Hamilton and the Report on Manufactures: A Suggestion." **Pennsylvania History** 32 (July 1965): 288-294.

3811. Meldman, L. L. "Tax Practice before the Internal Revenue Service." **Milwaukee Bar Association Gavel** 22 (November 1961): 13-19.

3812. Mendel, Judy. "Treasury Regulation Section 1.385 - Guidelines for Structuring Debt of a Closely Held Corporation." **Cumberland Law Review** 12 (Winter 1982): 139-153.

3813. Merline, D. A. "The Expanded Scope of the IRS Summons Power after United States v. Arthur Young and Company." **Southern California Law Review** 37 (Winter 1986): 307-333.

3814. Miller, R. N. "Reorganization of the Bureau of Internal Revenue - An Appraisal." **Taxes** 30 (December 1952): 967-973.

3815. Miller, R. S. "Administrative Agency Intelligence-Gathering: An Appraisal of the Investigative Powers of the Internal Revenue Service." **Boston College Industrial and Commercial Law Review** 6 (Summer 1965): 657-671.

3816. Mirarchi, R. E. "IRS Attacks the One-Man Professional Corporation." **Trusts and Estates** 118 (July 1979): 23-27.

3817. Monical, Steven E. "The Effect of Corporate Control on Valuation of Closely Held Corporate Stock for Federal Estate and Gift Tax Purposes." **University of Illinois Law Review** (Summer 1982): 775-798.

3818. Moses, B. S. "Issuance and Enforcement of IRS Summonses against Third-Party Recordkeepers." **Taxes** 60 (January 1982): 66-80.

3819. Mundheim, Robert H. "Treasury Counsel and Commissioner Kurtz Criticize Tax Attorneys on Shelters." **Journal of Taxation** (April 1980): 211-219.

3820. Murdoch, C. "Scope of the Power of the Internal Revenue Service to Reallocate under Section 482." **Boston College Industrial and Commercial Law Review** 6 (Summer 1965): 717-732.

3821. Murphy, J. H. "Internal Revenue Bureau Reorganization." **New York State Bar Bulletin** 25 (April 1953): 120-124.

3822. Nanes, Allan. "Federal Control of Firearms: Is It Necessary?" **Current History** 53 (July 1967): 38-42.

3823. Nash, M. J. "Effective Internal Revenue Service Appellate Division Practice." **New York University Institute on Federal Taxation** 35 (1977): 325-353.

3824. Neal, Harry E. **Six Against Crime: Treasury Agencies in Action.** New York: Messner, 1959.

3825. Nickel, H. "Mike Blumenthal Finally Puts His Act Together." **Fortune** 97 (January 30, 1978): 114-118.

3826. Nordwind, W. "Two Circuit Courts Now Hold That IRS Is Bound by Its Administrative Procedures." **Journal of Taxation** 34 (January 1971): 5-8.

3827. Olsen, A. F. "Revenue Agents' Tax Audits: Some Aspects of Policy and Procedures at the District Level." **New York Certified Public Accountant** 28 (November/December 1958): 783-794, 890-898.

3828. Pardee, Scott E. "Treasury and Federal Reserve Foreign Exchange Operations." **Federal Reserve Bulletin** 67 (June 1981): 486-487.

3829. Parker, D. S. "How the IRS Engineering and Valuation Branch Works: Its Policies on Depreciation." **Journal of Taxation** 10 (February 1959): 69-71.

3830. Parker, R. S. "Substitution of Escrow Will Destroy Benefits of Installment Sale Says IRS." **Journal of Taxation** 47 (December 1977): 346-349.

3831. Parnell, Archie. **Congress and the IRS: Improving the Relationship.** Washington, DC: Fund for Public Policy Research, 1980.

3832. Parnell, Archie. "Congressional Interference in Agency Enforcement: The IRS Experience." **Yale Law Journal** 89 (June 1980): 1360-1394.

3833. Parsons, W. W. "Installing Management Improvement in the United States Treasury Department." **Public Administration Review** 10 (Summer 1950): 176-180.

3834. Patten, J. H. "Judicial Review of Treasury Regulations." **National Income Tax Magazine** 5 (January 1927): 16-18.

3835. Penniman, Clara. "Reorganization and the Internal Revenue Service." **Public Administration Review** 21 (Summer 1961): 121-130.

3836. Peterson, J. M. "What You Need to Know about the IRS Model Profit-Sharing and Model Money Purchase Pension Plans." **Taxes** 56 (November 1978): 673-678.

3837. Phillips, Max D. "Study of the Office of Law Enforcement Coordination U. S. Treasury Department." **Journal of Criminal Law, Criminology and**

Police Science 54 (September 1963): 369-381.

3838. Pigg, J. H. "Enrollment to Practice before the Treasury Department of the United States and Practice and Procedure before the Bureau of Internal Revenue." **Kentucky State Bar Journal** 10 (December 1945): 65-84.

3839. Plumly, L. "Social Security Direct Deposit Is Only the Beginning." **Savings and Loan News** 99 (July 1978): 66-70.

3840. Ponn, G. W. "National Banks and the Future - One Regulator's Concerns." **Journal of Commercial Bank Lending** 57 (December 1974): 53-57.

3841. Premis, M. "Audit Review Process." **Creighton Law Review** 11 (March 1978): 755-763.

3842. Price, C. E. "Lawyers and the Internal Revenue Service." **Kentucky State Bar Journal** 17 (September 1953): 158-165.

3843. Raabe, W. "Parochial Schools and the IRS: The Scope of Administrative Control." **Taxes** 58 (July 1980): 494-499.

3844. Ratchford, Benjamin U. "Congress Studies Fiscal and Monetary Policies." **Southern Economic Journal** 19 (October 1952): 173-183.

3845. Raymond, J. J. "New Case Sets Limits on Service's Summons Power under Section 7602." **Journal of Taxation** 44 (March 1976): 172-174.

3846. Redman, L. "A Look at How the Reorganized Bureau of Internal Revenue Will Work." **Journal of Accountancy** 93 (May 1952): 571-577.

3847. Reichler, R., S. Friedmann and G. R. Ince. "Plan as a Service Audit Target: A Panel." **New York University Institute on Federal Taxation** 38 (1980): 13.1-13.52.

3848. Reid, Thomas R. "Public Access to Internal Revenue Service Rulings." **George Washington Law Review** 41 (October 1972): 23.

3849. Reiling, H. T. "Important Changes in Treasury Department Regulations." **National Income Tax Magazine** 7 (March 1929): 100-104.

3850. Reiling, H. T. "Tax Refunds over $200,200 Require Special Handling: Bureau Office Explains

Procedure." **Journal of Accountancy** 95 (May 1953): 567-571.

3851. Reilly, T. J. "Tax Practitioners and Circular 230." **Journal of Accountancy** 115 (January 1963): 63-66.

3852. Reismer, G. "Procedure under the Bureau of Internal Revenue Reorganization." **Marquette Law Review** 36 (Winter 1952-1953): 248-256.

3853. Richard, G. H. and J. A. Spanogle. "Accountability and Decision-making: A Study of Bank Charter Conversions." **University of Toledo Law Review** 12 (Winter 1981): 269-304.

3854. Richie, Richard W. and J. R. Alliston. "Impact of Office Automation in the Internal Revenue Service." **Monthly Labor Review** 86 (April 1963): 388-393.

3855. Ritholz, Jules. "Commissioner's Inquisitorial Powers." **Taxes** 45 (December 1967): 782-790.

3856. Robb, James D. "Attorney-Client Privilege and Work Product Doctrine - Application in the Corporate Context." **Wayne Law Review** 28 (Spring 1982): 1577-1600.

3857. Roberts, James E. "IRS Reconsidering Section 79." **CLU Journal** 31 (January 1977): 67-70.

3858. Robertson, Ross M. "Comptroller and Bank Supervision: A Historical Appraisal." **National Banking Review** 4 (March 1967): 49-61.

3859. Rodgers, G. L. "Commissioner Does Not Acquiesce." **Nebraska Law Review** 59 (1980): 1001-1039.

3860. Rogovin, Mitchell. "Four R's: Regulations, Rulings, Reliance, and Retroactivity." **Taxes** 43 (December 1965): 756-766.

3861. Rogovin, Mitchell. "Impact of Computers on Tax Practice Today: What They Can Do for the IRS and Tax Men." **Journal of Taxation** 25 (August 1966): 112-114.

3862. Roob, E. M. "As New Debt Manager Views Federal Financing." **Bankers Monthly** 90 (May 1973): 22-24.

3863. Rosapepe, J. S. "How to Collect $155 Billion." **Public Relations Journal** 24 (April 1968): 31-33.

3864. Rosen, G. R. "Quiet Rise of George Schultz."

Dun's Review 100 (October 1972): 48-51.

3865. Rosen, R. Eliot. "Treasury Circulates Unitary Tax Questionnaire." **Tax Notes** 15 (April 19, 1982): 239-241.

3866. Rosenbloom, H. David. "More IRS Information May Become Public Due to Amended Freedom of Information Act." **Journal of Taxation** 45 (November 1976): 258-263.

3867. Roth, D. M. "Retained Power to Substitute Corporate Trustees: Is Revenue Ruling 79-353 Correct?" **Trusts and Estates** 119 (April 1980): 42-50.

3868. Rothberg, H. J. "Study of the Impact of Office Automation in the IRS." **Monthly Labor Review** 92 (October 1969): 26-30.

3869. Rudow, D. B. "What Chances of a Return Being Examined? Practical View of IRS Audit Policy." **Journal of Taxation** 20 (March 1964): 170-174.

3870. Sacerdoti, G. "Concessions on Oil Payments." **Far Eastern Economic Review** 99 (January 1978): 73-74.

3871. St. John, J. "Revolutionary Consequences of the Income Tax." **American Opinion** 22 (December 1979): 37-39.

3872. Saltzman, Michael I. "Supreme Court's LaSalle Decision Makes It Harder to Successfully Challenge a Summons." **Journal of Taxation** 49 (September 1978): 130-135.

3873. Saltzman, Michael I. "What You Should Know about IRS Collection Procedures." **Practical Accountant** 11 (January 1978): 55-59.

3874. Sanders, R. E. "National Response Teams: AFT's Coordinated Effort in Arson Investigations." **FBI Law Enforcement Bulletin** 50 (December 1981): 1-5.

3875. Scherer, J. "Federal Credit Programs - The Achilles Heel of the Budget." **Challenge** 23 (January/February 1981): 55-57.

3876. Schmeckebier, Laurence F. **The Bureau of Internal Revenue: Its History, Activities and Organization.** Baltimore: Johns Hopkins University Press, 1923.

3877. Schmidt, Robert M. "Exchange of Information between the Michigan Department of Revenue and the Internal Revenue Service." **University of Detroit Law Journal** 38 (October 1960): 76-88.

3878. Schnee, E. J. and M. R. Taylor. "Accountants' Workpapers - Recent IRS Developments." **CPA Journal** 50 (February 1980): 13-17.

3879. Schneider, L. J. "Coping with the IRS' Unpublished Rules for Handling Accounting Method Changes." **Journal of Taxation** 48 (April 1978): 204-209.

3880. Schnepper, Jeff A. **Inside IRS.** New York: Stein and Day, 1978.

3881. Schubkegel, A. L. "Treasury's Reporting Rules Governing Transfers of Currency." **Taxes** 64 (June 1986): 339-364.

3882. Schwaigart, P. F. "Increasing IRS Emphasis on Inventories Stresses Need for Proper Practices." **Journal of Taxation** 19 (August 1963): 66-71.

3883. Schwartz, W. F. "Administration by the Department of the Treasury of the Laws Authorizing the Imposition of Antidumping Duties." **Virginia Journal of International Law** 14 (Spring 1974): 463-485.

3884. Schwerdtfeger, W. "Offers in Compromise of Federal Taxes." **Kentucky State Bar Journal** 16 (March 1952): 86-89, 96.

3885. Seeger, M. "Man to Watch in Washington." **Dun's Review** 94 (October 1969): 42-43.

3886. Shapiro, Leslie S. "Management and Operation of the Office of Director of Practice." **NYU Institute on Federal Taxation** 43 (1985): 1-28.

3887. Shapiro, Leslie S. "Professional Responsibility in the Eyes of the IRS." **Tax Adviser** 17 (March 1986): 136-143.

3888. Shefsky, L. E. "Publicly Offered Shelters: Can the SEC and IRS Be Served?" **Taxes** 53 (September 1975): 516-533.

3889. Sierra, Ralph J. "Possessions Corporations: Critique of Treasury Reports." **International Tax Journal** 7 (October 1980): 14-26.

3890. Silver, S. E. "IRS Sting Tactics under Attack in

the Courts." **Taxes** 60 (September 1982): 650-655.

3891. Silverman, C. S. "Case for National Labor Relations Board's Use of Rulemaking in Asserting Jurisdiction." **Labor Law Journal** 25 (October 1974): 607-617.

3892. Simmons, E. C. "Treasury Deposits and Excess Reserves." **Journal of Political Economy** 48 (June 1940): 325-343.

3893. Simmons, Sherwin P. "Eleven Questions - An Extraordinary New Audit Technique." **Tax Lawyer** 30 (Fall 1976): 23-35.

3894. Skerry, Peter. "Christian Schools versus IRS." **Public Interest** 61 (Fall 1980): 18-41.

3895. Skinner, R. G. "How the IRS Carriers on Its Unrelenting Search for Purchases of Goodwill." **Journal of Taxation** 29 (November 1968): 288-293.

3896. Smith, J. E. and R. R. Dince. "Consider the Banking Customer." **Bankers Magazine** 159 (Spring 1976): 58-62.

3897. Smith, W. H. "Electronic Data Processing in the Internal Revenue Service." **National Tax Journal** 14 (September 1961): 210-222.

3898. Smith, W. H. "What the IRS Is Now Doing to Improve Various Aspects of Tax Administration." **Journal of Taxation** 26 (January 1967): 56-58.

3899. Snyder, J. L. "Effects of the Recent FOIA Decision That IRS Must Publish Its Internal Memoranda." **Journal of Taxation** 52 (June 1980): 332-336.

3900. Snyder, J. W. "Reorganization of the Bureau of Internal Revenue." **Public Administration Review** 12 (Autumn 1952): 221-233.

3901. Sobeloff, Jonathan. "New Freedom of Information Act: What It Means to Tax Practitioners." **Journal of Taxation** 27 (September 1967): 130-142.

3902. Soule, A. B. "The United States Customs Boat Patrol on Lake Champlain during the Prohibition Era." **Vermont History** 48 (Summer 1980): 133-143.

3903. Sperry, R. "Classified, Selective Bibliography on the Administration and Operations of the Internal

Revenue Service." **National Tax Journal** 25 (March 1972): 65-74.

3904. Spiegel, H. H. "Current Operations in the Chief Counsel's Office." **Taxes** 38 (December 1960): 905-913.

3905. Spiegel, H. H. "Ex-CC Defends the IRS: Caught between Taxpayers and Congress, It Does a Good Job." **Journal of Taxation** 15 (August 1961): 108-113.

3906. Spiegel, H. H. "Why the Service Does What It Does." **Arkansas Law Review** 15 (Summer 1961): 274-287.

3907. Sproul, A. "Accord: Landmark in the First Fifty Years of the Federal Reserve System." **Federal Reserve Bank of New York Quarterly Review** 46 (November 1964): 227-236.

3908. Stang, Alan. "Tragedy in a Fight for Due Process." **American Opinion** 23 (November 1980): 39-43.

3909. Stelle, H. W. "The Chief Counsel's Office - Its Organization and Its Work." **Taxes** 24 (March 1946): 238-242.

3910. Stigamire, J. C. "Internal Revenue Service Case Settlement Procedures." **University of Southern California School of Law Tax Institute** 31 (1979): 1073-1084.

3911. Stine, G. T. "Working with the IRS." **Tax Adviser** 2 (September 1971): 563-576.

3912. Stowe, C. W. "Moral Responsibility in Tax Practice: Former IRS Official's View." **Journal of Accountancy** 107 (April 1959): 36-39.

3913. Stuart, R. A. "Some Pointers in Successful Negotiations with Internal Revenue Service." **Taxes** 40 (January 1962): 59-63.

3914. Sullivan, J. L. "Treasury's Collection Costs." **Taxes** 21 (June 1943): 335-336, 343-345.

3915. Surface, William. **Inside Internal Revenue.** New York: Coward-McCann, 1967.

3916. Surrey, Stanley S. "Comment on the Proposal to Separate the Bureau of Internal Revenue from the Treasury Department." **Tax Law Review** 8 (January 1953): 155-171.

3917. Surrey, Stanley S. "Treasury Department Regulatory Material under the Tax Code." **Policy Sciences** 7 (December 1976): 505-518.

3918. Swartz, H. T. "IRS Program to Up-Date Published Rulings." **William and Mary Law Review** 9 (Summer 1968): 951-969.

3919. Taggart, John Y. "Withholding on Foreigners' Original Issue Discount." **Tax Notes** 16 (August 30, 1982): 874-887.

3920. Taus, Esther R. **Central Banking Functions of the United States Treasury, 1789-1941.** New York: Columbia University Press, 1943.

3921. Taus, Esther R. **The Role of the U. S. Treasury in Stabilizing the Economy, 1941-1946.** Washington, DC: University Press of America, 1981.

3922. Taylor, H. D. "Automatic Data Processing in the Internal Revenue Service." **Journal of Accountancy** 119 (March 1965): 53-56.

3923. Taylor, Willard B. "Report on the U. S. Treasury Department Discussion Draft on Taxing Foreign Exchange Gains and Losses." **Tax Law Review** 36 (Summer 1981): 427-476.

3924. Teschner, P. A. "State Court, Decisions, Federal Taxation, and the Commissioner's Wonderland: The Need for Preliminary Characterization." **Taxes** 41 (February 1963): 98-104.

3925. Thomas, Kenneth F. and Robert E. Clayton. "Meeting with IRS Associate Commissioner." **Tax Adviser** 13 (December 1982): 753-756.

3926. Thomas, Kenneth F. and William R. Stromsem. "The Accountant-Advisor in Treasury's Office of Tax Legislative Counsel." **Tax Adviser** 11 (February 1980): 110-111.

3927. Thompson, E. G. "Disclosure and the Tax Reform Act of 1976." **National Tax Journal** 29 (December 1976): 391-397.

3928. Thoryn, M. "How to Straighten Out the IRS." **Nation's Business** 69 (April 1981): 74-76.

3929. Thrower, Randolph W. "IRS in Law Enforcement." **New York State Bar Journal** 43 (January 1971): 8-15.

3930. Tilzer, I. L. "May the IRS Ignore the Use of Diverted Funds in Criminal Tax Cases?" **Journal of Taxation** 46 (May 1977): 308-310.

3931. Trainor, H. J. "Functioning of the Inspection Service." **New York University Institute on Federal Taxation** 17 (1959): 495-505.

3932. Treusch, Paul E. "Chief Counsel's Office: A Dynamic View of Its Organization and Procedures: The Hows and Something of the Whys." **University of Southern California School of Law Tax Institute** (1960): 19-26.

3933. Treusch, Paul E. "District Conference - Can It Be Saved and Is It Worth Saving?" **Taxes** 56 (August 1978): 498-503.

3934. Treusch, Paul E. "Litigation Policy of the Chief Counsel's Office in Civil Tax Cases." **Taxes** 36 (December 1958): 958-967.

3935. Uretz, L. R. "Chief Counsel's Office." **Tennessee Law Review** 35 (Spring 1968): 467-481.

3936. Uretz, L. R. "Chief Counsel's Policy Regarding Acquiescence and Non-Acquiescence in Tax Court Cases." **Indiana Law Journal** 44 (Winter 1969): 206-215.

3937. Uretz, L. R. "Freedom of Information and the IRS." **Arkansas Law Review** 20 (Winter 1967): 283-298.

3938. Uretz, L. R. "How IRS Adapts Its Practice to Adverse Supreme Court Decisions." **Journal of Taxation** 26 (May 1967): 290-293.

3939. Uretz, L. R. "Settlement of Tax Controversies." **Taxes** 44 (December 1966): 794-806.

3940. Wakely, Maxwell A. H. "Practitioner's Guide to Achieving Favorable Tax Settlements with the IRS." **Journal of Taxation** 29 (October 1968): 220-223.

3941. Walsh, C. L. "Automatic Data Processing of Federal Corporation Income Tax Returns by Internal Revenue Service." **New York Certified Public Accountant** 36 (October 1966): 769-772.

3942. Walsh, J. "Functions of the Office of Administrative Hearings in OPA." **Missouri Bar Journal** 14 (October 1943): 267-272.

3943. Walters, J. M. "IRS Intelligence Division Operating Procedures: From 1040 through Criminal Trial." **New York University Institute on Federal Taxation** 32 (1974): 1195-1208.

3944. Wassenaar, R. C. "Internal Revenue Service: Financial Investigative Techniques Course." **Police Chief** 50 (June 1983): 49-50.

3945. Wasserman, M. G. "Proposed Reg. Sec. 1.61-16: An Example of Administrative Overreaching." **Taxes** 56 (May 1978): 243-250.

3946. Weinstein, Andrew H. and Mary T. Kogut. "IRS Audit of Attorney Trust Accounts." **Case and Comment** 88 (January/February 1983): 20-26.

3947. Weisbard, G. L. "Amended Returns: When, How to File, Rules Not Clear, Ethical Problems Arise." **Journal of Taxation** 16 (June 1962): 370-373.

3948. Weiss, Stanley. "Implementation of Debt-Equity Regulations Delayed." **Canadian Tax Journal** 30 (May/June 1982): 467-475.

3949. Weitzel, J. P. "Practice before the Treasury." **Journal of Accountancy** 109 (February 1960): 42-57.

3950. Wenchel, John P. "Procedure by Taxpayers before Treasury Department Tribunals." **Kentucky State Bar Journal** 10 (December 1945): 37-50.

3951. Whitaker, M. "Ruling Letters and Technical Advice: The Disclosure Crossroads." **Taxes** 53 (December 1975): 712-718.

3952. White, B. F. "Scope of Treasury's Power to Issue Non-Retroactive Regulations." **California Law Review** 38 (June 1950): 292-308.

3953. Willens, R. "Recent Decisions Open the Way for Trusts and Estates to Waive Stock Attribution." **Journal of Taxation** 51 (October 1979): 208-210.

3954. Williams, Ralph D. "Historical Development and Administrative Role of the Comptroller of the Currency in the National Banking System of the United States." Ph.D. dissertation, New York University, 1963.

3955. Winborne, S. A. "Internal Revenue Service: Addressing a Second Generation of Employee Plans Enforcement Problems." **Pension World** 18 (March

1982): 25-30.

3956. Wines, W. R. and B. Bugg. "IRS Should Eliminate the Penalty Tax Often Required for Delaying a Decision to File a Consolidated Return." **Taxes** 56 (July 1978): 384-388.

3957. Wolpe, F. "Thoughts for a Single Level of Appeal." **Taxes** 56 (May 1978): 267-271.

3958. Wormser, Rene A. "To the Commissioner of Internal Revenue: A Plea for Nonaggression." **Journal of Taxation** 20 (February 1964): 108-112.

3959. Worthy, K. M. "Chief Counsel's Office in the Seventies." **Taxes** 48 (January 1970): 5-13.

3960. Wright, L. H. "Inadequacies of Freedom of Information Act as Applied to IRS Letter Rulings." **Oklahoma Law Review** 28 (Fall 1975): 701-721.

3961. Yager, P. D. "When and How Should the Practitioner Ask for Rulings and Technical Advice?" **Journal of Taxation** 14 (January 1961): 38-45.

3962. Zalutsky, Morton H. "IRS-Issued Model Plans: A Simplified Procedure with Hidden Costs and Snares." **Journal of Taxation** 50 (February 1979): 98-102.

3963. Zelenak, L. "Should Courts Require the Internal Revenue Service to Be Consistent?" **Tax Law Review** 40 (Winter 1985): 411-448.

Chapter 15. U.S. Postal Service

3964. Ablard, C. D. and M. E. Harrison. "Post Office and Publishers' Pursestrings: A Study of the Second-Class Mailing Permit." **George Washington Law Review** 30 (April 1962): 367-374.

3965. Ague, Robert M. "Intent to Defraud in Postal Fraud Order Cases." **Temple Law Quarterly** 38 (Fall 1964): 61.

3966. Asher, Martin and Joel Popkin. "The Effect of Gender and Race Differentials on Public-Private Wage Comparisons: A Study of Postal Workers." **Industrial and Labor Relations Review** 38 (October 1984): 16-25.

3967. Baratz, Morton S. **The Economics of the Postal Service.** Washington, DC: Public Affairs Press, 1962.

3968. Bennett, James D. "Joseph Holt: Retrenchment and Reform in the Post Office Department, 1859-1860." **Filson Club Historical Quarterly** 49 (October 1975): 309-322.

3969. Berman, P. "Do We Really Need the Postal Service?" **Forbes** 123 (June 11, 1979): 47-49.

3970. Blaine, Harry R. "Grievance Procedure and Its Application in the United States Postal Service." **Labor Law Journal** 15 (November 1964): 725-733.

3971. Blount, Winton M. "Case for Postal Reform." **Nation's Business** 57 (September 1969): 52-54.

3972. Bolger, William F. "Electronic Mail: Room for a Partnership?" **Telephony** 197 (July 16, 1979): 28-30.

3973. Cohen, F. C. "Labor Features of the Postal Reorganization Act." **Labor Law Journal** 22 (January 1971): 44-50.

3974. Conkey, Kathleen. **The Postal Precipice: Can the U.S. Postal Service Be Saved?** Washington, DC: Center for the Study of Responsive Law, 1983.

3975. Cullinan, Gerald. **The Post Office Department.** New York: Praeger, 1968.

3976. Cunitz, Jonathan A. "The Impact of the Planning, Programming, Budgeting System on the Post Office Department." Ph.D. dissertation, Harvard University, 1968.

3977. Daly, J. J. "What's Ahead for the Postal Service?" **Public Relations Journal** 33 (January 1977): 15-17.

3978. Day, James E. "United States Post Office Department." **Business Lawyer** 17 (November 1961): 89-97.

3979. Flato, L. "Postal Automation: Millions for Zip." **Computer Decision** 8 (September 1976): 22-26.

3980. Fowler, Dorothy G. **Unmailable: Congress and the Post Office.** Athens: University of Georgia Press, 1977.

3981. Freidman, Jane M. "Erotica, Censorship, and the United States Post Office Department." **Michigan Academician** 4 (Summer 1971): 7-16.

3982. Gatell, Frank O. "Postmaster Huger and the Incendiary Publications." **South Carolina Historical Magazine** 64 (October 1963): 193-201.

3983. Geller, H. and Stuart Brotman. "Electronic Mailman." **Across the Board** 16 (June 1979): 28-37.

3984. Haldi, John. **Postal Monopoly.** Washington, DC: American Enterprise Institute for Public Policy Research, 1974.

3985. Harper, Dean. "Labor Relations in the Postal Service." **Industrial and Labor Relations Review** 17 (April 1964): 443-453.

3986. Kahn, Ely J. **Fraud: The United States Postal Inspection Service and Some of the Fools and Knaves It Has Known.** New York: Harper and Row, 1973.

3887. Loewenberg, J. Joseph. "The 1984 Postal Arbitration: Issues Surrounding the Award." **Monthly Labor Review** 109 (June 1986): 31-32.

3988. Long, Bryant. **Mail by Rail: The Story of the Postal Transportation Service.** New York: Simmons-Boardman, 1951.

3989. Mabert, Vincent A. and Michael J. Showalter. **Managing Productivity in the United States Postal Service.** LaFayette, IN: Krannert Graduate School of Industrial Administration, Purdue University, 1974.

3990. Mandel, Benjamin J. "Work Sampling in Financial Management - Cost Determination in Post Office Department." **Management Science** 17 (February 1971): 324-338.

3991. Mantell, Edmund H. "Factors Affecting Labor Productivity in Post Offices." **American Statistical Association Journal** 69 (June 1974): 303-309.

3992. Miller, W. H. "Growing Pains at the Postal Service." **Industry Week** 209 (June 29, 1981): 26-28.

3993. Mills, Harry N. "The Administration of Grievances at the Regional Level, Dallas Regions, United States Post Office Department, 1962-1968." Ph.D. dissertation, University of Oklahoma, 1971.

3994. Murphy, Richard J. "Postal Service." **Public Administration Review** 29 (November 1969): 647-653.

3995. Mustafa, H. "Agency Adaptation to Labor-Management Cooperation." **Labor Law Journal** 20 (July 1969): 428-437.

3996. Mustafa, H. "Cost Implications of Public Labor-Management Cooperation." **Labor Law Journal** 21 (October 1970): 654-662.

3997. Myers, Robert J. **The Coming Collapse of the Post Office.** Englewood Cliffs, NJ: Prentice-Hall, 1975.

3998. Pritchett, C. Herman. "The Postmaster General and Departmental Management." **Public Administration Review** 6 (Spring 1946): 130-136.

3999. Rosen, G. R. "Can the Mails Be Managed?" **Dun's Review** 94 (September 1969): 14-17.

4000. Rosen, G. R. "Is Business Subsidizing the Post Office?" **Dun's Review** 103 (March 1974): 66-70.

4001. Siegel, S. "United States Post Office, Incorporated: A Blueprint for Reform." **Michigan Law Review** 66 (February 1968): 615-628.

4002. Stanaback, Richard J. "Postal Operations in Territorial Florida, 1821-1845." **Florida Historical Quarterly** 52 (October 1973): 157-174.

4003. Stans, Maurice H. "Financial Reorganization in the U.S. Post Office." **Journal of Accountancy** 103 (June 1957): 53-64.

4004. Summerfield, Arthur E. **U.S. Mail: The Story of the United States Postal Service.** New York: Holt, Rinehart and Winston, 1960.

4005. Tierney, John T. "Government Corporations and Managing the Public's Business." **Political Science Quarterly** 99 (Spring 1984): 73-92.

4006. Tierney, John T. **Postal Reorganization: Managing the Public's Business.** Boston: Auburn House, 1981.

4007. Tuthill, M. "US Postal Service: A Monopoly Trying to Beat the Competition." **Nation's Business** 67 (May 1979): 38-40.

4008. Webber, Edwin W. "Personal Privacy - A Case of High Policy." **Public Administration Review** 20 (Summer 1960): 158-160.

4009. Wilmerding, Lucius. "Some Notes on Administrative History." **Public Administration Review** 15 (Spring 1955): 104-106.

4010. Woolf, D. A. "Labor Problems in the Post Office." **Industrial Relations** 9 (October 1964): 27-35.

Author Index

Subject Index

About the Compilers

ROBERT GOEHLERT is Librarian for Economics, Political Science, and Criminal Justice at the Indiana University Library. He has published numerous studies and bibliographies relating to government and politics and is a frequent contributor to scholarly journals in library science and other fields.

HUGH REYNOLDS is an Evaluator in the U.S. General Accounting Office in Dallas. His articles have appeared in *Government Publications Review* and other journals.